The Feminist Companion to the Bible

(Second Series)

8

Editor

Athalya Brenner

Sheffield Academic Press

A Continuum imprint

Prophets and Daniel

A Feminist Companion to the Bible
(Second Series)

edited by Athalya Brenner

Copyright © 2001 Sheffield Academic Press
A Continuum imprint

Published by
Sheffield Academic Press Ltd
The Tower Building, 11 York Road, London SE1 7NX
71 Lexington Avenue, New York, NY 10017-653

www.SheffieldAcademicPress.com
www.continuumbooks.com

British Library Cataloguing-in-Publication Data

A catalogue record for this book is available from the British Library

Typeset by Sheffield Academic Press
Printed on acid-free paper by The Cromwell Press, Trowbridge, Wiltshire

ISBN 1-84127-163-2

To the memory of

_____

Fokkelien van Dijk-Hemmes

תּ־נ־צ־בּ־ה׃

CONTENTS

II
DANIEL

ABBREVIATIONS

AB	Anchor Bible
ABD	David Noel Freedman (ed.), *The Anchor Bible Dictionary* (New York: Doubleday, 1992)
ANET	James B. Pritchard (ed.), *Ancient Near Eastern Texts Relating to the Old Testament* (Princeton: Princeton University Press, 1950)
AOAT	Alter Orient und Altes Testament
ASNU	Acta seminarii neotestamentici upsaliensis
ATANT	Abhandlungen zur Theologie des Alten und Neuen Testaments
ATD	Das Alte Testament Deutsch
BAH	Bibliothèque Archéologique et Historique
BBB	Bonner biblische Beiträge
BDB	Francis Brown, S.R. Driver and Charles A. Briggs, *A Hebrew and English Lexicon of the Old Testament* (Oxford: Clarendon Press, 1907)
BHS	*Biblia hebraica stuttgartensia*
Bib	*Biblica*
BibInt	*Biblical Interpretation: A Journal of Contemporary Approaches*
BK	*Bibel und Kirche*
BKAT	Biblischer Kommentar: Altes Testament
BN	*Biblische Notizen*
BR	*Bible Review*
BZ	*Biblische Zeitschrift*
BZAW	Beihefte zur *ZAW*
CAD	Ignace I. Gelb *et al.* (eds.), *The Assyrian Dictionary of the Oriental Institute of the University of Chicago* (Chicago: Oriental Institute, 1964–)
CBQ	*Catholic Biblical Quarterly*
CTA	A. Herdner (ed.), *Corpus des tablettes en cunéiformes alphabétiques découvertes à Ras Shamra–Ugarit de 1929 à 1939* (Paris: Imprimerie nationale Geuthner, 1963)
EncJud	*Encyclopaedia Judaica*
FzB	Forschung zur Bibel
FOTL	The Forms of the Old Testament Literature
FRLANT	Forschungen zur Religion und Literatur des Alten und Neuen Testaments

GKC	*Gesenius' Hebrew Grammar* (ed. E. Kautzsch, revised and trans. A.E. Cowley; Oxford: Clarendon Press, 1910)
HAT	Handbuch zum Alten Testament
HB	Hebrew Bible
HSM	Harvard Semitic Monographs
HUCA	*Hebrew Union College Annual*
ICC	International Critical Commentary
IDB	George Arthur Buttrick (ed.), *The Interpreter's Dictionary of the Bible* (4 vols.; Nashville: Abingdon Press, 1962)
IEJ	*Israel Exploration Journal*
Int	*Interpretation*
JAOS	*Journal of the American Oriental Society*
JBL	*Journal of Biblical Literature*
JCS	*Journal of Cuneiform Studies*
JFSR	*Journal of Feminist Studies in Religion*
JJS	*Journal of Jewish Studies*
JQR	*Jewish Quarterly Review*
JR	*Journal of Religion*
JSOT	*Journal for the Study of the Old Testament*
JSOTSup	*Journal for the Study of the Old Testament*, Supplement Series
KAT	Kommentar zum Alten Testament
KJV	King James Version
KUB	Keilschrifturkunden aus Boghaköi
NCB	New Century Bible
NICOT	New International Commentary on the Old Testament
NRSV	New Revised Standard Version
NT	New Testament
OBO	Orbis biblicus et orientalis
OTL	Old Testament Library
OTS	*Oudtestamentische Studiën*
PEQ	*Palestine Exploration Quarterly*
PW	August Friedrich von Pauly and Georg Wissowa (eds.), *Real-Encyclopädie der classischen Altertumswissenschaft* (Stuttgart: Metzler, 1894–)
RB	*Revue biblique*
RevistB	*Revista biblica*
RHR	*Revue de l'histoire des religions*
SAT	Die Schriften des Alten Testaments
SBLDS	SBL Dissertation Series
SBLMS	SBL Monograph Series
SBS	Stuttgarter Bibelstudien
TGl	*Theologie und Glaube*
ThWAT	G.J. Botterweck and H. Ringgren (eds.), *Theologisches Wörterbuch zum Alten Testament* (Stuttgart: W. Kohlhammer, 1970–)

TOTC	Tyndale Old Testament Commentaries
TUAT	Texte aus der Umwelt des Alten Testaments
UF	*Ugarit-Forschungen*
VT	*Vetus Testamentum*
VTSup	*Vetus Testamentum*, Supplements
ZAW	*Zeitschrift für die alttestamentliche Wissenschaft*
ZTK	*Zeitschrift für Theologie und Kirche*

LIST OF CONTRIBUTORS

Gerlinde Baumann, Fachbereich Ev Theologie, Philips Universtitat Marburg/Lahn, Lahn Tor 3, Marburg D-35037, Germany

Athalya Brenner, Biblical Studies, Dept of Theology and Religious Studies, University of Amsterdam, Oude Turfmarkt 147, 1012 GC Amsterdam, Netherlands

Esther Fuchs, Department of Judaic Studies, University of Arizona, Tucson, AZ 85721, USA

Mayer I. Gruber, Bible and Ancient Studies, Ben-Gurion University of the Negev, P.O.Box 653, Beersheva 84105, Israel

Judith M. Hadley, Department of Theology and Religious Studies, Villanova University, 800 Lancaster Avenue, Villanova, PA 19085, USA

Renate Jost, Augustana Hochshule, Theol. Hochschule der Ev.-Luth. Kirche in Bayon, Postfach 20, 91561, Neuerdettelsan

S. Tamar Kamionkowski, Reconstructionist Rabbinical College, Wyncote, 1299 Church Road, PA 19095, USA

Rainer Kessler, Heinrich-Heine-Str. 21, 35091 Cölbe, Germany

Julia M. O'Brien, Lancaster Theological Seminary, 555 W James Street, Lancaster, PA 17603, USA

Erin Runions, 228 Laurier Ouest, Montreal, QC H2T 2N8, Canada

Ulrike Sals, US Faculty of Theology, Ernst-Moritz-Arndt-Universität Greifswald, Rubenow-Platz 2/3, 17287 Greifswald, Germany

Emily Sampson, 8827 Bralorne Way, San Diego, CA 92126, USA

Mary E. Shields, Trinity Lutheran Seminary, 2199 East Main Street, Columbus, OH 43209, USA

Hans J.M. van Deventer, PO Box 11, Park South Vanderbijlpark, Guateng 1900, South Africa, 01127-168073341

INTRODUCTION

Athalya Brenner

This is the second Feminist Companion to prophecy (the first one was published in 1995 under the title *A Feminist Companion to the Latter Prophets*), and a first—if small—feminist contribution to Daniel studies. It is also the last volume of the Second Feminist Companion Series.

The first volume of the First Series, on the Song of Songs, was published in 1993. That the First and the Second Series together hold 20 volumes, published over just 8 years, is evidence of the growing body of feminist writing on the Bible—and its rigorous and critical quality.

When this Series was at the planning stage, approximately 10 years ago, there was a need to put together collections of feminist writings, focused on certain biblical books or groups of books, so that they could serve as representative pointers to the state of the young art of feminist Bible criticism. Such works on the HB (Hebrew Bible) are now numerous and widely available. Hence, this Series is discontinued since, fortunately, it is no longer necessary. On the other hand, the need is now felt for a similar collection on New Testament and related areas of study. This need will be fulfilled by a new series of Feminist Companion books edited by Amy Jill Levine with Marianne Bickenstaff.

Part I: *Prophecy*

So what is new or different in the present collection, apart from the addition of several works on the book of Daniel? The *Feminist Companion to the Latter Prophets* (First Series) had two main foci, the book of Hosea and the pornoprophetic 'marriage' metaphor, together with an assessment of the distrust towards women displayed by the Hebrew god in the so-called 'classical' prophetic books. In the present volume, which in general is in dialogue with the previous one, the emphasis on Hosea is gone. On the other hand, preoccupation with the 'marriage' metaphor remains and even grows: it is here being assessed and reinterpreted anew, and from fresh angles (Baumann, Shields, Runions, Kamionkowski, Sals, O'Brien, Gruber). So is the goddess image (Hadley and Sals), and the constructions of 'woman' and 'prophetess' in the Hebrew Bible (Fuchs, Jost, Kessler). This section contains numerous translations and reprints (Jost and Kessler on female prophecy, from the German; Shields on Jeremiah and Ezekiel; Sals on Ezekiel, again translated from the German; O'Brien on Malachi). In the spirit of re-consideration and readerly perspective modifications, Shields and O'Brien write retrospective self-responses to their work. As usual for the Feminist Companion collections, some of the contributors are well established and well known, whereas others are either younger and up-and-coming or else less known to the English speaking Guild.

a. *The Goddess Revisited*
Judith Hadley's major essay, 'The Queen of Heaven—Who is She?', opens this collection. Most studies of the 'Queen of Heaven' look at *either* the dating and structure of the Jeremiah passages in which she appears (chs. 7 and 44), *or* the origin/identity of the Queen and the nature of her cult. Rarely is there a discussion of the two together. Hadley provides this. She concludes that the Jeremiah passages are quite late and reflect a post-exilic understanding of the pre-exilic worship of goddesses, which by the time of writing had been eradicated. Did the use of the title 'Queen of Heaven' refer to a specific goddess, or generically to whatever goddess used to be worshipped 'back then' and, subsequently, was only dimly remembered by a title instead of by her name? This approach ties in with Hadley's general trend of following the 'depersonalization' of deities, especially the goddesses. In numerous previous works (see her essay for bibliographic references) Hadley has recorded the gradual 'devolution' of Asherah from a goddess, to merely her cult image, to a cult object owned and controlled by Yahweh. Here she questions whether the goddess behind the appellation 'Queen of Heaven' has undergone a similar process.

b. *Female 'Prophets' or 'Prophetesses'?*
Esther Fuchs's essays on feminist biblical criticism[1] were, when first published, an eye-opener for many. Fuchs's scholarly yet direct, challenging and angry voice made biblical scholars and students sit up and pay attention, and provoked many. Her work can and should be

---

1.   An updated collection of which is now published by Sheffield Academic Press under the title *Sexual Politics in Biblical Narrative* (2000).

considered pioneering. It is therefore a pleasure to include here a new essay by Fuchs, 'Prophecy and the Construction of Women: Inscription and Erasure'. Fuchs proceeds from a consideration of what a 'male' 'prophet' (נביא) is, which is far from clear. At any rate, prophets interpret truthfully God's intentions and communicate them to others. But women are constructed in a rather problematic relationship to Truth, notably to Truth mediated through words. Women deceive; and this may perhaps account for the ambiguous presentation of woman prophets and for the ambiguous presentation of women by the prophets, notably the latter prophets. Fuchs shows, step by step, how woman prophets in the prophetic books are derogated in/by the HB text to the point of erasure. From agents of speech they become sexual agents; in Fuchs's own words, 'The speaking organ, woman's discourse, has been replaced and displaced by her sexual organ, hence the obsessive focus of the latter prophets on what has been defined by some as pornography'.

What happens when 'The Daughters of Your People Prophesy'? Renate Jost examines precisely such a 'prophetic' text, Ezekiel 13, where—as Fuchs rightly claims—a distinction is made between male prophets and female prophets. The men are 'prophets', whereas the women 'prophesy'. There's a world of difference between the two descriptions. Jost proceeds to list the differences between the gendered groups of 'prophets' according to Ezekiel, concluding that 'Whether the women prophets prophesied in the name of Ishtar or in the name of Yhwh, it is apparent that they were influential enough to become dangerous opponents of the priestly circles in which the book of Ezekiel originated during the economic and religious crisis after 587 BCE, and that they were combated even more sharply than their male colleagues'.

The same basic question, 'what constitutes female prophecy?', is also at the background of Rainer Kessler's 'Miriam and the Prophecy of the Persian Period'. But Kessler's main concerns are different to those of the previous two contributors. He asks why Miriam (in Mic. 6 and in Num. 12) and other female prophets are made the textual representatives of prophecy, when male prophecy is so much more dominant in the HB. Kessler proceeds from an understanding that in Numbers 12 and Micah 6 alike a female figure—Miriam—represents prophecy, whereas male figures—Moses and Aaron respectively—represent the Torah and the cult. This understanding helps him to solve the problem of the apparently contradictory views of Miriam as a prophet in Numbers as against Micah, as well as to place her assessment as such in a politico-historical context within the early Second

Temple period. A discussion of the conflict between Nehemiah on the one hand, and on the other hand 'Noadiah and the other prophets', helps Kessler to arrive at his conclusions.

c. *The Pornoprophetic(?) 'Marriage' Metaphor*
In 'Prophetic Objections to Yhwh as the Violent Husband of Israel: Reinterpretations of the Prophetic Marriage Metaphor in Second Isaiah (Isaiah 40–55)', Gerlinde Baumann draws on previous discussions for reassessing the 'marriage' metaphor in the so-called Second Isaiah. In her opinion, two aspects have been neglected, or relatively so, in feminist interpretations of the metaphor: inner-biblical critique of Yhwh as a violent husband, especially as found in Second Isaiah; and alternative images of god that offset the 'violent husband' image somewhat. Baumann begins by presenting the main themes of the discussion concerning the prophetic marriage metaphor, which focus on Hosea, Jeremiah and Ezekiel. She then examines the terminology of the metaphor as well as alternative metaphors for Yhwh and Israel/Jerusalem. Next, she looks at Second Isaiah texts that can be viewed as objections to the prophetic marriage metaphor as outlined in Hosea, Jeremiah and Ezekiel. Finally she examines one other prophetic strategy which can be used as an alternative to the image of Yhwh. Her conclusion is sombre. Baumann concedes that even though Second Isaiah provides us with a new interpretation of the marriage metaphor, it is quite possible to go back to the old metaphor as expressed in the other books. And this is what we shall do in the essays that follow.

In 'Circumcision of the Prostitute: Gender, Sexuality, and the Call to Repentance in Jeremiah 3.1–4.4', Mary Shields agrees in passing that in Second Isaiah a reversal is to be found. As for the earlier texts, however, they are indeed harsh; and 'Jer. 3.1–4.4 represents an intermediate step in the development of the negative [marriage] metaphors, developing the imagery in terms harsher than those of Hosea, while not pushing to the extremes of Ezekiel'. Shields explores how gender-specific imagery and address construct the call to repentance in Jer. 3.1–4.4, as well as the implications of the ways in which gender itself is constructed by this passage. Gender is linked with 'overstepped boundaries', and women are positioned on the boundaries. In Shields's own words,

> Both the gender-specific metaphors and the alternating forms of direct address exert pressures on the male audience to change their behavior to conform to male rather than female subjectivity. In turn, this text constructs gender in that it reveals a disguised pressure for female readers

to conform to the patriarchal symbolic order. This imagery, however, works only as long as men hold the exclusive power to shape and define subjectivity. When women become resisting readers, the crisis in the patriarchal symbolic order is revealed.

This article, first published in 1995, is followed by a 'Self-Response'. A second reprinted article by Mary E. Shields, again followed by a 'Self-Response', is 'Multiple Exposures: Body Rhetoric and Gender in Ezekiel 16'. Once again, Shields is interested in how gender and the female body are constructed in/by the passage read, but also in how gender and the female body themselves construct the passage. In most treatments of this (to put it mildly) problematic passage, the male Yhwh character is hardly critiqued in the same way the 'female' character is, whereas the violence and the explicit body-naming of the 'female' character are played down. Therefore, in the first half of the study Shields discusses the female character, while in the second she focuses on the character of Yhwh. She shows how body rhetoric and gender characterization combine to expose Jerusalem while masking Yhwh completely, as well as presenting a portrayal of god's character 'which is, to say the least, difficult to reconcile with the picture of God's abundant love and mercy which many commentators would read into the text'.

In 'Violence and the Economy of Desire in Ezekiel 16.1-45', Erin Runions reads the same passage for the relationship between violence and desire, in the light of René Girard's theory of mimetic desire. In her own words,

> I first map out the relations of violence to desire, through an interrogation of the relationships, literal and metaphoric, between the key figures in the text (God, the woman Jerusalem, and the nations as lovers). Careful attention to the way the metaphor reconstructs literal violence and desire reveals an interesting interplay between the literal and the metaphoric, as well as raising some questions about the efficacy of the metaphor. Girard's theory is helpful in filling some of the gaps which open up between the literal and metaphoric in this interrogation, and in suggesting new ways to play the characters.

Ultimately, by reading with Girard a recasting of the two chief 'characters' is achieved—a project not unlike Shields's project, but differently formulated and executed.

Yet another reading of Ezekiel 16 is S. Tamar Kamionkowski's essay, 'Gender Reversal in Ezekiel 16'. Kamionkowski agrees with Shields's basic assessment of readers' responses to this troubled and troubling text, and of the privileging of the Yhwh character. She also concurs that this text is not only about politics and theology but concurrently, and on the deepest lever, about gender. However, she finds that feminists' responses to it are inadequate as well. Kamion-kowski disagrees with Shields's assertion that, in this text, the Yhwh character is the sole owner of power. On the contrary, she writes: had that been the case, 'there would be no conflict, no tension, and certainly no story'. The relationship described is chaotic: neither of the partners, divine/male or female/human, has full control of the situation. It is a story in which the disintegration of socio-political, cultural and religious 'truths' is symbolized by 'the breakdown of one of the most fundamental cultural and social institutions: gender'. Through a close reading of the Hebrew text Kamionkowski finds that, in it, 'wife' Israel/Jerusalem behaves like a male, transgressing gender boundaries even physically, thus reinstating chaos and embodying a subversion of the gender order decreed by Yhwh with the Creation. The blurring of pre-ordained gender identity is the true evil practised by the 'wife', to the speaker's consternation. Only such a crime is fit to metaphorize and explain the shocking experiences of the times.

At this point we move on to other prophetic books, but still on issues of reading, gender and gender interpretation. In 'Reading Zechariah 5.5-11: Prophecy, Gender and Hermeneutics', Ulrike Sals discusses the image of the woman in the איפה (*epah*)—'a woman shut up inside a grain measure that is closed with a lead lid, two women with stork's wings and finally a pedestal of the type that used to stand in the Jerusalem Temple', a woman who at least towards the vision's end is to be worshipped like a goddess, a woman whose evil is infectious and who is therefore carried away to Shinar. The figure is linked to its Proto-Zechariah politico-historical context (for the dating and background see also Kessler's essay in this volume). From the outset, Sals defines this text as misogynist. Her quest is to examine the woman figure, especially in the light of recent discussions about that figure as representative of a goddess. A close reading of the text is followed by a consideration of the Pandora myth and its (dis)similarities to the story of the *epah* woman, and some hermeneutic notes. Sals's concluding reminder, 'Mind the Gap'—that is, the multiple gaps in the text, between us and ancient texts, and in our own willingness to draw hasty analogies—is appropriate for this text and beyond.

In 'On Saying "No" to a Prophet', Julia M. O'Brien traces how her preoccupation with the book of Malachi for over a decade has unfolded and changed in tandem with her changing position as a person/reader. In her own words,

This essay explores my 10-year obsession with the book of Malachi. I consider the ways in which the change in my understanding of the book from March to November of 1995 is interwoven with a significant change in my personal location as a reader. While psychoanalytic and modern literary criticism has offered some insight into the relationship of my life and my reading, most beneficial have been Martha Nussbaum's volumes *Love's Knowledge* and *The Therapy of Desire*. Here I consider what Nussbaum's employment of literature in the task of moral philosophy and her argument for the cognitive content of emotions might offer me in the quest to understand my life with Malachi'.

O'Brien writes about how she came to reevaluate Malachi's message, harsh and abusive and 'collapsing under its own weight' as she still believes, but differently. Continuing to trace this process, 'In Retrospect... Self-Response to "On saying 'No' to a Prophet"', is Julia O'Brien's perspective after several more years (the original essay was published in *Semeia* 72 [1995]).

In the last article on prophecy in this volume, in 'Nineveh the Adulteress', Mayer I. Gruber looks again at the violent image of the 'adulteress' Israel and its inner-biblical afterlife, this time in Nahum. The book of Nahum, writes Gruber, shows many similarities to Hosea 1–2. In Hosea 1–2 Israel is defined as a זונה and adulterous woman, whose specific sin is worship of other gods; she is threatened with suffering and loss of modesty by physical exposure of her nakedness. This, from the speaker's perspective, is a 'measure for measure' punishment, as is often the case in the HB. However, Gruber questions the reapplication of both the designation and the punishment-by-exposure to Nineveh, a city representing Assyrian past glory and imminent demise, but which has no obligation to worship Yhwh. In other words, Nineveh's 'harlotry' and exposure in Nah. 3.4-5, for instance, metaphorize something other than the 'harlotry' and exposure of Samaria/Israel in Hosea 1–2. In other words, the same trope is used for different purposes; the due punishment is the same, but the sin differs in each case: in the one it is a matter of adultery/idolatry, in the other a matter of cruel policies and lack of common decency and ethics. Gruber tries to understand why the exposure fits the crime in the case of Nineveh, and we shall leave it to our readers to determine whether he succeeds or whether, more simply, the trope has been taken over in Nahum *as is*, well known and probably — for some audiences at least — a good attention-grabber. At any rate, as Gruber concludes, the trope of the 'whoring' city/woman remains popular and is applied to cities/ethnic groups/territories other than Yhwh's 'wives', and with similar theological and misogynist vigour. The trope of the 'fornicating woman' remains in evidence even when the so-called 'marriage metaphor' has ceased to be the issue—as in the cases of Nineveh, Babylon of the HB and the NT, and others. This should, it seems, cause further reflection on the origin and function of the violent prophetic images discussed in the articles of this section.

Part II: *Daniel*

Several foreign rulers, of diverse ethnic origins, are configured in the HB as obtuse: the unfortunate king of Daniel 5 features prominently among them. In 'Who's Afraid of Feminist Criticism? Who's Afraid of Biblical Humour? The Case of the Obtuse Foreign Ruler in the Hebrew Bible' (a reprint from 1994), I read this 'obtuse foreign male ruler' trope, or configuration, from two perspectives: humour and feminist concerns. The rulers are presented with bitter humour and malice for their [im]potence. Their reported inadequacy is satirized by reference to their maleness; their sexuality and body functions are inept. Furthermore, the rulers' ineptitude is enhanced by the mirrored images of women in their stories, women who are smarter by far than they are. The picture that emerges, in Daniel 5 as in other HB passages where this configuration appears, is as follows. 'Foreign' is a threat. Humour, the great weapon of the politically weak and powerless, is therefore used against the 'foreign' or 'other' in authority. The resourcefulness of females such as the queen in Daniel 5, by definition inferior social agents, serves—just like humour—as a literary device for amplifying the shortcomings of powerful 'foreign' males. This reprinted essay, like those by Shields and O'Brien, is followed by a 'Self Response'.

In 'Another Wise Queen (Mother): Women's Wisdom in Daniel 5.10-12?', Hans van Deventer reads Daniel 5 for other angles. To begin with, he focuses on the female character rather than on the male character, undoubtedly the smarter figure of the two. In dialogue with previous feminist scholarship, he explores the possibility that the 'queen' here—just as in Josephus Flavius—is not the king's spouse but his mother. By reading the 'queen' of the Aramaic text (מלכתא) as a so-called 'queen mother', he is able to invest her with the authority, experience, know-how and insight that are often attributed in the HB to older (read: less sexually threatening, past the child-bearing stage, overtly asexual), sometimes maternal, figures. This re-vision of the 'queen' will undoubtedly find favour with many woman readers, just as it may raise Freudian and other objections from other readers. At any rate, this interpretation enables van Deventer to relate the wise, son-rebuking 'queen mother' in Daniel 5 to the influential figure of

Modjadji, the rain-queen of the Lovedu people in Southern Africa. Such a comparison might serve to satisfy (at least to some extent) the aims of 'inculturation' and 'empowerment' of women (and of other Others). And he concludes: 'Our understanding of the role women played in ancient societies, linked to the role women still play in less male-dominated present-day societies (such as the Lovedu society), could set the tone for effecting change in the oppressive societies many women and children inhabit'.

Julia Evelina Smith is an unsung and pioneering heroine of female Bible translation in the nineteenth century, largely forgotten—but not quite. In 'Daniel, Belshazzar, and Julia: The Rediscovery and Vindication of the Translation of Julia E. Smith (1792–1886)', Emily Sampson does us the great service of, first, telling us the amazing story of Smith's life, character and passionate work (she made five translations of the Hebrew Bible from Hebrew, Greek and Latin, yet at the time and later her work was hardly appreciated); secondly, giving us samples of Smith's work, especially but not only from Daniel 5, as compared to standard translations and, thirdly, critiquing Smith's work with fairness and scrupulousness although, clearly, Sampson's own imagination and scholarly curiosity are fired by Smith's efforts. Smith's virtues are that she modernized the language of translation, introduced apt neologisms and rejected coyness in favour of directness, even where the text seemed to offend contemporaneous gentlefolk's sensibilities. Her shortcomings were her literal tendencies, her refusal to add words, her insistence on 'concordant congruity', and her treatment of the Hebrew verb system. Nevertheless, as can be seen also from her translation of Daniel 5, her work has value even for today's translator—and, may we remind ourselves, Bible translations and translation criticism do not boast too many female/feminist practitioners, even nowadays.

Part I

PROPHECY

A.

THE GODDESS REVISITED

THE QUEEN OF HEAVEN—WHO IS SHE?

Judith M. Hadley

The 'Queen of Heaven' (*mlkt hšmym*) is mentioned in two chapters in Jeremiah, chs. 7 and 44. To date, the discussion of most scholars on the topic can be divided into two categories: those who concentrate on the identity and cult of the Queen of Heaven,[1] and those who focus mainly on a literary analysis of the biblical text.[2] Only rarely is an attempt made to include both discussions.[3] This article will briefly

---

1. In this category see especially S. Ackerman, '"And the Women Knead Dough": The Worship of the Queen of Heaven in Sixth-Century Judah', in P.L. Day (ed.), *Gender and Difference in Ancient Israel* (Minneapolis: Fortress Press, 1989), pp. 109-24; *idem*, *Under Every Green Tree: Popular Religion in Sixth-Century Judah* (HSM, 46; Atlanta: Scholars Press, 1992), esp. Chapter 1, ' "And the Women Make Cakes for the Queen of Heaven": Jeremiah 7 and 44', pp. 5-35; S. Olyan, 'Some Observations Concerning the Identity of the Queen of Heaven', *UF* 19 (1987), pp. 161-74, among others.

2. This category includes, but is not limited to, commentaries on the book of Jeremiah. Cf. e.g. J. Bright, *Jeremiah* (AB; Garden City, NY: Doubleday, 2nd edn, 1965); W. Brueggemann, *A Commentary on Jeremiah: Exile and Homecoming* (Grand Rapids: Eerdmans, 1998); R.P. Carroll, *Jeremiah: A Commentary* (OTL; Philadelphia: Westminster Press, 1986); W.L. Holladay, *Jeremiah 1: A Commentary on the Book of the Prophet Jeremiah Chapters 1-25* (Hermeneia; Philadelphia: Fortress Press, 1986); *idem*, *Jeremiah 2: A Commentary on the Book of the Prophet Jeremiah Chapters 26-52* (Hermeneia; Minneapolis: Fortress Press, 1989); D.R. Jones, *Jeremiah* (NCB Commentary; Grand Rapids: Eerdmans, 1992); W. McKane, *A Critical and Exegetical Commentary on Jeremiah*. I. *Introduction and Commentary on Jeremiah I-XXV* (ICC; Edinburgh: T. & T. Clark, 1986); *idem*, *A Critical and Exegetical Commentary on Jeremiah*. II. *Commentary on Jeremiah XXVI-LII* (ICC; Edinburgh: T. & T. Clark, 1996); E.W. Nicholson, *The Book of the Prophet Jeremiah Chapters 1-25* (Cambridge: Cambridge University Press, 1973); *idem*, *The Book of the Prophet Jeremiah Chapters 26-52* (Cambridge: Cambridge University Press, 1975); J.A. Thompson, *The Book of Jeremiah* (Grand Rapids: Eerdmans, 1980).

3. To a limited extent, M. Delcor, 'Le culte de la "Reine du Ciel" selon Jer 7,18; 44,17-19, 25 et ses survivances', in W.C. Delsman *et al.* (eds.), *Von Kanaan bis Kerala* (AOAT, 211; Kevelaer: Butzon & Bercker; Neukirchen–Vluyn: Neukirchener Verlag, 1982), pp. 101-22; and for a more extended treatment see C. Frevel, *Aschera und*

consider both of these categories, beginning with a discussion of the biblical texts, in an attempt to identify the 'Queen of Heaven'.

Jeremiah 7

The first part of Jeremiah 7, especially vv. 1-15, forms a part of the 'Temple Sermon'.[4] Whereas many scholars separate vv. 16-20, in which the Queen of Heaven is mentioned, from the Temple Sermon that immediately precedes it,[5] the 'Queen of Heaven' passage is perhaps placed here due to the common theme of Jeremiah's attack on 'false' cultic practices.[6] The focus of the message shifts from the words of the Lord to the people (through Jeremiah) to the words of the Lord to Jeremiah himself. Jeremiah is told not to intercede for the people, who are performing actions 'in the towns of Judah', and 'in the streets of Jerusalem' (Jer. 7.17) in order to provoke Yahweh to anger (v. 18). Specifically, these actions are presented in Jer. 7.18 as follows: 'The children gather wood, the fathers kindle fire, and the women knead dough, to make cakes for the queen of heaven; and they pour out drink offerings to other gods, to provoke me to anger'. Before commenting on this passage further, it is obligatory to note that the Masoretic Text has vocalized the name as *mĕleket haššāmayîm*, thereby implying 'the works of heaven'.[7] Indeed, some of the manuscripts

der Ausschliesslichkeitsanspruch YHWHs, I (BBB, 94.1; Weinheim: Beltz Athenäum, 1995).

4. For more on Jeremiah's 'Temple Sermon' see the commentaries, including Brueggemann, *Jeremiah*, pp. 77-85; also Delcor, 'Le culte', pp. 101-102; K. Koch, 'Aschera als Himmelskönigin in Jerusalem', *UF* 20 (1988), pp. 97-120 (108-109) and the bibliography there.

5. Note the use of the different address: the 'as for you' of v. 16 changes focus from the people to Jeremiah himself. Cf. e.g. J.P. Hyatt, 'The Deuteronomic Edition of Jeremiah', in L.G. Perdue and B.W. Kovacs (eds.), *A Prophet to the Nations: Essays in Jeremiah Studies* (Winona Lake, IN: Eisenbrauns, 1984), pp. 247-67 (255); P.C. Craigie, P.H. Kelley and J.F. Drinkard Jr, *Jeremiah 1-25* (WBC, 26; Dallas: Word Books, 1991), p. 119; M.E. Biddle, *Polyphony and Symphony in Prophetic Literature: Rereading Jeremiah 7-20* (Studies in Old Testament Interpretation, 2; Macon, GA: Mercer University Press, 1996), p. 71.

6. Cf. e.g. Craigie *et al.*, *Jeremiah 1-25*, pp. 122-23; and see also K.M. O'Connor, *The Confessions of Jeremiah: Their Interpretation and Role in Chapters 1-25* (SBLDS, 94; Atlanta: Scholars Press, 1988), p. 126; Thompson, *Jeremiah*, p. 283; Jones, *Jeremiah*, p. 151.

7. As Frevel observes, nearly all of the articles on the Queen of Heaven have as the first footnote a comment concerning the vocalization of the consonantal text *mlkt hšmym*. Cf. e.g. Frevel, *Aschera*, p. 423 n. 1434; Ackerman, *Tree*, p. 5 n. 1.

have an added Hebrew aleph.[8] Robert Gordon has adequately shown that this 'aleph apologeticum' is an attempt to disguise the fact that the Queen of Heaven is referred to here.[9] Indeed, the LXX text has 'the hosts of heaven' instead of Queen of Heaven. However, the consensus among scholars is that originally the text read 'Queen of Heaven'.[10]

The activities being performed involve the whole family: children, fathers, and women. Peake believes that, at least in this chapter, the description of the activities indicates that worship of the Queen of Heaven was prevalent 'among the poorer classes, who have to collect firewood and do all the work themselves'.[11] It is interesting that 'women' (*nāšîm*) is the term used here, not mothers, in parallel with fathers. This designation appears to remove the women from the family unit, perhaps in anticipation of ch. 44, where they will take on more responsibility for the worship of the Queen of Heaven. Other scholars, such as Bauer, see this severing of family ties as a means of removing the male audience somewhat from the judgment soon to be announced.[12] Bauer also believes that 'by not naming mothers and daughters in particular, [this activity] is not limited to the private sphere, but allows for the possibility of cultic positions for these women'.[13] Indeed, the activities of the males, although integral to the end result, seem to be of secondary importance. It is the women who are making the cakes for the Queen of Heaven, which seems to be the main activity in this passage, together with the pouring out of

8. Cf. P.C. Schmitz, 'Queen of Heaven', in ABD, V, pp. 586-88 (586); A. Bauer, *Gender in the Book of Jeremiah: A Feminist-Literary Reading* (Studies in Biblical Literature, 5; New York: Peter Lang, 1999), p. 76 n. 2; W. McKane, 'Worship of the Queen of Heaven (Jer 44)', in I. Kottsieper, J. van Oorschot, D. Römheld and H.M. Wahl (eds.), *'Wer ist wie du, HERR, unter den Göttern?' Studien zur Theologie und Religionsgeschichte Israels für Otto Kaiser zum 70. Geburtstag* (Göttingen: Vandenhoeck & Ruprecht, 1994), pp. 318-24 (318); and see the discussion in McKane, *Jeremiah*, I, p. 170.

9. R.P. Gordon, 'Aleph Apologeticum', *JQR* 69 (1978), pp. 112-16.

10. Cf. e.g. C. Houtman, 'Queen of Heaven', in K. van der Toorn, B. Becking and P.W. van der Horst (eds.), *Dictionary of Deities and Demons in the Bible* (Leiden: E.J. Brill, 1995), cols. 1278-83 (col. 1279); Carroll, *Jeremiah*, p. 212; Holladay, *Jeremiah 1*, p. 251; M. Held, 'Studies in Biblical Lexicography in the Light of Akkadian', *Eretz-Israel* 16 (1982), pp. 76-85 (76) (Hebrew).

11. A.S. Peake, *Jeremiah and Lamentations. I. Jeremiah I–XXIV* (The Century Bible; Edinburgh: T.C. & E.C. Jack, n.d.), p. 150.

12. Bauer, *Gender*, pp. 77-78.

13. Bauer, *Gender*, p. 78; and see also R. Jost, *Frauen, Männer und die Himmelskönigin: Exegetische Studien* (Gütersloh: Chr. Kaiser Verlag/Gütersloher Verlagshaus, 1995), pp. 215-20, which was unavailable to me at the time of writing.

libations. More will be said about the cakes and the libations when we come to ch. 44, but note that here it is not specified who are the ones pouring out the libations. Furthermore, the deities to whom these libations are offered are not specified further than 'other gods', *ᵉlōhîm ᵃḥērîm*.

The motivation given for this activity is to provoke Yahweh to anger. However, it is unlikely that the participants in the cult would have considered that to be their motivation. Nevertheless, the punishment was to be severe and all-encompassing, as the anger of Yahweh would be poured out 'on human beings and animals, on the trees of the field and the fruit of the ground', and 'will burn and not be quenched' (Jer. 7.20). Obviously Yahweh would not tolerate such actions! Bird thinks that 'it is significant that the syncretistic rites with which Israelite women are explicitly connected are associated solely with female deities or with deities whose cult was predominantly female'.[14]

Scholars are divided concerning the dating of the book of Jeremiah, and a full analysis is beyond the scope of this article.[15] However, a few words are in order here. Opinion is divided over whether these passages concerning the Queen of Heaven reflect the actual situation of the time in which they are set, or if they were the product of a later deuteronomistic editor.[16] Those who believe that the account reflects actual historical events usually place this speech in the days of Jehoiakim, since the condemnation would not fit so well during the reign of Josiah, especially if his reforms were seen to be effective.[17] Nevertheless, most of these scholars consider that the cult of the

14. P.A. Bird, 'Images of Women in the Old Testament', in *idem, Missing Persons and Mistaken Identities: Women and Gender in Ancient Israel* (Overtures to Biblical Theology Series; Minneapolis: Fortress Press, 1997), pp. 13-51 (42 n. 77), and cf. *idem*, 'The Place of Women in the Israelite Cultus', in *Missing Persons*, pp. 81-102.

15. For more on the dating of Jeremiah see the sources in notes 16-18, as well as C.R. Seitz, *Theology in Conflict: Reactions to the Exile in the Book of Jeremiah* (Berlin and New York: W. de Gruyter, 1989).

16. Cf. e.g. Nicholson, *Jeremiah 26–52*, p. 152; R.P. Carroll, *From Chaos to Covenant: Uses of Prophecy in the Book of Jeremiah* (London: SCM Press, 1981), pp. 242 and 245; Jones, *Jeremiah*, p. 451.

17. Cf. e.g. Bright, *Jeremiah*, p. 58 and pp. 265-66; Brueggemann, *Jeremiah*, p. 77; Nicholson, *Jeremiah 26–52*, pp. 157-58; O'Connor, *Confessions*, pp. 149-57; M. Smith, 'The Veracity of Ezekiel, the Sins of Manasseh, and Jeremiah 44.18' *ZAW* 87 (1975), pp. 11-16 (15); Thompson, *Jeremiah*, p. 285; see also the discussion in McKane, *Jeremiah*, II, pp. 1087-88, but see Carroll, *Jeremiah*, pp. 736-37.

Queen of Heaven was initially introduced during the reign of Manasseh.[18] More will be said on the dating of this passage later.

Jeremiah 44

The situation is different for the speech in ch. 44. Here Jeremiah is addressing the Jewish community in Egypt, sometime after the destruction of Jerusalem as the punishment for the inhabitants who 'went to make offerings and serve other gods that they had not known' (Jer. 44.3 etc.). Carroll notes that 'it is an absurd feature of these sermons that the nation is accused of persistent idolatry throughout their existence yet always in terms of gods which they have not known! Either they worshipped them constantly or they did not know them, but hardly both.'[19] The language here certainly sounds deuteronomistic;[20] and now the judgment is coming to the remnant of Judah that has settled in Egypt.[21] They, too, will be rooted out and utterly destroyed.

Not only the setting is different in this account. The participants and even the language also differ. In a textually corrupt passage,[22] it appears that Jeremiah's answer shifts from all the assembled people to only the women. The women express their intent to continue their worship of the Queen of Heaven. 'We will do everything that we have vowed, make offerings to the queen of heaven and pour out libations to her, just as we and our ancestors, our kings and our officials, used to do in the towns of Judah and in the streets of Jerusalem' (v. 17). It will be noted that here the act of pouring out libations is identified as

18. Cf. C.L. Feinberg, *Jeremiah: A Commentary* (Grand Rapids: Zondervan, 1982), p. 74, who also notes that 'a female deity is foreign to OT theology; so the implication is that this cult was of non-Hebraic origin'; cf. also H. Cunliffe-Jones, *The Book of Jeremiah* (London: SCM Press, 1960), p. 85; Jones, *Jeremiah*, p. 151; J. Skinner, *Prophecy and Religion: Studies in the Life of Jeremiah* (Cambridge: Cambridge University Press, 1926), p. 343; M. Weinfeld, 'The Worship of Molech and of the Queen of Heaven and its Background', *UF* 4 (1972), pp. 133-54 (149); and McKane, 'Worship', p. 323 and the references there.

19. Carroll, *Jeremiah*, p. 729.

20. For a discussion of the composition of ch. 44 see Carroll, *Jeremiah*, p. 732; and McKane, *Jeremiah*, II, pp. 1083-86 and the references there.

21. J.G. Janzen, *Studies in the Text of Jeremiah* (HSM, 6; Cambridge, MA: Harvard University Press, 1973), p. 58; and cf. G.L. Keown, P.J. Scalise and T.G. Smothers, *Jeremiah 26–52* (WBC, 27; Dallas: Word Books, 1995), p. 263; McKane, *Jeremiah*, II, p. 1074.

22. Cf. Janzen, *Studies*, p. 133; Holladay, *Jeremiah*, II, p. 279; McKane, *Jeremiah*, II, pp. 1075-76.

being performed by the women, their ancestors, and kings and officials. The rite is also dedicated to the Queen of Heaven. In ch. 7, the libations were poured out to 'other gods', and the worshippers were not specified. The burning of incense (which is to be interpreted as sacrificing, see below) is also added as another aspect of worship.

The inclusion of the kings and officials changes the status of the worship of the Queen of Heaven. No longer is it seen as an act of private, family worship. Rather, here her worship is seen to pervade all of society and to include both men and women, royalty and subjects.[23] Obviously the Queen of Heaven, as portrayed in this passage, was a major deity who was worshipped by all Israelites. Evidently the author wishes to suggest that such all-pervading worship of a deity other than Yahweh was the reason for the destruction of the nation; therefore, the worship must be shown to include all segments of society.

The use of the word $m^e qat^e r\hat{o}t$, 'burning incense', is interesting. It may give us an insight into how the Queen of Heaven was worshipped,[24] but it could also be a euphemism for performing sacrifices to the Queen of Heaven (as well as the 'other gods' previously mentioned in this chapter).[25] In this way the extent of the 'evil' that the people were doing was euphemistically lessened, perhaps similar to the much later Masoretic euphemistic alteration of 'queen of heaven' to 'works of heaven' noted above. At any rate, the text makes it clear that no worship of 'other' deities can be on a par with the worship of Yahweh. Notice too that although the people and kings and officials are all said to be participating, at no point here is it stated that *priests* are performing sacrifices to the Queen.

Verse 15 gives the answer of the people that they intend to ignore Jeremiah's words and will fulfill their vows to make sacrifices to the Queen of Heaven. The fact that the verse begins 'Then all the men who were aware that their wives had been making offerings to other gods' removes the men themselves from this worship, and places it squarely on the shoulders of the women. But the use of the first person plural 'we' in v. 17 implies that the men also were involved in

23. Skinner (*Prophecy*, p. 334) believes that the women were themselves from leading families, perhaps even including princesses. Cf. also Jones, *Jeremiah*, p. 478.

24. Cf. Weinfeld, 'Worship', p. 153 and the references there.

25. Cf. e.g. the translation in Holladay, *Jeremiah*, II, pp. 278-79; McKane, *Jeremiah*, II, p. 1068; Carroll, *Jeremiah*, pp. 729 and 738; Bright, *Jeremiah*, p. 264 n. on v. 3; S.R. Driver, *The Book of the Prophet Jeremiah* (London: Hodder and Stoughton, 1906), p. 41; Peake, *Jeremiah*, I, p. 85; A.S. Peake, *Jeremiah and Lamentations. II. Jeremiah XXV to LII and Lamentations* (The Century Bible; Edinburgh: T.C. & E.C. Jack, n.d.), p. 203.

the worship of the Queen of Heaven specifically, if only as an example of the more general 'other gods' referred to in v. 15.

This forcefully direct answer has been suggested to be 'a response placed in the mouth of the Egyptian community by the prophetic tradition'.[26] The people may have been this defiant in their actions, but Brueggemann notes that such resistance in actual speech is far less likely, as one would normally attempt to compromise in a direct confrontation such as this.[27] He states that 'this resistant response either reflects a very hard-nosed community, prepared to challenge the prophet, or it is a device by the framers of the text to make the community of Egyptian Jews appear as ignoble as possible. In this answer (either a serious one or a contrived one to thicken the dispute) there is no signal of accommodation to the prophetic word.'[28] Elsewhere he notes that 'because the material makes a general theological point, it may indeed be that the ostensive answer to the prophet (vv. 15-19) is in fact not an answer but a deliberate foil designed to serve the larger argument'.[29] Indeed, Carroll believes that this account is written to show that 'only in exile, and then only among the Babylonian exiles, is there any hope for the future'.[30]

The women's comment in v. 19 that they worshipped the Queen of Heaven with their husbands' approval seems odd if the men also were involved in the cult, as the picture in ch. 7 shows and as the combined people's response in v. 17 implies. The statement can be interpreted as either an attempt on the women's part to 'pass the buck' in terms of ultimate responsibility for their actions, or as evidence of the men's complicity in the worship of the Queen of Heaven.[31] There may also be a reference here to Num. 30.1-17, especially vv. 6-8 concerning vows that a wife makes and which need her husband's approval. If the husband says nothing about the wife's vow, giving tacit approval, then she is bound by her vow. But if the husband expresses disapproval concerning the wife's vow, then the wife has to nullify her vow and Yahweh will release her from it. Admittedly, this passage in Numbers is generally considered to be quite late. Although some scholars believe that this law preserves an older legal practice; it may also serve to help illustrate the late

26. Brueggemann, *Jeremiah*, p. 407.
27. Brueggemann, *Jeremiah*, p. 407.
28. Brueggemann, *Jeremiah*, p. 407.
29. Brueggemann, *Jeremiah*, p. 404; and cf. Carroll, *Chaos*, p. 242.
30. Carroll, *Chaos*, p. 243.
31. McKane, *Jeremiah*, II, p. 1080; Carroll, *Jeremiah*, p. 735.

authorship of the Jeremiah passage.[32] Either way the text is read, the women are major participants in the cult, but they are nevertheless acting with the full approval of, and most likely the participation of, their husbands as well.

Although in his discussion and translation of the passage Morgan notes that both men and women indicated their intent to worship the Queen of Heaven,[33] he nevertheless entitles his chapter on Jeremiah 44 'Degenerate Womanhood'. Elsewhere he talks about 'the close and appalling connection between corrupt rulers, and polluted and frivolous womanhood'.[34] And yet later he seems unsure as to where to place the blame. 'The manhood of a nation is perpetually under the dominion of its womanhood; and yet the womanhood of the nation is influenced by what the manhood of the nation is.'[35] O'Connor notes that Jeremiah 44 'accuses women alone of worshiping the queen, whereas it reduces the husbands' offense to failure to control their wives... Hence, chap. 44 makes women the direct cause of the nation's collapse.'[36] She further notes that 'women were excluded from full participation in temple worship, and the predominant Israelite conception of God was masculine. The queen provided them with a female deity who offered them protection and prosperity.'[37] Ackerman further explains that 'texts describing activities like women baking cakes for the Queen of Heaven...seem not so much evidence of female heresy as they are testimony to the fact of the heavily male orientation of biblical Yahwism. This androcentric focus of the dominant cult could have left many ancient Israelite women with no option but to seek opportunities for religious expression elsewhere.'[38] O'Connor believes that 'it is even possible that women understood the queen of heaven to be connected in some way with the God of Israel. If that were the case, they would have intended no idolatry. It is difficult to explain why ch. 44 blames women for this worship, although 7.18 accuses entire families. Perhaps over time worship of the queen

32. Cf. McKane, *Jeremiah*, II, pp. 1079-80; *idem*, 'Worship', p. 321.

33. G.C. Morgan, *Studies in the Prophecy of Jeremiah* (London and Edinburgh: Oliphants, 1955), pp. 265-66.

34. Morgan, *Studies*, p. 270.

35. Morgan, *Studies*, p. 272.

36. K.M. O'Connor, 'Jeremiah', in C.A. Newsom and S.H. Ringe (eds.), *The Women's Bible Commentary* (London: SPCK; Louisville, KY: Westminster/John Knox Press, 1992), pp. 169-77 (172).

37. O'Connor, 'Jeremiah', pp. 172-73.

38. S. Ackerman, *Warrior, Dancer, Seductress, Queen* (New York: Doubleday, 1998), p. 117.

decreased among men and grew among women, or perhaps chap. 44 reflects a changed society in which misogyny had increased.'[39]

The motivation for the revival of the worship of the Queen of Heaven is simply that it works.[40] The argument is that as long as the people worshipped the Queen of Heaven all was well, but once they stopped worshipping her all was lost. As long as her worship continued 'we used to have plenty of food, and prospered, and saw no misfortune. But from the time we stopped making offerings to the queen of heaven and pouring out libations to her, we have lacked everything and have perished by the sword and by famine' (44.17b-18). The people are not arguing that the Queen of Heaven should be worshipped to the exclusion of the worship of Yahweh; rather, they are arguing that the worship of Yahweh and that of the Queen of Heaven are complementary. It was only when the worship of the Queen of Heaven was eliminated and the nation worshipped Yahweh alone that the trouble really started.[41] The complementary nature of the worship can be seen in the statements of the cult of the Queen of Heaven occurring 'in the towns of Judah and in the streets of Jerusalem' (v. 17, etc.). We should note that the temple is not mentioned for her worship. Although a temple is mentioned for the Queen of Heaven in Egypt in the Hermopolis letter 4.1, and although Olyan believes that this temple is the setting of the discourse in Jeremiah 44,[42] the case is not the same for Jerusalem. Yahweh, as the national deity, was worshipped in the Jerusalem temple. The Queen of Heaven, on the other hand, seemed to have had a much wider appeal amongst all segments of society, rich and poor alike. As long as both of these types of worship continued all was well. But the eradication of the worship of the Queen of Heaven was the first step to the eradication of the nation.[43] Indeed, as Bauer notes, 'by implication [the women's] assertion accuses Jeremiah's God for their present condition. Unlike the Queen of Heaven, YHWH did not provide.'[44]

Jeremiah's reply in vv. 20-23 is, not surprisingly, the direct opposite of this argument. Instead of the worship of the Queen of Heaven

39. O'Connor, 'Jeremiah', p. 173.

40. Cf. Brueggemann, *Jeremiah*, p. 407; Carroll, *Jeremiah*, p. 736; *idem, Chaos*, p. 246.

41. Cf. McKane, *Jeremiah*, II, p. 1088; *idem*, 'Worship', pp. 323-24; Jones, *Jeremiah*, p. 477.

42. Olyan, 'Observations', p. 173.

43. Cf. McKane, *Jeremiah*, II, pp. 1088-89; Thompson, *Jeremiah*, p. 679.

44. Bauer, *Gender*, p. 152.

being the source of blessing it is the cause of the destruction. This worship has so angered Yahweh that Yahweh has unleashed the destruction of the nation upon the people of Judah. And now that destruction will extend even to the remnant in Egypt, who are so intent on continuing the worship of 'other gods'. This argument is of course exactly the same as the one which the people present, only using the same evidence to come to the opposite conclusion.[45] To an objective observer, there is little to choose between the two sides, as there is no way to prove which view is the correct one, if, indeed, either one of them was correct, rather than both being mere coincidence. Yahweh therefore gives the people a sign through Jeremiah in vv. 29-30, concerning Pharaoh Hophra, to show that Jeremiah is indeed correct. The sign of course could be a deuteronomistic redaction,[46] but even if it were to be considered contemporary to the discussion between Jeremiah and the people, it would not do the people any good, as they would have to wait at least fifteen years in the context of the story to see this sign fulfilled.[47] The sign then may be more for the reader's benefit than for the people's, and would then go to strengthen the view that the whole confrontation was crafted by the deuteronomistic redactor in order to bolster the accusation against the Jews in Egypt.[48] It is interesting to note that Jeremiah thus answers the men with a historical argument, whereas he answers the women by merely saying to go ahead and sacrifice if that is their will (v. 25).[49]

45. Cf. Brueggemann, *Jeremiah*, p. 411; Carroll, *Chaos*, p. 246; *idem*, *Jeremiah*, pp. 737-38; McKane, *Jeremiah*, II, p. 1089; and cf. D.N. Freedman, 'The Biblical Idea of History', *Interpretation* 21 (1967), pp. 32-49 (33-37).

46. Cf. Nicholson, *Jeremiah 26–52*, p. 160.

47. Cf. the discussion in McKane, *Jeremiah*, II, pp. 1081-82.

48. For more on deuteronomistic influence in Jeremiah see J. Bright, 'The Date of the Prose Sermons of Jeremiah', in L.G. Perdue and B.W. Kovacs (eds.), *A Prophet to the Nations: Essays in Jeremiah Studies* (Winona Lake, IN: Eisenbrauns, 1984), pp. 193-212; H. Cazelles, 'Jeremiah and Deuteronomy', in Perdue and Kovacs (eds.), *A Prophet to the Nations*, pp. 89-111; E.K. Holt, 'The Chicken and the Egg— Or: Was Jeremiah a Member of the Deuteronomist Party?', *JSOT* 44 (1989), pp. 109-22; Hyatt, 'Deuteronomic Edition'; J.P. Hyatt, 'Jeremiah and Deuteronomy', in Perdue and Kovacs (eds.), *A Prophet to the Nations*, pp. 113-27; L. Stulman, *The Prose Sermons of the Book of Jeremiah: A Redescription of the Correspondences with the Deuteronomistic Literature in the Light of Recent Text-Critical Research* (SBLDS, 83; Atlanta: Scholars Press, 1986).

49. Cf. Holladay, *Jeremiah*, II, pp. 286 and 304; W.L. Holladay, *Jeremiah: A Fresh Reading* (New York: Pilgrim Press, 1990), p. 144.

'Cakes' for the Queen of Heaven

We turn now to the cakes that the women made for the Queen of Heaven. In Jer. 7.18 the women kneaded the dough in order to make the cakes for the Queen of Heaven, and here in 44.19 we get further information about these cakes. First, however, it should be noted that it was the women specifically who made the cakes in ch. 7, and here again in ch. 44 it is the women who take responsibility for making the cakes. Earlier, in v. 18, when presumably the men also were speaking, only 'burning incense' and pouring out libations were mentioned, but in v. 19 the women claim to have made cakes (*kawwānîm*) for the Queen of Heaven, marked with her image, or in order to portray her (*lᵉhaʿᵃṣîbāh*, BDB 781 'to fashion her').

The term *kawwānîm* is usually considered to be a loan word from the Akkadian *kamānu*, which is known from Neo-Assyrian texts as a cake sweetened with fig or honey.[50] This naturally calls to mind the 'raisin cakes' of Hos. 3.1.[51] This connection has caused some scholars to believe that the cakes for the Queen of Heaven, although not the same as Hosea's raisin cakes, were aphrodisiacs, and that therefore the Queen of Heaven was a goddess of love; but that is far from proven, and should be rejected.[52] Furthermore, the use of breadstuffs in the cult and for sacrifices is a very common characteristic of ancient Near Eastern religions. If the Queen of Heaven is to be considered a goddess of love because the women made cakes for her, are we then to consider Yahweh a god of love because of the shewbread that is continually on display in his temple?

The fashioning of cakes for the Queen of Heaven is perhaps the one aspect of her cult that has received the most attention by scholars. Culican has published terracotta figures of women baking bread;[53]

---

50. Cf. e.g. Holladay, *Jeremiah 1*, p. 254; Held, 'Studies', p. 77; Carroll, *Jeremiah*, p. 212; Houtman, 'Queen', col. 1280; Schmitz, 'Queen', p. 587; W.E. Rast, 'Cakes for the Queen of Heaven', in A.L. Merrill and T.W. Overholt (eds.), *Scripture in History and Theology: Essays in Honor of J. Coert Rylaarsdam* (Pittsburgh: Pickwick Press, 1977), pp. 167-80 (167-68); see also the discussion in McKane, *Jeremiah*, I, p. 170. For an alternate view see K.J.H. Vriezen, 'Cakes and Figurines: Related Women's Cultic Offerings in Ancient Israel?', in B. Becking and M. Dijkstra (eds.), *On Reading Prophetic Texts: Gender-Specific and Related Studies in Memory of Fokkelien van Dijk-Hemmes* (Leiden: E.J. Brill, 1996), pp. 251-63 (255).

51. Cf. Holladay, *Jeremiah 1*, p. 254.

52. Cf. Frevel, *Aschera*, p. 438 n. 1476.

53. W. Culican, 'A Votive Model from the Sea', *PEQ* 108 (1976), pp. 119-23.

Rast,[54] Schroer[55] and Vriezen[56] have discussed various bread moulds from Mari; others[57] have examined the practice of baking breadstuffs on ashes (which might be implied by ch. 7, which mentions children gathering wood, but no ovens), and the list goes on. Frevel[58] notes that it is true that no oven is mentioned, but neither is it mentioned that the bread is actually baked. Therefore, the statement that the children gather wood for the fathers' fire may not so much indicate that the cakes are ash-cakes as stress that the whole family was involved in the cult.

Another characteristic of these cakes that has intrigued scholars, especially in the context of ch. 44, is that they were made *leha'aṣîbāh*, in order to fashion her. Scholarly opinion is divided into two camps on this question: either some type of symbol was stamped upon the bread or cake in order to identify her, such as a star, dove, moon, pubic triangle or something similar;[59] or else the cake itself was made in a form that would depict the goddess,[60] perhaps resembling the terracotta female pillar figurines so commonly found in pre-exilic Judah.[61] The bread moulds from Mari mentioned above have been informative in this discussion, despite their perhaps limited applicability due to the fact that they pre-date the Jeremian cakes by over 1000 years. Furthermore, none of the moulds from Mari contains any evidence of having been baked, and so perhaps it is best to consider that many of these moulds, especially the deep ones, were used for milk products such as cheese, and not bread.[62] Schroer[63] has suggested

54. Rast, 'Cakes', pp. 172-74.

55. S. Schroer, *In Israel gab es Bilder: Nachrichten von darstellender Kunst im Alten Testament* (OBO, 74; Fribourg: Editions universitaires; Göttingen: Vandenhoeck & Ruprecht, 1987), pp. 276-81.

56. Vriezen, 'Cakes', pp. 261-62 and n. 53.

57. Ackerman, *Tree*, p. 31; Rast, 'Cakes', p. 175; and cf. Held, 'Studies', p. 77.

58. Frevel, *Aschera*, pp. 438-39.

59. Cf. Vriezen, 'Cakes', p. 255 and the references there, as well as L.E. Binns, *The Book of the Prophet Jeremiah* (London: Methuen, 1919), p. 72; Cunliffe-Jones, *Jeremiah*, p. 85; Jones, *Jeremiah*, p. 151; McKane, 'Worship', p. 319; Olyan, 'Observations', p. 173 and n. 78; and cf. Bauer, *Gender*, p. 154.

60. See the discussions in Holladay, *Jeremiah 1*, pp. 254-55; Rast, 'Cakes', p. 168; Frevel, *Aschera*, pp. 439-40; Ackerman, *Tree*, p. 32.

61. Vriezen, 'Cakes', p. 261; Schroer, *In Israel*, pp. 276-81.

62. A. Parrot, 'Les fouilles de Mari', *Syria* 18 (1937), pp. 54-84 (76); *idem*, *Mission Archéologique de Mari*. II. *Le Palais. Documents et Monuments* (BAH, 70; Paris, Librairie Orientaliste Paul Guethner, 1959), pp. 33-57; Vriezen, 'Cakes', p. 262 n. 56.

63. Schroer, *In Israel*, p. 277.

that perhaps some of the many terracotta moulds of female figurines that have been found in excavations may actually be dough moulds, and not for clay figurines. This suggestion is intriguing but not likely, since most of the moulds would be too small for any detail to be noted on the cake, and also there are complex problems with the consistency of the dough which would need to be satisfactorily resolved.[64]

In an attempt to solve this dilemma, Keel and Uehlinger[65] have suggested that a clay stamp from Ramat Rahel that depicts a female face, devoid of any other attributes or characteristics, illustrates the Queen of Heaven. If so, it would be strange that no symbols of divinity seem to be present on the stamp, and so perhaps another alternative is to be preferred.

Possible Identifications of the Queen of Heaven[66]

It is this use of sacrificial cakes, and especially the connection with the Akkadian loan-word *kamānu*, which leads many scholars to identify the Queen of Heaven with the goddess Ishtar. But there is certainly no concensus on this point. Other goddesses have been suggested as well, such as Shapshu, Anat, Asherah or the West Semitic equivalent of Ishtar, Astarte.[67] Still others prefer a combination of some of these deities, with a combination of Ishtar and Astarte being the most prevalent.[68] Finally, there are even some scholars who assert that it is

64. See also the discussion in Vriezen, 'Cakes', pp. 262-63; Frevel, *Aschera*, pp. 439-40; Ackerman, *Tree*, pp. 31-32.

65. O. Keel and C. Uehlinger, *Gods, Goddesses, and Images of God in Ancient Israel* (trans. H. Trapp; Edinburgh: T. & T. Clark, 1998), p. 340 and fig. 332.

66. A full analysis of the various possibilities, together with all the relevant inscriptional material, is beyond the scope of this article. For fuller discussions of the deities treated here see Ackerman, 'Dough', pp. 110-18; *idem*, *Tree*, pp. 8-35; Olyan, 'Observations'; and Frevel, *Aschera*, pp. 444-71; as well as the specific references below.

67. The scholars who support these candidates for the Queen of Heaven will be noted in the discussion of the relevant deity below.

68. Ackerman ('Dough', pp. 116-17 and *Tree*, p. 34) is perhaps the strongest advocate for the identity of the Queen of Heaven as a syncretistic deity who incorporates aspects of both Astarte and Ishtar. However, since there is such a close connection between these two deities anyway, most of the scholars noted below under either Astarte or Ishtar also acknowledge that the Queen of Heaven exhibits attributes of the other goddess. On a slightly different note, Keel and Uehlinger (*Gods*, pp. 339-40) support the linking of Ishtar with Asherah rather than Astarte.

impossible to determine who she was, especially given the little information which we have.[69]

We will briefly consider the case for Shapshu, Anat and Asherah
first, before turning to Ishtar and Astarte.

Shapshu

The main advocate for Shapshu as the Queen of Heaven is Dahood.
He bases his identification on *CTA* 23.54, which he translates 'Arise,
prepare cakes for Lady Shapshu and for the stars'.[70] Firstly, note that
Shapshu is here called Lady, and not Queen. Nevertheless, the title of
queen is certainly appropriate for any of the great goddesses (usually
considered to be Asherah, Astarte/Ishtar and Anat) and so presumably Dahood here equates 'Lady' with 'Queen'. However, nowhere is
Shapshu called queen, and so this identification may need to be re-
examined. More problematic is Dahood's translation of the Ugaritic
word which he renders 'cakes'. It is, of course, broken in the text,
reading *kn*, which Dahood reconstructs to read *kn[m]*. However, no
other scholars, even those who reconstruct the text to read *kn[m]*
(others preferring *kn[t]*), translate this word 'cakes', preferring as they
do to interpret the word as an adjective of the root *kwn*, meaning
'fixed'.[71] In short, Dahood's suggestion has received very little consideration from scholars, and Shapshu is no longer considered a
contender.[72]

Anat

The case for Anat is stronger.[73] She, at least, is called 'Anat, Lady of
Heaven, Mistress of all the Gods' on a stele from Beth-Shan. The title

69. Cf. e.g. Carroll, *Jeremiah*, p. 213, who says that a precise identification is
impossible.

70. M. Dahood, 'La Regina del Cielo in Geremia', *RevistB* 8 (1960), pp. 166-68.

71. See the comments and references in Held, 'Studies', p. 76; Ackerman, *Tree*,
pp. 11-12; and Frevel, *Aschera*, pp. 447-48.

72. For further criticisms of Dahood's suggestion see Culican, 'Votive Model',
p. 121; Held, 'Studies', p. 76; Ackerman, *Tree*, pp. 11-12; and Frevel, *Aschera*,
pp. 447-48.

73. Scholars who hold this view include W.F. Albright, *Yahweh and the Gods of
Canaan* (London: University of London, 1968), p. 113; M. Cogan, *Imperialism and
Religion: Assyria, Judah and Israel in the Eighth and Seventh Centuries BCE* (SBLMS, 19;
Missoula, MT: Scholars Press, 1974), pp. 85-86; F.F. Hvidberg, *Weeping and Laughter
in the Old Testament* (Leiden: E.J. Brill, 1962), pp. 115-17; F.O. Hvidberg-Hansen, *La
déesse Tnt, un étude sur la religion canaanéo-punique*, I (Copenhagen: Gad, 1979),
p. 96; B. Porten, *Archives from Elephantine* (Los Angeles and Berkeley: University of
California Press, 1968), p. 165.

'Lady of Heaven' is attributed to her on several inscriptions of Ramses II and elsewhere in Egypt.[74] There is also evidence from the fifth-century BCE Hermopolis Letter 4, which refers to the temple of the Queen of Heaven.[75] Although the Queen is not named, many scholars draw the obvious inference that she is to be identified with the Anat-Yahu and Anat-Bethel of the Elephantine papyri,[76] and that therefore the temple to the Queen of Heaven in Syene is to be considered a temple to Anat.[77]

And yet this identification is also uncertain. Most of the evidence is from the second millennium, and is therefore not even nearly contemporary with the Jeremiah passage. Also, the evidence that we have to date for the worship of Anat in Israel and Judah from the first millennium is only a few place names and personal names, which themselves largely hark back to the second millennium in origin.[78] As for the Elephantine material, although the date and location fit well with Jeremiah, the identification of Anat-Yahu and Anat-Bethel with the goddess Anat is far from proven. Indeed, scholars are not even convinced that the element *anat* in these names refers to a goddess, and believe that it may instead be understood as 'sign' or 'providence', thus referring to a hypostatized quality of the deity Yahu or Bethel.[79] Therefore there are difficulties with interpreting Anat as the Queen of Heaven as well.

---

74. Cf. Olyan, 'Observations', pp. 163-64; and Ackerman, *Tree*, p. 13 and the references there.

75. E. Bresciani and M. Kamil, 'Le Lettere aramaiche di Hermopoli', in E. Volterra, S. Moscati and G.L. Della Vida (eds.), *Atti della Accademia Nazionale dei Lincei: Rendiconti Mem. Scienze Morali 1966* (Ser. VII, 12.5; Rome: Accademia Nazionale dei Lincei, 1966), pp. 359-428 (398-403); J.T. Milik, 'Les papyrus araméens d'Hermoupolis et les cultes syro-phéniciens en Egypte perse', *Bib* 48 (1967), pp. 556-64; cf. Houtman, 'Queen', cols. 1278-79; Olyan, 'Observations', pp. 161-62; Ackerman, *Tree*, pp. 13-14; Frevel, *Aschera*, pp. 448-51.

76. For more on the Elephantine papyri see Porten, *Archives*, pp. 165, 168-71, 179, among others.

77. For arguments against this identification see Frevel, *Aschera*, p. 450 n. 1521.

78. Cf. Olyan, 'Observations', pp. 169-70; Ackerman, *Tree*, pp. 16-17; Frevel, *Aschera*, pp. 448-51.

79. A full analysis of the debate surrounding the Elephantine material is far beyond the scope of this article. For this debate, as well as other criticisms concerning the identification of Anat with the Queen of Heaven see, among others, Koch, 'Aschera', pp. 110-11; Olyan, 'Observations', pp. 169-71; Ackerman, *Tree*, pp. 16-20; and Frevel, *Aschera*, pp. 448-51.

Asherah

Before the discovery of the Khirbet el-Qom and Kuntillet Ajrud material, Asherah was seldom a serious contender for the title 'Queen of Heaven'. Now, however, she is increasingly being put forward as a likely candidate.[80] The first main champion for Asherah as Queen of Heaven was Koch.[81] He bases much of his argument for Asherah on the evidence that she was an important personage in the Bible, whose worship was closely connected to that of Yahweh.[82] He derives many of the conjectured astral qualities for Asherah from this connection, together with the interpretation of the *sēmel haqqinâ* in Ezek. 8.3, 5 as a representation of Asherah. Since Koch closely equates all of the so-called abominations in Ezekiel 8 together, and since worship of the sun is also condemned later in that chapter, he believes that it can be inferred that Asherah has astral qualities.[83] Additionally, she is mentioned alongside the Host of Heaven in Kings (cf. e.g. 2 Kgs 23), and Koch further identifies the aspect of 'burning incense' in the cult of the Queen of Heaven to refer to worship of astral deities.[84] Dijkstra concurs, and sees the identification of Asherah with the Queen of Heaven 'because of the Canaanite matrix of El-and-Asherah religion in the eighth c BCE and earlier centuries in Israel which implies that the Queen of Heaven can hardly be associated with someone else than Asherah'.[85]

Parts of this argument are compelling, whereas others are less convincing. The strongest argument for Asherah as the Queen of Heaven, to my mind, is that of her close association with Yahweh. Together they form the 'heavenly couple'. Apart from this connection, however, the evidence is less certain. For example, the mere juxtaposition of the objection of the *sēmel haqqinâ* in the same chapter as the condemnation of sun worship is hardly an argument for the astral qualities of Asherah. It has not been proven that the *sēmel haqqinâ* refers to a statue or symbol of Asherah, although I personally believe

---

80. Scholars who support this position include Freedman, 'Idea', pp. 34-35; B. Vawter, 'Yahweh: Lord of the Heavens and the Earth', *CBQ* 48 (1986), pp. 461-67 (464); Koch, 'Aschera', pp. 107-109; and M. Dijkstra, 'Goddess, God, Men and Women in Ezekiel 8', in Becking and Dijkstra (eds.), *On Reading Prophetic Texts*, pp. 83-114 (92).

81. Koch, 'Aschera', pp. 107-12.

82. Koch, 'Aschera', pp. 108-109.

83. Koch, 'Aschera', pp. 111-12.

84. Koch, 'Aschera', pp. 107-108.

85. Dijkstra, 'Goddess', pp. 92-93 n. 31.

that to be the case.[86] The atrocities presented in Ezekiel 8 are connected, but not in the sense that they are all the same type of worship; rather these are the types of things that are now happening in Yahweh's temple, where each action is portrayed as being more abominable than the previous one. Furthermore, as seen above, the word *qṭr*, 'burn incense', is most probably used as a euphemism for 'to sacrifice', and does not necessarily mean that incense was used in the Queen's cult.

Furthermore, it is possible that Asherah has too close a connection to Yahweh to be considered the Queen of Heaven. It is worth noting that objects sacred to Asherah were to be found in the temple of Yahweh, even planted next to Yahweh's altar (Deut. 16.21). Also, women wove hangings for the *asherah* that was to be found in the temple (2 Kgs 23.7). Furthermore, Asherah evidently had prophets (as well as priests?) dedicated to her service (1 Kgs 18.19). None of these connections with the temple or prophets is explicitly attested for the worship of the Queen of Heaven. Although she presumably had priests to perform her sacrifices, her worship is described as occurring in the streets of Jerusalem (Jer. 7.17, etc.). Of course, it is possible that the deuteronomistic authors of the Jeremiah passage wished to downplay the official acceptance of the cult of the Queen of Heaven, together with any connection to the temple, but it remains the case that what is known of the cult of the Queen of Heaven does not have much overlap with what is known of the cult of Asherah.[87]

What seems to be occurring here in the case of Asherah is rather that she is currently 'flavour of the month'. To paraphrase the well known saying, modern scholars are seeing Asherah in every goddess. Although it is possible that she is to be considered the Queen of Heaven, this identification too is far from certain from the evidence we have available.

Ishtar
We now return to Ishtar.[88] As mentioned above, one of the strongest arguments for considering Ishtar as the Queen of Heaven is the reference to the cakes. In Akkadian texts, *kamānu* cakes, especially ash

86. J.M. Hadley, *The Cult of Asherah in Ancient Israel and Judah: Evidence for a Hebrew Goddess* (Oriental Publications, 57; Cambridge: Cambridge University Press, 2000), p. 81.
87. For more comments and criticisms concerning Asherah as the Queen of Heaven see, for example, Olyan, 'Observations', p. 171; and Frevel, *Aschera*, pp. 462-69.
88. As mentioned above, many of the scholars who support Ishtar as the

cakes, are often associated with the cult of Ishtar. As noted above, many scholars believe ash cakes are referred to for the Queen of Heaven due to the lack of mention of an oven, but as we have seen that could be just to show the division of labour among the various family members. Ackerman notes a hymn to Ishtar which reads:

> O Ishtar, merciful goddess, I have come to visit you,
> I have prepared for you an offering, pure milk,
>   a pure cake baked in ashes (*kamān tumri*),
> I stood up for you a vessel for libations,
>   hear me and act favorably toward me![89]

Another text describes an ash cake being prepared in honour of Ishtar as part of a healing ritual.[90] It has also been suggested that the

Queen of Heaven also include references to Astarte. Therefore it is often difficult to determine exactly which goddess is being promoted, as so many scholars seem to 'hedge their bets'. Some of these will be noted here as they occur. The scholars who primarily support Ishtar include Binns, *Jeremiah*, p. 72; Bright, *Jeremiah*, p. 56, who notes, 'probably the Assyrian-Babylonian goddess Ishtar...but perhaps her cult had been identified with that of some Canaanite goddess'; Carroll, *Jeremiah*, p. 734, who notes, 'the queen of heaven probably refers to some form of the Ishtar cult or Isis as she would be known in Egypt'; Cunliffe-Jones, *Jeremiah*, p. 85; F. van Dijk-Hemmes, 'Traces of Women's Texts in the Hebrew Bible', in A. Brenner and F. van Dijk-Hemmes, *On Gendering Texts: Female and Male Voices in the Hebrew Bible* (Biblical Interpretation, 1; Leiden: E.J. Brill, 1993), p. 87; Feinberg, *Jeremiah*, pp. 74, 287 (but p. 286, 'apparently Astarte'); N.C. Habel, *Jeremiah, Lamentations* (Concordia Commentary; St Louis: Concordia, 1968), p. 92; R.K. Harrison, *Jeremiah and Lamentations* (TOTC; London: The Tyndale Press, 1973), pp. 87, 167, 'Ishtar (Canaanite Astarte)'; Held, 'Studies', p. 77; Holladay, *Jeremiah 1*, p. 254, 'the Palestinian manifestation of Ištar'; M.J. Hunter, *A Guide to Jeremiah* (Theological Education Fund Study Guide, 30; London: SPCK, 1993), p. 52, 'Astarte, the Babylonian goddess of fertility...the Assyrians called her Ishtar'; Jones, *Jeremiah*, p. 151; Peake, *Jeremiah*, I, p. 150; Peake, *Jeremiah*, II, p. 205; Rast, 'Cakes', p. 169, 'could well have been referred to Astarte or one of the other Palestinian deities, but it is doubtful that the strong associations of that title with Ishtar would have been absent'; Skinner, *Prophecy*, p. 343; A.W. Streane, *The Book of the Prophet Jeremiah together with the Lamentations* (Cambridge: Cambridge University Press, 1913), p. 54; Thompson, *Jeremiah*, p. 284, 'Assyro-Babylonian Astarte [Ishtar]', p. 679, 'Assyro-Babylonian goddess Ishtar, identified with Astarte'; Weinfeld, 'Worship', p. 150; R.E.O. White, *The Indomitable Prophet* (Grand Rapids: Eerdmans, 1992), p. 19; U. Winter, *Frau und Göttin: Exegetische und ikonographische Studien zum weiblichen Gottesbild im Alten Israel und in dessen Umwelt* (OBO, 53; Fribourg: Editions universitaires; Göttingen: Vandenhoeck & Ruprecht, 1983), pp. 564-66.

89. Ackerman, *Tree*, p. 31 and the references there; cf. Held, 'Studies', p. 77.
90. Ackerman, *Tree*, p. 31 and the references there.

moulds at Mari might be intended to portray Ishtar.[91] However, as
noted above, it is most likely that the deep moulds (which are the
ones that portray human forms) were used for dairy products.

Women were also prominent in the Ishtar cult, and the fact that
Ishtar's consort is Tammuz may prove to be instructive. Ackerman
draws a connection between the laments of Ishtar over her dead lover
Tammuz and the women who mourn the death of Tammuz in Ezek.
8.14, and thus suggests that 'this special role of women as ritual
mourners over Tammuz provides a significant parallel to the biblical
materials concerning the women who bake cakes for the Queen of
Heaven'.[92]

Ishtar is also certainly identified in Akkadian texts as Queen of
Heaven, *šarrat šamê*, or of course also *bēlet šamê*, Lady of Heaven. She
is also called 'Queen of Heaven and the Stars', 'Queen of Heaven and
Earth', 'Lady of Heaven and Earth', 'Sovereign of Heaven and Earth',
'Ruler of Heaven and Earth', and in a New Kingdom inscription from
Memphis which is dedicated to Hurrian Astarte, equal to Ishtar of
Nineveh, she is called 'the Lady of Heaven, the Mistress of the Two
Lands, the Mistress of all the Gods'. Finally, in Mesopotamia she is
equated with the Sumerian name of the planet Venus.[93]

Keel and Uehlinger also present several seals that show that Ishtar
was known in Palestine during the Iron Age.[94] However, they also
note that since none of these seals was found in Judah, 'to identify the
"Queen of Heaven" *exclusively* with the Assyrian deity Ishtar, and *no
other* possible deity, cannot be the last word on the subject'.[95] Therefore, although Ishtar seems to have a good case for being considered
the Queen of Heaven, there still may be other possibilities.[96]

Astarte

We therefore turn to Astarte.[97] Astarte, also, is called 'Lady of
Heaven' in many New Kingdom texts. She is also called 'Lady of
Heaven, Mistress of all the Gods' on a stele from Memphis from the

    91. Ackerman, *Tree*, p. 32.
    92. Ackerman, *Tree*, p. 33.
    93. For these epithets and references see Ackerman, *Tree*, pp. 28-29.
    94. Keel and Uehlinger, *Gods*, p. 293.
    95. Keel and Uehlinger, *Gods*, p. 294.
    96. For further comments and criticisms see Olyan, 'Observations', pp. 171-74;
Ackerman, *Tree*, pp. 28-34; and Frevel, *Aschera*, pp. 451-56.
    97. As noted above, many of the scholars who propose Astarte for the Queen
of Heaven also suggest Ishtar. Several of these comments will be included below.
These scholars include Bresciani and Kamil, 'Le Lettere', p. 400, 'Astarte identified

time of Merneptah, but she is also well attested as a queen in first millennium texts.[98] Perhaps most instructive for us here is that on the obverse face of the Kition tariff inscription, which lists the monthly expenditures for the temple of Astarte at Kition in Cyprus, Astarte is referred to as 'the Holy Queen' in l. 7 and 'the Queen' in l. 10.[99] Admittedly she is not mentioned by name in ll. 7 and 10, but that 'the title "queen" in an inscription concerned with the cult and temple of Astarte' refers to Astarte is not in doubt.[100] The identification of Astarte as the Queen of Heaven in this inscription is particularly interesting, due to the several parallels between this inscription and the situation in the book of Jeremiah. 'The inscription describes a festival, consisting of a procession through the city streets, accompanied by singing and lighting a fire to the Queen of Heaven.'[101] Furthermore, l. 10 refers to 'the two bakers who baked the basket of cakes for the Queen'.[102] This identification is also discussed by Culican,[103] who describes a Hellenistic votive model found off the Phoenician coast,

with Ishtar'; G.P. Couturier, 'Jeremiah', in R.E. Brown, J.A. Fitzmyer and R.E. Murphy (eds.), *Jerome Biblical Commentary* (Englewood Cliffs, NJ: Prentice-Hall, 1968), pp. 300-36 (310); Culican, 'Votive Model', p. 121; Delcor, 'Le culte', p. 119; Driver, *Jeremiah*, p. 43 n. b; J.A. Fitzmyer, 'The Phoenician Inscription from Pyrgi', *JAOS* 86 (1966), pp. 285-97 (287); Holladay, *Jeremiah* 1, p. 255; *idem*, *Jeremiah*, 2, p. 304; *idem*, *Fresh Reading*, p. 143; Hunter, *Jeremiah*, p. 52, 'Astarte, the Babylonian goddess of fertility...the Assyrians called her Ishtar'; McKane, *Jeremiah*, I, p. 170; R. du Mesnil du Buisson, *Etudes sur les dieux phéniciens hérités par l'empire romain* (Etudes préliminaires aux religions orientales dans l'Empire romain, 14; Leiden: E.J. Brill, 1970), pp. 12, 126-27; *idem*, *Nouvelles études sur les dieux et les mythes de Canaan* (Etudes préliminaires aux religions orientales dans l'Empire romain, 33; Leiden: E.J. Brill, 1973), pp. 56, 231; Milik, 'Les papyrus', p. 563; Nicholson, *Jeremiah 1–25*, p. 79, 'Astarte (Ashtoreth), though possibly Anat'; Olyan, 'Observations', pp. 169, 174; Rast, 'Cakes', p. 168, but also noting 'strong associations of that title with Ishtar'; M.S. Smith, *The Early History of God: Yahweh and the Other Deities in Ancient Israel* (San Francisco: Harper & Row, 1990), p. 90, 'may refer either to Astarte, the only West Semitic goddess bearing this title during the Iron Age, or to Ishtar', but p. 145, 'perhaps Astarte, or, less likely, Ishtar or Anat'; Thompson, *Jeremiah*, 679, 'Assyro-Babylonian goddess Ishtar, identified with Astarte', cf. n. 88.

98. For these texts see Ackerman, *Tree*, p. 20 and the references there. Cf. also Olyan, 'Observations', pp. 166-69.

99. Ackerman, *Tree*, pp. 20-21 and the references there.

100. Ackerman, 'Dough', p. 120 n. 10; cf. *idem*, *Tree*, p. 21.

101. P.J. King, *Jeremiah: An Archaeological Companion* (Louisville, KY: Westminster/John Knox Press, 1993), p. 107.

102. Ackerman, 'Dough', p. 113; and cf. *idem*, *Tree*, p. 26.

103. Culican, 'Votive Model', p. 122.

which has six figures positioned around a domed object. He interprets the domed object as a beehive oven, the standing pregnant female figure he interprets as Astarte, the male figure Culican suggests is a priest, and the four identical seated women are votaresses. He thus proposes that the scene is a cake-baking ritual in honour of Astarte.[104] This interpretation is far from proven, but the evidence from the Kition tariff inscription and Jer. 7.18 and 44.19, together with Astarte's popularity in the Phoenician and Punic realm in the late first millennium, makes it an attractive possibility.[105]

Concluding Remarks

And yet, of course, the figures on the votive model are not named, which is also the case for the Queen of Heaven in Jeremiah. I have discussed elsewhere the interesting fact that there is a tendency in the latest biblical texts either to misunderstand the situation that obtained in the pre-exilic period, or else deliberately to attempt to obscure the roles of deities other than Yahweh, especially in the case of Deuteronomy.[106] It may be instructive that here in Jeremiah the Queen of Heaven is not named. After all, I tend to think that perhaps we now in the twenty-first century are more interested in a precise identification of the Queen of Heaven than were the ancients in the first millennium BCE. In many texts and traditions we see a fluidity of deities and their attributes, where we would like much more rigidity. Houtman believes that

> the title Queen of Heaven was evidently a designation for the universal mother goddess, who according to the time and the place of her worship could have a different character. The use of the goddess' title without mentioning her proper name may be considered as a symptom of a religious atmosphere in which the qualities of a deity are held to be of more importance than her name.[107]

Barnett mentions a similar instance, in his discussion of the nameless grain deity at Arad. He prefers 'not to confer on this [Arad] figure the

---

104. Culican, 'Votive Model', pp. 119-20.

105. For more comments see Ackerman, 'Dough', pp. 110-14; *idem*, *Tree*, pp. 20-28; Olyan, 'Observations', pp. 166-69; Frevel, *Aschera*, pp. 457-61, among others.

106. J.M. Hadley, 'The De-Deification of Deities in Deuteronomy', paper delivered at the 16th Congress of the International Organization for the Study of the Old Testament (Oslo, Norway, 1998); *idem*, 'The Fertility of the Flock?: The De-Personalization of Astarte in the Old Testament', in Becking and Dijkstra (eds.), *On Reading Prophetic Texts*, pp. 115-33.

107. Houtman, 'Queen', col. 1281; and cf. Delcor, 'Le culte', pp. 115-19.

name of any special deity worshipped in a priestly cult, only to suggest that it depicts the nameless corn-spirit of ambiguous sex; probably honoured then as now at a popular level, which has survived until today largely because it is nameless'.[108]

Therefore, as long as the land is fertile and the people are prospering, the worshippers will gladly continue in their cultic practice. The argument of the women is compelling. As long as they faithfully performed their sacrifices for the Queen of Heaven, all was well. But since that worship was eradicated, the nation has been plunged into disaster. Therefore the Jews in Egypt are now intent on renewing their worship of the Queen of Heaven, in some form, perhaps even by worshipping a local Egyptian deity such as Isis.[109] If the text of the book of Jeremiah is contemporary with the events it describes, then the identity of the Queen of Heaven would have been crucial to the people, who would need to know exactly which deity they needed to worship again in order to get things back on track. However, if the text of Jeremiah derives from a much later time in the post-exilic period, it may be that exactly which deity the people were worshipping was not a matter of interest to the author, since by that time all of the duties of any other deities would have been absorbed into Yahwism, and Yahweh was the only deity needed. It is even possible that precisely which deity was responsible for what in those heady pre-exilic times was as confusing for the late post-exilic writers as it is for us today. Thus, all that was necessary for the writer to drive home the point was that there had been a time, generations ago, when the people worshipped the Queen of Heaven, who would represent, for the late author, *any* deity that was worshipped apart from Yahweh, be it in the past, the present, or, indeed, even the future.[110]

---

108. R.D. Barnett, 'From Arad to Carthage: Harvest Rites and Corn-Dollies', *Eretz-Israel* 20 (1989), pp. 1*-11* (3*).

109. It is interesting that most of the discussion of the identity of the Queen of Heaven has been limited to Northwest Semitic or Mesopotamian deities, and has not included Egyptian ones. Anat is the only one of the proposed candidates who has much of an Egyptian connection. Although I am not suggesting that Isis should be considered a serious contender for the role, it may be that one reason the author has chosen not to name the Queen of Heaven is so that the title may be applied to any deity apart from Yahweh that the Jews are tempted to worship, including now local indigenous ones.

110. Indeed, some have argued that the cult of the Queen of Heaven has continued up to the present day, namely in the veneration of the Virgin Mary (Regina Coeli); cf. Houtman, 'Queen', col. 1282; and O. Loretz, *Ugarit und die Bibel: Kanaanäische Götter und Religion im Alten Testament* (Darmstadt: Wissenschaftliche Buchgesellschaft, 1990), p. 88, among others.

B.

FEMALE PROPHETS OR 'PROPHETESSES'?

PROPHECY AND THE CONSTRUCTION OF WOMEN: INSCRIPTION AND ERASURE

Esther Fuchs

The very term נביא and the concept of prophecy in general, and their meaning especially in the context of the latter prophets, are far from clear. Some scholars tend to underplay the element of prediction and argue that a prophet is a messenger, a mediator between God and people, one whose function is to chastise the people and teach them right from wrong. Others tend to emphasize the element of prediction, arguing that the institution of prophecy was founded on the need of the king to know the results of specific military confrontations. Whether messengers or diviners of future events, prophets in the Hebrew Bible usually work with words. To transmit God's message, they use both symbolic and verbal communication, they perform and speak. The prophets whose names and lives are recorded in the biblical narrative, and the latter prophets we meet in the poetic segments, are presented as mouthpieces of God's Truth. They interpret truthfully God's intentions and communicate them to others, to individual kings or to a collective audience. But as I have argued elsewhere, women are constructed in a rather problematic relationship to Truth, notably to Truth mediated through words.[1] They often, if not always, use words so as to conceal or prevaricate with the Truth. Time and time again women deceive, for better or for worse, in one form or another; their utterances do not reflect the reality that is constructed in the text. This may perhaps account for the ambiguous presentation of woman prophets and for the ambiguous presentation of women by the prophets, notably the latter prophets.

---

1.   'Who is Hiding the Truth? Deceptive Women and Biblical Androcentrism', in Adela Y. Collins (ed.), *Feminist Perspectives on Biblical Scholarship* (Chico, CA: Scholars Press, 1985), pp. 137-44. See also, '"For I Have the Way of Women": Deception, Gender, and Ideology in Biblical Narrative', in J. Cheryl Exum and Johanna W.H. Bos (eds.), *Reasoning with the Foxes: Female Wit in a World of Male Power* (*Semeia*, 42; Society of Biblical Literature, 1988), pp. 68-83.

The latter prophets address an entire people; they chastise collect-ive behavior and predict dire consequences, a divine punishment for alleged cultic and ethical misconduct. The early prophets (e.g. Samuel, Nathan, Elijah) usually confront individual kings (e.g. Saul, David, Ahab), and castigate them for immoral behavior. Both categor-ies are presented in the biblical corpus in such a way as to exclude women. Huldah, who indirectly addresses Josiah, prophesies in the period of Jeremiah, but is not included among the fifteen latter prophets who are named and identified as individuals whose sermons have been collected and preserved. There are certainly no women among the early prophets. The women prophets we shall survey next are not shown to chastise a king, nor do they reprimand a collective audience. None of the women who could conceivably be categorized as early prophets is shown to perform a miracle. The ability to perform a miracle is presented as a complement to the early prophets' ability to utter true messages emanating from God. Though miracle-making is generally taken as an ancillary activity that is not necessarily a salient characteristic of the prophetic position, it is nevertheless a marker and index of divine approbation. The miracles wrought by Elijah and Elisha are often performed at the behest of women. Women are the receivers and beneficiaries of the prophets' miraculous powers. Even if we are to agree with Fokkelien van Dijk-Hemmes regarding the spiritual greatness of the Shunammite woman, the fact remains that it is Elisha, the male prophet, who predicts her pregnancy, and it is he who revives her son (2 Kgs 4.8-37).[2] It is Elisha who miraculously provides for the nameless penniless widow (2 Kgs 4.1-7), just as Elijah before him miraculously provides food for the nameless widow of Zarephath and eventually revives her son (1 Kgs 17.9-24). Women are affirmed in their helpless, passive and receptive roles. Women are *not* affirmed in their capacity as agents who them-selves possess numinous powers. The only reference to a woman possessing genuine numinous powers occurs in 1 Samuel 28 in con-junction with the woman of En-Dor. This nameless 'woman diviner' or בעלת אוב is shown to be capable of calling forth a ghost, not just any ghost but that of the prophet Samuel. And yet this activity is presented in highly ambivalent terms. She is not a prophet. She is incapable of having a dialogue with YHWH. Only the prophet is

---

2.   Fokkelien van Dijk-Hemmes, 'The Great Woman of Shunem and the Man of God: A Dual Interpretation of 2 Kings 4.8-37', in A. Brenner (ed.), *A Feminist Companion to Samuel and Kings* (Sheffield: Sheffield Academic Press, 1994), pp. 218-30.

shown to be able to transmit any truthful information about the
future. Only Samuel is shown to communicate divine intentions truthfully. What is then to be done if the male prophet is deceased? In the
absence of any other means of contacting YHWH with any measure of
success, the woman of En-Dor must resurrect the prophet's ghost. The
בעלת אוב is no match for God's prophet. With all her supernatural
talent, she cannot replace him. She is shown to use an illicit practice of
divination (קסם, v. 8). By her own cognizance she belongs to the
illegitimate group of the אובות and the ידעוני (v. 9), diviners who have
recourse to spirits, diviners who use magic and witchcraft, diviners
who are inferior, who are 'Other', who are construed as the opposite
of the prophets. The woman of En-Dor is limited in her abilities. She
does not recognize Samuel (v. 13). The story of the woman of En-Dor
juxtaposes the prophet of God Samuel with the misguided king Saul,
but it also satirizes the woman of En-Dor as the non-prophet par
excellence.[3] Eventually, even this extraordinary witch is domesticated,
shown to do what women (e.g. Sarah, Manoah's wife) do best: she
prepares a meal for the frightened King Saul (vv. 22-25).

נביאה is a term attributed to several women, such as Miriam,
Deborah and Huldah. Yet rarely does this label introduce a prophetic
discourse. More often than not the prophetic role of the woman in
question is obfuscated or suppressed. What we witness in the biblical
ambiguity but rather a process of suppression, which entails derogation and obfuscation. Suppression always results in some form of
palimpsestic tracing. The names of the women we encounter in the
text suggest that they have played meaningful roles, but the exposition is so sparse, there are so many informational gaps and lacunae,
that it is hardly clear what the prophetess's role consisted of. The
presentation of women as prophets is so fragmentary and so ambiguous that it is difficult if not impossible to reconstruct it as based on
the biblical record. It is of course possible to ignore the written text
and to reconstruct an institution of female prophecy based on other
sources. And yet it is important to remember that, for the most part,
such historical readings are no less imaginative than any other
interpretive reading.

In the case of Miriam in the book of Exodus, the term נביאה appears
in conjunction with a performative activity, singing and dancing. The
term נביאה describes a performative rather than a prophetic activity.

---

3.   The Pharaoh's חרטומים ('magicians'?) in the book of Exodus are also able to
perform miracles. Much like Moses, they are shown to have numinous powers, but
they lack Moses' prophetic powers.

In the case of Deborah, the term נביאה precedes the description of judicial and later military activities. Now both Miriam and Deborah are presented as prominent leaders, but not necessarily as prophetesses. Like Miriam, who praises YHWH for a successful deliverance from the hands of the Egyptians, Deborah too is shown to sing and give praise to God for a military defeat of national enemies, in this case the Canaanites. The connection between prophecy and poetry has already been recognized in scholarship. But is it coincidental that contexts describing the נביאה emphasize the poetic, psalmodic element, rather than the prophetic? Is it coincidental that the theme of military deliverance as divine victory is the theme that characterizes the public concern of both Miriam and Deborah, whereas the divine-human connection is the basic theme in Moses' prophecy? While Moses' messages are 'quoted' at great length, and while the early and certainly the latter prophets' discourses are represented in great detail, the woman prophets are terribly laconic, their discourses are minimal. Miriam's prophetic message is not represented at all in the text. Deborah's prophetic discourse is summed up in four verses (Judg. 4.6-7, 9, 14). The prophecy attributed to Huldah spans five highly formulaic verses, giving rise to speculations about its indebtedness to Jeremiah (2 Kgs 22.15-20). The case of Huldah is ambiguous enough to suggest that she may even have been a so called false prophet.[4] The narrative representation of women prophets differs from that of male prophets both qualitatively and quantitatively. The woman prophets lack the narrative expansiveness that characterizes the stories of Samuel, Elijah and Elisha. Their discourses are given short shrift, or erased altogether. Is it possible to argue that the fragmentary and ambivalent presentation of woman prophets is not coincidental? I would argue that the presentation of woman prophets reflects reluctance on the part of the narrator to admit or reveal the extent of women's prophetic activity. The narratorial ambivalence toward women's prophetic function is exposed in the suppression of the possibility of a female dialogue with YHWH. Even in the cases of the women who are labeled prophets, there is a reluctance to dramatize, using the third-person authoritative voice, the kind of dialogue male prophets are shown to have with YHWH. In other words, a נביאה may be shown to use the messenger formula, or a variation thereof, but there is no objective narratorial confirmation of the

---

4.   Diana Edelman, 'Huldah the Prophet—of Yahweh or Asherah?', in Brenner (ed.), *A Feminist Companion to Samuel and Kings*, pp. 231-50.

event.[5] While the formula 'YHWH spoke to Moses' or 'God spoke to Jeremiah' appears frequently, this formula does not appear in the context of female prophecy.

The first and only explicit reference to Miriam as נביאה occurs in Exod. 15.20. Yet, as noted earlier, the actions Miriam performs, her taking a תף (a drum) and leading other women in a victorious song and dance, are not the kind of activities usually attributed to prophets. Miriam offers a song of praise; she is not quoted as uttering a prophecy. Exodus 15.21 attributes to Miriam the verse 'Sing to YHWH, for he is highly exalted; the horse and the rider he has thrown into the sea'. The prophetic element in the song of the sea as quoted in vv. 14-18, describing the future conquest of Canaan, is ascribed to Moses (Exod. 15.1). Miriam leads other women 'with drums and with dances' (ובמחלת בתפים) as she herself holds a drum in her hand.

Carol Meyers argues that Miriam's musical activity, portrayed as it is within a female collective framework, alludes to a no longer known ancient Israelite institution of female singers and dancers.[6] But what is the connection between Miriam's musical performance and prophetic function? I would argue that the references to Miriam's musical performance, in the very context that invokes her as a prophet, substitute a non-verbal performance for the speech act which claims the authority of divine revelation. Miriam is denied the power of speech in the very context that presents her as a נביאה. To associate her prophecy with musical activity is to construct her as a lesser prophet, possibly one who depends on music for inspiration. The drum is mentioned among the musical instruments used by the 'bands of prophets' (חבל נביאים) described in 1 Sam. 10.5, whose prophetic activity is not taken seriously.

Miriam is neither represented as YHWH's messenger, nor as Moses' messenger, the role attributed to her brother Aaron. 'And YHWH said to Moses: Look, I have set you in God's stead to Pharaoh; and Aaron your brother will be your prophet' (נביאך, Exod. 7.1-2). Moses is God's prophet, he is in God's stead (נתתיך אלהים לפרעה), and Aaron is Moses' prophet. This hierarchical order implies that Aaron is the lesser authority. Exodus 15.20 presents Miriam as 'Aaron's sister'

5.   In the case of Deborah, the formula reads: הלא צוה ה' אלהי ישראל ('has not YHWH God of Israel commanded', Judg. 4.6). In the case of Huldah, the formula reads: כה אמר ה' אלהי ישראל (so says YHWH God of Israel', 2 Kgs 22.15).

6.   Carol L. Meyers, 'Miriam the Musician', in A. Brenner (ed.), *A Feminist Companion to Exodus to Deuteronomy* (Sheffield: Sheffield Academic Press, 1994), pp. 207-30.

rather than as **Moses'** sister, implying an association with the lesser prophet. I would like to suggest that both the association with Aaron, clearly the lesser male authority, and the description of the musical activity limit and redefine the meaning of the term נביאה. The text thus states that Miriam served as a נביאה, but at the same time it derogates, renders ambiguous, diminishes and understates the possible meaning of this term.

The hierarchical order establishing Moses as the supreme authority between YHWH and Aaron does not include Miriam. Numbers 12 attributes to Miriam a discourse that justifies her exclusion from this order. Miriam's speech subverts her authority and credibility, for she is shown to create problems rather than solve them. The only speech acts attributed to Miriam show her in fact not to speak in YHWH's name, and to misinterpret divine intention. The story begins with an incident involving Moses' Cushite woman: 'And Miriam and Aaron spoke against Moses regarding the Cushite woman he had taken, for he had taken a Cushite woman' (Num. 12.1). The text omits the most crucial facts that might help us judge whether Miriam's concern is reasonable or justified. The suppression of details subverts the validity of Miriam's concern. Her motivation is also negatively shaded, implying jealousy, sibling rivalry and a struggle for power and authority: 'Has YHWH indeed spoken only with Moses? Has He not spoken also with us?' (v. 2). It is in this context that the narrator makes sure we understand the lesser significance of Miriam's prophecy. The text explicitly states that there is a qualitative difference between Moses' prophetic abilities and those of his siblings. While Moses' prophecy is directly connected to YHWH, and while this prophecy entails a direct dialogue with God (פה אל פה), Miriam's and Aaron's prophecy is mediated by dreams (מואה), riddles (חידת) and images (תמנה, v. 8). Miriam and Aaron question Moses' authority, though he is the most modest (ענו) man on earth (v. 2). The only text that represents Miriam's speech, then, represents her as anything but a prophet. Rather than representing YHWH, she is rebuked and eventually punished by him. She and not Aaron becomes leprous (v. 10); and having no direct recourse to YHWH, she depends on both her brothers to intercede on her behalf. YHWH eventually cures her of her leprosy, but not before he compares her to a daughter who has been spat at by her father, and not before she is shut out of the camp for seven days (vv. 14-15). What the Miriamic texts describe is a woman who desires to be a prophet, but who fails to recognize her own limitations. Miriam does not recognize the simple fact that prophecy is the voluntary verbal communication of YHWH with a chosen agent. She misunderstands the divine will; she fails in her capacity as a prophet. The label נביאה which is applied to Miriam in Exod. 15.20 is thus progressively qualified, until it is emptied of meaning. I tend to agree with Phyllis Trible's assertion that Miriam prefigures a succession of woman prophets in the Hebrew Bible, but in my reading she prefigures their erasure, not their authority.[7] Trible suggests that we know so little about female prophets in the Bible because the tradition has been lost to us. Trible's meticulous reconstruction convinced me that there probably was a tradition of female prophecy in ancient Israel, but my point is that this tradition has been suppressed and not merely lost.

A similar ambiguity typifies the story of Deborah, who is also labeled נביאה in Judg. 4.4. And yet Judges 4 and 5, the prose version and the poetic version of her successful confrontation with the Canaanites, represent her military and strategic prowess, and certainly her poetic talent, rather than her prophetic skills. Having said that, I should hasten to clarify that of all the military leaders in the book of Judges, Deborah is the only one who shares her victory with another leader, a man, Barak the son of Abinoam (Judg. 4.10-16). Paradoxically, Deborah's direct involvement in the campaign against the Canaanites is purely verbal. Her involvement, the strategic instructions she gives Barak, is summarized in a few verses (Judg. 4.6-7). The text describes Deborah as going with (ותלך עם) Barak (v. 9), or going up with him (ותעל עמו, v. 10), suggesting that to some extent she follows his military lead. Deborah also shares her victory with yet another woman, the Kemite woman Jael, who is shown to be directly responsible for the defeat of the fearsome Canaanite officer Sisera (vv. 17-22). So in some ways, even Deborah's military prowess is somewhat curtailed by the narrative presentation of her 'assistants'. But it is in the context of her prophecy that the process of curtailment is especially jarring. In fact the label נביאה that is attributed to Deborah in Judg. 4.4 is complemented by yet another description. We are told that she is an אשת לפדות, which may be translated as 'the wife of Lapidot' (a male person's name). The information about Deborah's prophetic activities as well as her uxorial status is, to say the least, rather cursory. But perhaps more importantly, why is Deborah's uxorial status presented as a complement to her prophetic status? This is not the usual introduction of most male prophets, whose wives are rarely mentioned. Is there a necessary connection between

7.   Phyllis Trible, 'Bringing Miriam Out of the Shadows', in Brenner (ed.), *A Feminist Companion to Exodus to Deuteronomy*, pp. 166-86.

Deborah's prophecy and her married state? Verses 4 and 5 focus on Deborah's activities as a judge rather than as a prophet. The predicate that follows her introduction as prophet is שפטה ('is judging'). The root שפט appears again in v. 5 (in the word משפט, 'judgment'), presenting her in a judicial rather than a prophetic capacity.[8] Although Deborah is accorded less textual space than other male prophets, her story is repeated, appearing both as a narrative in Judges 4 and as a poem ascribed to herself and Barak the son of Abinoam in Judges 5. The label נביאה suggests some kind of direct communication between the subject in question and the deity. Yet it is in the figure of Gideon, who is not described as a prophet, that we are presented with YHWH's messenger. 'And the angel of YHWH appeared to him and said to him: "YHWH is with you, you mighty man of valor"' (Judg. 6.12). The description of the encounter between Gideon and YHWH's מלאך, 'messenger', takes up 12 verses (6.12-24). Additionally, the text freely quotes several dialogues between YHWH and Gideon in the course of the story. YHWH appears in a more indirect way in the Samson story. Once more the appearance is mediated through a divine messenger, a מלאך. At one point we read that 'The spirit of YHWH gripped Samson' (ותצלח עליו רוח ה', Judg. 14.19). Yet Samson is not described as a prophet. It is therefore peculiar that there is no report of any encounter or dialogue with the divine in the context of the story of Deborah.

What does Deborah's specifically prophetic role consist of? The narrator attributes to her a prediction: 'And Deborah said to Barak: "Arise, for this is the day YHWH will deliver (נתן) Sisera into your hands"' (Judg. 4.14). Indeed, the following verse confirms that YHWH was indeed involved in Barak's victory, making it clear that it was YHWH who 'overwhelmed' (ויהם) Sisera and the chariots and the entire camp 'before (לפני) Barak' (v. 15). Deborah then predicts that YHWH will deliver Sisera into the hands of Barak. The fact is that YHWH delivers Sisera into the hands of Jael. Nevertheless Deborah does predict that victory will be delivered by a woman. These predictions are attributed to Deborah without an objective narratorial description of a direct dialogue between the divine dispatcher and the female messenger.

The next chapter, the epic poem, renders the same story with different emphases.[9] Here there is next to nothing about Deborah's

---

8.   'And the children of Israel came up to her for judgment'.

9.   Mieke Bal offers a close reading of these chapters in *Murder and Difference: Gender, Genre and Scholarship on Sisera's Death* (trans. Matthew Gumpert;

prophetic status. She is presented as the composer, as the author of a song of victory, praising God for Israel's military victory over the Canaanites. The possibility that this song is 'authentic', in the sense that it may reflect a woman's voice, does not shed light on the question we are concerned with.[10] The meaning of the word נביאה is thus once again rendered ambiguous and diminished.

As in Deborah's case, Huldah is presented in the same verse both as a נביאה and as a married woman. But while the identity of Lappidoth is somewhat obscure, that of Shallum, the son of Tikvah, the son of Harhas is spelled out in some detail (2 Kgs 22.14). We are also told that Shallum was the 'keeper of the wardrobe' (שומר הבגדים). The information about Huldah herself refers only to the fact that she dwells in a particular area, the second quarter (משנה) in Jerusalem. Huldah, we are told, is sought out by a delegation of temple officers. Huldah's prophecy comprises five verses. Perhaps more importantly, Huldah is sought out by a righteous king, King Josiah, 'who did that which was right in the eyes of the Lord, and walked completely in the way of David his father, not deviating to the right or the left' (22.2). Indeed, while Hezekiah depends on Isaiah for guidance and survival, Josiah is shown to begin his reforms before he ever consults with Huldah, and to continue with his activities after he does. The text intimates that the king interpreted correctly YHWH's intentions. Even before he consults Huldah, Josiah proclaims that 'YHWH's wrath is great and is burning against us because our forefathers have not obeyed the words of this book' (2 Kgs 22.13). Having heard Huldah's prophecy, Josiah continues with his rehabilitative efforts. Her prophecy then changes neither the course of his actions nor the historical trajectory he maps out for the nation. While Hezekiah too is described favorably, he is shown to be castigated by Isaiah when he deviates from the proper path (2 Kgs 20.17-18). Huldah does not confront the king. Rather she affirms his interpretation of the book of Torah found by Hilkiah the priest (2 Kgs 22.10). Huldah transmits a divine message to the delegates the king sends to her rather than directly to the king.

Huldah's prophetic message is twofold: the monarchy is doomed,

10. Athalya Brenner and Fokkelien van Dijk-Hemmes, *On Gendering Texts: Female and Male Voices in the Hebrew Bible* (Leiden: E.J. Brill, 1993). For a thematic analysis of the poem see Susan Niditch, 'Eroticism and Death in the Tale of Jael', in Peggy L. Day (ed.), *Gender and Difference in Ancient Israel* (Minneapolis: Fortress Press, 1989), pp. 43-57.

but the king will escape. Verses 15-17 are addressed to Judah as a collective. The first part of the message is typically patterned as a prophetic message including the messenger formula (כה אמר ה'), an announcement of punishment, and an accusation that explains and justifies the punishment.[11] The punishment is described in rather general terms: 'I will bring evil upon this place' (v. 16). The phrase describing God's burning wrath (ונצתה חמתי, v. 17) uses the same idiomatic expression used earlier by Josiah (כי גדולה חמת ה' אשר היא נצתה בנו, v. 13). It has been argued that Huldah uses idiomatic expressions that are evocative of Jeremiah's style. This raised speculations about the authenticity of Huldah's role as a prophet, and the possibility that a late editor attributed to her a synthetic prophecy lifted from Jeremiah.[12] It has even been suggested that the mysterious Huldah may have been a prophet of the goddess Asherah, and that she was sought out in the hope of invoking divine mercy and forgiveness.[13] Yet, with all our misgivings about Huldah's indebtedness to Jeremiah, and despite our suspicions regarding her authenticity as a historical figure, Huldah is the only one to whom a prophecy of doom is attributed. What we find in the first part of her prophetic message is a process of inscription, the inscription of female prophetic agency.

This is hardly ascertainable in regard to the second half of the prophecy. Verses 18-20 are addressed individually to King Josiah. In these verses Huldah promises the king that he will be spared. Now, in the case of Isaiah the text is careful to describe a reality that complements the prophet's message. Thus, for example, Isaiah's message of doom against the Assyrians (2 Kgs 19.21-34) is followed by a vivid description of the destruction of the Assyrian army by YHWH's מלאך (19.35-37). Though Huldah seems to lack Isaiah's miraculously curative skills, she nevertheless promises Josiah that he will be spared. The prophecy attributed to Huldah describes Josiah as crying, as humbling himself and tearing up his clothes (v. 19). Only the last act is in fact reported by the narrator to have taken place (v. 11). Huldah's detailed description of Josiah's alleged repentance is more in keeping with the description of Hezekiah's behavior than with the description of Josiah's behavior (2 Kgs 20.3). In 22.20 Huldah promises that Josiah will die peacefully: 'I will gather you to your

---

11. By a 'typical' prophetic speech act I refer to a pattern that includes an address, an accusation and an announcement of judgment. See Claus Westermann, *Basic Forms of Prophetic Speech* (Louisville, KY: Westminster Press, 1991).

12. Edelman, 'Huldah the Prophet', pp. 232-39.

13. Edelman, 'Huldah the Prophet', pp. 243-48.

fathers, and you will be gathered to your grave in peace, and your eyes will not see the evil that I will bring on this place'. But the description of Josiah's demise at the hands of Pharaoh Necoh suggests that, contrary to Huldah's prophecy, Josiah died a violent death: 'In his days Pharaoh-Necoh king of Egypt went up against the king of Assyria to the river Euphrates; and King Josiah went against him, and he slew him at Megiddo, as soon as he saw him' (23.29). The text thus exposes the prophecy of Huldah as untrue. The veracity of Huldah's prediction is subverted by the description of Josiah's death in battle.[14]

Finally, we may add that while Isaiah is shown to have curative magic powers, much like Elijah and Elisha, Huldah lacks such powers. It is thus rather problematic to compare her either to Elijah and Elisha, the 'magical' early prophets, or to Isaiah and Jeremiah, the latter prophets whose sermons were preserved. Woman prophets are not just denied the sustained rhetorical ability of their male counterparts to pronounce and articulate divine messages, they also seem to lack the magical powers ascribed to both categories of male prophets. I would therefore argue that it is rather far-fetched to claim that the book of Kings offers us an egalitarian picture of male and female prophetic activity, as some scholars suggest. The book of Kings offers us images of needy nameless widows who benefit from the miraculous powers of Elijah and Elisha; it offers us the image of a latter prophet who is also capable of curing disease and prolonging life. This book affirms the discursive authority, veracity and numinous powers of male prophets in a way that completely overshadows the single episode regarding Huldah. Claudia Camp argues that 'prophecy was one religious vocation open to women on an equal basis with men'.[15] While I do not presume to know about ancient Israelite equal opportunity policies vis-à-vis woman prophets, I suggest that we read the text carefully enough to note its suppression and repression of the voice and activity of female prophets.

Yet another case in point is the reference to Noadiah. She too is labeled a נביאה but, whereas the previous references are ambiguous,

---

14. The discrepancy between Huldah's prophecy and Josiah's death is brought out a bit more dramatically in 2 Chron. 35.20-26. This text describes Josiah's insistence on a military confrontation with the Egyptian king, and the description of his defeat is more detailed. The king is described as gravely wounded by archers, and recognizing his demise. Finally, his death is mourned widely and also described with greater detail than in 2 Kgs 22.

15. Claudia V. Camp, '1 and 2 Kings', in C.A. Newsom and S.H. Ringe (eds.), *The Woman's Bible Commentary* (Louisville, KY: Westminster/John Knox Press, 1992), p. 109.

this reference is clearly negative. Noadiah is listed among Nehemiah's opponents. 'Remember Tobiah and Sanballat, O my God according to the things that they did, and also the prophetess Noadiah and the rest of the prophets who wanted to intimidate me' (Neh. 6.14). It is possible, and even probable, that historically speaking Noadiah was indeed a prominent woman, as Tamara Eskenazi argues.[16] But what do we know about her? Once again the introductory text, the text that labels a woman as נביאה, proceeds to obfuscate the 'facts' it describes, offering us no information about the prophetess in question. While we know that Tobiah was an Ammonite official who opposed Nehemiah all along, and while we know that Sanballat was the governor of Samaria, and while we infer that Nehemiah considers all three equally objectionable, Noadiah is the only one who remains a mystery.

Yet another reference to a נביאה occurs in the book of Isaiah. While Huldah the prophetess is described as Shallum's wife, here the נביאה is nameless. Her significance lies in her uxorial relationship to Isaiah: she is presented as his wife. Her own name is of no consequence; rather it is her son's names that the prophet uses as symbolic articulations of Judah's future. The נביאה emerges here as a sexual object and reproductive object that the prophet 'goes into' (קרב), thus domesticating the term and re-enclosing the concept within the male-dominated economy of marital relations. Needless to say, it is the prophet who names the son; the נביאה is both silenced and suppressed: 'And I went unto the prophetess (ואקרב אל הנביאה) and she conceived and bore a son. Then YHWH said to me: Call his name *Maher-shalal-hash-baz*' (מהר שלל חש בז, Isa. 8.3). The son's symbolic name drains the mother's suppression of significance. For why wonder about the nameless prophetess, when it is her husband's word that matters, and when it is her son's name that embodies the divine message? The label נביאה is thus associated with the nameless woman's uxorial and reproductive functions. The female prophetic word is replaced and displaced by the female body.

Is there a causal relationship between the inscription/erasure trope I see at work in the narrative portion of the Hebrew Bible, and the suppression of written records chronicling the prophecies of women? In other words, why have women not been featured among the fourteen latter prophets? Why is Jeremiah featured, and not Huldah? If indeed women prophets have been recognized and respected as such

16. Tamara C. Eskenazi, 'Out From the Shadows: Biblical Women in the Post-Exilic Era', in Brenner (ed.), *A Feminist Companion to Samuel and Kings*, p. 269.

in ancient Israel, as some scholars would have it, why does the biblical text refuse to admit it? I would like to suggest that there is a
direct correlation between the inscription and erasure noted in the
biblical narrative, and the similarly ambiguous if not downright
hostile presentation of women in the latter prophets. As Drorah Setel
and Athalya Brenner argued, the genre that best defines the
portrayals of women in Hosea 1–3, Jeremiah 2–3 and Ezekiel 16, 23 is
pornography.[17] Female images portray national corruption and way-
wardness in terms of deviant female sexuality. In this process woman
is objectified and slandered, the female body is associated with
danger and pollution, and woman as metaphor is constructed as the
appropriate victim of male violence because of the symbolic equation
of the male with the divine. But in addition to this important insight, I
would argue that woman in prophetic literature is presented as
fundamentally unbelievable, especially in her role as perpetrator and
victim of sexual sins. Women are dispossessed of language, speech
and a voice in prophetic literature.[18] To the extent that they speak at
all, either verbally or symbolically, their expressions are false and
unreliable. This prophetic trope is to a large extent an extension of the
pervasive association of women and deception in the biblical narrative, as I argued in a related article some years ago.[19]

Nowhere is the derogation of women as prophets more patent than
in Ezekiel 13. To be sure, Ezekiel attacks male prophets as well. But
the fact that he at least is a truthful prophet, according to his own conviction, exonerates men as a class from the global indictment that
women as a class cannot escape. Furthermore, the male prophets are
accused in metaphorical terms as 'foxes in ruins' and as daubing
broken walls with white plaster (Ezek. 4.10). These prophets are said
to deceive and mislead the people, by predicting peace (vv. 8, 10). The

17. T. Drorah Setel, 'Prophets and Pornography: Female Sexual Imagery in
Hosea', in Letty Russell (ed.), *Feminist Interpretation of the Bible* (Philadelphia:
Westminster Press, 1985), pp. 86-95; Athalya Brenner, 'Pornoprophetics Revisited:
Some Additional Reflections, in *'The Intercourse of Knowledge: On Gendering, Desire
and 'Sexuality' in the Hebrew Bible* (Leiden and New York: E.J. Brill, 1997), pp. 153-
74. See also related essays in Athalya Brenner (ed.), *A Feminist Companion to the
Latter Prophets* (Sheffield: Sheffield Academic Press, 1995); and Renita J. Weems,
Battered Love: Marriage, Sex and Violence in the Hebrew Prophets (Minneapolis:
Fortress Press, 1995).

18. Yvonne Sherwood, *The Prostitute and the Prophet: Hosea's Marriage in
Literary-Theoretical Perspective* (Sheffield: Sheffield Academic Press, 1996). See
especially pp. 306-22.

19. 'Who is Hiding the Truth?', pp. 137-44.

woman prophets, on the other hand, are accused not only of mis-leading the people, but also of intentionally discouraging righteous people by telling them lies, and by encouraging evil people to continue sinning (v. 22). These women are said to 'trap souls' and to 'kill souls that should not die and save souls that should not live' (v. 19). Not only are the woman prophets deceptive (vv. 17, 19) and murderous, they are cynical as well. They sell their false prediction in exchange for a fee, bread and barley to be precise (v. 19). Ezekiel describes women's prophesying as a kind of witchcraft: 'Woe to the women who sew magic bands for all wrists and head-veils for persons of every stature in order to catch souls. Will you kill souls belonging to my people and keep others alive for your profit?' (Ezek. 13.18).[20] Ezekiel's condemnation of woman prophets labels them prophets, but the description that follows suggests that they dabble in witchcraft for profit.[21] If indeed the woman prophets sell their services to individuals for a fee, their activities are less nefarious than the political predictions of the male false prophets addressing the nation as a whole. The women sell their services for a fee that buys them 'bread' and 'barley' — basic staples rather than luxuries. And yet the female false prophets are derided and denigrated in stronger terms than their male equivalents. It is not so much the message as the material means of communication that is being satirized here. And yet, have not the 'true' prophets including Ezekiel, used magic symbolic acts as part and parcel of their attempt to capture their audience's attention? [22] We may never know what the symbolic acts of the women described in Ezekiel's text refer to. It is possible to speculate that the prophet obfuscates the information he is offering, using ambiguous language in order to conceal both the reality of the women's behavior and its meaning. Ezekiel goes on to condemn the

---

20. This translation is based on Walther Eichrodt, *Ezekiel: A Commentary* (Philadelphia: Westminster Press, 1970).

21. The binding of sick people's wrists and other limbs was believed to bring about magic cures. The head-veils were the garment of the putative healer, and allegedly this long garment would trap the soul of the patient. But see a recent article suggesting that the women in Ezekiel are not involved in an inferior kind of prophecy, but rather in a distinct cultic ritual highly popular among women, especially among pregnant women. See Nancy R. Bowen, 'The Daughters of Your People: Female Prophets in Ezekiel 13.17-23', *JBL* 118.3 (1999), pp. 417-33.

22. As James L. Crenshaw argued, there are few clear criteria that may help us distinguish between 'true' and 'false' prophecies either in terms of content or in terms of the means of communication. See *Prophetic Conflict: Its Effect Upon Israelite Religion* (Berlin: W. de Gruyter, 1971).

woman prophets as follows: 'You have profaned me among my people for a few handfuls of barley and pieces of bread, in order to kill souls which should not die, and keep souls alive that should not live, by lying to this people of mine which listens so readily to lies' (Ezek. 13.20). The discourse that determines what is good and what is evil belongs to the male prophet. This discourse erases the women's words so thoroughly; all we know is that they are prophesying false-hoods and destroying innocent people. Their own words have been suppressed, so it is no longer possible to reconstruct an alternative meaning.

The existence and activities of woman prophets in the Bible are both inscribed and erased. The description of the positive prophets is often truncated and displaced, for often we are informed about mili-tary exploits or celebratory songs when the label attached to the female agents is unmistakably that of נביאה. The description of nega-tive prophets such as Noadiah is even more cursory, while the female false prophets in Ezekiel are shown to be murderous witches. Prophecy entails a rhetorical and numinous activity, symptomatic of a close relationship between a messenger and a divine source. The biblical text, both narrative and poetic, strenuously suppresses such a possibility in the context of female prophecy. Ezekiel's venomous description of women as false prophets all but erases the women's speech and presents their numinous powers as dangerous and destructive.

The inscription and suppression of early female prophets justifies their elimination from the important corpus of the latter prophets. Prophecy is the core and culmination of the monotheistic paradigm. The discursive intermingling of God's words and those of the male prophets represents the apotheosis of the andro-theistic infrastructure of monotheistic ideology.[23] This andro-theistic relationship must preclude female discourse. And yet to remain believable the biblical narrator must recognize female agency. The dual move of inscription and erasure recognizes female prophetic agency as minor, if not downright false in order to insure the unperturbed continuance of the andro-theistic dialogue of monotheistic religion.

By representing female prophetic discourse as minor, false, insig-nificant, abstruse, unreliable and peripheral the biblical redactor validates the elimination of women from the latter prophets. The

---

23. For an analysis of hierarchical relations and the monolithic character of monotheism see Regina M. Schwartz, *The Curse of Cain: The Violent Legacy of Mono-theism'* (Chicago and London: University of Chicago Press, 1997).

emphasis on woman's desecrated body in the latter prophets displays the shift from the mouth to the vagina, to use Luce Irigaray's metaphor.[24] The speaking organ, woman's discourse, has been replaced and displaced by her sexual organ; hence the obsessive focus of the latter prophets on what has been defined by some as pornography.

24. Luce Irigaray, 'When Our Lips Speak Together', in *This Sex Which is Not One* (trans. Catherine Porter; Ithaca, NY: Cornell University Press, 1985), pp. 205-218.

THE DAUGHTERS OF YOUR PEOPLE PROPHESY

Renate Jost

In Ezek. 13.17-21[1] the prophet speaks a word against the prophetic women of Judah. The prophets mentioned here are interesting for an exegesis in the context of feminist theology for two reasons: they are different from the male prophets mentioned earlier (Ezek. 13.2-9), and they constitute a group of woman prophets.

Women and Men as Prophets

While the men are dubbed 'prophets' (v. 2), just as Ezekiel himself lays claim to the status of a prophet who has been called (Ezek. 2.5; 33.33), the women are described as 'the daughters of your people who prophesy out of their own imagination'. Because of the use of the *hithpael* exegetes are fond of reading here a contemptuous undertone against the women,[2] but it seems to me that this is more a reflection of the attitude of the exegetes towards women than of the mood of the text, since the *hithpael* is also used for the behavior of Ezekiel himself (Ezek. 37.10).[3] The fact is that the *hithpael* is used to describe typical prophetic activity.

The woman prophets are explicitly accused of making their abilities available to all persons without distinction. With respect to prophets the text speaks metaphorically of an activity that goes beyond verbal prophecy, namely repairing a wall for the house of Israel (Ezek. 13.5). Hence the word against the woman prophets allows us to see them as artisans who make for themselves the garments required by their work and don them for their prophetic duties as well.

---

1. For a detailed discussion of Ezek. 13.17-21, see my *Frauen, Männer und die Himmelskönigin: Exegetische Studien* (Gütersloh: Chr. Kaiser Verlag/Gütersloher Verlagshaus, 1995).
2. Cf. Walter Zimmerli, *Ezechiel 1–24* (BKAT, 13.1; Neukirchen–Vluyn: Neukirchener Verlag, 1969), p. 296; Hans-Peter Müller, 'נביא', *ThWAT*, V (1984), p. 160.
3. Cf. Robert R. Wilson, 'Prophecy and Ecstasy: A Reexamination', *JBL* 98 (1979), pp. 321-37 (336).

An explanation for the women's use of the auxiliary items needed for their prophecy has been sought, for example, in comparable phenomena known to ethnologists[4] or in Assyrian-Babylonian parallels. But all attempts to explain the materials used by the women in this manner have proved unsatisfactory.

Is it possible that these may have been bands in the form of amulets to be fastened to the wrists, much like the *tefillin* that were later developed on the basis of a literal interpretation of Deut. 6.8 (cf. Deut. 11.18; Exod. 13.16)?[5] In Mt. 23.5 they are called phylacteries, which presupposes that they were understood as means of preservation and protection. Correspondingly, then, the head coverings or 'veils' could represent an early stage of the later *tallith*. This is an exciting suggestion because it would mean that, at that time, women wore the trappings of prayer that were later reserved for men. But perhaps they were also veils that women wore while prophesying? In 1 Cor. 11.5-16 Paul orders the women in Corinth to wear a veil when they pray or prophesy. Had that been customary during the period of the exile? These can remain suggestions only.

The woman prophets are accused of using their work to earn their bread, if only in a modest way. In contrast, the earnings of the male prophets are not mentioned here. While payment for the work of prophets was not regarded as offensive (cf. 1 Sam. 9.7; 1 Kings 14.3) in the pre-national situations and the early years of the kingdom in Israel (there is no corresponding text for Judah that reflects this period), earning one's living by prophesying was sharply rejected by later prophets in Judah (cf. Amos 7.10-12, and especially Mic. 3.5).[6]

---

4.   Thus, for example, Hans Ferdinand Fuhs (*Ezechiel 1–24* [NEB, 7; Würzburg: Echter Verlag, 1984], p. 73) considers it possible that the magical bands and head coverings could serve the purpose of self-binding as known among Asian shamans, so that liberation from the bindings may serve to prove the effective power of the spirits called upon. But this comparison is inaccurate because the woman prophets in Ezekiel also sew bands and veils for their women clients.

5.   Georg Braulik (*Deuteronomium 1–16*, 7 [NEB, 15; Würzburg: Echter Verlag, 1986], p. 57) draws an interesting link to the worship of Ishtar in his interpretation of Deut. 6.8: 'Besides personal knowledge of the Law the connection to YHWh in daily life is made universally evident through external symbols: a brooch on the turban... — as, for example, the hierodules of the goddess of love made known through the ornaments on their foreheads that they belonged to Ishtar — or an armband bearing the symbol of YHWh'. Unfortunately there is no supporting evidence for this. However, these may also have been bands made by women like those in Ezek. 13.17-23.

6.   In light of the modest incomes of the woman prophets, for whom it was primarily a question of mere survival, it seems to me that the formulation of

Were the male prophets in Ezek. 13.1-16 cult prophets, men from wealthy families? Did they prophesy without compensation, or does Ezekiel find their 'earnings' from prophecy inoffensive in contrast to those of the professional woman prophets? These are questions that must remain open.

The criticism of the male prophets consists in the accusation that they lie because they see peace where there is no peace. In contrast, the charge against the woman prophets is that they are acknowledged to be able to decide the life and death of individual persons.[7] The woman prophets are thus, for this and other reasons, connected by many interpreters with (black) magic and judged negatively in the context of the text itself.[8]

Magical practices by women outside the cult itself are mentioned in Exod. 4.24-26 without evaluation, and in 1 Samuel 28 under a clearly negative aspect. Exodus 22.17 is directed explicitly against 'witches'. But it is not only women who are accused as magicians and witches. Most of the texts concerned with this are aimed at both women and men (Lev. 19.31; 20.6, 27; Deut. 18.10-14). We should, however, note that magical rituals, some of which were taken over from the surrounding cultures, were incorporated in Israelite religion from an early period. These include divination with the *'urîm* and *tummîm*[9] as well as other rituals that must clearly be regarded as preventative or therapeutic magic. Ezekiel himself is depicted as a prophet who makes use of magical practices: in Ezek. 21.17 'MT 21.19' YHWH's command to prophesy is combined with a magical clapping of hands. Thus for him also 'prophesying' can have an immediate magical effect, fatal (Ezek. 11.13) or life-creating (Ezek. 37.7-10). Hence in the combination of prophecy and magic that kills or preserves human life he is by no means inferior to the women, but he denies them the right to act in the name of YHWH. The fact that equally competent

H.P. Müller, who speaks of 'magical ambitions' and 'desire for gain' among the women ('בְנֵאֹי', p. 160) is somewhat inappropriate.

7.   I find that Athalya Brenner's opinion *(The Israelite Woman: Social Role and Literary Type in Biblical Narrative* [Sheffield: JSOT Press, 1985], p. 74) that the activity of the woman prophets was completely ineffective is not confirmed by the text; it seems directed rather to an apologetic interest in protecting women from the accusation of practicing black magic. Ezekiel does, in fact, accuse them of just that. However, that does not say anything about the facts of the situation.

8.   Cf. Kurt Galling, *Hesekiel* (HAT; Tübingen: Mohr, 1936), p. 75.

9.   Deut. 33.8; 1 Sam. 14.41 LXX; 28.6; Exod. 28.30; Lev. 8.8; Num. 27.21; Ezra 2.63; Neh. 7.65; 1 Sam. 28.6; Num. 27.21 mention only the *urim*; Deut. 33.8 mentions *thummim* before *urim*.

'magicians' here confront each other is evident from the circumstance that in the case of the woman prophets (unlike the case of the men) Ezekiel addresses his prophecy directly to the prophetic women (Ezek. 13.17; cf. also 6.2; 21.2, 7; 4.7).[10] Thus magical practices are permitted for priests and male prophets as long as they are members of the 'official' cult, while 'freelance' magicians, male or female, are forbidden.[11]

Something similar is true for Mesopotamia. In *Maqlu* and *Schurpu*, the great magical compendia against wizardry that were very widely known in the first century, the same practices were used that were also attributed to 'witches'. It was a matter of importance whether magical actions were practiced in secret, that is, by a 'witch', or by appeal to and with the approval of the gods, that is, as legitimate, official defense. We must agree with Walter Farber's comment that this was 'undoubtedly often a very subjective distinction!'.[12] In Ezek. 13.17-23 the women are criticized in the first place not because of their magical practices, which Ezekiel himself apparently also used, if in a different form, but rather because their decisions about life and death are contrary to those of the prophet. What we have here are two opposed positions.

Woman prophets in Israel/Judah and Assyria

It is striking that Ezekiel here confronts a group of woman prophets because, although reference to prophetic groups in Israel is not uncommon,[13] this is the only instance in which a group of woman prophets is mentioned—unless we are to suppose that whenever there is an allusion to prophets, woman prophets are included.

Individual woman prophets are mentioned by name in texts that reflect Israel's pre-national period. In Exod. 15.20 Miriam is given the title of 'prophet', although her prominent role is questioned in the later tradition in Numbers 12; in Mic. 6.4 she is listed after Moses and Aaron. Miriam dances and plays the tambourine together with other women but she alone, as their leader, is called 'prophet'. Deborah, who judged Israel, is also called 'prophet' in Judg. 4.4. Common to both these women is the ascription of songs to them (Exod. 15.21;

---

10. Müller, 'בניא', p. 160.

11. Cf. Brenner, *The Israelite Woman*, p. 70.

12. Walter Farber 1386–1981 TUAT II, p. 262.

13. 1 Sam. 10.11; 28.6; 1 Kgs 18.4, 19; 22.6, 10, 12, 22; 2 Kgs 3.13; 17.13; 23.2; Neh. 6.7, 14; 9.32; Jer. 4.9.

Judg. 5.1-31). However, to say that they are called prophets only because they are singers[14] seems to me to underestimate their influence. Both are described as women who also intervened in political life either as advisors or as active agents.

It is striking that the beginnings of the royal era are followed by a long period in which no woman prophets are mentioned. Of the one in Isa. 8.3 we learn, apart from her being called 'prophet', only that she was attested by the priestly elite to be pregnant by Isaiah.

Huldah and Noadiah are also called prophets. Noadiah shows that a woman prophet could play a crucial political role even in the post-exilic period (Neh. 6.14). She, like the male colleagues mentioned along with her, was apparently responsible for advising the governor; she was influential enough to be regarded as an opponent of Nehemiah.[15] Huldah had an outstanding role comparable in significance to that of her contemporary, Jeremiah (cf. Jer. 37–38). It is therefore remarkable that she is not mentioned in the book of Jeremiah. Can it be that Jeremiah and those who preserved his words did not know her? That is improbable, because both worked in Jerusalem and their pronouncements took a similar direction. Is it possible that she was deliberately ignored because she was a powerful competitor? It was Huldah, not her contemporary Jeremiah, who gave the crucial divine sanction to the nation of Judah and the subsequent Josianic reform. Thus, in her function as adviser to the king, she was a unique figure even among her male colleagues.

Huldah's connection with the cult is obvious: she was sought out by the leading priests and she was the wife of a Temple official (2 Kgs 22.14; 2 Chron. 34.22). In light of all this Spieckermann has formulated an important thesis[16] regarding Ezek. 13.17-21, based on the dominant role of woman prophets in the new prophetic groups appearing in seventh-century Assyria:

> With regard to the situation in Judah we must ask whether the influential position of the prophet Huldah in the reign of Josiah…can only be understood against the background of contemporary Assyrian models. Ultimately woman prophets are a rarity in the Old Testament tradition and Huldah in her 'advisory function' to the king is a unique figure

14. Thus H. Junker, 'Die Frau im alttestamentlichen ekstatischen Kult', *TGL* 21 (1929), pp. 68-74, although he also deduces from this a broad cultic activity on the part of women. Cf. Zimmerli, *Ezechiel*, p. 295.

15. Cf. Zimmerli, *Ezechiel*, p. 295; Tamara C. Eskenazi, 'Out from the Shadows: Biblical Women in the Postexilic Era', *JSOT* 54 (1992), pp. 25-43 (41).

16. Hermann Spieckermann, *Juda unter Assur in der Sargonidenzeit* (FRLANT, 129; Göttingen: Vandenhoeck & Ruprecht, 1982), p. 296.

even among her male colleagues… A woman's achieving such great and generally acknowledged authority as a prophet reminds us of the woman prophets of Ishtar of Arbela whom Judahite vassals like Manasseh and Josiah certainly could have encountered in Nineveh and who may have inspired them to imitate that institution. Some decades later, at any rate, in Babylon itself the oracles of salvation were not without influence on the shape of Deutero-Isaiah's prophecy. But how little a prophecy of salvation directed specifically to the well-being of the king rests on the Old Testament prophetic tradition is sufficiently evident from Huldah's oracle in 2 Kings 22.15*: although it reveals a positive attitude toward Judah's ruler (cf. vv. 18ff.*), at the same time it is definitely part of the current of classical prophecies of destruction. True prophecy in Israel and Judah always attended to something other than the good will of the king and for that reason it was well armed against any attempt to force it into line.[17]

Although there is no documentation of woman prophets in the neo-Babylonian period, this thesis also has a certain plausibility for the woman prophets in Ezek. 13.17-21, for Assyrio-Babylonian influence could help to explain why it was only in the late royal era in Judah or in the Babylonian exile that woman prophets appear in roles equal to those of male prophets, and why they were singled out for attack in the struggles over true and false prophecy.

It is striking that the increased appearances of woman prophets in the neo-Assyrian period were connected with a manifestation of Ishtar as 'Ishtar of Arbela', the giver of oracles.[18] The dominant position of the woman prophets is documented in a collection of oracles for Asarhaddon (680–669 BCE). Because each oracle ends with the name of the person who conveyed its message, we can determine the gender proportions. According to the available information there were six cases involving a woman and only one involving a man.[19] As a rule the woman prophet who conveyed the message was called *raggintu*, 'the woman who calls out'. The messages consist of oracles of salvation addressed to the king or sometimes to the mother of the king (cf. Jer. 13.18-19), or to 'ordinary citizens'.

If the thesis that the group of woman prophets mentioned in Ezek. 13.17-21 is traceable to Assyrian influence is accurate, one may well

17. Spieckermann, *Juda* (1982), pp. 302-303.

18. Spieckermann, *Juda* (1982), p. 298; see especially the texts cited in n. 203. For translations of texts see Spieckermann, *Juda*, pp. 295-301, and Otto Kaiser *et al.* (eds.), *Texte aus der Umwelt des Alten Testamentes. II. Orakel, Rituale, Bau- und Votivinschriften, Lieder und Gebete*, pp. 56-59.

19. Spieckermann, *Juda*, pp. 297-98. For textual examples, cf. Kaiser *et al.* (eds.), *Texte*, II, pp. 56-65.

suspect that these could have been prophets who prophesied (also?) in the name of Ishtar, for in contrast to the male prophets it is not explicitly said of the women that they prophesy in the name of YHWH (cf. Ezek. 13.19). In addition, the use of the concept of 'profaning' that Ezekiel employs, for example, in connection with the worship of foreign gods (Ezek. 7.21-22; 20.16, 24, 39; 23.38-39) strengthens the suspicion. If the thesis is accurate we would be looking at a connection between the worship of a goddess, here Ishtar, and women's religious power.

Whether the woman prophets prophesied in the name of Ishtar or in the name of YHWH, it is apparent that they were influential enough to become dangerous opponents of the priestly circles in which the book of Ezekiel originated, during the economic and religious crisis after 587 BCE; and that they were combated even more sharply than their male colleagues.

MIRIAM AND THE PROPHECY OF THE PERSIAN PERIOD[*]

Rainer Kessler

1. *Miriam the Prophetess*

In Mic. 6.1-8 Yhwh reminds his people of the exodus from Egypt, the house of slavery. As leaders of the exodus whom Yhwh 'sent before you' he names 'Moses, Aaron, and Miriam' (v. 4). The listing of these three is remarkable because it coincides only superficially with the picture the Pentateuch draws of the exodus. To be sure Moses, Aaron and Miriam are named there too in connection with the exodus. But how different is the specific emphasis! Moses dominates everything, Aaron is clearly subordinate to him, and Miriam is altogether marginalized. What we find in the structure of the whole Pentateuch appears again in Exodus 15. This is demonstrated by the pushing aside of Miriam and her song to the second place (vv. 20-21) and the colonization and expansion of the song by 'Moses and the people of Israel' (v. 1).

By contrast, Mic. 6.4 stresses the equal rank of the three—Moses, Aaron and Miriam—in the exodus. Although the order of the list implies a certain hierarchy, the moment of equality is nevertheless emphasized beyond a hierarchy by the naming of all three in one and the same breath. But what interest is to be found behind the statement of Mic. 6.4? It would be too simple to say that justice should be done to Aaron and, especially, to Miriam in comparison to Moses. For what abstract interest in historical justice should motivate an author who writes centuries after the exodus—whether one thinks of an eighth-century Micah in whose name the text is transmitted or, which is more likely, of an author from the Persian period?

  * Originally published as 'Mirjam und die Prophetie der Perserzeit', in Ulrike Bail and Renate Jost (eds.), *Gott an den Rändern: Sozialgeschichtliche Perspektiven auf die Bibel* (Festschrift Willy Schottroff; Gütersloh: Chr. Kaiser Verlag/Gütersloher Verlagshaus, 1996), pp. 64-72. The English translation is mine. I wish to thank Keith Clarke, Michael Clarke and Katharina Pohl for their critical reading of the English version.

The question is, rather: What do Moses, Aaron and Miriam stand for in the time of the composition of the Micah text? The answer is quite simple and, as such, was given already a long time ago: 'Moses is the founder and mediator of theocracy' – today we would say that Moses stands for the Torah; 'Aaron is the representative of priesthood, Miriam is the prophetess, cf. Exod. 15.20'.[1] So Mic. 6.4 does not deal with the arrangement of historical figures, but with the relation of the subjects they stand for: Torah, cult and prophecy.

This view is confirmed by Numbers 12, another text in which Moses, Aaron and Miriam act. One might read this text as a countertext to Mic. 6.4. The basic conflict in this text is the relation of prophecy to what Moses stands for. Miriam and Aaron—in this order!—claim that Yhwh had not only spoken through Moses but also through them (v. 2). But Yhwh himself objects: 'If there is a prophet among you, I the Lord make myself known to him in a vision, I speak with him in a dream. Not so with my servant Moses; he is entrusted with all my house. With him I speak mouth to mouth, clearly, and not in dark speech' (vv. 6-8). To emphasize this, Miriam is afflicted with leprosy and only healed by the intervention of Aaron with Moses, and by Moses' intercession with God.

The message is clear. Moses, that is the Torah which he received 'mouth to mouth' from God (cf. Exod. 20.18-21; Deut. 5.23-33) and which was transmitted through him to everyone who is authorized to rely on the Torah of Moses,[2] stands above each and any form of prophecy with absolute authority. Prophecy besides Moses' prophecy or, worse, against him is a form of blasphemy. Aaron, the representative of the cult (cf. Lev. 1.5 etc.), is not punished like Miriam the prophetess. He takes the role of mediating between the sinner (v. 11) and Moses, who is totally on God's side.

---

1.   'Moses ist Gründer und Mittler der Theokratie, Aaron Repräsentant des Priesterthums, Mirjam die Prophetin, vgl. Exod. 15,20', J.T. Beck, *Erklärung der Propheten Micha und Joel nebst einer Einleitung in die Propheten* (Gütersloh: C. Bertelsmann, 1898), p. 180. On the other hand R.J. Burns (*Has the Lord Indeed Spoken Only Through Moses? A Study of the Biblical Portrait of Miriam* [SBLDS, 84; Atlanta, GA: Scholars Press, 1987]) totally plays down Miriam's role as a prophetess. She describes her in the first line as leader equal to Moses and Aaron, who originally had more affinities to cult. Her naming as a prophetess in Exod. 15.20 is, according to Burns, an anachronism (cf. esp. p. 122).

2.   See F. Crüsemann, *The Torah: Theology and Social History of Old Testament Law* (trans. Allan W. Mahnke; Minneapolis: Fortress Press, 1996) for the question of who stands behind the figure of Moses ('Moses as Institution? The Organizational Form of Israelite Law', pp. 59-107).

The two counter-texts, Mic. 6.4 and Numbers 12, provoke a double question. What is the historical background for the question of the specific arrangement of Torah, cult and prophecy discussed in our two texts and answered in such opposite manners? And why is the woman Miriam chosen as representative of prophecy alongside the two men Moses and Aaron? Let us begin with the second question.

2. *Women and Prophecy*

It has long been known that in Israel, besides the prophets, there also existed prophetesses. In the first place one has of course to remember Miriam herself, called 'the prophetess' in Exod. 15.20 and taken as representative of prophecy in Numbers 12. Furthermore Deborah (Judg. 4.4), Huldah (2 Kgs 22.14; 2 Chron. 34.22), Isaiah's wife (Isa. 8.3), Noadiah (Neh. 6.14) and, from later times, Anna (Lk. 2.36) are mentioned as 'prophetesses' as well. So there is certain evidence for the existence of prophetesses from the eighth century (Isaiah's wife), through the seventh (Huldah), and down to the fifth (Noadiah), which is exactly the period from which the prophetic writings of the Hebrew Bible stem.

But this record comprises only, so to say, the orthodox side of the prophetic phenomenon. If one considers the phenomenon in a wider sense and includes in it every form of contact with transcendent powers, the participation of women in it becomes even more broad-based. The law on the prophets in Deuteronomy (Deut. 18.9-22) clearly demonstrates that it is justified to speak of expanding the conception of prophecy. It is true that the law presents a sharp distinction between forbidden practices (vv. 10-14) and the orthodox form of Yhwh prophecy. However, both forms are treated in one and the same law. Moreover, one must mention the fact that orthodox prophecy is attacked and suspected in the same way as the heterodox practices. So officers call a prophet mad (משגע, 2 Kgs 9.11), so Amos is banished from the royal sanctuary at Bethel (Amos 7.10-17), so a priest calls for the temple police because of Jeremiah, and the same priest is the supervisor of the prophets called mad (משגע) also here (Jer. 29.26-27).

When all the practices declared to be prohibited by the deuteronomic law on prophecy (Deut. 18.10-14) are taken as the basis for argument, we see that such practices are not only executed by men but also by women. 1 Samuel 28 tells the story of a woman described as a 'medium' (v. 7). Leviticus 20.27 speaks of 'a man or a woman who is a medium or a wizard'. Ezekiel 13 criticizes the (male) 'prophets of Israel' (vv. 1-16), followed by polemics against women accused of magic practices of saving or destroying human lives (vv. 17-23), whose activities are defined by the same word—'to prophesy'—as those of their male counterparts (v. 17). Isaiah 57.3 knows 'sons of the sorceress'. 2 Kings 9.22 speaks of the 'sorceries' of Queen Jezebel, and in Rev. 2.20, her name is applied to a prophetess from Thyatira accused of seducing the community.

All the above mentioned practices are also attributed to men; and the question must be left unanswered whether, in the grammatically masculine forms of the Hebrew language, women are included too—a question to which, nevertheless, an affirmative answer is highly probable. But the formulation of Exod. 22.17, with its exclusively feminine forms, proves that this field of handling transcendent powers was seen as the domain of women: 'You shall not permit a sorceress to live'.

When we look beyond the borders of Israel, these observed phenomena are confirmed. Thus the Middle Assyrian Laws from the end of the second millennium[3] threaten the practice of sorcery, by men or by women, with death, which is comparable with the stipulations of the Israelite Covenant Code. And as far as prophecy itself is concerned, in the first half of the second millennium in Mari many women act as prophetesses besides men, either in a cultic context (as *apiltum*, 'answerer', *muhhutum*, 'ecstatic' and other senses) or as lay women.[4] And the Assyrian prophecies of the seventh century, which fall within the period of the Old Testament prophetic movement, were even given mostly by women called *raggintu* = caller.[5]

Taking all these hints together we see a picture of broad female participation in this field, connected with prophecy in a wider sense. The panorama ranges from sorcery, to invocation of spirits of the dead, to singing that is imagined as divinely inspired (Exod. 15.20-21, cf. 1 Sam. 10.5 for ecstatic prophecy and 1 Chron. 25.1-3 for the temple music), through to official consultation of a prophetess by the king (2 Kgs 22). In that last case we must even suppose that, according to

---

3. Cf. *ANET*, pp. 180-88; William W. Hallo (ed.), *The Context of Scripture*, II (Leiden: E.J. Brill, 2000), pp. 353-61.

4. See F. Ellermeier, *Prophetie in Mari und Israel* (Theologische und Orientalistische Arbeiten, 1; Herzberg: Verlag Erwin Jungfer, 1968), pp. 83-84.

5. See the discussion of the texts of the Assyrian prophecies of the seventh century in H. Spieckermann, *Juda unter Assur in der Sargonidenzeit* (FRLANT, 129; Göttingen: Vandenhoeck & Ruprecht, 1982), pp. 295-303 and of the contribution of prophetesses in general in F. Nötscher, 'Prophetie im Umkreis des alten Israel', *BZ* NS 10 (1966), pp. 161-97, esp. pp. 183-85.

the opinion of the authors of the text, Huldah holds the Mosaic prophetic office provided in the deuteronomic law on the prophets (Deut. 18.9-22) and equipped with the highest authority.[6]

We have to take into consideration that women in Israel had no access to priestly functions in the cult of Yhwh. Then we comprehend all the more why they play such an important role in the field that can be understood as prophetic, in its wider meaning, and why they are mentioned in such a continuous fashion as true prophetesses of Yhwh. Against this background it is thus easy to see why, according to Mic. 6.4 and Numbers 12, Miriam the woman is representative of prophecy in general.[7]

3. *The Prophecy of the Persian Period*

If we now turn to the question of the historical situation in which the relation between the Torah represented by Moses, the cult represented by Aaron, and prophecy represented by Miriam could have become a problem in society, we are soon referred to the Persian period.

On the one hand there is the prerequisite that Moses represents the Torah. This is stated only by Deuteronomy and the literature influenced by it. At the beginning of the Covenant Code we still read (as words of God): 'You have seen for yourselves that I have talked with you from heaven' (Exod. 20.22b).[8] It is only Deuteronomy that is styled as a speech of Moses. It is also in Deuteronomy that we see a tendency, which then comes to its climax in Numbers 12 and which one could call the taming of prophecy. It works in two ways. On the one hand, prophecy is restricted by rules in the law concerning the prophets (Deut. 18.9-22), legitimate practices are separated from non-legitimate ones, and pointers are given on how to differentiate between true and false. On the other hand, in the same law Moses is styled as a sort of paramount prophet from whom all other prophecy is derived. Prophecy is thus both made part of the Torah represented by Moses and, at the same time, made subordinate to Moses' Torah. It

6. See U. Rüterswörden, 'Die Prophetin Hulda', in M. Weippert and St Timm (eds.), *Meilenstein* (Festschrift Herbert Donner; ÄAt, 30; Wiesbaden: Otto Harrassowitz, 1995), pp. 234-42.

7. Burns, *Miriam*, though judging the attribution of the prophetic role to Miriam to be an 'anachronism' (isn't that judgment an anachronism in itself?), sees the reason for this attribution in 'the fact that prophetesses did function as authentic oracular figures in various stages of Hebrew religion' (p. 79).

8. Cf. Crüsemann, *Torah*, pp. 199-200.

is therefore no surprise that, in Deuteronomy, Miriam is mentioned only as the one punished by leprosy (Deut. 24.9).

We cannot deal here with the controversial issue of when Deuteronomy and, especially, the laws about functions—part of which is also the law concerning the prophets—are to be dated. But, even with an early date, one would only come back to late monarchical times. General considerations of development indeed give reason to proceed a little further and to assume the Persian period as the background of the conflict dealt with in Numbers 12 and Mic. 6.4.

It is true that the late monarchical period was already a period of dispute about prophecy, and it is also true that this conflict is the background for the formulation of the deuteronomic law on prophecy. But still, this conflict is a dispute between individual prophets: for example the conflict between Jeremiah and Hananiah (Jer. 28), or the fact that a fictitious Isaiah (2 Kgs 18–20; Isa. 36–39) is advanced as argument against the prophecies of Jeremiah and Ezekiel.[9] In the Persian period, in contrast, prophecy *as such* is disputed.

The socio-political background is determined by the fundamental question of whether the Jewish community should arrange itself in line with Persian supremacy. This arrangement would mean that the province of Judah is restricted to relative autonomy in the province of Judah, but achieving firm political and also religious preferential conditions in return. The alternative would be to dream the dream of political independence, of restitution of the Davidic monarchy, of the temple of Jerusalem being the centre of the whole world and—connected with all this—the dream of world-wide peace and global social justice. The course of in-line arrangement with the Persian authorities is most clearly pursued by Nehemiah and Ezra. It finds its final form in the declaration of the 'law of the God of heaven', in whichever form, that is identical with the Moses' Torah as the obligatory law for the province of Judah and for the Jews in the satrapy of Transeuphrates (Ezra 7).

The other course is the prophetic one. It begins with Haggai and Zechariah and fails with these two prophets. For, in its final aim, the anti-Persian dream of Zerubbabel as messiah (Hag. 2.20-22) and of a temple that in a little while will be the centre of the world (Hag. 2.6-9) is not fulfilled. The temple remains a local sanctuary of relatively

---

9.   Cf. the interpretation of the Isaiah stories by C. Hardmeier, *Prophetie im Streit vor dem Untergang Judas: Erzählkommunikative Studien zur Entstehungssituation der Jesaja- und Jeremiaerzählungen in II Reg 18–20 und Jer 37–40* (BZAW, 187; Berlin and New York: W. de Gruyter, 1990).

modest significance in the Persian Empire, and Judah remains in total dependence on Persian supremacy. From then on prophecy will be in opposition to the powers that support the arrangement with the Persians.[10]

That is why deep mistrust exists towards this sort of prophecy, and Nehemiah utters it explicitly. Before his note about the successful completion of the construction of the Jerusalem wall (Neh. 6.15-16) he inserts, almost as a *ritardando al fine*, a longer passage on obstructions against the construction of the town wall (vv. 1-14). At first he speaks of opponents in the leadership of the province of Samaria (vv. 1-9). Then he mentions a certain Shemaiah and his 'prophecy' (v. 12), which consists of warning Nehemiah that his enemies will kill him, and who gives him the advice to hide in the temple (v. 10). Nehemiah interprets the warning and advice as a perfidious attempt to prevent him from constructing the wall and to discredit him in the people's eyes (vv. 11-13). The report ends with the prayer: 'Remember Tobiah and Sanballat, O my God, according to these things that they did, and also the prophetess Noadiah and the rest of the prophets who wanted to make me afraid' (v. 14).

At the end of the report a new person appears, Noadiah.[11] We hear two things about her. She is given importance by being mentioned by name amongst a larger group of prophets (we may once again assume that under the masculine plural form of prophets there are to be found prophetesses also). And she and the others would frighten Nehemiah—as he sees it. But how do they achieve it?

When reading v. 14 after vv. 10-13, one could imagine that Noadiah and the others would have warned Nehemiah of his enemies and would have provoked him into a harmful over-reaction, as Shemaiah had attempted. But this is quite unlikely. First, Shemaiah's warning is fully right even in the eyes of Nehemiah, and the proposal for Nehemiah to hide in the temple is rather harmless because Nehemiah has only to ignore the proposal. And second, it is difficult to understand why not only a Shemaiah but also a Noadiah and other prophets are needed to make such a harmless proposal.

---

10. This view is especially supported by R. Albertz, *A History of Israelite Religion in the Old Testament Period* (Louisville, KY: Westminster/John Knox Press, 1994), pp. 454-58.

11. For K. Galling (*Die Bücher der Chronik, Esra, Nehemia* [ATD, 12; Göttingen: Vandenhoeck & Ruprecht, 1954], p. 228), the position at the end of the report is reason enough to annihilate one of the prophetesses of the Old Testament in the name of textual criticism.

But Nehemiah himself tells us indirectly, in v. 6, how Noadiah and the other prophets could really scare him. There he quotes an 'open letter' (v. 5) from his Samarian opponents in which they threaten him, claiming that the construction of the Jerusalem wall is only a first step to revolt against the Persians. Nehemiah is supposed to be interested in becoming king of the Jews, and to have ordered prophets to proclaim in Jerusalem that he is king in Judah. Nehemiah denies any intention in this direction (v. 8), and then states that they wanted to 'frighten' him (v. 9) — the same words he later uses also for the actions of Noadiah.

And indeed it is obvious that Noadiah and the other prophets proclaimed just this: independence from the Persians and Nehemiah as their king. By this they really could 'frighten' Nehemiah. For whether he himself had commanded these prophets, as they said in Samaria, or whether he denies this and fights these prophets, the mere fact that they appear on stage highly jeopardizes his position with the central Persian authorities. This is stressed by the fact that in the beginning of the reign of Artaxerxes I, in whose twentieth regnal year the construction of the Jerusalem wall takes place, the Samarians were able to prevent a first attempt to reconstruct the wall by referring to eventual desires for separation (Ezra 4.8-24).

But why does Nehemiah then speak in such an enigmatic way just of 'Noadiah and the rest of the prophets who wanted to make me afraid', without stating the real reason? It is because he must veil the real reason. For the mere acknowledgment that such prophecies proclaiming Nehemiah king indeed existed in Jerusalem would decisively weaken his position towards his opponents in Samaria (and in the Judean upper class, as mentioned immediately in the following verses, in Neh. 6.17-19).

Understanding the true character of the conflict between Nehemiah on the one hand and Noadiah and the prophetic circles connected with her on the other hand, we come back to Mic. 6.4 and Numbers 12. I have already mentioned that Numbers 12 follows the line of thought aimed at taming prophecy, beginning in Deuteronomy and continuing with Nehemiah and Ezra. In this position the prophets are only preachers of repentance from the past, who called the people back to the Torah and whom the people did not follow, to their own detriment. This reception of prophecy by subordinating it to the Torah entered the books of Ezra and Nehemiah in the large communal confessions of guilt; cf. Ezra 9.10-11: 'We have forsaken thy commandments, which thou didst command by thy servants the prophets'; or Neh. 9.26: 'They cast thy law behind their back and killed thy prophets, who had warned them in order to turn them back to thee'.

The other position is directly opposed to the previous one. It insists on political independence from the Persians in favour of the idea of being a worldwide centre, and connects this target with the idea of social justice and peace. This second position is represented by Miriam in Mic. 6.4 where, in contrast to Numbers 12, Miriam is not subordinate to Moses and Aaron but rather coordinated with them. And it is precisely the book of Micah that contains numerous oracles of the sort that 'frightened' Nehemiah. It speaks of the temple as centre of the world (Mic. 4.1-4), of the restoration of the former monarchy (4.8), of a Judean ruler of the world coming from Bethlehem (5.1-4), but also of worldwide peace (4.3-4; 5.4) and of social justice, as the transmission of the old social denunciations of Micah 2 onwards demonstrates. And Mic. 6.1-8 insists that these prophetic traditions have the same rights concerning Israel's relation with its God alongside what Moses and Aaron stand for. The cultic way of relation with God is even seen critically (vv. 6-7). The famous words of v. 8, 'He has showed you, O man, what is good ...', are formulated in a way that is not unambiguously related to either Torah or prophetic traditions. And since, as in the conflict between Nehemiah and Noadiah, here too it is a prophetess who plays the prominent role, we understand better why in Mic. 6.4 it is Miriam the female who represents prophecy.

4. *The Sayings of the Prophetesses*

When with Noadiah a woman forms the front line of prophetic opposition against Nehemiah; when in Numbers 12 as well as in Mic. 6.4, defining the prophetic position in an oppositional way Miriam the female represents prophecy; when finally women in general play an important role in the history of prophecy—then, of course, the question arises: where are their sayings handed down to us? For, besides the sayings of Miriam in Exod. 15.20-21 and Num. 12.1-2, the sayings of Deborah in Judges 4 and 5, and those of Huldah in 2 Kgs 22.15-20, no oracle of a prophetess is transmitted, certainly not in a separate book attributed to a prophetess.

Yet this question can be answered very easily. In principle, they are to be found in the books of Isaiah, of Jeremiah, of Ezekiel, and of the twelve so-called Minor Prophets, that is to say, under the names of male prophets. Thus they suffer the same fate as, later on, those women who took part in the formation and transmission of the Jesus tradition, whose contribution also disappears behind the names of the male Evangelists.[12]

On the other hand, at the present state of the discussion, it is impossible to say which specific texts in the prophetic books stem from a prophetess. The notions on the book of Micah mentioned above show us of what sort such texts might indeed be. But this is no substitute for proof in any single case. And it seems clear that, concerning the form and content of their oracles, prophetesses did not speak in a different voice from that of their male colleagues. They are not reduced to a special female field within prophecy but represent, as Miriam does, prophecy as a whole. This is not only demonstrated by the thoroughly classical oracle of Huldah (2 Kgs 22.15-20), but is also evidenced outside Israel by the Assyrian collections of prophetic oracles about the kings Asarhaddon and Assurbanipal. There we find on two tablets oracles of prophets and, more often, of prophetesses, without being able to differentiate between male and female in relation to language or content.

In the future too it will remain difficult or even impossible to prove whether a certain text stems from a prophetess or not. The prophetic books of the Old Testament are transmitted under the names of male prophets, but we cannot be sure how large the female contribution is. In spite of this it must be maintained, against an androcentric view of Old Testament prophecy, that there is a contribution of prophetesses in the prophetic books of the Old Testament. Micah 6.4 and Numbers 12 make allowance for this fact by making Miriam the representative of prophecy in general.

---

12. Cf. L. Schottroff, *Lydia's Impatient Sisters: A Feminist Social History of Early Christianity* (trans. Barbara Rumscheidt and Martin Rumscheidt; Louisville, KY: Westminster/John Knox Press, 1995), pp. 56-57.

C.

The Pornoprophetic(?) 'Marriage' Metaphor

PROPHETIC OBJECTIONS TO YHWH AS THE VIOLENT HUSBAND OF ISRAEL: REINTERPRETATIONS OF THE PROPHETIC MARRIAGE METAPHOR IN SECOND ISAIAH (ISAIAH 40–55)

Gerlinde Baumann

> The holiest vow that man can make,
> The golden thread in life,
> The bond that none may dare to break,
> That bindeth man and wife;
> Which, blessed by thee, whate'er betides,
> No evil shall destroy,
> Through careworn days each care divides,
> And doubles every joy.
> (Godfrey Thring, 1823–1903)[1]

1. Introduction

YHWH as the husband of Israel or Jerusalem has been treated for a long time under the heading, 'the love of God', but especially in the last two decades has been recognized as a highly problematic metaphor. This topic has also been widely discussed in feminist exegesis in the last decade.[2] It is the aspect of violence in the divine husband's

---

1.   I would like to thank Dale J. Provost for remarks on style and language and for discussion of the article. He also found Thring's words in the *Service Book and Hymnal* (authorized by the Lutheran Churches Cooperation on the Liturgy and Hymnal; Minneapolis: Augsburg, 1958), no. 301.

2.   I will reference feminist critics in relation to the biblical texts they examine. Some of the authors examine several texts: see, e.g., A. Brenner and F. van Dijk-Hemmes, *On Gendering Texts: Female and Male Voices in the Hebrew Bible* (Biblical Interpretation Series, 1; Leiden: Brill, 1993); R.J. Weems, *Battered Love: Marriage, Sex, and Violence in the Hebrew Prophets* (Overtures to Biblical Theology, Minneapolis: Fortress Press, 1995) and E. Seifert, *Tochter und Vater im Alten Testament: Eine ideologiegeschichtliche Untersuchung zur Verfügungsgewalt von Vätern über ihre Töchter* (Neukirchener Theologische Dissertationen und Habilitationen, 9, Neukirchen-Vluyn: Neukirchener Verlag, 1997), and also my own work: G. Baumann, *Liebe und Gewalt: Die Ehe als Metapher für das Verhältnis JHWH-Israel in den Prophetenbüchern* (SBS, 185; Stuttgart: Katholisches Bibelwerk, 2000). I will summarize the most important results of my book in this article.

behaviour which causes problems with the metaphor. Another facet of the problem is the assumed historical effect in ancient Israel and the potentially recurring effect of the metaphor[3] on its readers today as well: if YHWH is presented as a violent husband, the violent behaviour of 'earthly' husbands might then in return be legitimized by the metaphor.[4]

The feminist critique of the metaphor is very enlightening. Two aspects, however, have not been treated in great depth. The first is the inner-biblical critique of YHWH as a violent husband. While the marriage metaphor tries to explain the exilic fate of Zion/Jerusalem, these texts, mainly to be found in Second Isaiah (Isa. 40–55), offer us an alternative explanation. I will examine the texts below and explain how they transform the marriage metaphor of Hosea, Jeremiah and Ezekiel.

The second aspect is the wider literary context in which the marriage metaphor is used. In some of the prophetic books, we find other images than those of YHWH as a violent husband and Israel/Jerusalem as the 'adulterous wife'. These counter-images should certainly

---

3. In the feminist discussion about the marriage metaphor, the most important theoretical outlines are: G. Lakoff and M. Johnson, *Metaphors We Live By* (Chicago and London: University of Chicago Press, 1980); P. Ricœur, *The Rule of Metaphor: Multi-Disciplinary Studies of the Creation of Meaning in Language* (London: Routledge & Kegan Paul, 1977); *idem*, 'The Metaphorical Process as Cognition, Imagination, and Feeling', *Critical Inquiry* 5 (1978), pp. 143-59; J.M. Soskice, *Metaphor and Religious Language* (Oxford: Clarendon Press, 1985); Max Black, *Models and Metaphors: Studies in Language and Philosophy* (Ithaca, NY and London: Cornell University Press, 1962). An outline for the feminist theory is given by C.V. Camp, 'Metaphor in Feminist Biblical Interpretation: Theoretical Perspectives', *Semeia* 61 (1993), pp. 3-36. Several monographs in the feminist discussion of the marriage metaphor also give summaries of these theories. For feminist critique mainly of the concept of Lakoff and Johnson see M. Bal, 'Metaphors He Lives By', *Semeia* 61 (1993), pp. 185-207.

4. Black (*Models*, p. 44) shows how the two parts of the metaphor are interconnected. 'If to call a man a wolf is to put him in a special light, we must not forget that the metaphor makes the wolf seem more human than he otherwise would be'. Black is one of the scholars who created the theory of the metaphor as an interaction between its parts. One can easily transfer the metaphor of God as a violent husband to this model. A consideration of Ricœur is also important for a feminist critique of the marriage metaphor: Since feelings are involved in perceiving and interpreting a metaphor (Ricœur, 'Process', p. 155), it is very difficult to do so objectively from a critical distance. As a consequence, it is nearly impossible not to be influenced by a highly emotional metaphor such as YHWH as a husband and Israel/Zion as his 'whoring' wife. Feminist critique of the marriage metaphor can be seen as an attempt to gain a critical intellectual distance.

be taken into account, for they can be evaluated as prophetic objections to the violent imagery of the marriage metaphor.

First, I will present the main themes of the discussion concerning the prophetic marriage metaphor, which focus on Hosea, Jeremiah and Ezekiel (Section 2). I will examine the terminology of the prophetic marriage metaphor as well as alternative metaphors for YHWH and Israel/Jerusalem. Secondly, I will look at the Second Isaiah texts which can be viewed as objections to the prophetic marriage metaphor (Section 3). The question here will be what these texts say which can be connected to the prophetic marriage metaphor, and in which way they can be read as objections to it. To what extent can we find some kind of inner-biblical critique in these texts to counter the prophetic marriage metaphor and the way it is outlined in Hosea, Jeremiah and Ezekiel (Section 4)? Last but not least, I will examine one other prophetic strategy which can be used as an alternative to the image of YHWH as a violent husband (Section 5).

2. *YHWH as a Violent Husband in the Prophetic Marriage Metaphor*

Hosea

Parts of Hosea 1–3 are probably the texts in which the prophetic marriage metaphor was used for the first time.[5] In some of the texts, we cannot be certain whether Hosea's and Gomer's marriage is the subject, or if the texts are speaking about YHWH and his metaphorical 'wife' Israel. As Yee summarizes: 'The tragic human story of the prophet interconnects with the metaphorical tale of Yahweh and Israel, so that the two stories become essentially one. The prophet creates in this fusion the powerful marriage metaphor to articulate the special covenant relationship between God and Israel.'[6] Israel

---

5.   For further examination of the prophetic marriage metaphor in Hos. 1–3 see, e.g., Y. Sherwood, *The Prostitute and the Prophet: Hosea's Marriage in Literary-Theoretical Perspective* (JSOTSup, 212; Gender, Culture, Theory, 2; Sheffield: Sheffield Academic Press, 1996); M.T. Wacker, *Figurationen des Weiblichen im Hosea-Buch* (Herders Biblische Studien, 8; Freiburg: Herder, 1996); R. Törnkvist, *The Use and Abuse of Female Sexual Imagery in the Book of Hosea: A Feminist Critical Approach to Hos. 1–3* (Acta Universitatis Upsaliensis, Uppsala Women's Studies, A. Women in Religion, 7; Uppsala: Uppsala University Press, 1998); and several articles in A. Brenner (ed.), *A Feminist Companion to the Latter Prophets* (Feminist Companion to the Bible, 8; Sheffield: Sheffield Academic Press, 1995).

6.   G.A. Yee, 'Hosea', in C.A.Newsom and S.H. Ringe (eds.), *The Women's Bible Commentary* (Louisville, KY: Westminster/John Knox Press, 1992), pp. 195-202 (198-99).

worships other Gods, which is metaphorically described in a degrading[7] manner as 'whoring' (זנה). She 'commits adultery' (נאף; Hos. 2.4; 3.1) with Baal, instead of upholding the marital relationship with her husband YHWH. She even accepts the wages of a whore (אתנן; Hos. 2.14; 9.1). YHWH reacts by proclaiming a divorce (Hos. 2.4a), and he 'uncovers' (גלה) her 'nakedness'[8] (2.12).[9] This has been recognized in feminist critique as a scene of pornography[10] and sexual violence.[11] Later on, YHWH tries to reestablish the relationship (2.21 onwards).

Feminist critique has also pointed out that the picture of YHWH's 'wife', Israel, represents culturally negative images of certain groups of women who live beyond the borders of the patriarchal family.[12] Her punishment in a scene of sexual violence not only portrays YHWH as a violent husband, but also legitimizes such behaviour

7.   Cf. P.A. Bird, ' "To Play the Harlot": An Inquiry into an Old Testament Metaphor', in P.L. Day (ed.), *Gender and Difference in Ancient Israel* (Minneapolis: Fortress Press, 1989), pp. 80-89. F. van Dijk-Hemmes ('The Imagination of Power and the Power of Imagination: An Intertextual Analysis of Two Biblical Love Songs: The Song of Songs and Hosea 2', *JSOT* 44 [1989], pp. 75-88) points to the fact that the female concept of a marital relationship, which can be reconstructed from the Song of Songs, is different from the male one; but only the male concept is acknowledged in Hosea. 'The woman who expresses her desire for her lover becomes in the Hosean context a harlot who, in a shameless way, goes after her lovers' (p. 82). H. Schulte ('Beobachtungen zum Begriff der Zônâ im Alten Testament', *ZAW* 104 [1992], pp. 255-62), states that the term זנה has not always had a negative connotation.

8.   The word נבלת is a *hapax legomenon*; for the translation, see the discussion in Wacker, *Figurationen*, p. 69 n. 5.

9.   The expression 'to uncover the nakedness' (גלה ערוה) is used in Lev. 18.6-19; [20.11, 17-23] for sexual intercourse. Therefore, it is likely that not only public humiliation by being stripped naked is meant in the prophetic text, but the rape of the woman as well. Cf. P. Gordon and H.C. Washington, 'Rape as a Military Metaphor in the Hebrew Bible', in Brenner (ed.), *A Feminist Companion to the Latter Prophets*, pp. 308-25 (316-18); F.R. Magdalene, 'Ancient Near-Eastern Treaty-Curses and the Ultimate Texts of Terror: A Study of the Language of Divine Sexual Abuse in the Prophetic Corpus', in Brenner (ed.), *A Feminist Companion to the Latter Prophets*, pp. 326-52 (328-34); Seifert, *Tochter*, pp. 296-97.

10.   The first to use the term 'prophetic pornography' is T.D. Setel, 'Prophets and Pornography', in L.M. Russell (ed.), *Feminist Interpretation of the Bible* (Oxford: Basil Blackwell, 1985), pp. 86-95 (87-88).

11.   R.J. Weems ('Gomer: Victim of Violence or Victim of Metaphor?', *Semeia* 47 [1989], pp. 87-104) examines the text of Hos. 2.4-25 and discovers that sexual violence in this passage is not simply a motif, but a decisive element of the textual structure.

12.   Cf. n. 7 above.

against actual[13] women by ascribing this kind of conduct to God. As Weems points out: 'In this case, a risky metaphor gives rise to a risky deduction: here, to the extent that God's covenant with Israel is like a marriage between a man and a woman, then a husband's physical punishment against his wife is as warranted as God's punishment of Israel'. [14]

In the search for a metaphor against that of YHWH as a violent husband we find a scene of reconciliation between Hosea and Gomer in Hosea 3, and between YHWH and Israel in Hos. 2.18-25. We can assume, however, that this reconciliation does not last long, because in Hos. 4.15 Israel is again referred to as a 'whore'. We can also examine some passages in Hosea 2, 4, 11, and 14. Wacker discovered that the imagery of a goddess is applied to YHWH here.[15] Additionally, we can take into account Hos. 11.1-4.[16] The description of a peaceful and harmonious relationship between Israel and YHWH does not, however, use the prophetic marriage metaphor in this case: In Hosea 11, 'Ephraim' is YHWH's beloved son and not his wife. As such, we are not given a positive image with which we can counter the 'whoring' Israel of Hosea 1–4.

Jeremiah

Like Hosea, the book of Jeremiah also uses the metaphor of marriage.[17] The Hosean metaphor, however, is adapted and transformed. Diamond and O'Connor list the parallels and differences: Jeremiah only describes two 'heavenly' marriages between YHWH and Israel and Jerusalem; 'she' is pictured as more monstrous and animalistic[18]

---

13. I use this term as the opposite of 'metaphorical'; it denotes women of flesh and blood.

14. Weems, 'Gomer', p. 100.

15. M.-T. Wacker, 'Traces of the Goddess in the Book of Hosea', in Brenner (ed.), *A Feminist Companion to the Latter Prophets*, pp. 219-41.

16. H. Schüngel-Straumann ('God as Mother in Hosea 11', in Brenner [ed.], *A Feminist Companion to the Latter Prophets*, pp. 194-218) sees YHWH as a mother. This is achieved through a connection of Hos. 11.1-7 with vv. 8-11. I do not, however, share Schüngel-Straumann's opinion that נחומי in v. 8 should be changed to רחמי and be translated as 'womb'. Therefore, I doubt that YHWH is seen exclusively as a mother in Hos. 11.1-11.

17. For feminist examinations of the book of Jeremiah, see K.M. O'Connor, 'Jeremiah', in Newsom and Ringe (eds.), *The Women's Bible Commentary*, pp. 169-77; and A. Bauer, *Gender in the Book of Jeremiah: A Feminist-Literary Reading* (Studies in Biblical Literature, 5, New York: Peter Lang, 1999).

18. A. Brenner ('On Prophetic Propaganda and the Politics of "Love": The Case of Jeremiah', in *idem* [ed.], *A Feminist Companion to the Latter Prophets*, pp. 256-74

than in Hosea; YHWH does not only punish her, but also divorces her; Jeremiah sees no chance for the restoration of the marriage and puts the blame on the 'wife', and the children are seen as the only survivors of the family tragedy: 'Jeremiah reads an old metaphor and writes a new narrative'.[19]

In Jer. 2.1–3.5, the young Jerusalem has become YHWH's bride.[20] Although her 'whoring' (זנה) with other gods is a burden on the relationship with YHWH, he is not yet willing to divorce her as he did with Israel before. She gets a second chance to come back to him. In the following chapters, the sins and transgressions of the — predominantly male part of the — Israelite people are numbered. Therefore, it is doubtful whether the prophet will be able to turn the people back to YHWH.[21] In Jeremiah 13, the marital separation of YHWH and Jerusalem culminates in a scene of sexual violence: in v. 22, 'for the greatness of her sins' her 'hem' or her 'genitals' (שׁול*)[22] are

---

[262-64]), points to a degrading of women through the comparison of their sexual lust to that of animals.

19. For a comparison of Hos. 1–3 and Jer. 2–5, especially with respect to the marriage metaphor see A.R.P. Diamond and K. O'Connor, 'Unfaithful Passions: Coding Women Coding Men in Jeremiah 2-3 (4.2)', *BiblInt* 4 (1996), pp. 288-310 [306-307]. A broader examination from a non-feminist perspective is given by A. Weider, *Ehemetaphorik in prophetischer Verkündigung: Hos. 1–3 und seine Wirkungsgeschichte im Jeremiabuch. Ein Beitrag zum alttestamentlichen Gottes-Bild* (FzB, 71; Würzburg: Echter Verlag, 1993), and M. Schulz-Rauch, *Hosea und Jeremia: Zur Wirkungsgeschichte des Hoseabuches* (Calwer Theologische Monographien, 16; Stuttgart: Calwer Verlag, 1996).

20. Diamond and O'Connor ('Passions', p. 289) find the marriage metaphor in Jer. 2–5 to be a 'root metaphor'.

21. M.E. Shields ('Circumcision of the Prostitute: Gender, Sexuality, and the Call to Repentance in Jeremiah 3.1-4.4', *BiblInt* 3 [1995], pp. 61-74; reprinted with a response in this volume) notes that the positive images and the possibility of change are ascribed in Jer. 3.1-4.4 exclusively to male figures, whereas women figures do not find positive identification in this text.

22. The word שׁול*, is difficult to translate in its different contexts. In Isa. 6.1, for instance, it is clearly not meant to indicate YHWH's genitals (against L. Eslinger, 'The Infinite in a Finite Organical Perception [Isaiah VI 1-5]', *VT* 45 [1995], pp. 155-69); this would not only have been extremely offensive, but completely contradicts the rest of the Old Testament texts, where YHWH's private parts are never mentioned (see, e.g., H. Eilberg-Schwartz, 'God's Body: The Divine Cover-Up', in J.M. Law [ed.], *Religious Reflexions on the Human Body* [Bloomington: Indiana University Press, 1995], pp. 143-57). It is probably meant as the hem of his garment; similarly שׁול*, for the priest's clothing in Exod. 28.33-34; 39.34-36. The expression 'to uncover (חשׂף/גלה) the שׁבל/שׁול' (Jer. 13.22, 26; Nah. 3.5; Isa. 47.2) has a different emphasis. The verb גלה can refer to the thing or person uncovered as well as the

'uncovered' (גלה ni.), which means that she is stripped naked. The last two words of the verse, however, state more clearly what is meant: 'your "heels" will be violated' (נחמסו עקביך). 'Heel' (עקב) is another euphemism for the genitals, and the verb חמס is one of the strong Hebrew expressions used to designate violence of all kinds. Therefore a severe form of sexual violence, probably rape, is meant here.[23] Whereas in v. 22 the passive form is used (perhaps as *passivum divinum* which would point to YHWH, but this is not clear), in v. 26 the subject of the action is named: it is YHWH himself who 'uncovers' (חשׂף) the 'hem' or genitals 'over her face'[24], so that her 'shame' (קלון) can be seen. This is the only passage in the Old Testament where YHWH himself performs the act of sexual violence against one of his own 'wives'.[25] So the exilic fate of Jerusalem is described as a scene of sexual violence, within the context of the prophetic marriage metaphor.[26]

Although in Jeremiah 30–31 post-exilic texts that tell us about the restoration of Jerusalem can be found, the image of YHWH as a husband who punishes his wife by means of sexual violence is hardly

---

thing which is removed in the act of uncovering. This is not the case with חשׂף. In the Old Testament, its objects are only those persons or things that are uncovered and never that which is removed (for further examination, see Baumann, *Liebe*, pp. 60-61). How does this fit together with שׁבל/שׁול? If we assume that the context of stripping the genitals naked is meant here, we have to consider the problem of sexual metaphors. As Brenner says, genitals are rarely directly depicted in the Old Testament: 'biblical designations of human erogenous zones, primary and second-ary and of both sexes, are in general euphemistic' (A. Brenner, *The Intercourse of Knowledge: On Gendering Desire and 'Sexuality' in the Hebrew Bible* [Biblical Inter-pretation Series, 26; Leiden: E.J. Brill, 1997], p. 33; see also my own remarks in Baumann, *Liebe*, pp. 42-43). Mostly, they are metaphorized, which means that other expressions are used instead of the precise medical terms we choose nowadays. So, it is possible that in this case a 'hem' or 'skirt' actually describes what is normally covered by it, which is the body and, in this context, especially the genitals.

23. Cf. Magdalene, 'Treaty Curses', p. 329 n. 4, or Bauer, *Gender*, p. 104.

24. This is another problem with the understanding of the passage in Jer. 13.26 and Nah. 3.5. It is nearly impossible to determine the exact meaning of the expression על פניך (literally: 'over your face') in relation to גלה. It probably means something like 'against you'; cf. Baumann, *Liebe*, pp. 63-64.

25. Against the foreign city Nineveh (Assyria), however, YHWH is active in Nah. 3.5-6.

26. The background of the metaphor is probably the ancient Near Eastern laws about divorce or adultery as well as the connection of war and rape which was common in the ancient Near East. This is reflected in the treaty-curses against vassals (cf. Magdalene, 'Treaty-Curses', pp. 341-46 and the discussion of several theses in Baumann, *Liebe*, pp. 78-90).

revoked or corrected by other texts in the book of Jeremiah. Rather, it is simply reinforced again: in a quotation from Jer. 13.22 in Jer. 30.15, YHWH states that his punishment against her was completely just and adequate.[27] Even though Jerusalem/Zion will be restored, this is not expressed in terms of the marriage metaphor. When it comes to restitution and hope, the 'son' Jacob is the one who is named; Israel remains, still, the rebel daughter (31.22).[28]

Ezekiel

In Ezekial 16 and 23, we find the two longest allegories of the prophetic marriage metaphor.[29] Ezekiel transforms the previous version, which he probably knows from the book of Jeremiah.[30] In Ezekiel 16, we are presented with the allegory of Jerusalem who is found by YHWH as a baby. She grows up, and he marries her.[31] Thereafter, she 'whores'[32] with other 'men'. These 'men' are not only other gods as in Hosea and Jeremiah, but also the political allies of Israel/Jerusalem (Egypt, Assyria, Babylonia) and their gods. The story ends tragically:[33] in her 'whoring', she first 'uncovers her nakedness' by herself

---

27. In Jer. 30.17 YHWH is the one who restores the health and heals the wounds of Zion; this is, however, more the image of YHWH as a healer than as a husband (cf. O'Connor, 'Jeremiah', p. 176).

28. O'Connor notes: 'Much, but not all, of Jeremiah's God language justifies violence against women and subordinates them to their human kings, judges, and fathers' ('Jeremiah', p. 172). Cf. also: 'Although the book portrays God primarily in male terms, God escapes the narrow confines of patriarchal imagery in some passages' (p. 176). She refers to Jer. 7.1-15; 8.1-12; 8.19–9.3; 30.17; 31.20, 31-34; 33.6 (pp. 176-77).

29. For a detailed study of the female Jerusalem in Ezekiel, see J. Galambush, *Jerusalem in the Book of Ezekiel: The City as Yahweh's Wife* (SBLDS, 130; Atlanta: Scholars Press, 1992). Suggestions for teaching these texts are made by K.P. Darr, 'Ezekiel's Justifications of God: Teaching Troubling Texts', *JSOT* 55 (1992), pp. 97-117.

30. For the relationship between Ezekiel and Jeremiah, with no special attention to the marriage metaphor, see D. Vieweger, *Die literarischen Bezüge zwischen den Büchern Jeremia und Ezechiel* (Beiträge zur Erforschung des Alten Testaments und des antiken Judentums, 26; Frankfurt: Peter Lang, 1993).

31. Seifert (*Tochter*, pp. 262-68), points to the fact that in Ezek. 16.1-14 we can find motifs of sexual abuse of children by their fathers (YHWH as the foster-father marries his foster-child).

32. Only in Ezekiel do we have the noun תזנות from the root זנה; this verb and its derivatives are used more often than in the other prophetic books.

33. C. Maier ('Jerusalem als Ehebrecherin in Ezechiel 16: Zur Verwendung und Funktion einer biblischen Metapher', in H. Jahnow *et al.*, *Feministische Hermeneutik*

(גלה ערוה, 16.36), and then YHWH does the same with her in front of her ex-lovers (16.37).[34] It is not stated definitively, but it can be assumed that she will be gang-raped (as Weems puts it),[35] or subjected to other forms of sexual violence (16.39). In the end, she is cut to pieces by her former lovers (16.40).

The end of the story resembles that in Ezekiel 23. Here we are given the allegory about two sisters, Samaria (Ohola) and Jerusalem (Oholiba), who have 'whored' with men since their youth. This is, however, the textual interpretation of the sexual violence of their 'lovers' against them (23.3, 8, 21).[36] First, Samaria's 'nakedness' is 'uncovered' (גלה ערוה) by her Assyrian 'lovers', and then she is murdered (23.10). Although her sister Jerusalem saw what had happened, she did not alter her behaviour. As in Ezekiel 16, she is the one who exposes herself first (23.18), and later her 'nakedness is uncovered' by her 'lovers' (23.29) before she is killed.

This extremely pornographic, violent and cruel allegory is one means Ezekiel uses to tell the history of Israel/Samaria and Jerusalem that led to their exilic fate. For the 'women', there is no chance of a new life. Galambush explains why this is so:

> Ultimately, the metaphor of Jerusalem as wife is itself a problem, always threatening to transform Yahweh's marriage into a marriage between the Holy and the unclean. Ezekiel therefore depicts Yahweh as ultimately driven to destroy his hopelessly polluted temple. Morover, just as Yahweh destroys the temple, so also must he preside over the death

und Erstes Testament: Analysen und Interpretationen [Stuttgart: W. Kohlhammer, 1994], pp. 76-101) examines the text with respect to its development. The original text did not have the sexual violence or the death penalty for the woman; the verses Ezek. 16.30-31, 34, 36-38, 41b-63 were probably added by several redactors later.

34. M.E. Shields ('Multiple Exposures: Body Rhetoric and Gender Characterization in Ezekiel 16', *JFSR* 14 [1998], pp. 7-13; reprinted with a Self Response in this volume) points out that whereas 'her' body is uncovered in some detail for the reader, we do not know anything about 'his' body.

35. Weems, *Battered Love*, p. 60.

36. Van Dijk-Hemmes (in Brenner and van Dijk-Hemmes, *Gendering Texts*, p. 173) speaks (with Setel) of the 'misnaming of female experience': 'It would have been more adequate to describe the events during the sisters' youth in the following manner: "They were sexually molested in Egypt, in their youth they were sexually abused". This way, justice would have been done to the fate of these metaphorical women, and the audience would not have been seduced into viewing women or girls as responsible for and even guilty of their own violation. In short, there would have been no question of "blaming the victim".'

of his metaphorical wife (16.40), not only to vindicate his dishonored name, but to remove the potential for future defilement that the city's feminine persona represents.[37]

Thus Jerusalem is restored as a city. In Ezekiel 40–48 we get a detailed vision of the New Jerusalem. In the entire book of Ezekiel, however, YHWH *as a husband* does not deviate from his role of imposing (and carrying out) the death penalty on his wife; nor is Jerusalem *as a wife* given the chance to gain reconciliation. Thus Shields concludes: 'Woman is written out of the restoration (as far as she can be)'.[38]

Lamentations
The use of the marriage metaphor in Lamentations 1 is different from the above texts in several aspects. First, we are not told the story of YHWH's and Jerusalem's marriage. Obviously, one has to know it from Hosea, Jeremiah or Ezekiel. Secondly, Lamentations is not a prophetic book, although tradition[39] ascribes it to Jeremiah. As the Latin title of this short book suggests, it consists of laments and not of prophetic speech. In some verses, Jerusalem/Zion speaks herself (e.g. 1.9b, 11b-16, 18-22),[40] which is different from most of the prophetic texts. Nevertheless, in vv. 8-9 her fate of suffering is the consequence of her sins. In Lamentations 1, a doubled shame is ascribed to her: she becomes 'unclean' without having the chance to clean herself; and she is to blame for her sins and for her uncleanliness, as a result of the sexual violence she suffered as punishment. Consequently, she is completely isolated from her community.[41] Her former admirers now

37. Galambush, *Jerusalem*, p. 88.
38. Shields, 'Exposures', p. 13 (see also in this volume).
39. O. Kaiser ('Klagelieder', in H. Ringgren, W. Zimmerli and O. Kaiser, *Sprüche. Prediger. Das Hohe Lied. Klagelieder. Das Buch Esther* [ATD, 16; Göttingen: Vandenhoeck & Ruprecht, 3rd edn, 1981], p. 295), says that 2 Chron. 35.25 can be interpreted as referring to the Jeremian authorship of Lamentations.
40. This fact is appreciated by K.M. O'Connor ('Lamentations', in Newsom and Ringe [eds.], *The Women's Bible Commentary*, pp. 178-82 [181]): 'Daughter Zion's voice evokes the pain of women who have lost their children, who know sexual abuse, who are victims of war and famine. To pray with daughter Zion is to join with the struggles of women around the globe. It is to reject victimhood by embracing the anger that can provide energy to transform relationship.'
41. 'Uncleanliness' is a problematic word, which in biblical texts carries a different meaning than in common language; cf., e.g., I.J. Petermann (Bathmartha), 'Machen Geburt und Monatsblutung die Frau "unrein"? Zur Revisionsbedürftigkeit eines mißverstandenen Diktums', in L. Schottroff and M.-T. Wacker (eds.), *Von der Wurzel getragen: Christlich-feministische Exegese in Auseinandersetzung mit Antijudaismus* (Biblical Interpretation Series, 17; Leiden: E.J. Brill, 1996), pp. 43-60 (44-45): טמא

despise her because they have seen her 'shame/nakedness' (עְרוֹה) and the uncleanliness of her 'skirts/hems' (שׁוּל*). This is most probably an allusion to sexual violence.[42]

This is what makes Lamentations 1 realistic in its depiction of the woman, as O'Connor concludes: 'Daughter Zion blames herself for the excesses of her abusers and, like contemporary victims of domestic violence, appears to have no self-esteem left'.[43] This, however, could be fatal for battered women today. The roles of man and woman are fixed in this biblical text as those of a violent husband, who acts within the accepted legal bounds of society; and a woman, who is completely victimized by her circumstances and her surroundings. Finally, we do find in Lamentations numerous metaphors of YHWH's violence that are not limited to a female victim: in Lamentations 3 a male figure speaks as a victim of divine wrath. This, however, does not provide us with much hope, as Lamentations definitely is a book dominated by destruction and severe suffering.

Summary

In Hosea, Jeremiah, Ezekiel and Lamentations, we find different forms of the prophetic marriage metaphor.[44] There are, however, common motifs. In each of the texts, Israel/Jerusalem is called a 'whore' or 'adulteress'. We also find in all of these texts scenes of sexual violence. YHWH is always involved in the punishment of his wife, although he is not always the one who directly attacks or rapes her.

Other than in Lamentations, we can find positive imagery for God. In none of these books, however, is YHWH described in positive terms

---

is not a hygienic or aesthetic classification, but rather one of ritual meaning.

42. U. Bail (*Gegen das Schweigen klagen: Eine intertextuelle Studie zu den Klagepsalmen Ps 6 und Ps 55 und der Erzählung von der Vergewaltigung Tamars* [Gütersloh: Chr. Kaiser Verlag/Gütersloher Verlagshaus, 1998], p. 190) compares Lam. 1.8b with Jer. 13.22, 26; Ezek. 16.37, and Nah. 3.5-7. She assumes that also in Lam. 1.8b rape is meant. The same conclusion is reached by B.B. Kaiser, 'Poet as "Female Impersonator": The Image of Daughter Zion as Speaker in Biblical Poems of Suffering', *JR* 67 (1987), pp. 164-82 (175). Seifert (*Tochter*, p. 285) points to Lam. 2.4, 8, and 9, where the metaphor of rape can also be seen: 'Wenn Gott seinen Zorn in ihr Zelt gießt (2,4) und Mauern und Riegel zerbricht (2,8.9), werden Assoziationen geweckt, die sich mit der gewaltsamen Penetration einer Frau beim Geschlechtsverkehr verbinden lassen'.

43. O'Connor, 'Lamentations', p. 180.

44. For a comparison of the different motifs cf. G. Baumann, 'Connected by Marriage, Adultery and Violence: The Prophetic Marriage Metaphor in the Book of the Twelve and in the Major Prophets', *SBLSP* 1999, pp. 556-66.

as the husband of Israel/Jerusalem *after* the scenes of violence. The prophetic marriage metaphor is not used to express restoration.

3. *Objections in Isaiah 40–55 to YHWH as a Violent Husband*

I shall begin by reviewing First Isaiah (Isa. 1–39) with regard to the use of the prophetic marriage metaphor which, by comparison to the other prophetic books, is hardly mentioned. Only in 1.21 is the city of Jerusalem called a 'whore'. This verse is most probably a post-exilic addition to First Isaiah.[45] Such is obviously the case with two other texts that refer to foreign cities,[46] one of which also uses the metaphor of the city as a 'whore': in Isa. 23.12, the city of Sidon is depicted as a virgin who has been violated.[47] The city of Tyre (23.15-18), on the other hand, is called a 'forgotten whore' and her fate has already been planned. These three texts are the only allusions to the terminology of the prophetic marriage metaphor that we find in First Isaiah. Therefore, as with Lamentations 1, we have to assume that the readers of Second Isaiah have learned of the marriage metaphor from Hosea, Jeremiah or Ezekiel.

There are four complexes of metaphorical speech in Second Isaiah that can be related to the prophetic marriage metaphor. We will look at the texts which use this metaphor in a prophetic announcement of judgment against Babylon (Isa. 47) and in connection with the image of 'Zion' as a wife, partly with YHWH as her husband (Isa. 49.17-21; 50.1 and Isa. 54.1-10). Two other complexes of metaphors deal with YHWH as mother (Isa. 42.14; 45.10; 46.3-4; 49.15), and Zion as the female equivalent to the theologically important figure of the 'Servant of YHWH' (עבד יהוה; Isa. 42.1-4; 49.1-6; 50.4-9; 52.13–53.12).

Jerusalem's former fate is now Babylon's: Isaiah 47
A text which closely resembles the scenes of punishment of Israel and Jerusalem in Hos. 2.12; Jer. 13.22, 26; Ezekiel 16; 23 and Lam. 1.8-9 can be found in Isa. 47.2-3:

---

45. Cf. O. Kaiser, *Das Buch des Propheten Jesaja. Kapitel 1–12* (ATD, 17; Göttingen: Vandenhoeck & Ruprecht, 5th edn, 1981), pp. 56-58.

46. O. Kaiser, *Der Prophet Jesaja. Kapitel 13–39* (ATD, 18; Göttingen: Vandenhoeck & Ruprecht, 2nd edn, 1976), pp. 138-40.

47. For a brief discussion of the verb עשׁק in Isa. 23.12, see Baumann, *Liebe*, p. 187.

(2)   Take the handmill and grind meal,
      remove your veil, lift up (חשׂף) the robe, uncover (גלה) your thighs,
      walk through the river.
(3)   Your nakedness (ערוה) shall be uncovered (גלה),
      and your shame (חרפה) shall be seen.
      I will take revenge, and I will not deal kindly with anyone.[48]

There are several Old Testament texts in which parallels to Isaiah 47 can be found. Aside from the marriage metaphor, there are even more similarities to Lamentations 1, similarities that Willey has examined in detail: in Isaiah 47, 'Daughter Babylon's humiliation is imagined point for point as Jerusalem's was portrayed in Lamentations'. [49]

In Isa. 47.2-3 the same (mis)treatment with which YHWH handles Israel/Jerusalem is repeated: a woman will be forced to lift her skirts and to be publicly humiliated. The terminology which is used is the same as in the texts of the prophetic marriage metaphor, discussed above (Section 2): 'to uncover' (גלה) in Hos. 2.12; Jer. 13.22 and Ezek. 16.36-37; 23.10, 18, 29; or 'to lift up' (חשׂף) in Jer. 13.26. The objects are the 'robe' or 'hem' of the garment (שׁבל or שׁול) in Jer. 13.22 and 26, or the 'nakedness' (ערוה) in Ezek. 16.36-37; 23.10, 18, 29. Thus in Isa. 47.3a we find evidence of sexual violence or, perhaps, even the rape of the metaphorical woman. The rapist is not mentioned explicitly in v. 3a, although in v. 3b YHWH is the subject. Thereby, the niphal in v. 3a (תגל) can be understood as *passivum divinum*, which would point to YHWH as the rapist.

This time, however, it is not Jerusalem who is the victim of violent vengeance—it is Babylon. Isaiah 47 is the only example of violence against a foreign nation in Second Isaiah. Therefore, we do not see YHWH as a battering husband here, but rather in a role of a raping soldier.[50] In Nah. 3.4-7, another parallel to Isa. 47.2-3, YHWH is clearly described as the rapist. The object or victim is the city of Nineveh, the Assyrian capital, which is called a 'whore' (זונה). This is not the case with Babylon in Isa. 47. Galambush notes that 'the reason for

48.   The translation of this difficult passage in v. 3b follows C.A. Franke, *Isaiah 46, 47, and 48: A New Literary-Critical Reading* (Biblical and Judaic Studies from the University of California (San Diego), 3; Winona Lake: Eisenbrauns, 1994), p. 118; for the discussion see pp. 118 and 119.

49.   P.T. Willey, *Remember the Former Things: The Recollection of Previous Texts in Second Isaiah* (SBLDS, 161; Atlanta: Scholars Press, 1997), p. 167; the comparison of Isa. 47 and Lam. 1 on pp. 167-70.

50.   M. Franzmann ('The City as Woman: The Case of Babylon in Isaiah 47', *Australian Biblical Review* 43 [1995], pp. 1-19 [13]) puts it this way: 'Yahweh the warrior-rapist takes inexorable vengeance against Babylon'.

Babylon's punishment [in Isa. 47] is not "adultery". Pride is the chief
sin of which she is accused (vv. 7-8, 10, 12), though "evil" (v. 10) and
"enchantments" (v. 12; cf. Nah 3.4) are also named'.[51] Both Nah. 3.4-7
and Isa. 47.2-3 can be interpreted as a reversal of YHWH's punishing
actions against his wife Israel/Jerusalem. Franke sees Isaiah 47 as a
'major division within Second Isaiah'. The text 'can also be seen to
play an important dividing role within xl–lv. There is a dramatic
build-up in chs. xl–xlvi, in which Jacob/Israel is weary and
exhausted, disheartened and ashamed, imprisoned and sitting in
darkness, a people plundered and without a rescuer. This build-up
culminates in xlvii where the tables are turned upon Babylon'.[52]
YHWH's wife is no longer the victim of violence. It is 'her' enemy,
metaphorically described as the woman Babylon, who experiences
this fate. This shift in the focus of YHWH's vengeance to Israel's
enemies was probably written to comfort the Israelites by YHWH's
taking revenge on their enemies. Although the metaphor has been
altered somewhat, YHWH continues to act in a similar manner. He is
pictured as a man, probably a soldier in this case, committing sexual
violence against a woman.

This aspect of the metaphor in Isa. 47.2-3 has been criticized by
feminist theologians. YHWH as 'a warrior-rapist' is a very frightening
image of God, and by no means more positive than YHWH as a
battering and raping husband,[53] even though his violence is directed
against women other than his own wife. Such a metaphor carries
specific consequences for readers throughout the ages:

> Violence done to women is a normal part of everyday life in a
> patriarchal society, and members are not socialized to feel sympathy for
> the victims of such violence. When people in such a society describe
> God by using male metaphors, then the danger is inevitable that 'he'
> will not be able to escape what is regarded as normal behaviour for men
> in this context. To use the image of Yahweh as warrior is to make
> possible Yahweh's acting as a soldier rapist. [54]

---

51. Galambush, *Jerusalem*, p. 43.

52. C.A. Franke, 'The Function of the Satiric Lament over Babylon in Second
Isaiah (XLVII)', *VT* 41 (1991), pp. 408-18 [417]. Cf. Also C. Westermann, *Das Buch
des Propheten Jesaja. Kapitel 40–66* (ATD, 19; Göttingen: Vandenhoeck & Ruprecht,
4th edn, 1981), p. 152. He makes a remark on North's observation that there are 40
words in Isa. 47 which only occur here in Second Isaiah.

53. Franzmann, 'City', p. 17.

54. Franzmann, 'City', p. 18.

YHWH and Zion as a Couple: Isa. 49.14, 17-21; 50.1, and 54.1-10
After Isaiah 47 there is no further mention of Babylon. With her story
at an end, we now find positive allusions to the marriage of YHWH
and Zion.[55] The first such instance can be found in Isa. 49.14-21[56] (or
49.14-26[57]). The form of this paragraph is a point of discussion among
scholars. We can accept the compromise suggested by Koole: 'these
vv. [14-21] can be regarded as a discussion with elements of the pronouncement of salvation (Beuken) or as a pronouncement of salvation
with elements of the discussion (Whybray)'.[58] In Isa. 49.14 we listen to
Zion in a verse where she is mourning over her fate:

> And Zion said: 'YHWH has forsaken (עזב) me,
> and the Lord (אדני) has forgotten me!'

We cannot say clearly whether this verse alludes to the prophetic
marriage metaphor or not. In the event that it does, we would expect
YHWH to be called בעל 'master', 'husband' and not simply אדני 'lord'.
Another argument against an allusion to the marriage metaphor here
is that the following verse (49.15) does not refer to marriage but,
instead, compares YHWH to a mother, thereby making use of the
parent-child metaphor. We will take a closer look at 49.15 below,
within the context of YHWH as a mother in Second Isaiah. On the
other hand, 'forgetting' (עזב) is meaningful in the context of marriage,
although it most likely means 'to separate from' instead of 'to be
divorced'.[59] That this is an adequate description of the legal situation

---

55. Zion in Second Isaiah is, however, a figure with many facets: she is
YHWH's wife and daughter, a 'virgin' (בתולה, which refers to an unmarried young
woman) as well as a mother.

56. This is the passage according to J.L. Koole, *Isaiah 49–55* (HOT, 3.2; Leuven,
1998), pp. 48-68, and K. Baltzer, *Deutero-Jesaja* (KAT, 10.2; Gütersloh: Gütersloher
Verlagshaus, 1999), pp. 405-14.

57. The passage includes vv. 14-26 in the view of Westermann, *Jesaja*, pp. 175-
80; R.P. Merendino, 'Jes 49,14-26: Jahwes Bekenntnis zu Sion und die neue Heilszeit', *RB* 89 (1982), pp. 321-69; and A. Schoors, *I am God Your Saviour: A Form-
Critical Study of the Main Genres in Is. XL–LV* (VTSup, 24; Leiden: E.J. Brill, 1973),
pp. 104-21.

58. Koole, *Isaiah 49–55*, p. 51; cf. W.A.M. Beuken, *Jesaja deel II B* (Die Prediking
van het Oude Testament; Nijkerk: Callenbach, 1983), p. 53, and R.N. Whybray,
Isaiah 40–66 (NCB; London: Oliphants, 1975), p. 143.

59. Baltzer, *Deutero-Jesaja*, p. 406: 'Damit ist die Frau rechtlich gesehen in einem
miserablen Status zwischen Ehe und Scheidung. Als Geschiedene kann sie wenig-
stens ihren Brautpreis (mōhar) zurückverlangen und in das Haus ihrer Familie
zurückkehren oder sich neu verheiraten.'

between YHWH and Zion is strengthened by Isa. 50.1, another verse
we shall examine more closely later in this section.

Isaiah 49.17-21 does in fact come back to the marriage metaphor
and alludes to some of its common features:

> (17) Your builders hurry;
> your destroyers and those who laid you waste go away from you.
> (18) Raise your eyes all around and see;
> they all gather, they come to you.
> As I live, oracle of YHWH,
> you shall put on all of them like an ornament (עדי),
> and you shall bind them
> (חקשׁלים) like a bride (בכלה).
> (19) For your ruins and your desolate places
> and the land of your devastation—
> now, you will be too crowded for your inhabitants,
> and those who destroyed you will be far away.
> (20) Still do they say in your ears, the children of your childlessness:
> 'The place is too narrow for me; come near to me, so that I can dwell'.
> (21) Then you will say in your heart: 'Who has borne me these?
> I was childless and barren, exiled and put away—
> and these, who has brought them up?
> See, I was left alone—where have these come from?'

In vv. 17-18, the metaphorical speech of marriage is not easy to recognize. The 'builders'[60] as well as the 'destroyers', who go away from
her, point to the metaphor of Zion as a city. The connection between
land or city on the one hand and wife on the other hand can be found
in most of the prophetic marriage metaphor's texts.[61] In the texts
about YHWH's punishment of Israel or Judah, Hosea combines
YHWH's destruction of the land's fertility (Hos. 2.11-12, 14) with the
stripping of 'his' wife (vv. 12, 15); and Jeremiah links the sins and the
people's exilic fate (Jer. 13.21, 24-25, 27) to the stripping of YHWH's
wife (Jer. 13.22, 26-27). Ezekiel's metaphor of YHWH's marriage to
Oholah (Samaria) and Oholibah (Jerusalem) is even more transparent
with regard to the historical reality.[62] Ezekiel speaks of the military
devastation of the land (23.24) together with the 'wife's' punishment

---

60. The *Biblia Hebraica Stuttgartensia* and most of the commentators suggest (in
opposition to the Masoretic text and in agreement with the Septuagint and the
Qumran version, and others) 'builders' (from the verb בנה) instead of 'your
children' (from the noun בן).

61. For this connection, see, e.g., O.H. Steck, 'Zion als Gelände und Gestalt:
Überlegungen zur Wahrnehmung Jerusalems als Stadt und Frau im Alten Testament', *ZTK* 86 (1989), pp. 261-81 (261-64, 274-75); Maier, 'Jerusalem', pp. 87-88.

62. See a summary of this in Baumann, *Liebe*, pp. 171-74.

(23.25). Isa. 49.17 uses the same metaphors of punishment and devastation, this time to announce that there will be no more devastation
and destruction, but rather a rebuilding of the city and a gathering of
the people.[63] Within this context, the restored city is depicted as a
bride in v. 18, with the Israelites who come back out of exile as bridal
ornament for Zion.

Many allusions to Jeremiah 13 can be found in Isaiah 49. Willey
gives a summary of the metaphors and the way they are transformed
from Jeremiah 13 to Isaiah 49:

> Echoes of Jeremiah's words in chapter 13, which is closely related to
> chapter 3, may also be heard in this section in language such as 'lift up
> your eyes and see' (Isa. 49.18, see Jer. 13.20), the imagery of the
> scattered/returning flock (Isa. 49.9-10, see Jer. 13.20), 'you will say in
> your heart' (Isa. 49.21, see Jer. 13.22), labor pains and birth (Isa. 49.21,
> see Jer. 13.21), exile (Isa. 49.21, see Jer. 13.18), and the humbling of kings
> and queens (Isa. 49.23, see Jer. 13.18). In all these cases, imagery that
> was used to communicate devastation is here reversed to sum up
> restoration: what Zion sees is not her coming enemies but her coming
> children, no longer her flock being driven away but her flock being led
> back; what she says in her heart expresses no longer dismay but
> surprised delight; what she experiences is no longer labor without birth
> but birth without labor. She is no longer exiled but restored; and it is no
> longer her royalty, but that of other nations, who are humbled. They
> come bowing down before Zion.[64]

So Jerusalem/Zion is restored, her fate in Jeremiah 13 is figuratively
and literally reversed using the same terminology. In Isa. 49.20-21, the
mother who lost her children will soon have so many that she needs
more place to accommodate all of them. The underlying metaphor
here is that of Zion's motherhood which is used in several texts,
mainly in Second and Third Isaiah[65] In Isa. 49, the dreadful exilic fate

    63. This vision is repeated in Isa. 60.4.
    64. Willey, *Remember the Former Things*, pp. 203-204.
    65. K. Nielsen (*There is Hope for a Tree: The Tree as Metaphor in Isaiah* [JSOTSup,
65; Sheffield: Sheffield Academic Press, 1989]), names 49.14-15; 54.1-2; 60.1 onwards; 62.4 and 66.7 onwards. She adds a remark on the connection to the
narratives in Genesis: 'This motif is also repeated in the patriarchal narratives,
which played an important role particularly during the period of the Exile. The
ancestresses experienced the same fate: first childlessness, then the long-expected
child is born. The people's earlier history and their present history are thus perceived as reflected images of one another' (p. 183). See also H. Schüngel-Straumann ('Mutter Zion im Alten Testament', in T. Schneider and H. Schüngel-
Straumann [eds.], *Theologie zwischen Zeiten und Kontinenten: Für Elisabeth Gössmann*
[Freiburg: Herder, 1993], pp. 19-30), who examines Isa. 49.14-26; 66.7-14 and also
Ps. 87.

of the 'mother' and land Zion is revoked and turned into the joyful life of a mother with a large family. This is not the marriage metaphor in a strict sense because there is no mention of a husband. There are, however, several expressions—in particular in Jer. 2.32—which allude to the prophetic marriage metaphor: the Hebrew word for 'ornament' in Isa. 49.18, עֲדִי, is not very common, but is often used in texts containing the marriage metaphor (Jer. 2.32; 4.30; Ezek. 16.7; 23.40). Willey also remarks that the expression 'can (someone) ever forget' (שׁכח and the particle ה) occurs in the Old Testament only here and in Jer. 2.32. Two other words connect both verses: to *bind* (קָשַׁר) the ornament like a *bride* (כלה).[66]

The allusions to other texts of the prophetic marriage metaphor emphasize that the story of the unfaithful and 'whoring' wife Zion/ Jerusalem lies in the past and is being changed and transformed into the opposite. The fate of Zion is told using similar words but with a completely different outcome.

As stated above, the husband is still lacking for the complete form of the prophetic marriage metaphor. When he finally enters the stage in Isa. 50.1, the roles are clearly identified. The marriage of YHWH and Zion is touched upon in this verse; their divorce, however, is denied. In a rhetorical question, YHWH asks the Israelites:

> Where is your mother's certificate of divorce (ספר כריתות)
> with which I sent her away? [...]
> For your transgressions your mother has been sent away.

The 'certificate of divorce' refers to Jer. 3.8, where YHWH's divorce from Israel—not from Jerusalem/Zion—is recalled. What followed the divorce was the fall of Samaria and the end of the kingdom of Israel. The fate of Israel/Samaria is described in Jer. 3.8 to threaten the inhabitants of Jerusalem; they are to stop their false behaviour and return to YHWH. In Isa. 50.1, however, the threat is taken away. Obviously the relationship between YHWH and Jerusalem still exists, as there is no certificate of divorce. The imagery is 'that of YHWH as Zion's estranged—but not divorced—husband'. [67]

At the end of Isa. 50.1, Zion/Jerusalem is again referred to as a mother, but not in a metaphorical way as in 49.20-21. She is directly called 'your mother'. This title is used for Israel in Hos. 2.4, 7: The

---

66. Willey, *Remember the Former Things*, pp. 198-99.

67. Willey, *Remember the Former Things*, p. 202. Similarly K.P. Darr, *Isaiah's Vision and the Family of God* (Literary Currents in Biblical Interpretation; Louisville, KY: Westminster/John Knox Press, 1994), pp. 66 and 176; cf. Baltzer, *Deutero-Jesaja*, p. 406.

Israelites as children of the 'whoring' mother Israel are urged to indict their mother for her 'harlotry'.[68] Unlike Hosea and Ezekiel, Second Isaiah takes this motif up and changes it slightly: now it is not the 'mother' Israel or Jerusalem who has sinned, but rather 'her' children, the Israelites themselves. The female figure is the one who bore the consequences of her children's misbehaviour.[69] She is no longer called a 'whore', but is looked upon as a mother in a positive role; she takes responsibility for her children. As Darr puts it:

> Yahweh's and Jerusalem's children are held responsible for the family's estrangement. Though the husband concedes that Zion was 'sent away', her dismissal resulted from the children's rebellion, and not from misdeeds on her part. … Once again, Jerusalem is exculpated at Israel's expense. [70]

As a voice of feminist critique on Isa. 50.1, Brenner mentions the reinforcing of gender roles and the setting of the patriarchal marriage in this text:

> […]there is no bill of divorce, v. 1 claims; but the wording, together with the parallels in Jer. 3.8 and Deut. 24.1-4, imply that a man divorces and a woman is divorced; a man writes the relevant document and a woman accepts it; a man stays in the household and she leaves it. [71]

We can conclude the following: In Isa. 50.1, there is a denial of YHWH's divorce from Jerusalem. She is not a sinner; her children are to blame. The imagery of Jerusalem remains, however, within the framework of the patriarchal marriage. Nonetheless, only YHWH plays an active role, whereas the wife is completely passive and is being acted upon.

(Re-)Marriage for Eternity: Isaiah 54
In this passage, the joy of Jerusalem's (re-)marriage (54.1-3, 4-5) is announced as well as the promise that YHWH will never leave her again (54.6-8, 9-10). In the oracle of salvation (vv. 4-6) and in the

---

68. There is also a 'mother' in Ezek. 16.3, 44-45; 23.2; however, Israel/Jerusalem is not meant here, but their mother who is a foreign country. This is to emphasize Israel/Jerusalem's proclivity towards worshipping other gods.

69. Willey, *Remember the Former Things*, p. 203: 'Though Jeremiah attributes these [the sins and transgressions] to the wife, Second Isaiah blames the children'.

70. Darr, *Isaiah's Vision*, p. 176.

71. A. Brenner, 'Identifying the Speaker-in-the-Text and the Reader's Location in Prophetic Texts: The Case of Isaiah 50', in *idem* and C. Fontaine (eds.), *A Feminist Companion to Reading the Bible: Approaches, Methods and Strategies* (Sheffield: Sheffield Academic Press, 1997), pp. 138-50 (145).

pronouncement of salvation (vv. 7-8),[72] several terms of the marriage metaphor are used.[73]

> (4) Do not fear, for you will not be ashamed (בוש);
>   do not shame, for you will not be disgraced (כלם).
>   For you will forget the shame (בוש) of your youth,
>   and you will not remember (לא זכר) the dishonour (חרפה)
>   of your widowhood (אלמנות) any more.
> (5) For your husband (בעל) is your creator;
>   his name is YHWH Zebaoth;
>   and your redeemer is the Holy One of Israel;
>   God of the whole earth is he called.
> (6) For as a deserted wife and one with distressed spirit,
>   YHWH calls you;
>   and the wife of the youth (אשת נעורים):
>   can[74] she be rejected (מאס), spoke your God.
> (7) For a brief moment I left (עזב) you,
>   but with great compassion (רחמים גדלים) I will gather you.
> (8) In a flood of anger I hid my face from you for a moment,
>   but with everlasting grace (חסד עולם) I will have mercy (רחם) on you,
>   says your redeemer YHWH.

The recipient of the salvation oracle is Jerusalem.[75] She is depicted as a woman who shares the bitterest fate of an Israelite woman:

---

72. For a discussion of the form, see Koole, *Isaiah 49–55*, pp. 347-49.

73. For allusions to Lam. 5 which do not use the marriage metaphor, see Willey, *Remember the Former Things*, pp. 233-39.

74. I translate this expression with, e.g., M.C.A. Korpel ('The Female Servant of the Lord in Isaiah 54', in B. Becking and M. Dijkstra [eds.], *On Reading Prophetic Texts: Gender-Specific and Related Studies in Memory of Fokkelien van Dijk-Hemmes* [Biblical Interpretation Series, 18; Leiden: E.J. Brill, 1996], pp. 153-67 (157 n. 17), as 'a reference to a rhetorical question'.

75. Jerusalem/Zion, however, is not mentioned explicitly in the text. I do not agree with J.F.A. Sawyer ('Daughter of Zion and Servant of the Lord in Isaiah: A Comparison', *JSOT* 44 [1989], pp. 89-107), who suggests that the woman in the text is not Jerusalem: 'It is not a story about Jerusalem, any more than the servant songs are about Israel or Jesus or the prophet. It is about a woman, and to neglect this is to miss the dynamic of the passage' (p. 94). In my opinion, the description of YHWH's marriage points too clearly to the figure of Jerusalem/Zion to be disregarded. Only in the context of the prophetic marriage metaphor can this passage be understood; otherwise these allusions do not make sense. Neither does Darr (*Isaiah's Vision*, p. 178) agree with Sawyer. There is also, in this passage, metaphorical speech which points to Jerusalem. Perhaps Baltzer is correct when he suggests that a higher degree of abstraction and universality is achieved through the ommission of the name (Baltzer, *Deutero-Jesaja*, p. 543).

infertility, desolation (v. 1) and widowhood (v. 4).[76] To have no family meant to be without any economic basis and without legal protection. For Jerusalem, however, this is history: YHWH, the husband who left her 'for a short moment', is her husband (בעל) again. Willey carefully examines the allusions of this text to its predecessors in the wider range of the marriage metaphor, 'adultery' and reconciliation, Jeremiah 3 and 31:

> Here [in Isa. 54.4], the two synonyms of shame used in Jer. 3.25 (כלמה, בשת) and the three used in Jer. 31.19 (בשת, כלם and חרפה) are recollected together—a density unique to these passages. As in the Jeremiah passages, this shame has been hers since her youth... [In] Isa. 54.6, Jeremiah's word נעורים reappears in a description of Zion as אשת נעורים, 'wife of youth.
>
> YHWH's response in Jer. 3.26 is an exhortation to return (שוב), which is repeated in Jer. 31.21. But discussion of return is significantly missing in Isaiah 54. It is not Jerusalem who is imagined needing to return in Second Isaiah, but rather YHWH (52.8) and the exiles (44.22; 49.5-6; 51.11) who return to Jerusalem. Before the exhortation to return, Jer. 31.20 added a note of grace, in which YHWH emphatically claims to remember the pity of Ephraim (רחם ארחמנו...זכר אזכרנו). In Isa. 54.4, it is Jerusalem who will not remember (לא תזכרי) her shame, and in both Isa. 54.8 and 10, YHWH repeats promises to pity (מרחמך/רחמתיך) and show steadfast love (חסד), thus restoring Jerusalem to the original marital devotion that Jeremiah had envisioned. And whereas Jeremiah repeatedly accused her of having abandoned YHWH (Jer. 2.13, 17, and 19), now YHWH repeatedly promises not to abandon her (Isa. 54.6, 7).[77] The verb 'to leave' (עזב) is the same as in Isa. 49.14.

The comparison of Jeremiah 3 and 31 with Isaiah 54 sheds a different light on the exile of Israel/Jerusalem. The line of argumentation in Hosea, Jeremiah and Ezekiel comes close to the deuteronomistic theology, which sees the exile as YHWH's punishment for the sins of Israel/Jerusalem (mainly, worshipping other gods).[78] In Isaiah 54 it is, however, no longer YHWH's violent punishment of 'her', as in Hosea 2 and Jeremiah 13, or YHWH's summoning 'her' former lovers to

---

76.   Zion as 'widow' (אלמנה) is also mentioned in Lam. 1.1. In Isa. 47.8, Babylon denies the possibility of ever becoming a widow or being childless—but this is exactly what she will be, once YHWH attacks her (see above, section 3). Here in Isa. 54, the title 'widow' was probably chosen to allude to Lam. 1, and not to the marriage metaphor, since YHWH as the 'husband' of Jerusalem certainly did not die.

77.   Willey, *Remember the Former Things*, p. 245; I quote the Hebrew words without the vowels here.

78.   Cf. Baumann, *Liebe*, pp. 232-33.

execute the (death) penalty, as in Ezekiel 16 and 23. YHWH is now depicted as a husband who comes back to the wife he had abandoned. During the time of the exile, her suffering was made possible because YHWH left her unprotected from her enemies. He 'looked away' from her, and others could harm her. It is still YHWH, however, who has made this violation possible. This is in line with Second Isaiah's image of God: YHWH, who created the universe and claims to be the only existing God, is also completely responsible for Zion's fate. YHWH's punishment, however, is not described as battering or sexual violence against her, but as his abandonment of her in a state of wrath. Now YHWH comes back to his wife and promises to stay with her in an everlasting relationship.[79] As Sawyer puts it: 'He takes prime responsibility for the tragedy and swears he will never again be angry with her or rebuke her'.[80] I do not think one has to go as far as Sawyer does, claiming that YHWH 'comes to her, on bended knee as it were, to plead with her to let bygones be bygones and start again'. [81] But I agree with Sawyer that this text is about reconciliation, that YHWH's words are apologetic and remorseful.[82] The basis, however, is the patriarchal marriage, and only in this context can the passage be understood: 'She is physically weaker than he is and socially dependent on him. He has the power to give her happiness and dignity and freedom; she knows he also has the power to punish, humiliate and abuse her. So he has to convince her that he really loves her and that she can trust him.'[83]

This is the point where feminist critique needs to start. Although YHWH's punishment is revoked to a certain degree and is no longer described as sexual violence, the setting of the patriarchal marriage itself has been neither changed nor transformed. The difference is in the behaviour of husband YHWH, and the suffering of the wife Jerusalem varies slightly. It is still she, however, who had been blamed and who had been shamed; and it is still his voluntary decision to leave her or to come back. The marital relationship, with the wife's complete dependence on the husband, is still implied as the only situation in which a woman can live safely.

---

79. The metaphor is also transparent for the actual Israelites and their situation: YHWH will gather them again from Babylonia. The title בעל denotes YHWH as the 'lord' of the Israelites in Jer. 3.14; 31.32.

80. Sawyer, 'Daughter', p. 94.

81. Sawyer, 'Daughter', p. 96.

82. Sawyer, 'Daughter', p. 95.

83. Sawyer, 'Daughter', pp. 95-96.

Perhaps Second Isaiah 'deconstructed' the image of YHWH as the husband of Zion in a different way—by stepping out of the marriage metaphor and by using imagery that is not often related to God in the Old Testament: that of God as a mother. I will now examine the Second Isaiah texts which are thought to depict YHWH in this role.

YHWH as Mother in Second Isaiah: Isa. 42.14; 45.10; 46.3-4 and 49.15
In Isa. 42.14; 45.10; 46.3-4 and 49.15, YHWH is compared to a mother in different ways.[84] In Isa. 42.14, in the context of an oracle of salvation, the powerful image of a woman in labour pains is linked to YHWH, directly after YHWH is compared to a warrior (v. 13):

> For a long time I have been silent, I kept still and restrained myself;
> like a woman in labor (כיולדה) I will cry out, I will gasp and also pant.

According to Gruber, in this verse the female activity in childbearing is emphasized.[85] Trible sets the focus differently: the product, the new creation, is the subject of this metaphor.[86] In this verse, however, the poetic device is a simile. The particle כ indicates that YHWH is not *actually* a woman in labor; he just *acts* the way she does. Darr explains this as follows:

> When the poet likens Yahweh's behavior to that of a travailing woman, this does not necessarily mean that Yahweh is giving birth, in a meta-phorical sense, to *anything*. It is one thing to say, as Ps 90.2 says, that Yahweh gave birth to mountains, land, and world. It is one thing to say, as Deut 32.18 says, that Yahweh writhed in labor pains with Israel. But it is quite another thing to say that Yahweh will in some sense *act like a woman acts when she is in labour*. Yet it is precisely this latter idea which is stated in our text. [87]

So we see that the focus in the text lies on YHWH's activity of groaning and breathing like a woman in labour. The expression ילד

---

84. See, e.g., M.L. Gruber, 'The Motherhood of God in Second Isaiah', *RB* 90 (1983), pp. 351-59, or J.J. Schmitt, 'The Motherhood of God and Zion as Mother', *RB* 92 (1985), pp. 557-69. An examination of the verb 'to writhe' (חיל) is given by J.A. Foster, 'The Motherhood of God: The Use of *ḥyl* as God-Language in the Hebrew Scriptures', in L.M. Hopfe (ed.), *Uncovering Ancient Stones: Essays in Memory of H.N. Richardson* (Winona Lake: Eisenbrauns, 1994), pp. 93-102 (looking at Isa. 49.9-11 on pp. 98-99).

85. Gruber, 'Motherhood', p. 355.

86. P. Trible, *God and the Rhetoric of Sexuality* (Philadelphia: Westminster Press, 1978), p. 64.

87. Darr, 'Like Warrior, like Women: Destruction and Deliverance in Isaiah 42.10-17', *CBQ* 49 (1987), pp. 560-71 (565).

('to give birth, to beget') is often used in the Old Testament in the context of 'desperate circumstances'.[88] Yet this is not meant in Isa. 49.14. The verbs of the second stichos 'effectively communicate a sense of the force of Yahweh's breaths, which in this context are likened to the breath of a woman in travail'.[89] This divine breath is often destructive; Darr references Isa. 40.7, 24, for example. That is not the case, however, in Isa. 42.14:

> Here the simile 'like a travailing woman' has been transformed from one connoting fear-induced pain to one bespeaking power and might— an image which is equal in intensity to the warrior image that precedes it. Yahweh goes forth like a warrior, shouting a war cry, and demonstrates prowess over foes. Yahweh gasps and pants like a woman in travail, and the breath of God desiccates the earth.[90]

This simile has other aspects as well, and not all of them are touched on in the depiction of YHWH as a warrior in v. 13. Baltzer notes that the mention of the birth as the end of the pregnancy adds the aspect of inevitability and consistency to YHWH's behaviour.[91]

We can conclude that even if YHWH is not a woman in labour here, the simile of the woman in labour for YHWH's activity in rescuing his people can bind together several aspects that cannot otherwise be linked in one image. The positive notion of this image in Second Isaiah is competely different from the use of the birth metaphor in Jeremiah, as Bauer summarizes.[92]

88. Darr, 'Warrior', p. 567.
89. Darr, 'Warrior', p. 569.
90. Darr, 'Warrior', p. 570.
91. Baltzer notes: 'Nicht so sicher ist, was das *tertium comparationis* ist. Es kann das "Schreien" sein. Ich meine aber, dass in v. 14 auf der Bildebene des Vergleichs ein einheitlicher Vorgang dargestellt wird: Am Ende der Schwangerschaft kommt es zur Geburt! Ihre Unausweichlichkeit und Folgerichtigkeit ist das *tertium comparationis*' (*Deutero-Jesaja*, p. 194). Koole too points to this aspect: 'God's plan to liberate his people was long established, long 'formed', 46.11. However, the execution of God's purpose must abide God's time. As soon as this times comes, God's apparent absence ends and salvation must break through against all opposition. Then God cannot refrain from showing his presence—like a woman giving birth' (*Isaiah 40–48*, p. 255).
92. Bauer, *Gender*, p. 162: 'The use of the childbirth metaphor (e.g., Jer. 4.19-21; 4.31; 13.21; 22.23; cf. 30.5-7), woman writhing in labor pain serves as an image for the suffering of the people. Without bringing new life into the world, the childbirth metaphor in Jeremiah tips towards death. The image is reduced to the pain and the threat of death alone; it does not lead to the joy of new life'.

Isa. 45.9-13 mentions YHWH in a disputation as a God of sovereignty and enormous power. His superiority over the Israelites or
even all human beings is illustrated with the help of several
metaphors:

> (9) Woe to anyone who strives with his maker,
>   a vessel among earthen vessels:
>   Does clay say to the one who forms it:
>   'What are you doing?' and 'Your work has no handles!'
> (10) Woe to anyone who says to a father:
>   'What are you begetting (ילד)?'
>   And to a woman: 'With what are you writhing in labor (חיל)?'
> (11) Thus says YHWH, the Holy One of Israel, and its creator:
>   Will you question me about my children,
>   and command me concerning the work of my hands?

In these verses, 'products' that question their creator's plans or
actions are cast in a negative light. The 'creators' are potter, father and
mother. The imagined audience with whom the dispute is held is put
into the position of the creation/product, which has no right to
question its creator's plans or actions. Verse 11 relates this message to
YHWH and connects the two metaphorical contexts of pottery and
parenthood, as Naidoff has noted.[93] We can summarize that YHWH is
not only compared to a mother here, but also to a potter or father, and
that YHWH's relation to all three is vague. The point of the text is not
to call YHWH a potter, a father or a mother but, is rather, the behaviour of the addressee.[94] The aim of the verse, then, is to question this
behaviour.

It is not the image of the woman in labour, but of a parent
who bears a child, which is proclaimed in an oracle of salvation in Isa.
46.3-4.

> (3) Listen to me, o house of Jacob,
>   and all the remnant of the house of Israel,
>   who have been borne from your womb (בטן),
>   carried from the womb (רחם);

---

93. B.D. Naidoff, 'The Twofold Structure of Isaiah 45, 9-13', *VT* 31 (1981),
pp. 180-85 (183). The work of the hands in v. 9 is tied together with the same theme
in v. 11bβ, and the same with the procreation in v. 10 and 11bα.

94. See, e.g., J.L. Koole, *Isaiah 40–48* (HOT, 3.1; Kampen, 1997), p. 455: 'the
particle מה asks not so much about the result ("what") as about the right of the
addressee to act in this way: why are you doing this, what are you venturing to do,
desist from this'. Similarly Baltzer, *Deutero-Jesaja*, p. 305: 'Beide Doppel-Voten
kommen zum gleichen Ergebnis und verstärken sich damit gegenseitig: der
Mensch kann das Handeln Gottes nicht hinterfragen noch bestimmen'.

(4) even to the old age I am he,
　　and even to grey hair I will bear.
　　I have made, and I shall carry; I shall bear, and I shall save.

Even if the men in Israelite society carried their children from time to time, the image in Isa. 46.3-4 is predominantly a gynocentric one. Childcare was the task of the mothers.[95] In this description, however, YHWH is once again a kind of 'better mother'. YHWH does not only carry young children like human mothers do, but he will carry them on into adulthood and even as old men and women.

This tendency is present in the next passage, 49.15, as well. In v. 14, Zion complains that YHWH forgot her and left her. YHWH replies in v. 15:

Can a woman ever forget (שׁכח) her baby,
have no[96] mercy with the child of her womb (בטן)?
Even these may forget, but I will not forget (שׁכח) you.

It is just as unlikely for YHWH to forget Israel/Jerusalem as it is for the mother of a small infant to forget her child. Again, the verse does not say that YHWH *is* a mother. YHWH *acts* like a mother, or, in the strict sense of the second stichos, acts better than a mother. A mother can, under extreme conditions, forget or even sacrifice her child,[97] but YHWH will never forget Israel. The following verse (v. 16) emphasizes this message with the image of YHWH 'inscribing' Zion on the palms of his hands.

In the four texts examined above, YHWH is compared in different ways to women, with special attention to the typical things a mother does. In Second Isaiah, however, YHWH is not called 'Mother' (אם).[98] In each of these verses we find, clearly, a simile or a direct

95. See, e.g., C.L. Meyers, 'Everyday Life: Women in the Period of the Hebrew Bible', in Newsom and Ringe (eds.), *The Women's Bible Commentary* (Historical Commentary on the Old Testament; Kampen: Kok Pharos), pp. 244-51 (248).

96. The מן with the infinitive of רחם here has the meaning of a 'private marker'; it marks what is missing or unavailable (B.K. Waltke and M. O'Connor, *An Introduction to Biblical Hebrew Syntax* [Winona Lake: Eisenbrauns, 1990], p. 214). Similarly A.E. Cowley, *Genesius' Hebrew Grammar* (ed. E. Kautsch; Oxford: Clarendon Press: Oxford, 1910 [1957]), §119y.

97. Koole mentions two extreme examples of cannibalism in times of famine: 2 Kgs 6.26-31 and Lam. 4.10 (*Isaiah 49–55*, p. 55).

98. YHWH in Second Isaiah is nonetheless more closely related to a mother than to a father. In Isa. 51.2, Abraham is named as father (אב) of the Israelites. In Third Isaiah, both titles are related to YHWH: YHWH is called a 'father' in Isa. 63.16; 64.7, and compared to a mother—in the same indirect way as in the Second Isaiah texts—in Isa. 66.13.

comparison. Nevertheless, there always remains a certain distance between YHWH and the motherly role. This is achieved by the addition of other social roles within the context, or by using the particle כ ('as'). Despite these restrictions, we have to keep in mind that no other book in the Old Testament comes closer to female imagery of YHWH than Second Isaiah does.

How can these motherly images of YHWH be linked with the prophetic marriage metaphor? Unlike the other books that contain the prophetic marriage metaphor, Second Isaiah uses an alternative imagery for God. YHWH is not only metaphorized as a husband or as a raping warrior, but also as a mother. The result is ambiguous; several images of God exist side by side in this part of the book of Isaiah.[99] Although Second Isaiah leaves no doubt that YHWH is the one and only God of the universe, it leaves room for different images of this one God. YHWH is a husband in the texts that recall and correct the prophetic marriage metaphor; YHWH is a raping warrior when fighting the enemy of Israel, Babylon. YHWH, however, also has facets that can be compared to the feelings and actions of a mother when it comes to creating a new life for the Israelites, his redeeming deeds, and his unchangeable will to rescue Israel from the Babylonian exile. YHWH changes his role according to the task he has to fulfill. It is interesting to note, in this context, that male imagery is used when Second Isaiah speaks about older Israelite traditions and what has happened in the past. Female imagery is closely related to YHWH's rescuing actions toward the Israelites.

Zion as a Figure Similar to the Ebed

In a recent discussion, the so-called 'Servant of YHWH' (the 'songs' are found in Isa. 42.1-4; 49.1-6; 50.4-9; 52.13–53.12)[100] and the figure of (daughter) Zion in Second Isaiah are seen as being related to each other.[101] In the context of Isaiah 50[102] and 54,[103] for example, the

---

99. Cf. Korpel's general remark in 'Female Servant', p. 162: 'This prophet has no difficulty in switching from the collective to the singular and from the masculine metaphor to the feminine'.

100. In the scholarly debate, we find many titles on this subject (cf. H. Haag, *Der Gottesknecht bei Deuterojesaja* (Erträge der Forschung, 233; Darmstadt: Wissenschaftliche Buchgesellschaft, 2nd edn, 1993). Most of this literature, however, does not relate the *Ebed* to Zion.

101. See, e.g., Korpel, 'Female Servant', with reference to W.A.M. Beuken ('Isaiah XIV: The Multiple Identity of the Person Addressed', *OTS* 19 [1974], pp. 29-70), L.E. Wilshire ('The Servant-City: A New Interpretation of the "Servant of the Lord" in the Servant Songs of Deutero-Isaiah', *JBL* 94 [1975], pp. 356-67),

division of the text and the connection to both figures is debated. Do these texts deal with just one of these figures—and if so with which one?—or with both? I do not want to outline the entire discussion here, but rather present the information relevant to this context. Korpel examines both figures and compares them. They mainly share a negative past and a positive future.[104] Korpel concludes:

> Apparently Zion and the servant or the Israelites in general are to some extent interchangeable concepts'.[105]

> In spite of the close parallels between the male and female servants of YHWH on the one hand and the Israelites on the other, a full identification is not what the prophet has in mind. Zion is distinguished from her children as her male colleague is from the older generation.[106]

What we can gain from this comparison is that, compared to Hosea, Jeremiah and Ezekiel, the image of Zion as the wife of YHWH is different here. She is not the only one who is punished by YHWH or who has to bear the guilt. The servant of YHWH, who is recognized as a male figure, also suffers for the sins of the people (e.g. Isa. 53.4-5). In Jeremiah and Ezekiel, this role is played by Israel or Jerusalem as the wife of YHWH. Now this fate is shared by both—a male and a female figure.

4. Conclusions

Which are the topics in Second Isaiah that can be seen as objections to the prophetic marriage metaphor with YHWH as a violent husband, and what are the limits of these objections?

One difference between Second Isaiah on the one hand and between Hosea, Jeremiah and Ezekiel on the other hand is the change

---

T.N.D. Mettinger (*A Farewell to the Servant Songs: A Critical Examination of an Exegetical Axiom* [Scripta minora K. Hamanistika Vetenskapssamfundet i Lund 1982–1983, 3; Lund: C.W.K. Gleerup, 1983]) and Sawyer, 'Daughter'. Willey (*Remember the Former Things*), points to Isa. 54.17, where the "servants of YHWH' appear for the first and only time in connection with Zion' (p. 232).

102. Cf. Brenner, 'Speaker', pp. 141-44.

103. Cf. Beuken, 'Isaiah XIV', pp. 31-63. Beuken uses the concept of the 'corporate personality' (pp. 63-70) to explain the 'multiple identity' (p. 63) of the woman who 'is throughout the chapter the one person addressed, first by the prophet, then by God himself' (p. 63). Cf. also Korpel, 'Female Servant', pp. 155-62.

104. Korpel, 'Female Servant', pp. 163-66.

105. Korpel, 'Female Servant', p. 164. I will give only one example: YHWH will not forget (נשׁה ni.) the *Ebed* (44.21), nor will he forget (שׁכח) Zion (49.15).

106. Korpel, 'Female Servant', p. 166.

in the form of the prophetic speech where the prophetic marriage metaphor is used. In Second Isaiah we find the metaphor in oracles of salvation—in some texts mixed with other forms—and not in procla-mations of punishment. The oracle against the foreign nation Babylon, in Isaiah 47, is the only exception. Secondly, YHWH's 'wife' Zion is no longer the recipient of YHWH's punishment. YHWH himself does not raise his hand against his wife; he partly regrets what he has done. This is a clear objection to the image of YHWH as a violent husband. The theological model used to explain the exile is being transformed by Second Isaiah, and this prophetic school creates a new model by changing the social roles of husband and wife. YHWH remains the husband, but he no longer violates his wife. Zion remains the wife, but she is no longer the guilty party. The divine marriage is (re-)established by a reunion of the couple in an eternal perspective and can never be destroyed.

Second Isaiah uses the exact terminology of the marriage metaphor from Hosea, Jeremiah and Ezekiel to describe the change in Jerusalem's fate, although he could have chosen other words to give his message. That Second Isaiah chose exactly these words is an indi-cation of the fact that these later texts not only wanted to express a change in Zion's fate, but also intended to change the metaphor itself. Jerusalem is YHWH's beloved wife again, and YHWH himself gives a different explanation for her exilic suffering. The pattern of punish-ment for her 'whoring' (זנה) or 'committing adultery' (נאף) has been abandoned in Isa. 40–55. None of these words are used in Second Isaiah. Now 'she' bears the guilt of her sinful children, the Israelites, but it is not her own guilt. In this respect, Zion can be compared to the figure of the *Ebed*, the 'Servant' of YHWH, who bears the sins of 'the many' (Isa. 53.12).

There are additional metaphors other than the image of YHWH as a husband in Second Isaiah. It is open to the reader to decide whether or not this is an objection to the prophetic marriage metaphor. In my opinion it is so, although the metaphorical connections between YHWH and a mother are not (syntactically) as close as the bonds between YHWH and a husband. This change in metaphors has, at the very least, a disturbing effect on the reader. We find a broader range of metaphors in this text, and both genders are utilized to explain YHWH's actions. The exclusion of women and the female from the imagery for God[107] has been revoked. At the same time, the gender roles of the marriage metaphor are dissolved by the fact that not only

107. Cf., e.g., Wacker, 'Traces', pp. 219-20.

YHWH, but also Zion as his wife are depicted as 'mothers'.

There are, of course, certain limits to the Second Isaiah objections against YHWH as a violent husband of Israel. The school of Second Isaiah does not provide a *completely* different image of God here. It does, however, change it significantly. YHWH is seen as the one and only God of the universe.[108] Within this monotheistic theology, images of God that had been abandoned before can now be tolerated; and some of these are female images, although many others are male.[109]

Still other images—for example, the violent aspect of YHWH as a warrior-rapist, such as we find in Isa. 47.2-3—remain stable. Perhaps one can explain this imagery as a reaction to the experience of violence and extreme suffering in war, deportation and exile. Its fatal consequences for the image of God and of women, however, do remain.

What also remains stable is the marriage metaphor, still being used for YHWH and for Zion. Although there are other metaphors for YHWH here, this 'old' one is still being adapted to the new situation. One reason for this could be the change in the theological model that was to be expressed by the change in the metaphor. This has, however, a double effect: the marriage metaphor is transformed and reshaped, but it is also reinforced. The new content confirms the old form. YHWH is still the husband, albeit not one who uses direct violence against his own wife. Zion/Jerusalem is still the wife whose weal and woe depend on her husband's will. The imagery still functions within a patriarchal family setting. She is the dependent and passive one, and he plays the active part. As Brenner puts it:

> I find it difficult to rejoice at the mother image... It should be remembered that the metaphorical wife-mother of Isaiah 40–66 is suffering terribly. She will be restored, and this is good; however, her dependent state—she is her divine master's legally covenanted possession, to cherish and keep or to be sent away solely according to his judgment—deconstructs her... She, as woman or city/land/community, has no significant autonomy, no life without the male's good will. This is a central message. [110]

We do have to keep in mind, however, that the image of YHWH as a husband corresponds to the image of God in Second Isaiah. It is a

---

108. See Isa. 43.10, 12-13; 44.6, 8; 45.5-6, 14; 46.9 and 48.12.

109. See, e.g., S. Ackerman, 'Isaiah', in Newsom and Ringe (eds.), *The Women's Bible Commentary*, pp. 162-68 (163).

110. Brenner, 'Speaker', pp. 145-46.

concept of God that differs from that of the other prophetic books: God is predominantly the one who has mercy on Jerusalem and therefore rescues it from the Babylonian exile. This fits in with the image of God as husband, which is also different from the other texts of the prophetic marriage metaphor: YHWH has mercy on his 'wife' and comes back to her after the exile. He is the active one, and she is being rescued.

As a feminist theologian, I regret to say that Second Isaiah does not measure up to all my previous expectations. I fail to find a completely different imagery of YHWH here. YHWH is still violent against his enemy. And yet, when taking into account the limits of a patriarchal society in times of war and violence, I still find the different image of God in Second Isaiah quite remarkable.

Outlook

As we have seen, there are certain objections in Second Isaiah to YHWH as a violent husband, as in the prophetic marriage metaphor. These objections are limited. Even in the book of Isaiah, the Second Isaiah interpretation has not been elaborated within the Second Isaiah line of argumentation, as we can see when looking at Third Isaiah (chs. 56–66). Isaiah 57.3-13 explains what the people of Israel have done according to the main line of the prophetic marriage meta-phor.[111] Even though the Israelites are called 'children of an adulterer' (מנאף), and of a 'whore' (זנה)[112] in 57.3, no direct form of punishment is announced here. We find scenes of a (re-)marriage of YHWH and Zion in Isa. 62.2-5, which pick up on Isa. 54.5-6 and elaborate on it. The motif of YHWH's 'wrath' (קצף) is used in Isa. 60.10b in analogy to Isa. 54.8a. But now, probably as an allusion to the marriage metaphor in Hosea, Jeremiah and Ezekiel, YHWH has 'struck' (נכה hi.) his wife, before his 'favour' (רצון) 'shows mercy' on her (רחם, Isa. 60.10b, cf. Isa. 54.8b). With this slight change of the metaphor, Third Isaiah, goes back to the pattern of punishment of the wife who is guilty and punished legitimately by her husband. In Isa. 60.3-5, however, Zion will experience new motherhood, as in Isa. 49.20-23. We also find an alternative image for God in Third Isaiah: YHWH can be called a

---

111. Cf., e.g., M.E. Biddle, 'The Figure of Lady Jerusalem: Identification, Deification and Personification of Cities in the Ancient Near East', in K.L. Younger, Jr, W.W. Hallo and B.F. Batto (eds.), *The Biblical Canon in Comparative Perspective* (Scripture in Context, 4; Ancient Near Eastern Texts and Studies, 11; Lewiston, NY: Mellen Press, 1991), pp. 173-94.

112. This passage causes textual problems: Literally, the Israelites are 'children of an adulterer, and she whored'. The translation given follows G.

father (63.16; 64.7) or can be described as a mother (66.7-13) of the Israelites. In conclusion, we can say that Third Isaiah takes some of the new and positive metaphors of Second Isaiah, but mixes them with the 'old' pattern of YHWH punishing his wife for her sins.

Nevertheless, Second Isaiah's way to object to the prophetic marriage metaphor has not been the only one. At the end of the book of the Twelve and of the prophetic canon (נביאים), we find a 'final word' on the marriage metaphor. Malachi develops another strategy for undermining the enormous power the marriage metaphor once had.[113] Again, we find an interesting interpretation in a passage with a difficult text.[114] In Mal. 2.10-16,[115] Judah undergoes a change of gender. In v. 11a, the subject is the 'treacherous Judah' (בגדה יהודה) we have met in Jer. 3.7, 8, 10 and 11. In Mal. 2.11b, Judah is addressed as a masculine figure:

> Judah has profaned the sanctuary of YHWH, which he loves,
> and has married (בעל) the daughter of a foreign god.

It is possible to interpret the passage with Isaksson: YHWH is the wife of the male Judah.[116] By switching the gender roles of YHWH and Israel/Judah, it is made difficult to use the marriage metaphor again with its previous unambiguous meaning. O'Brien has pointed to the power of this gender change: 'Whatever actual practice the book is

---

113. For a survey on Mal. 2.10-16, cf. Baumann, *Liebe*, pp. 222-28.

114. I have noticed that textual problems are characteristic for passages which describe YHWH with female imagery (or as a violent man). I explain this by the assumption that these texts troubled those who handed them down to us, and that they tried to change them in some way.

115. There is a scholarly debate over whether Mal. 2.10-16 is to be understood symbolically or literally; cf. G.P. Hugenberger, *Marriage as Covenant: A Study of Biblical Law and Ethics Governing Marriage Developed from the Perspective of Malachi* (VTSup, 52; Leiden: E.J. Brill, 1994), pp. 7-8 n. 51.

116. A. Isaksson, *Marriage and Ministry in the New Temple: A Study with Special Reference to Mt. 19.3-12 and 1. Cor. 11.3-16* (Acta Seminarii Neotestamentici Upsaliensis, 24; Lund: C.W.K. Gleerup, 1965), p. 33: 'However, the expressions "the wife of your youth" and "the wife of your covenant" [in vv. 14-15] need not be reduced to meaning the worship of Yahweh or belief in Yahweh. It is really Yahweh himself who is given these designations. And the reason why he, who is otherwise represented as the husband in the marriage between Yahweh and Israel, is mentioned in this verse quite unexpectedly as the wife is simply that the prophet is continuing to use the same image as in v. 11. There Judah is mentioned as the man who has married the daughter of a foreign god. This marriage means treachery towards Yahweh, the wife of his youth and the wife of his covenant. In order to enable the author to carry on using the image from v. 11, Yahweh must be represented as the wife.'

decrying, the prophetic discourse of idolatry as adultery has over-written its own argument'.[117]

Not all of the later adoptions of the prophetic marriage metaphor are so deconstructive and open to new perspectives on the image of God. The 'old pattern' of the marriage metaphor, with the female part as a sinning 'whore', is taken up in the New Testament in the book of Revelation (Rev. 17). In Rev. 17.16, we are told again the story of a women who is being stripped naked; in this text, she is the 'whore Babylon'. In v. 17, YHWH is again the one who causes this form of punishment.

In spite of Second Isaiah's progress in transforming the metaphor, the 'old' form is still present in the Scriptures—allowing sexist, porno-graphic and misogynic interpretations. Even though Second Isaiah provides us with a new interpretation of the marriage metaphor, it is quite possible to go back to the old metaphor. As readers and inter-preters of the biblical Scriptures, we have to take care that both forms of the metaphor are recounted.

---

117. J.M. O'Brien, 'Judah as Wife and Husband: Deconstructing Gender in Malachi', *JBL* 115 (1996), pp. 243-52 (249). See also O'Brien in this volume.

CIRCUMCISION OF THE PROSTITUTE: GENDER, SEXUALITY, AND THE CALL TO REPENTANCE IN JEREMIAH 3.1–4.4[*]

Mary E. Shields

The move from accusation to promise in Jer. 3.1–4.4 is mirrored by a move from female imagery to male imagery. Within the prophetic literature there are several other texts, extending from the early eighth century (Hosea) through the exilic period (Lamentations and Second Isaiah), in which both female and male imagery are used and in which Israel is addressed both as female and male. It is notable that in the pre-exilic texts, negative female imagery predominates—the images primarily used are those of overstepped sexual boundaries (adultery/harlotry/prostitution), whereas the later texts of Second Isaiah (e.g. Isa. 54) portray a reversal of such imagery.[1] The earliest texts, Hosea 2 and 4, liken Israel to a prostitute while retaining the positive aspects of the metaphorical husband/wife relationship between God and Israel. Ezekiel 16 and 23, the latest pre-exilic/exilic texts, take the imagery to its negative extreme with a vituperative, at times almost pornographic, portrayal of Israel as harlot, with no redeeming imagery, male or female. Within the scope of the pre-exilic texts, however, Jer. 3.1–4.4 represents an intermediate step in the development of the negative metaphors, developing the imagery in

*   This article has been revised and expanded from a paper presented at the 1991 Annual Meeting of the Society of Biblical Literature in Kansas City, MO. I would like to thank Carol Newsom and David Gunn for their helpful comments on the paper and early drafts of this article. Originally published in *BibInt* 3.1 (1995), pp. 61-74. Reprinted by permission.
    1.   This negative imaging of Israel has its counterpart in later literature, especially in the image of the Strange Woman in wisdom literature. See Claudia V. Camp, 'What's So Strange about the Strange Woman?', in David Jobling, Peggy L. Day and Gerald T. Sheppard (eds.), *The Bible and the Politics of Exegesis: Essays in Honor of Norman K. Gottwald on His Sixty-Fifth Birthday* (Cleveland: Pilgrim Press, 1991), pp. 17-31, for an excellent description of the development of the Strange Woman metaphor and its connections to prophetic literature (esp. pp. 20, 24 and n. 10).

terms harsher than those of Hosea, while not pushing to the extremes of Ezekiel.

In Jer. 3.1–4.4 there are not just shifts from female imagery to male imagery, however, but also shifts in the mode of address: the move from accusation to promise is equally mirrored by a move from feminine direct address to masculine direct address. The prophet, who speaks for God, quotes God as 'I' and addresses the audience as 'you'. In patriarchal society, where the males are the citizens, the primary audience is male. The object of the discourse is to convince the audience of something, to subject them to it—to cause them to identify as subjects of the discourse. The author seeks the dominance of one discourse over others, namely, those advocating/allowing the worship of gods other than YHWH, and those advocating the establishment of foreign alliances. In the case of Jer. 3.1–4.4, gender-specific metaphors and forms of address are the vehicle used to persuade the audience. This paper will explore how gender-specific imagery and address construct the call to repentance in Jer. 3.1–4.4, as well as the implications of the ways in which gender is itself constructed by this passage.

Emile Benveniste, an influential linguist, shows language, discourse and subjectivity to be inseparable. Language constitutes reality. Discourse is any use of language, written or verbal, which assumes a speaker and a hearer, in which the speaker intends to influence the hearer.[2] Thus, any discourse is inherently ideological: it persuades the audience toward one version of reality over others. There are various modes of discourse (for instance, economic, social, political), each of which seeks to change an audience's self-definition. There may also be dominant modes of discourse, modes used by those in power to mold society in a certain way. These modes of discourse seek to construct people's subjectivity, that is, they seek to get people to define themselves in a certain way. Louis Althusser, a Marxist philosopher, discusses subjectivity in terms of 'hailing'. In the well-known analogy of a police officer hailing someone on the street, 'Hey, you there!', the person hailed, by turning and answering, takes up the position of subject. She or he recognizes that the hail was addressed to her or him rather than anyone else.[3]

---

2.   Emile Benveniste, *Problems in General Linguistics* (trans. Mary Elizabeth Meek; Coral Gables: University of Miami Press, 1971), pp. 208-209.

3.   Louis Althusser, *Lenin and Philosophy* (trans. Ben Brewster; London: Monthly Review Press, 1971), p. 174.

In discourse, a speaker uses direct address, 'hailing', to persuade. Bruce Lincoln, in *Discourse and the Construction of Society*, sees discourse as working both ideologically and affectively (through the 'evocation of sentiment'): 'it is through these paired instrumentalities—ideological persuasion and sentiment evocation—that discourse holds the capacity to shape and reshape society itself'.[4] The rhetoric itself and the way it is presented must not only be persuasive cognitively, they must hook people on the emotional level; they must cause them to re-draw boundaries (I identify with this rather than that, or, I am this kind of person rather than that kind of person).[5]

It is just such a reconstruction of subjectivity, through re-drawing boundaries, which concerns the prophets. The prophet and prophetic language are often in conflict with the dominant institutions, and thus with the dominant discourses produced by those institutions.[6] Prophetic language is persuasive language which seeks to change people's behavior. It offers a competing, often subversive, discourse which seeks to reconstruct the audience's subjectivity. The intended effect is that once people identify themselves in a new way, their behavior will also change. Jer. 3.1–4.4 offers such a competing discourse; it seeks to re-draw the boundaries and to reconstruct subjectivity so as to produce a change of behavior.

When one is seeking to offer a new discourse, to re-draw the boundaries, an effective way is to evoke boundaries already central to society. In a patriarchal world, where men are the citizens, the ones with power (and where they are the main audience), boundaries are effectively evoked through reference to women (the Other, the 'not-men'), the ones at the margins.[7] Thus, the discourse of Jer. 3.1–4.4 begins with the metaphor of a marriage in which the woman, the wife, has overstepped the boundaries. In order fully to understand what is going on in this passage, however, it is necessary to move

---

4. Bruce Lincoln, *Discourse and the Construction of Society: Comparative Studies of Myth, Ritual, and Classification* (New York: Oxford University Press, 1989), pp. 8-9.

5. Lincoln discusses such boundaries in terms of social borders, which he defines as 'those imaginary lines that distinguish one group of persons from another' (*Discourse*, p. 9). He also refers to the 'numerous and varied factors' which 'may help to mark and enforce such borders' (p. 9). These factors would include customs and laws specific to a particular society.

6. In the case of Jeremiah, see, e.g., Jer. 36, 37. This is true of other biblical prophets, too. See, e.g., 1 Kgs 17 and 2 Kgs 1 for similar conflict between Elijah and the throne.

7. For a more complete discussion of women's marginality and that marginality's association with boundaries, see below.

back to the larger context to include Jeremiah 2, where we find the clues to the competing discourses, as well as the introduction of the primary image which will be in the background of everything that follows.

In Jer. 2.2 God, the husband, addresses Israel as his wife: 'I remember the devotion (*ḥesed*) of your youth, your love as a bride, how you followed me in the wilderness, in a land not sown'. The direct address asks the male audience to take the subject position of a woman. In patriarchal marriage, the wife's sexuality is controlled by and reserved for her husband alone. This is pictured as the natural, the 'common-sense' way things ought to be. Yet the conflict between behavior and ideology is almost immediately made apparent: Jer. 2.5 reads, 'What wrong did your ancestors find in me that they went far from me and went after worthless things (*hebel*)...'. The rest of the chapter takes up the issue of the nature of the 'worthless things', giving us a relatively clear picture of the discourses the author is competing against.

The accusations addressed to the audience are primarily of two kinds: the worship of other gods and foreign political alliances. According to the author, God the husband is competing against rivals for his allegiance. With respect to the worship of foreign gods, Israel is addressed in the masculine plural: ' "Therefore once more I accuse you", says the Lord' (2.9). In Jer. 2.10-12 the author appeals to what is natural or 'common-sense' in asking whether any other nation would exchange their gods for what are not gods. Verse 28 clearly summarizes the competing discourse, again addressing the audience as masculine: 'Where are your gods that you made for yourself? Let them rise up, if they can save you, in your time of trouble; for you have as many gods as you have towns, O Judah'. With respect to foreign political alliances, Israel is once again addressed in the feminine singular. References to foreign alliances with Egypt and Assyria are made in v. 18 and in vv. 36-37.

A third accusation receives less emphasis, but is nonetheless important. Its focus is social justice/injustice; it is illustrated by the metaphor of a thief used in relation to the political and religious leaders in v. 26. In v. 34 as well, the accusation includes allusions to justice issues: 'on your skirts is found the lifeblood of the innocent poor'. The next phrase connects it specifically with the earlier thief metaphor: 'you did not find them [the innocent poor] breaking in'. The issues of justice (*mišpaṭ*) and righteousness (*sᵉdāqāh*) appear again in 4.1-4. Here these issues are connected with circumcision of the heart, also

connected closely with justice in Deuteronomy.[8] The negative consequences of all three activities fall primarily into two spheres,
economic (lack of profit or prosperity) and political (destruction),
although the cosmic sphere is also represented in Jer. 3.3 (cf. 4.23-28).

It is v. 20, however, which explicitly connects Israel's activity to
gender and sexuality: 'On every high hill and under every green tree
you sprawled and played the whore (*zōnāh*)'. Moreover, this imagery
is coupled with images of overstepped boundaries: 'long ago you
broke your yoke and burst your bonds' (v. 20). The images of broken
boundaries multiply in the rest of the chapter: the choice vine planted
by YHWH that has become wild (v. 21); the wild ass in heat whose
unrestrained lust emphasizes the lack of sexual boundaries (v. 24); the
thief who will be shamed when caught (v. 26); and the promiscuous
woman who has something to teach the prostitute: 'How well you
direct your way to seek love, so that you even teach wicked women
your ways!' The NRSV reads, 'How well you direct your course to
seek lovers (*'ahªbāh*)!' Nowhere else in the Hebrew Bible does *'ahªbāh*
refer to the objects of love (i.e., lovers). Moreover, the parallelism here
argues for a meaning referring to actual sexual practices, not other
people. Note that the female 'you' of the discourse is differentiated
from the 'wicked women' (i.e., prostitutes, who are conceived of as
wicked and are treated as outcasts in patriarchal society). The differentiation emphasizes the status of the 'you' as wife. It is this very
status of Israel as the wife who has overstepped the boundaries that is
exploited in Jer. 3.1–4.4.

Jer. 3.1-5 begins by merging the coupled images of gender and
overstepped boundaries. Through the quotation of a law, the legal
boundary is invoked along with sexual boundaries in phrasing the
question of the possibility of repentance: ' "If a man divorces his wife
and she goes from him and becomes another man's wife, can he
return to her? Would not such a land be greatly polluted? You have
played the whore with many lovers; and yet would you return to
me?" says the Lord' (Jer. 3.1).

The use of gender-specific language is a particularly powerful way
to indicate the breaking of boundaries in a patriarchal context such as
the Bible. In the patriarchal symbolic world, where the self is defined
as male, the primary image of the 'other', that which is not self, is

8.   Cf. Deut. 10.16-19; also Deut. 30, where circumcision of the heart includes
obedience to YHWH's commandments, many of which have to do with issues of
social justice and righteousness (e.g., the jubilee legislation of Deut. 15; Deut. 16.18-
20; the legislation regarding kings in Deut. 17.14-20; and Deut. 24.17-22).

woman. Being situated at the margins of male society,[9] woman is a figure of ambivalence: she represents both the attractive and the dangerous. Toril Moi further connects women's marginality with limits:

> if patriarchy sees women as occupying a marginal position within the symbolic order, then it can construe them as the *limit* or borderline of that order. From a phallocentric point of view, women will then come to represent the necessary frontier between man and chaos; but because of their very marginality they will also always seem to recede into and merge with the chaos of the outside. Women seen as the limit of the symbolic order will in other words share in the disconcerting properties of *all* frontiers; they will be neither inside nor outside, neither known nor unknown.[10]

It is thus the very marginality of women, their place at the boundaries of patriarchal society, which makes the imagery work so well.

Jeremiah employs both the attractive and the dangerous aspects in representing Israel: the attractive representation of women is that of 2.1 – the devoted wife. The dangerous representation was already introduced in 2.20 when Israel is portrayed as acting promiscuously. The dangerous image is developed further in Jer. 3.2, where Israel is portrayed as a prostitute: 'Look up to the bare heights, and see! Where have you not been lain with? By the waysides you have sat waiting for lovers, like a nomad in the wilderness. You have polluted the land with your whoring and wickedness'. The irony of the danger is that it leads to infertility for the land: 'Therefore the showers have been withheld, and the spring rain has not come' (3.3). God, the male husband, withholds divine seed from the (female) land. Just as in the patriarchal social fabric the woman who oversteps the boundaries is punished either by legal means (divorce, public humiliation) or by

9. See Toril Moi's convincing argument that women are seen 'as occupying a marginal position within the symbolic order' in a patriarchal system: *Sexual/Textual Politics: Feminist Literary Theory* (London: Routledge, 1985), p. 167.

10. Moi, *Sexual/Textual Politics*, p. 167. In biblical studies the issues of ambiguity, limits and frontiers have been dealt with in reference to the female imagery in Proverbs in two recent articles, one by Claudia V. Camp ('Wise and Strange: An Interpretation of the Female Imagery in Proverbs in Light of Trickster Mythology', *Semeia* 42 [1988], pp. 14-36) and the other by Carol Newsom ('Woman and the Discourse of Patriarchal Wisdom: A Study of Proverbs 1-9', in Peggy L. Day [ed.], *Gender and Difference in Ancient Israel* [Philadelphia: Fortress Press, 1989], pp. 142-60). While Camp uses anthropological theory, Newsom comes to some similar conclusions using socio-linguistic theory.

social means (ostracism), so in Jer. 3.3 the land is punished because of Israel's misbehavior.[11]

What gives the language of this image its potency, however, is the rhetorical strategy of addressing the male audience with the feminine form of address. Such a strategy asks men both to identify themselves as the promiscuous woman and to resist that identification. As husbands (present, past, or future), the 'natural' identification, and thus, the subtle pressure, is to identify with the male voice, the righteous husband—God. Yet the address forces them first to take the subject position of the promiscuous wife.[12]

The dual nature of the pressures of subjectivity (i.e., of self-identification) exerted in the text is illustrated in 3.1-18.[13] As noted above, the audience is addressed as the promiscuous wife in vv. 1-5.[14] Then

11.   Note the connection between women and chaos (or at least disorientation in the natural world) here, which Moi mentions in the quotation above. Note, too, that the connection between woman and the land has already been made in 3.1. The connection between woman and land includes questions of paternity and fertility, which in turn are part of a larger issue of identity: to whom does Israel belong? to whom should Israel be faithful?

12.   The alternation of masculine and feminine forms of address signifies that the metaphors do not refer literally to sexual cultic practice, but rather that promiscuity is a general metaphor for non-allegiance to YHWH. This supports Phyllis Bird's conclusion that the term *zônâ* 'has, in itself no cultic connotations' (Phyllis Bird, '"To Play the Harlot": An Inquiry into an Old Testament Metaphor', in Peggy L. Day [ed.], *Gender and Difference*, p. 88. For a full discussion of the term and its connotations, see the entire article, pp. 75-94).

13.   Scholars are unanimous in seeing several levels of tradition in Jer. 3.1-18. The usual divisions include 3.1-5; 3.6-11. Verses 12-18 have been divided in various ways, but virtually all scholars view v. 17 and v. 18 as exilic or post-exilic additions. Many scholars also view 3.19-4.4 as the original continuation of 3.1-5, with 3.6-11 consisting of additions to that original unity (see, for example, John Bright, *Jeremiah* [AB; Garden City, NY: Doubleday, 1965], p. 25; Wilhelm Rudolph, *Jeremia* [HAT; Tübingen, 1958: J.C.B. Mohr (Paul Siebeck), pp. 21, 27]). For a full discussion of the redaction history see Mark E. Biddle, *A Redaction History of Jeremiah 2.1–4.2* (ATANT; Zürich: Theologischer Verlag, 1990). I would agree with most scholars that Jer. 3.1–4.4 contains several levels of material. However, I see this chapter as a mosaic unity, with a coherent development of theme and thought.

14.   Jer. 3.1-5 is that portion of 3.1–4.4 which has generated the most literature. The literature on these verses focuses on two major issues: its form (see, for example, U. Simon, 'The Poor Man's Ewe Lamb', *Bib* 48 [1967], pp. 207-42; and Burke O. Long, 'The Stylistic Components of Jer. 3.1-5', *ZAW* 88 [1976], pp. 376-90), and its relation to a parallel law in Deut. 24.1-4 (see, for example, James D. Martin, 'The Forensic Background to Jeremiah III 1', *VT* 19 [1969], pp. 82-92; T.R. Hobbs, 'Jeremiah 3.1-5 and Deuteronomy 24.1-4', *ZAW* 86 [1974], pp. 23-29; G.J. Wenham,

the author steps back to paint an allegorical picture in vv. 6-11[15] of two rival sisters, 'Turning back' or 'Apostasy' Israel and 'Treachery' Judah. Judah saw the consequences of Israel's behavior, 'She saw that for all the adulteries (*n'p*) of that faithless one, Israel, I had sent her away with a decree of divorce' (v. 8), and yet she still followed her paths. This is the basis for the judgment that Judah is more guilty than Israel (v. 11), as well as for an appeal to Israel to repent and return (vv. 12-18).[16] When the promises connected with repentance are given, however, the address changes to masculine plural. The audience is asked to take the subject position of sons: 'Return, O faithless sons', saying of YHWH, 'for I am your Baal' (v. 14).[17] The promises which follow include return to the land and good rulers ('shep-

'The Restoration of Marriage Reconsidered', *JJS* 30 [1979], pp. 36-40; and R. Yaron, 'The Restoration of Marriage', *JJS* 17 [1966], pp. 1-11.

15. On the basis of the switch from poetry to prose, as well as the move to allegory, most scholars see vv. 6-11 as a later level of tradition. See, for example, W. McKane, 'Relations between Poetry and Prose in the Book of Jeremiah with Special Reference to Jeremiah iii 6-11 and xii 14-17', in J.A. Emerton (ed.), *Congress Volume, Vienna, 1980* (VTSup, 32; 1981), pp. 220-37; also in Leo G. Perdue and Brian W. Kovacs (eds.), *A Prophet to the Nations: Essays in Jeremiah Studies* (Winona Lake: Eisenbrauns, 1984), pp. 269-84. Although vv. 6-11 may indeed be a later addition, I disagree with the assumptions that an author cannot change his or her style of writing (e.g. from poetry to prose) or expression (e.g., from metaphor to allegory). In fact, vv. 6-11 are an extension and interpretation of vv. 1-5 which lead to the ultimate issue of the passage: the appeal to repent and return in vv. 12-18.

16. Again, most scholarly work has focused on identifying the different redactional levels of these verses, or dealing with specific issues, such as the use of Zion imagery in vv. 14-18, and the significance of the mention of the ark in v. 16 (see, for example, M. Haran, 'The Disappearance of the Ark', *IEJ* 13 [1963], pp. 46-58; Rudolph, *Jeremiah*, pp. 23, 25; J.A. Soggin, 'The Ark of The Covenant, Jeremiah 3,16', in P.-M. Bogaert [ed.], *Le Livre de Jérémie* [Leuven: Leuven University Press, 1981], pp. 215-21, as well as P. Volz, *Studien zum Text des Jeremia* [Beiträge zur Wissenschaft vom Alten Testament, 25; Leipzig: J.C. Hinrichs, 1920], p. 23; and Bright, *Jeremiah*, p. 27 for various views on the disappearance of the ark which are used to date this section). The connection of vv. 12-18 with vv. 1-11 has not been dealt with in any substantive way.

17. The use of the word 'Baal' here has several levels of meaning. On one level, it continues the marital imagery—Yahweh is the people's metaphorical husband. On another level, it is a reminder of the covenantal relationship between the people and Yahweh: the term may mean 'master', thereby indicating the requirement to obey the overlord. Finally, the term may be an ironic reference to Baal worship. Contrary to their prior belief, it is Yahweh who is their true Baal. (J.A. Thompson has also noted these possibilities in *The Book of Jeremiah* [NICOT, Grand Rapids: Eerdmans, 1980], p. 201.)

herds')[18] who will teach 'knowledge and understanding'. The implication is that the repentance itself will allow the audience to resume
their status as male subjects.

Jeremiah 3.19–4.4 repeats the general structure of 3.1-18 with a new
emphasis: Israel's uniqueness. Verses 19-21 restate the situation of vv.
1-11, again asking the audience to take a female subject position, this
time through a father-daughter metaphor: 'I thought how I would set
you [fem. sing.] among my sons, and give you a pleasant land, the
most beautiful heritage of all the nations. And I thought you would
call me, "My Father", and would not turn from following me'
(v. 19).[19] The image of the daughter inheriting is highly unusual in the
Hebrew Bible. There are only two occasions where daughters inherit.
The first of these is Job 42.6, where Job's daughters are given an
inheritance with his sons (note, however, that there is no mention of
land). The only other occasion where daughters inherit land is the
case of the daughters of Zelophehad (Num. 27). In their case, they
inherit solely because there were no sons in the family. Here, however, daughters not only inherit with the sons, they inherit 'the most
beautiful heritage of all the nations' (v. 19).

While there is mention of the apportionment of nations and
boundaries in Deut. 32.8-9, which has a similar emphasis on Israel's
uniqueness and privilege, the father-daughter metaphor is particularly apt here. Just as with the earlier feminine singular address,
this image would shock a patriarchal audience. Further, since the
emphasis of this section is Israel's unique status and its separation
from other nations, the father-daughter metaphor is a striking way to
make the point: the fact that the daughter is the one to inherit the best
portion further emphasizes her uniqueness, and further separates her
from the rest of the heirs (the other nations).[20]

Again the audience is asked to take the subject position of
woman—this time a positive, unique position. But almost immediately that position is undermined. The various English translations
of v. 20 obscure the continuing reference to Israel as daughter by
translating *îššâ* as 'wife' rather than 'woman' and *mērē'âh* as 'husband'

18. The use of the shepherd metaphor for the leadership of Judah/Israel also
occurs elsewhere in Jeremiah as well. Cf. Jer. 23.

19. Most scholars try to avoid the issue of daughters inheriting the land by
deleting the feminine form of address and emending the text to the second person
singular masculine address. There is, however, no textual basis for this.

20. The idea of separation from other nations is also a subtle way to suggest
that Israel does not need those nations. In other words it is implying that Israel
does not need foreign alliances.

rather than the more usual 'companion' or 'friend',[21] which also indicates close association, and in the case of *r'h* III, an object of desire.[22] I translate, 'Instead, as a woman has become faithless to her lover, so you have been faithless to me, O house of Israel', saying of YHWH. The father-daughter metaphor stresses Israel's unique position among the nations, yet the metaphors in v. 20 connect the daughter's actions with sexual boundaries. Just in case the male audience failed to take up the subject position of woman in the foregoing section (vv. 1-18), the author makes the necessity of this position explicit through the simile of v. 20.

Verse 20 marks the end of the feminine form of address. From v. 21 on, the audience is again asked to take the subject position of sons, while God retains the position of father. It is as this subject that Israel is given the conditions of and promises for repentance. The text has claimed for God the authoritative position of patriarchal father and has attempted to discredit the other rival discourses by showing that they push the audience's behavior beyond legal and ethical boundaries. What is at stake is honor: the sons are quoted as saying, 'Let us lie down in our shame, and let our dishonor cover us; for we have sinned against the Lord our God...' (v. 25). Patriarchy maintains authority through control, including control of women's sexuality. The male audience as husbands (present, past, or future) and as sons have a stake in maintaining the order, the status quo. When women take control by transgressing the boundaries (sexual or otherwise) that men have set, the entire order of patriarchy is challenged. Such behavior leads to dishonor. It is through asking the audience to identify themselves as the adulteress/prostitute that the discourse makes the audience's behavior clear. Equally, it is through this identification that pressure is exerted to return to the subject position of son through change of behavior.

Like what has gone before, the conditions and promises for repentance in Jer. 4.1-4[23] reveal the concern for order by their connection

21. See BDB, p. 946. A.S. Peake also made this suggestion in *Jeremiah*, I (The Century Bible; Edinburgh: T.C. & E.C. Jack, 1910), p. 113.

22. I have also taken the *bāḡᵉdâ* as *qal* third person feminine singular (cf. parallel *bᵉḡaḏtem*).

23. Scholars are equally divided as to whether to end this unit with 4.2 or 4.4. Those who end with 4.2 view 4.3-4 either as transitional material or as the beginning of the next section which continues through ch. 6. For a full discussion of this view, see Jeremiah Unterman, *From Repentance to Redemption* (JSOTSup, 54; Sheffield: Sheffield Academic Press, 1987), pp. 30-32, and Winfried Thiel, *Die deuteronomistische Redaktion von Jeremia 1–25* (Neukirchen–Vluyn: Neukirchener Verlag,

with boundaries. Likewise they reveal the concern for the formation of identity by being set out in exclusively male terms.[24] The promise connected with sincere change of behavior in 4.2, 'then nations shall be blessed [*Hitpael*] by him...', is an allusion to the blessing accompanying the promise to Abraham in Gen. 12.3 and 22.18, and to Isaac in Gen. 26.4. In Gen. 22.18 and 26.4 (which correspond more directly with Jer. 4.2) the promise of blessing is explicitly associated with descendants (seed): 'all the nations of the earth shall gain blessing for themselves [*Hitpael*] in your descendants (*zr'*)'. The implication is that if the audience take up the subject position of son, they will be the agents of the blessing promised to the patriarchs.

The link to the patriarchs is continued in 4.4 where the issue of the uniqueness and separation of Israel raised in v. 19 is resolved in the exclusively male metaphor of circumcision. Just as the promise to the arch-patriarch, Abraham, is linked with a physical sign of separation and uniqueness, so in 4.4, the sons are reminded of the physical sign of their uniqueness and separation through the call to circumcise themselves (not just physically, but with their hearts) to YHWH. By its very nature, this imagery of circumcision excludes women. The patriarchal symbolic order may thus be maintained or re-established through stopping their promiscuous behavior and by preserving their uniqueness as sons. In the case of the male audience, once they have identified with and rejected the negative female metaphors, they return to the comfortable subject position of sons to God's father in the patriarchal symbolic order. They are called no longer to identify themselves as promiscuous women/worshippers of other gods/makers of foreign alliances, but can now identify themselves as new Abrahams, worshipping YHWH alone and preserving their distinction from other peoples. Or, perhaps, are they to identify themselves as faithful women (cf. 3.12-13, the first call to return; significantly, also the one call to return which uses feminine address)?

The foregoing analysis has attempted to illustrate how the choice of feminine imagery works powerfully and effectively within the patriarchal social order. But, having discovered, unmasked, and put to flight two rival discourses, that which advocates the making of foreign alliances and that which advocates/allows the worship of foreign gods, the question remains whether there is something at stake in the

---

1973), pp. 93-95. However, I see vv. 3-4 as being integrally connected to what goes before (see my discussion below).

24. The conditions and promises in Jer. 4.1-4 also reflect the concern for social justice by their terminology (*mišpāṭ/ṣᵉdāqâ*).

feminine imagery itself. In other words, is the imagery merely metaphorical or is there yet another rival discourse underlying this text?
The following raises more issues than it answers, but it is a beginning
reconstruction of what may be behind this imagery.

In her article dealing with discourse and female imagery in Proverbs
1-9, Carol Newsom notes that any symbolic thinking which uses a
specific group of people cannot simply be symbolic—it also has an
implication for the behavior of that group of people.[25] This is especially true in a patriarchal text that uses symbolic language referring
to women. When it is only males in the society who enter into public
discourse, one does not notice such implications. Once, however,
women enter into public discourse by taking the subject position and
speaking as subjects (rather than being merely the object of discourse), the symbolic language becomes confused. When a woman
reads this text, she 'cannot occupy the same symbolic relation to
herself that she does to man'.[26]

As Newsom suggests, when a woman reader is subjected to and
becomes the subject of this discourse, something different happens.
As a subordinate social group, women have a different relationship to
language.[27] Although the discourse is disguised as neutral (the
devoted wife is the 'natural' order of things, sexually promiscuous
women have transgressed the 'natural' boundaries), it acts ideologically to exert pressure on the woman to be a faithful wife, mother
and daughter, the only positive roles allotted to her within the boundaries created by patriarchy. The consequences for women who over-
step the boundaries are the same as they were for the male audience:
drought (connected with the fertility of the land, and implicitly with
the fertility of women as well) and destruction (2.15; 3.3; 4.4b). Yet
woman remains to a large extent excluded from subjectivity in this
text, both through the shifts to the masculine address when the conditions and promises for repentance are offered, and through the use
of the metaphor of circumcision as a symbol of loyalty to YHWH.

To illustrate this point in a more personal way, as a woman, I see
this text as arguing for a change of (male) behavior on the religious
and political planes, planes defined and governed by males. However, with regard to female behavior, this text, by virtue of its
imagery, confines women (and myself as a female reader) to two
roles—faithful wife and daughter. Any behavior taking women

25. Newsom, 'Discourse', p. 155.
26. Newsom, 'Discourse', p. 155.
27. Moi, *Sexual/Textual Politics*, p. 154.

outside these roles identifies them as prostitutes. Even the imagery of circumcision (which, to be sure, could include women, since it is circumcision of the *heart*), functionally excludes women (and myself as a female reader) from complete membership in society. It is only men who carry the sign of circumcision—implicit in the image itself is physical circumcision which then *extends* to the heart. Thus, the entire symbolic world of the discourse operates to marginalize women and women's interests.

If women read this discourse through the patriarchal symbolic structure, they are most often not even aware of the pressure to confine themselves to these roles, since they are presented as 'natural' or 'common sense'. However, the seeds for unmasking the patriarchal symbolic structure are carried within the text itself. As noted above, the rival discourse in which people worship other gods is also portrayed as unnatural (2.9-13). But whereas that discourse is unmasked and put to flight, the patriarchal discourse becomes even more powerful because it is left masked. In fact, it has been disguised so well that it takes a discourse from our time to see it. By making a preoccupation with competing discourses evident, the way is opened for the reader to see the other discourse. When women resist taking the object position, they step out of the patriarchal symbolic order long enough to see the pressure that is being exerted. This resistance opens the reader's eyes to see that woman in this passage is not the speaking subject, but rather the effect of someone else's speech. Such a realization makes it clear that the patriarchal discourse is itself competing against something; there is a subtext to this text.

This paper has attempted to show that gender is an important factor in the construction and interpretation of this text. Both the gender-specific metaphors and the alternating forms of direct address exert pressures on the male audience to change its behavior to conform to male rather than female subjectivity. In turn, this text constructs gender in that it reveals a disguised pressure for female readers to conform to the patriarchal symbolic order. This imagery, however, works only as long as men hold the exclusive power to shape and define subjectivity. When women become resisting readers, the crisis in the patriarchal symbolic order is revealed.

SELF-RESPONSE TO 'CIRCUMCISION OF THE PROSTITUTE'

Mary E. Shields

This article was an early reading of Jeremiah 3.1–4.4, the focus of my doctoral dissertation. I came to the text because I was interested in intertextuality, particularly the ways in which Jer. 3.1–4.4 takes up a law also found in Deut. 24.1-4. However, there was something that always bothered me about the text. It took me a long time to realize that it was the way in which gender was used; the shifts in direct address which so many historical critical scholars take as signs of redaction and/or sources, actually have a logic to them. That logic is reflected in the shifts in imagery, from husband/wife to father/son to circumcision. This article was an early attempt to address the move from feminine to masculine imagery, and an accompanying shift: the move from female to male address.

Since 1993, Renita J. Weems has published a short section on the use of the marriage metaphor in Jeremiah in her book, *Battered Love*.[1] Although we were working completely independently of one another, many of our observations and conclusions were similar. For instance, we both talk about the shock value of addressing a male audience and calling them whores, as well as the rhetorical power of such address. While my analysis of Jer. 3.1–4.4 is deeper than that of Weems, Weems goes further than my article in her consideration of how other texts in Jeremiah use this imagery, thus situating the passage within the broader context of Jeremianic rhetoric.

Due to space considerations, my article was necessarily an overview of how the rhetoric of gender worked in Jer. 3.1–4.4. My 1996 doctoral dissertation allowed me the space to explore the implications of that rhetoric more fully. I have taken the material in this article further in my dissertation by expanding and deepening the discussion

1.   Renita J. Weems, *Battered Love: Marriage, Sex, and Violence in the Hebrew Prophets* (Overtures to Biblical Theology; Minneapolis: Fortress Press, 1995), pp. 52-58.

of rhetoric in general and how strategies, not only of gender, but also intertextuality and metaphor, work together rhetorically. I have also shown that the author uses certain theological, cultural and social ideals to reinforce the rhetoric of the passage as a whole. In addition, my analysis of the text itself is much more detailed in the dissertation.

There are at least three areas that I plan to expand further as I rework the dissertation for publication.[2] The first is a closer look at the part which God plays in this rhetoric. I intend to take the same step that I took in my analyses of one of the two Ezekiel texts using the marriage metaphor, Ezekiel 23,[3] that is, looking at the dangers of this imagery theologically. A second area is further attention to the ways in which this imagery not only relies upon but also prescribes particular kinds of male/female relationships and the implications of the type of prescription given. Third, I will propose that Jer. 3.1–4.4 is based on a root metaphor for procreation, seed and soil, with soil representing women and seed representing men. I argue that this metaphor helps to explain the way gender and cultural ideals using gender are used rhetorically in the piece. Using anthropological theory as well as a broad definition of intertextuality that includes a text's interaction with cultural ideals, I will seek to show how Jer. 3.1–4.4 exemplifies what Carol Delaney suggests about 'the seed-soil theory of procreation', upon which this passage is based. Delaney argues that this theory of procreation goes beyond male-female relationships by being projected onto the deity, thereby becoming part of God's creative power. Moreover, 'because of the structural and symbolic alliance established between men and God, men partake of this power; as a result their dominance seems natural and given in the order of things. This association is part of the power behind these patriarchal systems, for it is the glorification, not just of the male, but of the male as "father"'.[4] These ideas are worked out in the text of Jer. 3.1–4.4, partially explaining the shifts from: a) marriage imagery when God is accusing Israel as well as its connection with fertility of the land; to b) father/son imagery when the possibility of repentance and obedience arises; and, finally, to c) the final images of breaking up

2. Forthcoming in the JSOT Supplement Series.
3. Mary E. Shields, 'An Abusive God? Identity and Power, Gender and Violence in Ezekiel 23', in A.K.M. Adam (ed.), *Postmodern Interpretations of the Bible: A Reader* (St Louis: Chalice Press, 2001), pp. 129-51.
4. C. Delaney, *The Seed and the Soil: Gender and Cosmology in Turkish Village Society* (Berkeley: University of California Press, 1991), p. 35.

fallow ground and circumcision (which Howard Eilberg Schwartz and Nancy Jay have linked to fertility). This work will enable me to address more extensively the issue of how the marriage image as used in the prophets does violence not only to women, but to both male–female and human–divine relationships.

MULTIPLE EXPOSURES:
BODY RHETORIC AND GENDER IN EZEKIEL 16*

Mary E. Shields

The extended metaphor telling the story of Jerusalem in Ezek. 16.1-43 opens and closes with images of exposure. Yet the exposure of the infant, the pubescent girl, and the adulterous woman are not the only exposures contained in this passage. The entire chapter is a series of exposures—views of one observer, the narrator Yahweh. We see only what the narrator allows us to see, and what is hidden is as important to the passage as what is revealed. This study will look at the body and gender rhetoric—the ways in which gender and the female body both construct and are constructed by this chapter. The first half of the study will be devoted to a discussion of the female character, while the second half will focus on the character of Yahweh. I will seek to show how body rhetoric and gender characterization combine to expose Jerusalem while masking Yahweh completely, as well as how this chapter presents a portrayal of God's character which is, to say the least, difficult to reconcile with the picture of God's abundant love and mercy which many commentators would read into the text.

By any account, Ezekiel 16 is a problematic passage and the most extreme case among the prophetic oracles of accusation using marital and sexual imagery. Although it has folkloric overtones[1] and is told in

*   This study is substantially revised and expanded from two papers: 'Body Rhetoric and Gender: Ezekiel 16', and 'Gender Characterization in Ezekiel 16', given at the 1993 and 1996 annual meetings of the Society of Biblical Literature respectively. I wish to thank J. Cheryl Exum, David Gunn and Claudia Camp, for their careful readings, helpful advice, and encouragement at the early stages of this article; my thanks also to Peter Browning, Karen J. Taylor and Philip Krummrich, colleagues at Drury College, for their astute editorial suggestions. Any remaining inadequacies are, of course, my own responsibility. Originally published in *JFSR* 14 (1998), pp. 5-18. Reprinted by permission.

1.   See, e.g., Keith W. Carley, *The Book of the Prophet Ezekiel* (Cambridge Bible Commentary; Cambridge: Cambridge University Press, 1974), p. 95; Walther Eichrodt, *Ezekiel* (OTL; Philadelphia: Westminster Press, 1970), p. 202. More recently,

striking imagery, the extended metaphor of the foundling Jerusalem is the only text banned from use in the synagogue.[2] It is the story of an infant who is exposed, and found and married by Yahweh. Critics suggest that she turns to whoring in ungratefulness.[3] She is punished through gang rape[4] and mutilation, but then restored after a fashion. Whereas the earlier oracles (in Hosea and Jeremiah) retain some of the positive aspects of the metaphorical husband/wife relationship between God and Israel, Ezekiel 16 represents a completely negative and vituperative portrayal of Israel.

The problems begin with the Hebrew. Virtually all the English translations of this passage gloss over and tone down the ways in which body parts are named. They also subdue the violence of the imagery. The problems are complicated by the commentaries, which do attend to the specificity of the imagery—one recent commentary described it as 'painful and embarrassing…often disgusting detail'[5]— but which again gloss over the most problematic aspects of the passage. Although mention is made of the 'almost pornographic'[6] nature of the rhetoric and imagery, the universal (masculinist) scholarly opinion of this chapter has been that it is 'one of the Bible's strongest statements about unconditional election based solely on the grace of God. It is God's unmerited favor which links the beginning and end of the passage'.[7]

Recent studies of Ezekiel 16 which have taken into account the problematic nature of the imagery, with few exceptions, have focused exclusively on the characterization of the child/woman in the text, and her relation to the protagonist, the husband Yahweh. A recent

Ronald M. Hals has questioned the folkloric connection (*Ezekiel* [FOTL, 19; Grand Rapids: Eerdmans, 1989], p. 109).

2. *m. Meg.* 4.10; *b. Hag.* 131.

3. See, for example, Donald E. Gowan, *Ezekiel* (Atlanta: John Knox Press, 1985), p. 67; and Eichrodt, *Ezekiel*, p. 218.

4. Cf. Renita J. Weems, *Battered Love: Marriage, Sex, and Violence in the Hebrew Prophets* (Overtures to Biblical Theology; Minneapolis: Fortress Press, 1995), p. 60.

5. Joseph Blenkinsopp, *Ezekiel* (Interpretations; Louisville, KY: John Knox Press, 1990), p. 78.

6. Blenkinsopp, *Ezekiel*, p. 76.

7. Gowan, *Ezekiel*, pp. 66-67. See also Aelred Cody, *Ezekiel: With an Excursus on Old Testament Priesthood* (Old Testament Message: A Biblical Theological Commentary, 11; Wilmington, DE: Michael Glazier, 1984), p. 79; F.B. Huey, Jr, *Ezekiel, Daniel* (Layman's Bible Commentary, 12; Nashville: Broadman, 1983), p. 44; and Lamar Eugene Cooper, Sr, *Ezekiel* (The New American Commentary, 17; Nashville: Broadman & Holman, 1994), p. 179.

study by Julie Galambush,[8] for example, takes the discussion into a new realm, paying close attention both to the extended metaphor and to its power within the worldview of Ezekiel and his times. She argues that the woman as 'other', as dangerous, is a powerful vehicle to convey two deep concerns of Ezekiel: 'the purity of the Temple and the honor of Yahweh, both of which must be protected if Yahweh is to dwell among the people of Israel'.[9] Galambush also makes a convincing argument for the symbolic identification of the Temple with the woman,[10] whose behavior has so defiled the Temple that it (and symbolically, the woman herself, through judgment) must be destroyed. Moreover, Yahweh, as the one with authority over the woman's body/sexuality, is shamed and dishonored by her behavior. Her exposure and punishment restores Yahweh's honor, thus turning the destruction of Jerusalem and the Temple into a victory for Israel as a monotheistic people. I would agree in substantial measure with this view, even going so far as to say that for Ezekiel, a priest concerned with issues of purity, woman was a natural image of defilement. For instance, her connection with blood, through both menstruation and birth, automatically places her on the boundaries of society.[11] Yet Galambush's study, because of its focus, does not discuss the character of Yahweh directly.[12] This study seeks, in part, to address the latter issue, by looking at *both* sides of the metaphor to see how both the woman and Yahweh are characterized in terms of gender.

Ezekiel 16 is, in fact, structured in such a way as to deflect attention from the character of Yahweh: the entire chapter is in I-you language,

---

8. *Jerusalem in the Book of Ezekiel: The City as Yahweh's Wife* (SBLDS, 130; Atlanta: Scholars Press, 1992).

9. Galambush, *Jerusalem in the Book of Ezekiel*, p. 161.

10. Cf. Galambush, *Jerusalem in the Book of Ezekiel*, p. 87.

11. In the Hebrew Bible blood can preserve life through sacrifice, or defile through spilled or discharged blood (e.g. through murder, menstruation and birth). Women's blood is exclusively defiling blood; between menstruation and giving birth, a woman would spend most of her life in an unclean state. While I do not want to make too much of the issue of blood here, what I wish to emphasize is that blood pollutes anyone who is not a priest. To touch or lie in blood is to stress the margin. Thus, the fact that the infant in Ezek. 16 lies in her blood places her outside of societal norms. See, for example, Mary Douglas, *Purity and Danger* (London: Routledge and Kegan Paul, 2nd edn, 1978).

12. Galambush's notes deal with some of the problematic aspects of Yahweh in this metaphor, while at the same time describing them in terms of threats to God's power and honor (see, for example, *Jerusalem in the Book of Ezekiel*, p. 94 n. 14).

with the 'I' representing Yahweh's speech and the 'you' representing the female figure, Jerusalem. This I-you language constitutes Yahweh as subject and the child/woman Jerusalem as object. Even in the scenes depicting Jerusalem's breaking of bonds through adultery, the reader never sees the woman's viewpoint: the narrator continues the I-you language, so that the reader views the woman's actions through Yahweh's eyes. Moreover, the woman never speaks in this passage. She is therefore never constituted as a separate subject apart from Yahweh's speech and view.

The woman of the metaphor is objectified not only by the structure of the piece, but through the narrator's preoccupation with the woman's body. The chapter begins with a series of three vignettes, each one detailing an aspect of infant Jerusalem's life through focus on her body. In the first vignette (vv. 1-5), Yahweh begins the characterization of Jerusalem by casting aspersions on her birth and ancestry—a Canaanite heritage is hardly a complimentary one. Body rhetoric is first used in v. 4 to describe the infant: none of the usual things done for an infant (cutting the navel cord, washing with water, rubbing with salt, wrapping in cloths—all actions focused on the infant's body) were done for this infant. Rather, like many females in the ancient Near East, she was abandoned and exposed—a usual way to get rid of an unwanted infant, particularly a girl.[13] Not only was she unloved—the text says she 'was abhorred'. From the very beginning her gender counted against her, almost causing her death.

The next two vignettes begin identically: 'I passed by and saw you' (ואעבר עליך ואראך), each time followed by Yahweh's view (vv. 6 and 8). In v. 6, Yahweh passes by and sees her, he commands her to live. Verse 7 begins with a second command: 'Grow up like a sprout of the field'. This decree is followed by a picture of the girl's early youth. The image of v. 7 is that of a wild vine or plant; the metaphors emphasize the fertility of the plant. The Hebrew reads, 'a multitude like a sprout of the field, I made you; you expanded[14] and grew up and you came into the ornaments of ornaments [that is, 'the best of

---

13. See Aline Rousselle, *Porneia: On Desire and the Body in Antiquity* (Oxford: Basil Blackwell, 1988), ch. 3, esp. p. 50, who deals with both female exposure and the rituals of cleansing an infant at birth. A more recent treatment of proper care of an infant at birth, dealing specifically with the ancient Near East, is Meir Malul, 'Adoption of Foundlings in the Bible and Mesopotamian Documents: A Study of Some Legal Metaphors in Ezekiel 16.1-7', *JSOT* 46 (1990), pp. 97-126.

14. I would translate רבבה in keeping with the imagery of צמח here: 'expanded' or 'spread'.

ornaments']: breasts were firmed and your hair sprouted'.[15] The imagery here contrasts greatly with what the commentators would see. The usual description places Yahweh in the role of the nursemaid or father[16]—caring tenderly for and nursing this child back to life.[17] On the contrary, the imagery itself reveals no tender care, no love, indeed no compassion at all until she exhibited the 'ornaments of ornaments': breasts and pubic hair. In fact God's disdain for the girl/woman is emphasized by the final words: 'You were naked and bare'. Moreover, no mention is made of the proper things being done for her by God—she is neither washed nor clothed.[18]

The second time Yahweh 'passes by' and 'sees' (v. 8), his attention is focused on her pubescent state. The emphasis is on his view, which is introduced by the particle הנה, followed by his perception of the young woman: 'you were at the time for love' (v. 8). The Hebrew word for love here is the same term used in the Song of Songs for

15. Many scholars would emend the text to read 'the time of menstruation' instead of 'ornaments of ornaments'. While, to be sure, this verse describes a state of puberty, the emphasis is on Yahweh's gaze, on what he sees. Therefore, I would hold to the Hebrew with its stress on the details of those ornaments: breasts and pubic hair.

16. Seeing Yahweh as an adoptive father gives rise to the notion of incest in our culture. However, such an idea would not be an issue in ancient Israel, where father/daughter incest is conspicuously absent from the types of incest prohibited in the Levitical legislation (Lev. 18–20). The absence of this specific prohibition makes sense for a patrilineal society: a daughter's bearing her father's son does not blur the lines of descent. See my discussion of this issue in my doctoral dissertation dealing with another of the biblical marriage metaphors: 'Circumscribing the Prostitute: The Rhetorics of Intertextuality, Metaphor and Gender in Jeremiah 3.1–4.4' (1996), a revised version of which is forthcoming in the JSOT Supplement series.

17. Cf. Hals, *Ezekiel*, p. 106; Cooper, *Ezekiel*, pp. 169, 171; Blenkinsopp, *Ezekiel*, p. 79. F. Zimmerli is more careful, speaking of 'Yahweh's pitying love' which 'brings a decisive change' to her life twice, each time at a critical point (*Ezekiel I: A Commentary on the Book of the Prophet Ezekiel, Chapters 1–24* [trans. R.E. Clements; Hermeneia; Philadelphia: Westminster Press, 1979], p. 339). He nevertheless glosses over the lack of care the child received and attributes love of a sort to God. Galambush, in contrast, correctly connects the words 'multitude' and 'expanded' with the literal growth of Jerusalem the city, as well as noting the way in which the images 'reinforce the connection between the growing girl and the wild and uncultivated realm without' (*Jerusalem in the Book of Ezekiel*, p. 93). She does not stress, however, the ways in which these words emphasize the girl's fertility even before she becomes a woman.

18. The first instance of care for the girl's/young woman's body is in v. 9, where Yahweh cleanses her and covers her.

sexual love, דדים.[19] Note again that, counter to the commentators, who wax eloquent about God's love or his 'falling in love'[20] with the young woman, the text itself attributes only desire, i.e. sexual feelings, to God.[21] Perhaps the commentators have equated lust with love.

Yahweh's actions in the next section of the text also focus on the woman's body: 'I spread the edge of my cloak over you, I covered your nakedness, I made an oath to you, I entered you with a covenant, saying of the Lord Yahweh, and you became mine' (v. 8). Verse 9 describes Yahweh's washing (ritually cleansing) and anointing of the woman, the first time her body is cared for in the text.

Thus far the body rhetoric has focused on her bloodiness and nakedness. In v. 6, when Yahweh passes by and sees, she was 'kicking out in [her] blood'. His command to live also emphasizes her bloody state: 'I said to you in your blood, "Live"'.[22] When Yahweh makes her his, he cleanses: 'I washed you with water and cleansed the blood [plural] from upon you' (v. 9). In the latter description, the plural use of blood fuses the image of the infant kicking out in her birth blood, the blood of menstruation associated with her pubescent state, and the hymeneal blood associated with her marriage to Yahweh.[23] Each of these types of blood is associated with the female gender alone. In addition, each type of blood causes contamination which requires ritual cleansing. Such references to blood emphasize the woman's body and associate that body with uncleanness.

References to nakedness likewise problematize the woman's body, associating its natural state with shame. As noted above, nakedness is stressed in the description of the child's development into puberty, 'yet you were naked and bare' (v. 7). This stress is reinforced by the use of two terms for nakedness instead of one. The second term, עריה,

19. Cf. also Moshe Greenberg, *Ezekiel 1–20* (AB; Garden City, NY: Doubleday, 1983), p. 277.

20. Cf. Eichrodt, *Ezekiel*, p. 205.

21. Here again there is a great contrast between what commentators tend to see in this passage and what the text actually says. Peter C. Craigie, for example, suggests that Yahweh has 'made provision' for the child 'over many years' (*Ezekiel* [Daily Study Bible Series; Philadelphia: Westminster Press, 1983], p. 108). He says further that 'the whole story is rooted in God's love' and 'God's love is not conditioned by external factors' (p. 108). On the contrary, I would argue that the focus is precisely on 'external factors', as evidenced by Yahweh's gaze.

22. This phrase is repeated in the MT. With the editors of the *BHS* I delete the repetition as a dittography.

23. Greenberg sees this reference to blood as a cleansing of menstrual blood, but he also suggests that the mention of blood links backward to v. 7 and forward to v. 22 (*Ezekiel 1–20*, p. 278).

carries connotations of shamefulness and ritual uncleanness.[24] In this verse, the young woman's nakedness exposes her womanly attributes to the male gaze, inspiring sexual desire in her future husband. Yet her nakedness must also be covered properly so as to preserve her from the gaze of other males. The woman's body becomes acceptable only through cleansing, clothing and adorning (vv. 8-9). Further, the only beauty the woman has is not her own, but rather the beauty of her adornments which reflect her husband's power and honor.

The body rhetoric, by focusing on nakedness, blood and the physical attributes of the onset of womanhood, not only objectifies the infant/girl/woman, but also associates the woman with those aspects of the female body which are most problematic in a patriarchal worldview. Thus, even though the woman's desirability is conveyed through attention to her body, that body, and therefore the woman herself, is indelibly stained (cf. v. 63).

The next verses (vv. 10-14) depict Yahweh clothing and adorning the woman's body. The actions are all God's; she is a mannequin, an object to be acted upon. The marks of ownership, the best and richest of clothing, the jewelry and the 'glorious crown', indicate her husband's status.[25] In v. 13, she is also fattened up—given the food of fertility and royalty.[26] After all these things God does, she grows beautiful, fit for royalty. Moreover, the text emphasizes that it is God's actions that make her beautiful instead of untouchable (unclean), and that her beauty is intended to reflect his glory. Verse 14 reads, 'Your fame spread among the nations on account of your beauty for it was perfect because of my splendor that I had bestowed on you, saying of Yahweh'.[27]

---

24. Exposure of a woman's nakedness is the quintessential punishment for adultery (cf. Hos. 2.3; Jer. 13.22, 26; Nah. 3.5; Isa. 47.3). The sexual taboos in Leviticus are framed in terms of uncovering nakedness (cf. Lev. 18, 20).

25. Galambush also notes their connection with the tabernacle and priestly vestments (*Jerusalem in the Book of Ezekiel*, p. 95).

26. These foods are not only the best (royal), but are 'offerings prescribed for the tabernacle (e.g. Lev. 2.7; Num 6.15, 7.13, 19; 8.8)' (Galambush, *Jerusalem in the Book of Ezekiel*, p. 95). Katherine Pfisterer Darr has also noted that '[d]escriptions of her fine accoutrements invoke cultic associations' ('Ezekiel's Justifications of God: Teaching Troubling Texts', *JSOT* 55 [1992], p. 104). More on the implications of this link below.

27. This verse is singled out by some to illustrate the idea that, to use the words of one commentator, the woman 'contributed no merit or worthiness of her own: it was all of grace' (John B. Taylor, *Ezekiel* [TOTC; Downer's Grove, IL: InterVarsity Press, 1969], p. 137). Cf. Cody, *Ezekiel*, p. 79; Cooper, *Ezekiel*, p. 179; and Huey, *Ezekiel*, p. 44.

In these verses the woman's clothing and jewelry serve not only to beautify her, but also to constrain her, to show her husband's control over her. The very terms used in vv. 10-12, 'I clothed you... I bound you...and covered you... I adorned you... I put on...' are connected to words of binding and chaining. This story actually implies that the very attributes which enable a woman to produce and sustain life must be controlled so that her life-producing capacity is available only to one man, her husband. Apart from his control, her body and her sexuality are dangerous.

The danger of uncontrolled sexuality is illustrated by the woman's actions in vv. 15-34. As in the previous verses, the rhetoric used to describe her foreign alliances and her worship of other gods is focused on what she does with her body. In each case her over-stepping of bounds is described in terms of unbridled and insatiable sexuality. Her undiscriminating choice of sexual partners is empha-sized in relation to a description of idol worship (vv. 15-22), and her insatiability is described with regard to foreigners, whom she pays for sex (v. 34).

As Keith W. Carley notes, in vv. 15-20 'four accusations are intro-duced with the words "You took" (verses 16, 17, 19, 20)'.[28] Here the woman systematically undoes everything which Yahweh has done for (or to) her. She makes shrines to other gods out of her clothes (which, we are reminded, were really God's, v. 16); she makes idols out of the jewelry which God gave her (v. 17); she gives away God's oil and incense (v. 18); she sacrifices God's bread (v. 19) and God's children 'whom you had borne to me' in v. 20—described also as 'my children' in v. 21. The culmination is reached in v. 22, where God reminds her of the first days and, repeating the terms for nakedness and bareness from her time of puberty as well as the image of the infant kicking in her blood, stresses her former state of uncleanness. Verse 22 reads, 'in all of your abominations and your whorings you did not remember the days of your youth when you were naked and bare, kicking out in your blood'. The implicit charge: ungratefulness (the implication of v. 22 is: 'you did not remember how I "rescued" you from unclean-ness and shamefulness'). In addition her actions, both sexual and sacrificial, place her once again in the realm of uncleanness.

In the verses discussing her intercourse with foreigners (vv. 23-34) the language increases in violence, accusing her of being insatiable, not just cultically, but also politically: political alliances with Egypt, Assyria and Chaldea are named as instances of prostitution. Here the

28.   Carley, *Ezekiel*, p. 99.

charge is that Jerusalem acted in this way with the intent to 'provoke me to anger' (v. 26). Verse 32 sums up Jerusalem's actions with an exclamation: 'The adulterous wife: instead of her husband, she receives strangers!' The term זרים, strangers, incorporates both the cultic and the political aspects of her behavior. The final image in v. 34 stresses Jerusalem's contrariness and the extremity of her over-stepping of sexual boundaries: rather than being paid, like a prosti-tute, she actually pays her clients for sex.

The woman's punishment is described in vv. 35-43. The woman's body remains the focus: her exposure, leaving her once again 'naked and bare' in v. 39, and the bloody imagery in v. 40, return her to her infantile state, unclean and abhorred (it is her lovers who have turned on her, v. 37; cf. v. 5). These verses, in a sense, obliterate her identity. Moreover, since her punishments will take place 'in the sight of many women' (v. 41), her raped and mutilated body becomes an object lesson for others of her gender.

The way in which the rhetoric of vv. 15-34 slips in and out of histor-ical reality, referring transparently to worship of idols and to foreign alliances, makes v. 41 disturbing.[29] It is all too easy for readers here to make the jump from the narrative world to their contemporary world. If taken in this way, v. 41 makes the metaphorical woman in Ezekiel 16 an object lesson for women living in Ezekiel's day.[30] The message is even more overt in the sister narrative, Ezekiel 23, which also uses an extended metaphor to describe the relationship between Yahweh and Jerusalem: 'Thus I will put an end to lewdness in the land, so that all women may take warning and not commit lewdness as you have done' (v. 48). Even though the language is symbolic, it can neverthe-

29. The first direct slippage into historical reality is actually in v. 14, where Yahweh says, 'Your name went forth *among the nations*'. As M.G. Swanepoel notes, בגוים 'is a term that has political meaning' ('Ezekiel 16: Abandoned Child, Bride Adorned or Unfaithful Wife?', in Philip R. Davies and David J.A. Clines [eds.], *Among the Prophets: Language, Image and Structure in the Prophetic Writings* [JSOTSup, 144; Sheffield: Sheffield Academic Press, 1993], p. 88). As noted above, there are further parallels: the Hebrew words used to describe the woman's clothing in v. 13 are those used for the 'materials and furnishings of the tabernacle' (Galambush, *Jerusalem in the Book of Ezekiel*, p. 95). Since the slippage of the meta-phor into historical reality already occurs in vv. 10-14, when the woman commits adultery using these fabrics in vv. 15-22, the reader has already been prepared through the imagery to see slippage between the metaphorical world and actual cultic practices.

30. In this regard it is suggestive that her beauty goes forth 'among the nations' (v. 14), but her punishment takes place 'in the sight of many women' (v. 41) rather than in the sight of the nations.

less be applied to real-life husband-wife relationships. The character of the woman becomes representative of her gender—all women are tarred with the same brush in that they are so often ritually unclean (through menstruation and childbirth), and there is always the husband's underlying fear that he cannot control her sexuality (the emphasis on the woman as an example to other women).

Unlike vv. 1-43, the last two sections of the chapter do not focus on the female body. Verses 44-58 depict the woman as being worse than her 'sisters', two cities that are described elsewhere in the Hebrew Bible as acting in a sexually lascivious manner (e.g. Gen. 19 [Sodom] and Hosea [Samaria]), primarily in order to justify Yahweh's punishment. The final section, which re-establishes Yahweh's covenant with Jerusalem, makes no mention of her body, other than to proclaim that she shall 'no longer open [her] mouth' (v. 63), a curious statement given that she never speaks in this text.[31] However, the emphasis on the woman's ongoing shame in v. 63 reminds the reader—as well as the woman in the narrative—that her body is the source of shame and uncleanness.

This reading of Ezekiel 16 has raised several problems about the portrayal of the woman and of God. It is clear from the beginning that the infant, child and woman are portrayed in terms associated with uncleanness and shame. The very associations of this type of language with taboos and uncleanness link real women and their bodies with uncleanness as well. The only time the woman is clean in this passage is when Yahweh washes and clothes her. By repeatedly connecting women with uncleanness, the text places women completely outside the boundaries. No longer do women represent the limits of society, they seem to be excluded completely.

This rhetoric stresses women's total exclusion in several other ways. The clothing and binding imagery noted above emphasizes the woman's objectification, her lack of freedom and of power—indeed, her lack of a self. She is merely the property of the husband. There is, moreover, no sense of an individual personality here. She is entirely what Yahweh has made of her. When she acts in a fashion which surprises and confounds her male benefactor, she is returned to her

---

31. When one considers the explicitness and vulgarity of Ezekiel's language, perhaps the comment is not so curious after all. Perhaps the 'mouth' in v. 63 may be the 'mouth' which Jerusalem 'opens' to all her lovers. If this is the case, the implications are intriguing and unsettling. Although she is denied speech, she acts with her other 'mouth' in the very way which is most threatening to patriarchy. According to v. 63, then, after the horrific punishment, she may never desire to open that 'mouth' again.

unclean, shameful state, thus taking away any possible identity she has apart from Yahweh.

Women are completely circumscribed by this text: they are unclean and therefore unholy; their bodies and their sexuality are to be for one man alone; they are bound and covered possessions with no freedom of movement, no speech—no power. In this regard, it is notable that Galambush finds that after the Temple is destroyed in Ezekiel, the city is never again personified as a woman. The building of the new Temple carefully omits any overt connections between the Temple, the city, and a woman or woman's body. In fact, the city is no longer 'Jerusalem', but 'Yahweh is there'.[32] Woman is written out of the restoration (at least as far as she can be).

Although the woman is the focal point of the entire chapter, there is another primary character as well: Yahweh. Since Yahweh does all the speaking in this text, it is striking that neither in the text itself, nor in interpretations of the text, are God's actions and speech exposed as clearly as are the actions of the woman.

With rare exceptions, and those are recent,[33] most commentaries or articles on this text attribute emotions and actions to God which the text simply does not support. Most emphasize God's care for the child,[34] and his falling in love with the young woman[35] (although love is never mentioned). Most even try to downplay the rage and jealousy in vv. 35-43, the most explicit and shocking section of the piece. Peter C. Craigie goes so far as to say '[t]he rage that characterizes this passage is rooted in love; it is not so much anger…but horror…'.[36]

---

32. Galambush, *Jerusalem in the Book of Ezekiel*, pp. 145-57.

33. See Galambush, *Jerusalem in the Book of Ezekiel*; Weems, *Battered Love*; Jon L. Berquist, *Surprises by the River: The Prophet of Ezekiel* (St Louis: Chalice Press, 1993), pp. 45-49; and Darr, 'Ezekiel's Justifications of God', pp. 97-117.

34. See n. 14 above.

35. Cf. Eichrodt, *Ezekiel*, p. 205; Craigie, *Ezekiel*, pp. 109-11; Cody, *Ezekiel*, p. 78; and Huey, *Ezekiel*, p. 41. In contrast, Paul Joyce is one of the few who do not read love into the text. Of v. 8 he says, 'the relationship between Yahweh and his people is here expressed in terms of marriage. It should be noted, however, that all the phrases used in this verse appear to be either legal or sexual; we do not find here much evidence of real warmth or affection' (*Divine Initiative and Human Response in Ezekiel* [JSOTSup, 51; Sheffield: Sheffield Academic Press, 1989], p. 100).

36. Craigie, *Ezekiel*, p. 117. Others merely try to downplay the rage or justify the extremeness of God's actions. Eichrodt, for example, says, '[t]he way in which God's wrath and jealousy are heaped up is to denote the inexorable, yet wholly personal manner in which he reacts against any attempt to deny or ridicule his giving of himself' (*Ezekiel*, p. 209).

I believe it is dangerous, however, to let the male figure off the hook here, even if that figure is God (perhaps *because* that male figure is God). The very fact that commentators and translators alike try to neutralize or downplay the language should be a warning signal that something is wrong with a facile reading of this text. If we step back and look at Yahweh as a character in this story, we find that there are a number of structures which are being obscured. As we have seen, the I-you focus not only draws attention to the 'you', but also draws attention away from the 'I'. Readers are led by the very language of the text not to question the I-figure. Second, the I-figure is Yahweh. Yahweh is a privileged figure in any interpretation; it is very difficult to step far enough away from the story to question God. Third, one of the effects of the narrative being structured in such a way as to focus solely on the body and actions of the woman is to emphasize the power of the male figure — God. Throughout this text power resides in one person: Yahweh. It is he who sees the infant and pronounces that she should live, and who marries, washes and adorns the young woman. It is he who allows the woman no speech in this text. It is his power which the woman challenges by her actions, causing shame, and it is his power which is reasserted through the punishment, its justification, and the partial reconciliation in the second half of the chapter. The extremity of the punishment reaffirms both his power and his honor: the purpose of re-establishing his covenant with a subdued and shamed Israel in vv. 59-63 is that 'you shall know that I am Yahweh'. His power, in the end, is absolute.

Moreover, while the rhetoric of the piece continually focuses on the body of the woman, nowhere is the body of the central male figure described or even mentioned. The only actions which allude to the protagonist's body are the 'passing by' and 'seeing' in vv. 6 and 8; and the spreading of his cloak, the covering, entering, washing and clothing in vv. 9-12. Even the sex act is glossed over by euphemisms (spreading his skirt over her, covering her nakedness, entering into covenant [with] her).[37] It is only through the references to 'my children' (v. 21), 'whom you had borne to me' (v. 20) that it is clear that this marriage included sexual intercourse between the husband and wife. Not only is the male body obscured in vv. 1-34, but Yahweh distances himself still further. In the horrific punishment in vv. 35-43,

37. It is somewhat odd that most commentators avoid addressing Yahweh's sexuality in the text, focusing instead on the covenant or bond between Yahweh and the woman. See, e.g., Swanepoel, 'Ezekiel 16?', p. 87; Eichrodt, *Ezekiel*, p. 206; and Zimmerli, *Ezekiel I*, p. 340.

it is the lovers who are gathered together by Yahweh to carry out the rape and battery; he does not himself take part. Thus the body of the male figure is completely obscured, while the female figure is repeatedly exposed.

Despite the distance created through the structure and the avoidance of male body rhetoric, as Yahweh accuses the woman of systematically divesting herself of all the bindings and controls which Yahweh has placed upon her, Yahweh's corresponding emotional response begins to leak through. Yahweh's anger is increasingly easy to see in the text, particularly in his continued emphasis on his ownership of all the things (clothing and jewels) and children she used in her idol worship (vv. 15-21), and in the reminder of the uncleanness and shame of her origins (v. 22 reads, 'In all your abominations and whorings, you did not remember the days of your youth, when you were naked and bare, kicking out in your blood'). Other emotions also begin to slip out in the description of her foreign alliances. At the beginning of his description of her adulteries with foreigners (v. 23), he ejaculates 'Woe, woe to you!', indicating his growing fury. In v. 26, his snide reference to the largeness of the Egyptians' male organs indicates his jealousy (he characterizes the Egyptians as 'large of flesh' — is this penis envy?). Verse 30 voices his disgust: 'how sick is your heart'. Finally, his direct address to her as זונה (whore) in v. 35 indicates the rage which results in her rape and mutilation.

Verses 35-43 contain a graphic and horrifying depiction of the abuse the woman suffers as a punishment. The description itself is easily passed over, until one realizes that it uncannily resembles the cycle of spousal abuse which is only now in our time being discussed openly. Following a period of escalating tension (vv. 15-34), the rage and jealousy of Yahweh are 'satisfied' through rape and battery, after which Yahweh 'will become calm, and will be angry no longer' (v. 42). As with the rhetoric of the abuser in spousal abuse, the victim is entirely at fault and has caused this rage and violence. The battery itself satisfies the abuser's rage and is followed by a calm which lasts until the next episode.[38]

38. The cycle itself includes three primary phases. Phase one is an escalation of tension, which includes minor battering incidents, including psychological abuse. The tension building phase can be seen in vv. 15-34 in this text. Phase two is the 'acute battering incident', in this case exemplified by the punishment scene in vv. 35-41. This phase is followed immediately by a period of calm and usually a sort of honeymoon phase, where the abuser 'woos' the victim back into the relationship. See Lenore E. Walker, *The Battered Woman* (San Francisco: Harper & Row, 1979), pp. 56-70, for a clear description of these phases. It is important to note

In the biblical story, the woman's actions that led to the punishment are portrayed in extreme enough terms so that any audience, male or female, would be appalled. The story sets up the reader to rationalize the rape and mutilation. Yet what the story obscures is the male partner's part in adultery. The abuser in this case retains a certain distance from the punishment: he merely passes judgment and gathers the other lovers around his spouse. They are the ones who carry out the punishment, although they are guilty as well. By having the lovers carry out the punishment Yahweh remains one step removed from the action, thus preserving the privilege which surrounds him. Yet the result is disturbing: he himself is not a spouse batterer; he has others do the battering for him. Put in these terms, the spousal abuse seems more extreme. Rather than being done in private, as most spousal abuse is done, the battery here is public (and therefore an example for all, especially women, v. 41). Equally disturbing is the fact that having the lovers carry out the retribution deflects attention from the one who is ultimately responsible: because that character is God, and therefore not only privileged but unrepresentable, the effect is more global. Moreover, the very fact that the I-figure in the text is God makes the reader even less likely to question the justice of that figure's action. But it is precisely at this point that gender characterization is the most dangerous.

If we as readers do not resist this type of characterization, we run the risk of identifying all women as being, through their very bodies, unclean or potentially unclean. At the same time we may fail to give critical consideration to the actions or bodies of the other gender. Both the structure of this piece and its identification of Yahweh as the husband conspire to keep the reader from questioning male privilege, male dominance, even male rape and abuse. The question which arises from these observations is: what is Ezekiel so afraid of? What happens if we turn the story on its head and look at the character of God in the text? Why is the text so constructed as to keep many generations of scholars from doing so?

My hunch is that we avoid looking at the character of God in this text because, if we dare to look at his character, we will be repelled by what we see. Moreover, the actions which are so appalling have the potential to cause us to re-evaluate our theology, or, at the very least, to call into question this text's validity as 'the word of God'. For example, what kind of a God could, even in a metaphorical world, not

that while Ezek. 16 includes a calm phase, there is here no wooing or contrite behavior on the part of Yahweh.

only stand by but actively gather men to rape and mutilate his wife? Most of us do not want to be confronted with such a picture of God, so it is very easy to let God remain in the privileged position, not to question the justice of God's extreme actions, in short, to settle for the status quo.[39]

Renita J. Weems is one of those who is not afraid to deal head-on with the problematic nature of God's character in this chapter. Unlike most scholars, she confronts the problems associated with God's cruelty and viciousness as the husband in the metaphor, particularly in Ezekiel 16. She acknowledges that 'in Ezekiel, the husband does not apologize for his rage, knows of no restraints in the punishment he metes out, and even fully intends to brutalize his wife until he feels satisfied and avenged'.[40] She talks about Ezekiel's use of this metaphor as revealing 'Israel's experience of God as the source of both good and evil'.[41] She adds, '[t]he prophets were careful to acknowledge that just as God was capable of profound acts of mercy and compassion, there was also a side to God that was mysterious and adversarial'.[42] She suggests further that the metaphor also 'permitted the prophets to capture the inexplicably menacing, dark side of God's dealings with Israel'.[43]

Weems also addresses the difficulty that this metaphor produces in twentieth-century readings of this text. Although she does not put it in precisely this way, she recognizes that the slippage of the imagery (e.g. into historical idol-worship and historical foreign alliances) leads some readers to apply it to human marital relationships.[44] In addition, Weems attempts to rehabilitate the marriage metaphor as reflective of power structures and politics gone awry. On the one hand, she advocates reading from a woman's perspective, which could involve

---

39. Some might get around the theological problem by emphasizing the metaphorical nature of the text, and/or the character of the one who wrote it. By placing the burden of this view of God on Ezekiel, readers can again avoid addressing the problems posed by this characterization of God. In this type of reading, Ezekiel is the one who has problems. See, e.g., Edwin C. Broome, 'Ezekiel's Abnormal Personality', *JBL* 65 (1946), pp. 277-92; and Ned H. Cassem, 'Ezekiel's Psychotic Personality: Reservations on the Use of the Couch for Biblical Personalities', in Richard Clifford (ed.), *The Word in the World* (Cambridge, MA: Weston College Press, 1973), pp. 59-63.

40. Weems, *Battered Love*, p. 74.

41. Weems, *Battered Love*, p. 75.

42. Weems, *Battered Love*, p. 75.

43. Weems, *Battered Love*, p. 76.

44. Cf. Weems, *Battered Love*, pp. 110-12.

'[s]eeing ourselves through the eyes of a woman, however defiled, depraved, incorrigible, and battered'.[45] Such a reading would, she argues, 'help us finally glimpse some of the ways in which we have been wounded by patriarchy'.[46] This reading, however, does not deal with the fact that it is God who does the wounding in the meta-phorical world. On the other hand, she privileges God again in her final, tentative attempt to justify the metaphor when she argues that 'the marriage metaphor permits us to believe in the most unbelievable of all possible responses to our woundedness, namely grace'.[47]

Using the marriage metaphor cannot achieve both ends. If one views the metaphor from a woman's perspective, then God's charac-ter is problematized as abusive, wounding and cruel. The final picture of God as somehow ultimately compassionate does not square with the ways in which the woman is treated in the metaphor. Nor does it square with the final picture of Ezekiel 16, in which Yahweh 'restores' Israel but allows her no speech, retains all power for himself, and emphasizes her ongoing shame. If one lets Jeremiah 31 have the last word, as Weems does in her chapter focusing on the character of God in the texts using the marital metaphor,[48] then one may be able to justify finding a compassionate God in the metaphor, but not in Ezekiel 16 itself. Within Ezekiel there is no reconciliation, no restoration which includes forgiveness and absolution. Moreover, it is Ezekiel who, canonically at least, has the last word.[49]

Although her interpretation of the marriage imagery is nuanced, Weems's answer to the question of God's character is just a little too

---

45. Weems, *Battered Love*, p. 113.
46. Weems, *Battered Love*, p. 113.
47. Weems, *Battered Love*, p. 114.
48. Cf. Weems, *Battered Love*, pp. 82-83.
49. Weems' account of Ezek. 16 also does not deal with the arbitrariness of God's character at the very beginning of the text: she mentions 'courtship' and 'their idyllic life together as devoted bride and generous, protective husband' in relation to her discussion of Ezek. 16 (*Battered Love*, p. 59). Thus, although she avoids the common characterization of Yahweh as nursemaid, or one who falls in love with Jerusalem, she nevertheless glosses over the details of vv. 1-14. To do Weems justice, however, she does recognize that in Ezek. 16, 'rather than describing a reconciliation based on romance and seduction, like those in Hosea and Jeremiah, the prophet focuses...on the woman's profound sense of humilia-tion and shame as the basis of their getting back together' (*Battered Love*, p. 98). Thus, what I am suggesting is that her choice of texts with which to conclude her evaluation of God's character in the marital metaphor obscures the power and danger of Ezekiel's imagery.

facile for me (although I would love to have the relative comfort of her explanation). Instead I would argue that, particularly in light of the ways in which the metaphor collapses and therefore can be applied to human relationships, the metaphor itself is just too dangerous. By highlighting God's grace or compassion, and not critiquing the violence of God's actions, readers endorse violence against women. In our culture, where domestic violence is on the rise, and those who participate rely on scriptures such as Ezekiel 16 for their warrant, this text is even more problematic. The metaphor, and God's character within it, must be deconstructed, and deconstructed in such a way that it may no longer be used to justify male violence and abuse of any group in our society.

This study has dealt with a text which is problematic from a number of angles. Through looking at the ways in which body rhetoric and gender characterization both construct and are constructed by Ezekiel 16, this study has revealed problematic implications of the imagery and the rhetoric for the position of women. I have also attempted to unmask what is so effectively masked by the structure and rhetoric: the figure of God; in short, to expose the relational and political implications of the metaphor and God's character in Ezekiel 16.

SELF-RESPONSE TO 'MULTIPLE EXPOSURES'

Mary E. Shields

The author/compiler of Ezekiel[1] had a difficult dual task: on the one hand, to establish that God was indeed still God despite the defeat of Judah; and on the other hand, to provide a theological justification for the humiliation and exile of Judeans to Babylon. He was doing, in my students' terms, 'constructive theology'. In many ways he succeeded beautifully: the portable throne-chariot which made YHWH present in Babylon, and which was depicted as leaving the city defiled in chs. 8–11, but which returns to the rebuilt and cleansed city and temple in chs. 40–48, is one example of how old ideas that God had chosen Jerusalem and would maintain it inviolably forever were blown apart by new imagery and rhetoric. Likewise, portraying the people's actions in terms of violating God's honor, and showing that God would both punish and restore the people to re-establish his honor ('so that they will know that I am YHWH'),[2] showed that God was not a defeated God and had not abandoned them, but rather was the one God they should worship and follow. This notion had a deep impact on the development of strict monotheism in the Second Temple community. However, in seeking to construct a powerful identity for YHWH, Ezekiel also constructed a violent and abusive identity for him. This violence and abuse are nowhere more evident than in Ezekiel 16 and 23. Following the examples of Hosea and Jeremiah, who take a relationship with which all of society had some knowledge of, either as children of married parents or as spouses themselves, he constructed a 'biography'[3] for Jerusalem which made her YHWH's wife. In giving this metaphor the slant he did, however, Ezekiel also constructed an abusive, violent, wife-battering God.

---

1. For the sake of simplicity, the author/compiler(s) of Ezekiel will hereinafter be called Ezekiel.

2. An omnipresent refrain throughout the book.

3. Moshe Greenberg's term, see *Ezekiel 1–20* (AB; Garden City, NY: Doubleday, 1983), p. 299.

This article was the second in a series of three studies of the marriage metaphor depicting YHWH as husband and Israel as an adulterous wife. Each time I have tackled a new text I have come up against the metaphorical picture of YHWH. In this study I discussed the gender and body rhetorics of the text, rhetorics that act to privilege YHWH's character, and to mask his violent actions against Israel. What I was not ready to take on when I did this study was a clear view of the implications of the characterization of God in the text. Although I acknowledged the danger of the imagery, and some of the problems that imagery poses for human male–female relationships, I did not explore the theological danger of the imagery, that is, what it means for an abusive God to appear in Scripture. Yet, in my work with this marriage metaphor, I felt increasingly compelled to do so. Therefore, in my last article in the series, 'An Abusive God? Identity and Power, Gender and Violence in Ezekiel 23',[4] I began to address this issue. What I found as I studied Ezekiel 23 is equally true of Ezekiel 16: although the text is constructed so as to show the power residing in the male partner of the relationship, YHWH, in actuality the female character in Ezekiel 16 steps outside of that power relationship to act independently. In other words, by portraying her actions of vv. 15-29 as actions directed against YHWH, the narrator (YHWH in the piece) implicitly indicates that YHWH does not have absolute power. It is at this point that the power dynamics of Ezekiel 16 unravel, allowing for a deconstruction of the figure of YHWH as portrayed in the text. As I argued in my article on Ezekiel 23, the character of YHWH here needs to be deconstructed because of the multiple problems that character poses for divine–human relationships as well as male–female human relationships. Rather than being swept under the rug, I believe this text needs to be exposed as the theologically problematic text it is. The implications of a violent, abusive God are wide-ranging: allowing some to see the Holocaust, for example, as divine punishment; allowing others to continue to see God as supportive of nuclear arms build-up and war; and allowing still others, as I said in this article, to justify spousal abuse because the Bible ('the word of God') gives it divine warrant. My hope is that exposing this text enables readers to look critically at the Bible's portrayal of God in a way that will result in new, constructive theologies which are non-violent and non-abusive.

4. In *Postmodern Interpretations of the Bible: A Reader* (ed. A.K.M. Adam; St Louis: Chalice Press, 2001), pp. 129-51.

VIOLENCE AND THE ECONOMY OF DESIRE IN EZEKIEL 16.1-45

Erin Runions

Ezekiel 16.1-45 is a troubling text, inhabited by images of brutal violence toward a woman in return for her sexual desire and activity. Along with many feminist biblical critics,[1] I find this image of a woman cruelly punished for her desire and assertive sexuality deeply disturbing. On first reading, the passage appears, though troubling, to present an image consistent with the biblical tradition of carefully regulating women's sexuality, under threat of violence; here the application of censure seems straightforward: the woman Jerusalem's intercourse with many nations is rewarded with violence. Yet I cannot push away the questions which plague me: why this kind of extended pornographic violence? Why not just stick to the violence prescribed by law for promiscuity (death by stoning)[2] and be done with it? Why must this text describe the woman's promiscuity for a full twenty verses and her punishment for another nine?

Reluctant to settle for the response 'the Bible is just like that', I have pursued the relation of violence to desire in this passage. In an effort to illuminate how and why desire provokes this kind of violence in this text, I turn to René Girard's theory of mimetic desire and conflict as a heuristic device.[3] Girard's theory prompts me to re-read Ezek. 16.1-45, taking into account the relations of violence to desire, and of the metaphoric to the literal. This theoretical intrusion into the textual

---

1. For an excellent sampling, see especially Athalya Brenner (ed.), *A Feminist Companion to the Latter Prophets* (Sheffield: Sheffield Academic Press, 1995). See also Julie Galambush, *Jerusalem in the Book of Ezekiel: The City as Yahweh's Wife* (SBLDS, 130; Atlanta: Scholars Press, 1992); Renita J. Weems, *Battered Love: Marriage, Sex and Violence in the Hebrew Prophets* (Minneapolis: Fortress Press,1995); J. Cheryl Exum, *Plotted, Shot and Painted: Cultural Representations of Biblical Women* (JSOTSup, 215; Gender, Culture, Theory, 3; Sheffield: Sheffield Academic Press, 1996).

2. See Lev. 20.10-12 and Deut. 22.20-24.

3. James Williams (*The Bible, Violence and the Sacred* [San Francisco: Harper, 1991], pp. 20-25), planted the seed for this kind of reading, by bringing Girard's thinking on the sacrificial victim together with the idea of metaphor.

world has the subsequent result of recasting the characters of both the deity and the woman. In this new *mise en scène*, the deity appears as a parental figure (either masculine or feminine), with sexual preferences for men; the woman-as-a-whore-to-be-punished appears as figurative surrogate victim in a literal economy of desire and violence.

My method is as follows: I first map out the relations of violence to desire through an interrogation of the relationships, literal and metaphoric, between the key figures in the text (God, the woman Jerusalem, and the nations as lovers). Careful attention to the way the metaphor reconstructs literal violence and desire reveals an interesting interplay between the literal and the metaphoric, as well as raising some questions about the efficacy of the metaphor. Girard's theory is helpful in filling some of the gaps which open up between the literal and the metaphoric in this interrogation, and in suggesting new ways to play the characters.

In teasing out a new staging, I am not trying to establish a definitive way of understanding the text, but rather looking at new options for reading the metaphors, options that can no longer serve as models which justify violence against women. While working on this project, I have been asked a number of times 'why not just reject this text?' The answer is political and theological. I am concerned by the way in which the metaphorical language can be taken as prescriptive for real-life interactions. I wish to re-read this metaphor, and metaphors like it, so that they can no longer be used as normative for violent gender relations by those who read the Bible as instructive.

Mapping the Relations

Violence and desire characterize the relationships found in Ezek. 16.1-45. In the text, Yahweh muses over the metaphorical woman Jerusalem, whom he found as a bloody baby and raised into a beautiful woman. Clothing and ornamenting her naked body (with developing breasts and growing hair), the deity delights in her beauty until she becomes sexually active and independent about it (without a pimp or a father to market her wares). For this she is called whore, a woman of insatiable desire (vv. 28-29), one who never has enough of her lovers. Yahweh's overwhelming anger and violence are unleashed upon her, inciting in turn her lovers (the nations) against her. They, having appeared for the most part as passive beneficiaries of the woman's affections, turn violent, stoning and slashing and burning the woman and her possessions (vv. 39-42).

Close examination of the literal and metaphoric relations between

the three key characters in the passage (Yahweh, the woman Jerusalem, and the nations as lovers) shows that violence and desire do
not seem to function in the metaphor as expected. Assuming that the
metaphor is used in this passage as a way of exposing a problematic
literal situation (and this is, I suppose, a large assumption about prophetic literature), I would expect to find a fair level of correspondence
between the literal and the figurative, especially in the context of
relationships involving desire and violence, since these are the dominant tropes. Indeed, with regard to violence, as I will try to show, the
literal and the figurative are inseparable in places. However, where
the metaphor inserts desire as a motivation for this violence, it does so
in a way that bears no resemblance whatsoever to the literal situation.
Perhaps this metaphoric divergence from the literal is the beauty (?)
of the metaphor; but if this is the case, then it cannot be read in the
straightforward allegorical fashion that it often has been read by
commentators.[4]

The first divergence from allegory appears in the relationship
between the woman Jerusalem and her lovers, the nations. The metaphor does not portray the link between desire and violence in this
relationship as might be expected in an allegory. In the metaphor, the
woman desires her lovers, and they respond with violence. The metaphor seems to be a figuration of the literal violence attending the
unstable political relation between Judah and the nations, with whom
it sought to form alliances in order to secure its independence.[5] In
vv. 40-41 metaphoric and literal violence meet and fuse: the violence,
though metaphorically enacted by the lovers against the woman, is
the literal violence of war, employing sword and fire. If this were to
be read as allegory, I should expect to find a similar literal/meta-
phoric fusion between the literal cause of the nations' violence against
Jerusalem and the metaphoric reason for the lovers' violence against
the woman. But the lovers do not attack the woman for reasons that
fuse metaphoric (sexual) and literal (political): she is not attacked
because she has angered them, or because they are jealous, or because

4.   For example Walther Zimmerli, *A Commentary on the Book of the Prophet
Ezekiel, Chapters 1–24* (trans. Ronald E. Clements; Hermeneia; Philadelphia: Fortress Press, 1979), pp. 334-35.

5.   Moshe Greenberg (*Ezekiel 1–20: A New Translation with Introduction and
Commentary* [AB, 22; Garden City, NY: Doubleday, 1983], p. 13), suggests on the
basis of ancient letters that Judah made anti-Babylonian political alliances with
Egypt, and that Judean troops fought for Egyptian Psammetichus II in 593 BCE.
Likewise, Zimmerli posits Egyptian-initiated resistance against Babylon (*Ezekiel
1–20*, pp. 13-15).

she has threatened their power. In fact the metaphoric/sexual relationship between the lovers and the woman does not seem to provide
any motivation (short of outright abuse) for the violence. One wonders either why the nations are characterized as lovers; or why the
lovers previously enjoying free, and by all appearances amicable, sex
would turn on the woman.

Then why do the woman's lovers turn on her? According to the
text, it is because they are provoked by Yahweh (vv. 27, 37-39) in the
relation between Yahweh and the nations as lovers. This relation
seems to be a one-sided competition for the loyalty of the woman
Jerusalem. Yet unlike most tales of competition or jealousy, neither of
the parties defeats the other. Rather it is the woman who is defeated,
even though the lovers are given no incentive to carry out this violence. Another fusion appears here between the literal and metaphoric levels of the text: that is, an overlap of the agents of violence.
The text portrays the violence as both Yahweh's violence and the
nations' violence. But Yahweh's violence is, for the most part, carried
out by the lovers, *qua* nations. The difficulty is that the lovers' violence is Yahweh's violence, but the lovers do not represent Yahweh in
the metaphor. The passage is certainly not strictly allegorical, as there
is no direct correlate for Yahweh in the imagery. One wonders why
the lovers are needed to carry out the violence. What is the relationship then between Yahweh and the nations' seemingly unmotivated
violence?

It is only in the metaphoric relation between Yahweh and the
woman Jerusalem that the motivation for violence appears. Yahweh
desires the sexual loyalty of the woman Jerusalem. When this loyalty
is not forthcoming, the deity enlists the lovers (as nations) against the
woman and violence ensues. But why such warfaring brutality?

Many commentators read the relationship between the deity and
the woman Jerusalem as a sexual relation, and the violence as the
understandable(!) reaction of a husband to sexual infidelity. For
instance, Wevers claims that Ezekiel picks up other biblical images of
Israel as an adulterous wife, arguing that 'Ezekiel does not admit a
primeval period of blissful innocence; Jerusalem's origins were pagan.
Nor is divine forgiveness of an erring bride contemplated, or even the
possibility of a repentant wife'.[6] The implication here is not only that
the woman is bad through and through, but that the violence is

6.   John. W. Wevers, *Ezekiel* (The Century Bible; London: Thomas Nelson and
Sons, 1969), p. 119.

justified if no repentance is evident (or possible). Zimmerli echoes this view of the text[7] but carries the justification of the violence further, continuously referring to the woman's action as adultery. He seems to revel in the violence and Yahweh's vindication, replaying the violence in his commentary (as do other commentators), with comments such as 'the lovers…attack the adulteress herself, robbing her of her clothes and jewelry, leaving her naked and bare. In this way Yahweh accomplishes indirectly the divorce'.[8] In the same vein, Greenberg notes that 'fury and passion pertain to a betrayed husband', citing Prov. 6.34, 'the fury of a husband will be passionate'.[9] Even feminist scholars read the violence as reaction to adultery, though not justified.[10]

The deity's desire is almost without exception read as sexual desire, and thus the violence is justified (understandable/expected) as that of reaction to sexual infidelity. Though often this kind of reading is problematic in and of itself, I am not convinced that this passage is about marital fidelity, rather than about filial loyalty. It is surprising that no one ever seems to comment on the tension that a reading of a sexual relationship creates with the first thirteen verses of the chapter, which point to a parent/child relationship between Yahweh and the woman. To read the relationship between the woman and the deity as a sexual relationship is either to ignore the obvious parental imagery of vv. 1-13 (where the deity cares for the baby, washes it, clothes it, and feeds it) or to tacitly condone incest. It seems to me that the features portraying a parental relationship between Yahweh and the woman are very prominent, more so than features which are *possibly* sexual.

There are a number of *ambiguous* textual features in the passage which are usually read in a way (frequently with the aid of intertexts) that results in a sexual/marital relationship between Yahweh and the woman. I would like to point out how they might also be read

---

7.   Zimmerli, *A Commentary*, pp. 336-37.

8.   Zimmerli, *A Commentary*, p. 346.

9.   Wevers, *Ezekiel*, p. 286.

10.   See Fokkelien van Dijk-Hemmes, 'The Metaphorization of Woman in Prophetic Speech: An Analysis of Ezekiel 23', in Brenner (ed.), *A Feminist Companion to the Latter Prophets*, p. 246; Katheryn Pfisterer Darr, 'Ezekiel', in Carol A. Newsom and Sharon H. Ringe (eds.), *The Women's Bible Commentary: Expanded Edition* (Louisville, KY: Westminster/John Knox Press, 1998), pp. 197-98; Galambush, *Jerusalem*, pp. 84-85; Exum, *Plotted*, p. 108; Weems, *Battered Love*, who finds the metaphor problematic for modern readers, but—strangely for a feminist critic dealing with violence against women—restates the prophetic metaphor as one in which God, 'himself a victim…has been driven to extreme measures'.

differently. For instance, many scholars read v. 8, 'I stretched my hand to you and I covered your nakedness and I swore to you and brought a covenant to you' (my translation), as a metaphor for marriage,[11] because of the combination of ברית with פרש כנף. This reading is based on Mal. 2.14 and Prov. 2.17, the two occasions in the Hebrew Bible where ברית *might* be said to relate to marriage; and on Ruth 3.9, where פרש כנף may be taken in the context of marriage. But this reading ignores the other kinds of agreement that the covenant could enact, perhaps of adoption[12] rather than marriage; and it ignores the other ten uses of the expression פרש כנף[13] in the Hebrew Bible, many of which are in reference to the wings of eagles or cherubim,[14] and which may point here simply to a sign of protection. Notably, Deut. 32.10-11 describes, in a surprisingly similar passage, how Yahweh found Jacob in the desert and protected him like an eagle spreading its wings over its young.

Similarly, the use of the word נאף (to commit adultery), which occurs twice in this passage (19.32, 38), has led scholars to understand the woman as an adulteress, rather than merely a prostitute. However the verb that is consistently used of the woman is זנה (to prostitute), which implies sexual license but not necessarily infidelity. The use of נאף in this passage is not clear: in neither instance is it conjugated as an active verb which clearly modifies the woman, and in both cases it could be said to be *comparative*.

In the first instance, scholars assume that the adulterous woman in v. 32, who takes strangers instead of her husband (האשה המנאפת תחת אישה תקח את־זרים) is Jerusalem, reading the verse as an accusation of Jerusalem's adultery. 'Adulterous woman' (האשה המנאפת) is thus translated as vocative,[15] even though the verb takes a simple prefix

11. Cf. Galambush, *Jerusalem*, p. 94 n. 15; Zimmerli, *Ezekiel*, p. 340; and Wevers, *Ezekiel*, p. 121. Greenberg is the exception here: he argues that the language is of oath and covenant, but not necessarily marriage (*Ezekiel 1–20*, p. 278); yet ultimately he reads the relationship sexually, and the woman as an adulteress (p. 286).

12. The covenant of God with Abraham, Isaac and Jacob can be viewed as a sort of adoption-agreement. God adopts Abraham and his descendants as God's people in return for a certain loyalty. Or this may just be an instance where the metaphoric and literal merge, and the covenant here just means the literal covenant between God and Israel, as in Ezek. 16.59-63.

13. Exod. 25.20, 37.9; Deut. 32.11; 1 Kgs 6.27, 8.7; 2 Chron. 3.13, 5.8; Job 39.26; Jer. 48.40, 49.22.

14. Exod. 25.20, 37.9; 1 Kgs. 6.27, 8.7; 2 Chron. 3.13, 5.8.

15. Cf. Greenberg, *Ezekiel 1–20*, p. 271; Wevers, *Ezekiel*, p. 127; Zimmerli does not translate as a vocative, but does say, 'V. 32 with its mention of האשה המנאפת must be a subsequent definition which corresponds fully with the whole outline of

third person singular form (future tense), whereas hitherto the woman Jerusalem is always modified by second person suffix or waw consecutive verb forms (past tense). As I read it, this sudden shift in verb form, matched by the simple prefix form used in the next sentence to describe other prostitutes, could indicate that the 'adulterous woman' here is a *comparison* with the woman Jerusalem's flagrant prostitution. In the second instance, Jerusalem is told in v. 38 that she will be judged with the judgments of adulteresses (ושפטתיך משפטי נאפות). Again this can be read as a comparative statement: her punishment will be the same as that of the adulteress.

Nowhere in the text does it explicitly say that she is an adulteress.[16] Even the parable raised against her in v. 45 does not accuse her of adultery; it merely compares her with her mother and sisters who loathe their men. Given the thoroughness of the description of her sexual activities, and the vehemence with which they are condemned, if the woman is truly engaging in adultery, why is the text so reticent about it?

There is one textual feature which remains to explain: the sudden appearance of sons and daughters which the woman 'bore for' Yahweh (v. 20), and which she sacrifices to the images with whom she is prostituting (vv. 21-22). The introduction of children has typically been read as proof of a sexual relationship between Yahweh and the woman. However, just as the parental images of vv. 1-13 are read to fit a sexual context, this textual feature can be read to fit the parental context. For instance, if Ruth is to be used as an intertext with Ezekiel 16 (as for v. 8), it might be used to point to the parental custom of claiming an adopted daughter's baby as their own. In Ruth 4.17, Ruth's son is described as, 'a son born to Naomi' (ילד בן לנעמי). On

Ezek. 16 which deals with the immorality of a married woman' (*Ezekiel*, p. 346). The New International Version goes so far as to translate אישה as having a second person prenominal suffix ('your husband'). Galambush is more moderate, and like Zimmerli translates it as an explanatory aside, but without the gloss (*Jerusalem*, p. 66).

16. Usually the other uses of נאף in Ezekiel are taken into account here, all of which occur in Ezek. 23 (23.37 [×3], 45), which is commonly read in conjunction with Ezek. 16. In Ezek. 23 it is clearer that Jerusalem (Oholibah) is called an adulteress, along with Samaria (Oholah). What is not quite evident in Ezek. 23 is the actual relationship between Yahweh and the sisters. Though at one point (23.5) Oholah is accused of prostituting with her lovers while she belonged to Yahweh, and at another (23.35) Oholibah is accused of forgetting Yahweh, it is nowhere suggested that either of them is married to Yahweh, nor that their adultery is against him.

this basis (which is surely as firm as the intertexual reading of v. 8 as a marriage image) Jerusalem could be read as an adopted daughter, providing the deity with offspring.

However, if I do not read these ambiguous textual features as indicative of sexual desire on Yahweh's part, I am left asking why a parental desire for sexual modesty would elicit this kind of violent reaction. Is it just an indignant reaction to loss of control? It seems somewhat excessive. Even *if* the relationship is read as sexual, the questions are the same: the metaphor does not seem to account for the intensity of the violence.

Having scrutinized the relationships in the passage, I am left with a great unease. It is disturbing enough that in all three of these metaphoric relations, it is the woman Jerusalem who is the recipient of violence, and that in every case the deity is responsible for the violence. But worse, the metaphor tries to connect two separate conflicts, the literal conflict between Jerusalem and the nations, and the metaphoric conflict between Yahweh and Jerusalem, by inserting a woman's desire as some kind of reason for all the violence. The metaphor strains terribly to account for violence. Because the sexual imagery cannot account on its own for the lovers' violence, the metaphor relies on a third, inordinately violent, deity figure. Thus configured, the success of the metaphor hinges on the fact that the deity must have good reason to be so violent;[17] yet, as shown above, the typical reading of 'just desert' for infidelity does not seem to cohere, either with typical relationships of jealousy between two competing parties or with the type of relationship between Yahweh and the woman. Thus, if no reason is found for this excessive violence, we are left with a text which gratuitously links violence to women's sexuality and absolves it as righteous violence. While this possibility cannot be ruled out, I wish to see whether other factors, hidden in the shadow cast by dominant readings, may be operating here. So I turn to Girard, to see if his theory of mimetic desire and conflict can shed any light on what motivates the violence in this metaphor.

---

17. I should note here that the woman is accused of performing violent sacrifice of her children (vv. 20, 21, 36). Some may argue that this is enough to evoke such a violent response, but the sacrifice of children is not here portrayed as an issue of justice, but as one more thing which the deity has given to her that she has turned and offered to others.

Mimetic Desire and Conflict

In Girard's view, desire (and desire here is not limited to the sexual, by any means) is a result of imitation, or mimesis, which in turn leads to violence. Humans imitate each other in their search for fulfillment, in their search for being.[18] Desires, like anything else, are imitated. One person desires what another desires because she or he 'looks to that other person to inform him of what he should desire in order to acquire that being'.[19] In other words, if I see someone I wish to become like (because I feel they are closer to fulfillment than me) I imitate that person, including their desires. This puts me into a relationship of competition and eventual conflict with that person. Conflict will always arise when two people want the same thing, especially if it is only available to one of them. As Girard puts it, 'two desires converging on the same object are bound to clash... one cannot respond to that universal human injunction, "Imitate me!" without almost immediately encountering an inexplicable counter order: "Don't imitate me!" (which really means, "Do not appropriate my object")'.[20] Thus mimetic desire leads to a continual violent crisis.[21] Girard goes on to say that the violence produced by this conflict of desires is often dealt with by sacrifice, either intentionally through ritual, or unconsciously through scapegoating.[22] Violence is directed toward a surrogate victim, one who is chosen so that the violence is not taken out on members of the community, yet one who is not completely foreign to the community either, that is, one marginal to the community.[23]

Girard's theory helps make sense of the economy of violence and desire underlying the metaphor in Ezek. 16.1-45. When applied to each of the relations of violence and desire discussed thus far, Girard's theory illuminates the elusive operation of violence. Within each of these relations, it is useful to identify the conflict that arises,

18. René Girard, *Violence and the Sacred* (trans. Patrick Gregory; Baltimore: The Johns Hopkins University Press, 1977), p. 146.

19. Girard, *Violence and the Sacred*, p. 146.

20. Girard, *Violence and the Sacred*, pp. 146-47.

21. For a fuller explanation of mimetic desire, see René Girard, 'Generative Scapegoating', in Robert G. Hamerton-Kelly (ed.), *Violent Origins* (Stanford: Stanford University Press, 1987), pp. 122-23; and Girard, *Violence and the Sacred*, pp. 143-48.

22.   René Girard, *Things Hidden Since the Foundation of the World* (trans. Stephen Bann and Michael Metteer; London: Athlone Press, 1987), pp. 73-95.

23. Girard, *Violence and the Sacred*, p. 271.

the object of desire in each relation, and the mimesis which plays to produce this desire.

In the literal relationship between Jerusalem and the nations the conflict is obviously political. Judah, as an unwilling colony of Babylon, is obviously in conflict with more dominant political powers who, having no intention of giving up any of their control would forcibly deter attempts to climb the political ladder. Using a Girardian model, this might be seen as a case of mimetic desire: the object of desire is political independence and control, which Judah, seeing in others, wishes to reproduce for itself. Judah's imitation of the nations seems also to extend to religious practice, as evidenced by the constant juxtaposition of sexual desire and cultic imagery (vv. 16, 19, 24-25, 31).[24] Following Girard then, violence on the part of the nations would be a natural result of Judah's politically driven imitation of them.

Yet the simple pattern of mimesis and violence between two political entities is obscured and transformed by the metaphoric overlay. As noted earlier, Jerusalem's political desire appears as a woman's sexual desire while Yahweh and the nations converge as agents of violence. In the metaphoric relationship between Yahweh and the woman, conflict is not produced in the same way as in the literal situation. Since Yahweh is not portrayed as a political entity, political independence can no longer be seen as the object of desire and the catalyst for mimesis and subsequent conflict. Now the nations as lovers are the object of desire. The difference in the operation of mimesis in the metaphoric situation is subtle: in the literal situation, Jerusalem wishes to be independent like the nations and thus *imitates the nations*; in the metaphoric situation, the woman's object of desire *is the nations as lovers*. Since the object of desire shifts in the metaphoric relation, the question becomes: whom is the woman imitating, whom does she want to be like?

Applying Girard's theory, the woman's desire for the nations as lovers must be imitation of something; and since Yahweh responds to it with a violence meant to suppress her desire, it would seem that her desire is an imitation of the deity's own desire for the nations-as-lovers.[25] Finally a metaphoric motivation appears for the violence,

---

24. Zimmerli, *Ezekiel*, pp. 344-45; Wevers (*Ezekiel*, pp. 125-26) and Greenberg (*Ezekiel 1–20*, pp. 281-82), consider 'harlotry' to be a figure for the political alliances themselves.

25. Yahweh's desire for the nations is a theme that recurs throughout the Hebrew Bible; for instance, there are passages in Isaiah (2.3-4; 19.23-25; 66.18-21); and Micah (4.1-3; 7.12) that look forward to the nations being gathered to Yahweh. In Ezekiel, this theme is more covert and the desire is usually accompanied by

alleviating some of the discomfort produced by the incoherence in the metaphor. The violence of Yahweh toward the woman is a result of the conflict produced by mimesis; it is the violence directed against one encroaching on the deity's sexual territory. This motive for the violence in the text not only solves the mystery of Yahweh's excessive violence, but it also has a number of implications for understanding the gender and role of Yahweh and for reading the metaphor of the woman.

Recasting the Characters

This reading affects the characterization of the deity. If the woman desires the nations-as-lovers because she is imitating Yahweh, and if the lovers are characterized as male, as they are in this passage,[26] she must therefore be imitating a preference for sexual activity with men.[27] This could either mean that the deity has homoerotic preferences, or that the deity is a heterosexual feminine figure. Since the passage is an address of the deity in the first person throughout, the deity's gender is ambiguous, though elsewhere in the book the deity is referred to in the masculine.

If the deity is read as a feminine heterosexual figure, the descriptions of finding the bloody baby, washing it, clothing it and rearing it become definitely maternal. If I place this maternal image alongside the image of the deity competing with the woman Jerusalem for the

violence when the nation in question becomes arrogant and too available to the other nations. For examples see the prophecies against Tyre in Ezek. 26, 27, 28, which depict the male Tyre trading with a great number of nations (27.12-27) as arrogant (28.5, 17) and also as incredibly beautiful (27.11; 28.12-14); and the depictions of Assyria as a great cedar in Ezek. 31, also arrogant (31.10), available to other nations (31.6) and beautiful. If one were more accustomed to looking for male–male desire, one could read 28.12-14 and 31.1-9, to be descriptions of Yahweh's desire, as easily as 19.7-15.

26. See v. 17, 'you made for yourself images of men and you prostituted with them'; v. 26, 'sons of Egypt'; v. 28, 'sons of Assyria'; and the masculine participle אהבים in vv. 36-37.

27. In support of a deity with male sexual preferences, we might even read the deity's description of Egyptians in v. 26 (taking בשׂר as a euphemism for penis, see Gen. 17.11, 14, 23, 24, 25; Exod. 28.42; Lev. 15.2-19; Ezek. 23.20; 44.7, 9) as 'ones with big penises' (גדלי בשׂר), an erotic image (for some). Certainly, in Ezek. 23.20 there is a fascination with the Egyptian lovers' large genitals, as David J. Halperin points out in *Seeking Ezekiel: Text and Psychology* (University Park, PA: Pennsylvania State University Press, 1993), p. 146. Halperin takes this in another direction though, and suggests an Oedipal conflict at work (*Seeking Ezekiel*, p. 21).

same lovers, a larger picture emerges of a mother who is jealous of her daughter's sexual activities. If the deity is read as a masculine figure (perhaps a homosexual or bisexual father) the scene does not change all that much—the same kind of parental jealousy is present and the violence does not go away; but such a reading does have the extra-textual effect of challenging the predominant heterosexist reading of the character of Yahweh.

Second, this reading does not allow the (usual) status of sexual object to be conferred upon the woman. Whether the deity is a masculine or feminine figure, the point is that the deity's desire is directed toward the nations; the woman is no longer the object of the deity's sexual attention.[28] While the deity obviously longs for the woman and her loyalty in some way, this longing can be read as non-parental. Reading in an asexual context makes the descriptions of her nakedness and sexual activity less titillating[29] and more matter of fact, removing the stigma of sexual object. Whatever other objectification this passage may pose for the figure of a woman (she is obviously still considered as property of the parent), removing the ability to read her as primarily the sexual object of male desire liberates her considerably. Moreover, the violence directed toward her can no longer be understood as 'just reward' for her sexual activity, but rather it can be seen as the outcome of the deity's inability to deal with mimetic desire.

Thus far, I have only accounted for the mimetic relation that sets up the nations as the object of desire in the passage; this does not explain how the woman Jerusalem becomes the object of the deity's desire, even if this desire is not sexualized. What sets her up as an object of desire; who is being imitated? Finding an answer to this question requires examination of the relation between Yahweh and the nations as rivals. Unfortunately, not much is said about this relation in the text, so any reading of it is bound to be hypothetical. Yet it is clear that throughout the book of Ezekiel Yahweh is in competition with the nations for control. In the quest to be like each other with respect to power, and perhaps divinity,[30] Yahweh and the nations fix their sights on the same object of desire, the woman Jerusalem. Under this model, I would expect to find Yahweh's desire for control of the

---

28. Of course, this does not consider the possibility of an incestuous relationship.

29. One may be less tempted, for instance, to read שַׂעַר in v. 7 as pubic hair, as Zimmerli does (*Ezekiel*, p. 339), rather than any other kind of hair.

30. For instance, in Ezek. 28 there seems to be some contest over divinity.

woman heightened by the threat to his monopoly on this prized possession, and Yahweh's violence directed against the nations trying to appropriate his territory. But, as pointed out, this is not what appears here in the text. Instead, Yahweh's violence is directed toward the woman. Is the violence misdirected, from the competitor to the prize herself? Why does violence not evolve as expected against the nations, given this particular relation of mimetic desire?

Metaphorical Sacrifice

This brings me to Girard's notion of scapegoat or surrogate victim as a way of accounting for the interplay between the literal and meta-phoric relations of violence and desire in this passage. Here the metaphorical conflict between Yahweh and the nations is apparently being taken out on the woman Jerusalem. In other words, the woman Jerusalem becomes a surrogate victim for the violence that should properly be directed at the nations. But why should such scape-goating occur here? I would like to suggest that the woman Jerusalem is a metaphoric construction, functioning to provide a scapegoat or surrogate victim for the violence that was ready to erupt or was erupting in Israel's literal political context. The interplay between the literal and the figurative sets up a situation outside of the real world in which a *metaphorical* 'sacrifice' can be offered to try to deal with a literal situation of political violence. Prophetic and religious language is perhaps being used here not only as a way of explaining the political situation, but also as a way of trying to alleviate the violence of that situation.

The choice of the metaphor of a woman who is called a prostitute as a surrogate victim makes perfect sense according to Girard's theory. A prostitute is part of the community, but marginal to it by virtue of her 'deviant' sexual behaviour and by virtue of her gender. Girard's description of the role of women as sacrificial victims in Dionysiac rites seems particularly pertinent: 'the woman qualifies for sacrificial status by reason of her weakness and relatively marginal social status. That is why she can be viewed as a quasi-sacred figure, both desired and disdained, alternately elevated and abused'.[31] Likewise, the woman Jerusalem vacillates between the common and the quasi-sacred. Because she is viewed both as sexually active at the top of every street (thus common) and as property/child of the deity (thus

---

31. Girard, *Violence and the Sacred*, p. 142.

sacred), she is able to take on the role of victim which mediates between the sacred and the profane.

But what are the implications of this kind of reading? One could argue that moving the image from the status of conjugal violence to that of sacrificial victim is not exactly an elevation; one would hardly choose the image of sacrificial ewe as an icon for feminist biblical criticism. But an understanding of this metaphor in its function as surrogate victim allows us to account for the extreme violence against a woman in this text; it transforms the figure of the woman by rendering her a heroine of sorts, and it brings the image of prostitute from the despised margin to the valued center. The woman becomes an important salvific figure, in that she obviates violence in the community. This also brings the figure into line with other biblical prostitutes who forestall violence in the community and act as salvific figures (for instance, Tamar who prevents herself from being killed, and becomes a forebearer of David; or Rahab who keeps spies from being killed, allowing them to bring a favourable report for the claiming of the land).

Conclusions

Girard's theory not only answers questions raised by careful observation of all the relations of desire and violence in the text, both metaphorical and literal; it also opens up possibilities for reading that help subvert dominant interpretations. When Girard's theory is read alongside the text, the deity is forced to take responsibility for the violence, as a function of his or her own jealousies; and the woman is freed from her shackles of sexual objectivity, regaining her standing as a valuable member of the community.

These readings are part of an effort to liberate images of women from being the objects of pornographic titillation—whose 'wantonness' is exposed along with their body parts, and who are punishable for being sexually active. It is time to reclaim these images, so that they can no longer be read in their canonized, authorial position as validation for patriarchal oppression and violence against women. It is time to chip away at the monolithic conception of Yahweh until a new figure emerges: one that takes responsibility for, rather than righteously justifying, violence against women.

GENDER REVERSAL IN EZEKIEL 16

S. Tamar Kamionkowski

אלּיעזר אומר אין מפטירין בהודע את־ירושלים
R. Eliezer says: We do not read the chapter, 'Cause Jerusalem to know' as the concluding recitation following a Torah reading.[1]

This rabbinic statement prohibits the liturgical reading of Ezekiel 16 along with a handful of other texts, including the rape of Tamar and David's seduction of Bathsheba. The rabbis were troubled and embarrassed by these biblical accounts of sexual violence and indiscretion, and they attempted to hide these potentially dangerous texts. This discomfort is shared by critical commentators as well. As G.A. Cooke wrote in his 1936 commentary, 'There is much in this ch[apter] which is repulsive to our taste'.[2]

Ezekiel 16 tells a story about an abandoned baby girl, rescued by a man who later marries her and provides her with clothing, food and riches. The bride repays her husband's generosity by seeking other lovers to whom she passes on her riches and gifts. Enraged, the husband punishes his wife through public shaming, physical abuse and near death. Seeing his wife humbled and put back in her place, he forgives her adultery and takes her back in love. Of course, in this extended metaphor, the husband is YHWH and the young woman is Jerusalem, i.e. the people therein.

Ezekiel bothered the rabbis because of its inconsistencies with Levitical law,[3] because of the visions of the divine throne, and, specifically in Ezekiel 16, because of its explicit sexual language and its implication that Israel's roots were heathen.[4] Only the most sophisticated

---

1. *m. Meg.* 4.10.
2. G.A. Cooke, *A Critical and Exegetical Commentary on the Book of Ezekiel* (ICC; Edinburgh: T. & T. Clark, 2nd edn, 1967), p. 160.
3. *b. Šab.* 13b credits Hananiah ben Hezekiah with the reconciliation of Ezekiel's legislation and the Torah, without which the book of Ezekiel would have been 'withdrawn' (נגנז).
4. *b. Meg.* 25a-b.

reader could safely enter into the text of Ezekiel. In modern readings of this text, dangers also abound for the unsophisticated reader. An overly simplistic reading of the marital metaphor between God and Israel may lead to the conclusion that a proper husband–wife relationship is one of mastery and submission, or that God condones rape as a suitable punishment for female adultery.[5]

This text is not only dangerous for the reasons the rabbis provide, nor is it profoundly disturbing simply because it sanctions domestic violence and misogyny. Ezekiel 16 reflects a voice of desperation which can make its reader nervous and anxious. Ezekiel 16 demolishes a structure only to rebuild it with ever more reinforcement. The prophet's words put into question fundamental gender categories and provide a glimpse of a non-polarized gender system only to designate that system 'chaotic' and to reassert the dominant view with a greater vigor. In this study I argue that gender reversal is the backbone against which Ezekiel 16 can be understood.

Ezekiel 16 is about an exploration of gender ambiguities and reversals. Read in this light, wife Jerusalem's wrongdoing does not just concern political and religious matters and it is not just about unfaithfulness. The abomination of 'wife Jerusalem' is that she is attempting to pass for a male (i.e. aggressive, independent), that she is crossing gender boundaries and upsetting the world order. In other words, Ezekiel constructs a metaphor whereby the Judean/exilic male community poses as a female (personified Jerusalem) who in turn passes for a male (independent and aggressive). The claim that Israel's sin is not just a matter of being unfaithful to her husband, but also of subverting the defined roles within that relationship, is a subtle but significant change in perspective. This story is one of confused gender scripts, ensuing chaos, and a re-ordering through the reinforcement of strictly defined gender scripts.

1. *Recent Treatments of Ezekiel 16*

To date, research on Ezekiel 16 has broadly consisted of studies that emphasize the theological teachings of the forgiving nature of God, even in those cases where the sins are extreme;[6] and feminist critiques

---

5.   See Susan Brooks Thistlethwaite, 'Every Two Minutes: Battered Women and Feminist Interpretation', in Letty M. Russell (ed.), *Feminist Interpretation of the Bible* (Philadelphia: Westminster Press, 1985), p. 107, and Naomi Graetz, *Silence is Deadly: Judaism Confronts Wifebeating* (Northvale, NJ: Jason Aronson Press, 1998), pp. 35-52.

6.   See, for example, Joseph Blenkinsopp, *Ezekiel* (Interpretation: A Bible Commentary for Teaching and Preaching; Louisville, KY: John Knox Press, 1990); M.G.

which condemn the 'pornographic' and sexist aspects of the text.[7] Traditional commentators tend to empathize with God and focus on the deity's forgiving nature, even in the face of Israel's horrific wrong-doings.[8] Commentators generally provide an uncritical exposition of the prophet's point of view. They participate in Ezekiel's rhetoric and even further the image by calling Jerusalem, in the words of Blenkinsopp, the 'nymphomaniac bride'. Additionally, they provide an apology for God's violence. Note Blenkinsopp's description: 'Ezekiel describes the corruption of the human will in even darker colors than his older contemporary [Jeremiah]. The story of the nymphomaniac bride expresses this conviction in violent language, at the risk of sickening the reader, in order to set over against it the saving will of God and the possibility of renewal'.[9]

Since Drorah Setel's 1985 article on Hosea, feminist readers have created a new paradigm for reading Ezekiel in which the primary empathy lies with the woman Jerusalem. These interpreters, many whose works have been featured in Athalya Brenner's *A Feminist Companion to the Latter Prophets*, empathize with wife Israel and the abuse to which she is subjected by God. Most recently, Mary Shields has written on the ways in which the format of the text 'masks' the violence perpetrated by Yahweh. She demonstrates how God is automatically a privileged figure and how the male figure is never described, never embodied; he simply resides in the background,

Swanepoel, 'Ezekiel 16: Abandoned Child, Bride Adorned or Unfaithful Wife?', in Philip R. Davies and David J.A. Clines (eds.), *Among the Prophets: Language, Image and Structure in the Prophetic Writings* (JSOTSup, 144; Sheffield: JSOT Press, 1993), pp. 84-104.

7.   See especially the collection of essays found in Athalya Brenner's *A Feminist Companion to the Latter Prophets* (Sheffield: Sheffield Academic Press, 1995). See also T. Drorah Setel, 'Prophets and Pornography: Female Sexual Imagery in Hosea', in Russell (ed.), *Feminist Interpretation of the Bible*, pp. 86-95; and Renita J. Weems, *Battered Love: Marriage, Sex and Violence in the Hebrew Prophets* (Minneapolis: Fortress Press, 1995).

8.   Weems writes: 'Only an audience that could relate to and identify with the metaphorical husband's outrage and horror could possibly perceive his reactions as plausible and legitimate... Only those who had a certain relationship to power could appreciate some of the assumptions embedded in the metaphor. That is, the metaphor expected its audience to sympathize with the rights and responsibilities that came with power and to understand the threat that women could pose to male honor' (*Battered Love*, p. 41). By consistently reading the text on the side of the male God, commentators, again and again, fail to approach the text critically, fail to step outside of the metaphoric frame to analyze the metaphor itself.

9.   Blenkinsopp, *Ezekiel*, p. 78.

while the woman is exposed time and time again. One of the conclusions which Shields makes from these observations is that

> Throughout this text, power resides in one person: Yahweh. It is he who sees the infant and pronounces that she should live, and who marries, washes, and adorns the young woman. It is he who allows the woman no speech in this text. His power, in the end, is absolute.[10]

Ultimately, traditional and feminist interpreters agree that YHWH has the sole power in the relationship. The points of difference reside in the reader's sympathies. Is Israel's powerlessness a positive sign of submission to God? Or is the powerlessness a reflection and reinforcement of women's subordination? Are God's actions justified as a fit punishment motivated by an ultimately forgiving nature? Or are these actions abusive and derived from jealousy and uncontrolled rage? While both of these approaches yield valuable insights, neither method captures the full complexity of the text.

I would respectfully disagree with Shields's statement that '[t]hroughout this text, power resides in one person: Yahweh'. Power does not reside in only one character throughout the story—if this were the case, there would be no conflict, no tension, and certainly no story. What is actually so remarkable about this text is that God does not have all the power! The story begins and ends in a fantasy or a myth of an all-powerful God and a completely submissive wife or people. However, the material embedded within this frame reveals a different perspective. The center of the story expresses a much more volatile, chaotic relationship—one in which the deity does not have full control and in which wife Israel is not completely submissive. I will argue that this is a story about cultural upheavals, social disintegration and theological crises, all expressed through the breakdown of one of the most fundamental cultural and social institutions: gender.

2. *The Text of Ezekiel 16*

A matter that should give a reader of Ezekiel 16 pause is that the writer, discussing idolatry and foreign alliances, does not draw from the common stock of idioms available to him.[11] Certainly it has been

---

10. Mary Shields, 'Multiple Exposures: Body Rhetoric and Gender Characterization in Ezekiel 16', *JFSR* 14 (1998), pp. 5-18 (14). Reprinted with Self-Response in this volume.

11. פסל ומסכה or פסל ומצבה: Exod. 20.4; Lev. 26.1; Deut. 4.16, 23, 25; 5.8; 27.15; Judg. 17.3, 4; 18.14, 17, 30, 31; 2 Kgs 21.7; Isa. 40.19; 42.17; 44.9, 15, 17; 45.20; 48.5; Jer. 10.14; 51.17; Nah. 1.14; Hab. 2.18; Ps. 97.7; 2 Chron. 33.7.

noted that Ezekiel's biblical Hebrew reflects the beginning of Late
Biblical Hebrew (LBH) and that the text is highly corrupt; nonetheless, the text is filled with unique phrases and unusual words which
cannot be wholly accounted for through current characterizations of
textual corruption and LBH. A careful lexical and syntactical study of
Ezekiel 16 reveals that many of the unusual idioms and ambiguities in
this text are rooted in gender, and once this becomes clear, we are in a
better position to read the clues necessary for a deeper, more nuanced
reading of the text.

The first fourteen verses of the chapter describe the miraculous
rescue of an abandoned baby girl.[12] The text emphasizes both the vul-
nerable and helpless state of the foundling and the generous saving
acts of God. God clothes, feeds and finally marries young Jerusalem,
bestowing on her gifts and riches. In every respect, the young woman
is a passive recipient of her husband's actions. Beginning with v. 15
the story takes a radical turn, and it is this section which will be the
focus of our attention. From the first verse of this section, the woman
is described with active verbs. We no longer hear about her state of
being, or how she is acted upon; rather, she acts. Commentators take
this observation for granted or do not notice this at all. Instead, they
focus on the nature of the woman's actions, rather than on the fact of
her acting at all. However, the extreme change of syntax is an indi-
cator that the *fact* of her action is just as significant as the *content* of her
actions. This is also supported in YHWH's woe in v. 22. YHWH
laments that the woman does not remember and hold fast to her days
of nakedness, vulnerability and helplessness.

a. *Women's Ejaculation*

In the early part of YHWH's tirade against his wife (v. 15) he accuses
her of sexual promiscuity with the phrase, וַתִּשְׁפְּכִי אֶת־תַּזְנוּתַיִךְ, vari-
ously translated as 'you lavished your favors' or better, Greenberg's
'you poured out your harlotry'.[13] Greenhill expresses a common
understanding of this phrase: 'The word pouring out sets forth the
vehement and insatiable desire she had to sin…'[14] The verb שׁפך, in
figurative usage is restricted primarily to three contexts in biblical

---

12. For a detailed analysis of the beginning of Ezek. 16, see my *Gender Reversal
and Cosmic Chaos: Studies on the Book of Ezekiel* (Sheffield: Sheffield Academic Press,
Forthcoming).

13. Moshe Greenberg, *Ezekiel 1–20* (AB; Garden City, NY: Doubleday, 1983),
p. 270.

14. W. Greenhill, *An Exposition of Ezekiel* (Edinburgh and Carlisle, PA: Banner
of Truth Trust, 1645–67), p. 367.

literature:[15] murder (שָׁפַךְ דָּם),[16] erecting siege mounds (שָׁפַךְ סוֹלְלָה),[17] and the expression of God's fury (שָׁפַךְ חֵמָה).[18] The latter two phrases always appear in the context of violence and destruction, whether the violence is initiated by men (in war) or by God (violent release of fury expressed through invasion or natural devastation). The phrase שָׁפַךְ דָּם usually signifies murder, that is, the killing of an innocent person. This phrase appears ten times in the book of Ezekiel. The writer uses this phrase most often to describe the actions of the leaders of Jerusalem, as in Ezek. 22.6:

הנה נשׂיאי ישׂראל איש לזרעו הֿיו בך למען שפך־דם

The princes of Israel in your midst, each one used his power for the shedding of blood.

In 22.3, the grammatical feminine is used to describe the violent actions which take place in the midst of the city Jerusalem. In 16.38 and 23.45 the phrase appears as a parallel to נָאַף, adultery, referring to the evils of personified Jerusalem. The verse in ch. 23 reads:

ואנשׁים צדיקם המה ישׁפטו אותהם משׁפט נאפות ומשׁפט שׁפכות דם
כי נאפת הנה ודם בידיהן

Righteous men shall punish them with the judgments for adultery and for bloodshed, for they are adulteresses and blood is on their hands.

In 31 out of 33 total occurrences of this verb in the book of Ezekiel, it is used in one of these three manners. Our phrase, שָׁפַךְ תַּזְנוּת, appears only in ch. 16 and once in 23.8. There the text reads:

ואת-תזנותיה ממצרים לא עזבה כי אותה שׁכבו בנעוריה והמה עשׂו דדי
בתוליה וישׁפכו תזנותם עליה

She did not give up the promiscuous behavior that she had undertaken with the Egyptians, for they had violated her in her youth; that is, they had touched her virgin nipples and had ejaculated [lit. poured out their lust] upon her.

15. שָׁפַךְ נֶפֶשׁ expresses the pouring out of one's soul in grief, cf. 1 Sam. 1.15; Job 30.16; Lam. 2.11.

16. 10 times in Ezekiel; cf. also Gen. 9.6, 37.22; Lev. 17.4; Num. 35.33; Deut. 19.10; 1 Sam. 25.31; 1 Kgs 2.31, 18.28; 2 Kgs 21.16, 24.4; Isa. 59.7; Jer. 7.6, 22.3, 17; Joel 4.19; Zeph. 1.17; Ps. 79.3, 106.38; Prov. 1.16, 6.17; Lam. 4.13; 1 Chron. 22.8, 23.3.

17. 4 times in Ezekiel; cf. also 2 Sam. 20.15; 2 Kgs 19.32; Isa. 37.33; Jer. 6.6; Dan. 11.15.

18. 10 times in Ezekiel; cf. also Isa. 42.25; Jer. 6.11, 10.25; Ps. 79.6; Lam. 2.4, 4.11.

Several important observations can be made about this verse. First of all, the sexual act described here is not consensual sex, it is rape.[19] The action is executed by men upon a woman; she is the object, the passive recipient. The men's violations culminate with their climax, their ejaculation, which is the ultimate act of aggression in this verse. Within this context, שׁפך תזנות is an aggressive act perpetrated by men. It is only in Ezek. 16.15 that a female is the subject of the verb, a verb which has strong connotations of aggression, power and violence. And if, in fact, the meaning of this phrase is connected to ejaculation in ch. 23, we can only wonder as to the nuance of the meaning(s) in ch. 16.

Related to the phrase שׁפך תזנות, we find the phrase הׁשׁפך נחׁשׁתך in v. 36. This phrase has been a crux which has been interpreted in a variety of ways. Moshe Greenberg relates the word (נחׁשׁתך) to the Akkadian *nuḫšātu*, 'hemorrhage'.[20] In Mesopotamian ritual and medical texts, this term seems to refer to a gynecological disorder characterized by a genital discharge. So, for example, one medical prescription concludes: *ina šērim la patan išatti naḫšātu ipparrasā*, 'Let her drink of it in the morning, not having eaten; the discharge will then stop'.[21] According to the citations provided in the *CAD*, the medical problems could include an unusual flow of blood during pregnancy: *ša naḫšātu marṣat sinništu ša ina mērešu damū ītanammarū*, 'a

19. The verb שׁכב can take one of two prepositions to indicate sexual intercourse: עם and את. Alternatively, the verb can be followed immediately by the direct object marker. In those cases where את does not have an attached pronominal suffix, it is impossible to determine whether the preposition or the direct object marker is intended (cf. Gen. 26.10, 35.22; Lev. 18.22; 1 Sam. 2.22). (It should be noted that the distinction between preposition and direct object marker is only a matter of Masoretic vocalization and not orthography.) A study of those cases in which the suffix does distinguish between the two leads to no sharp distinctions with regard to semantic differences. The preposition עם appears in a variety of contexts including, for example, Gen. 19.32-35, where Lot's daughters seduce Lot into sexual intercourse; Gen. 30.5, which describes a sexual encounter between Jacob and his wife Leah; Exod. 22.15 and Deut. 22.25, 28, which include legislation regarding the seduction or rape of an unmarried, sexually inexperienced young woman, etc. The priestly writer(s) use the direct object with שׁכב to indicate sexual intercourse in Lev. 15.18, 24 within the context of acts that induce a state of טמאה (impurity), and in regard to the trial of the suspected adulteress in Num. 5. The most interesting case is that of 2 Sam. 13, in which the two different forms of the verb phrase occur side by side within the same narrative.

20. See M. Greenberg, 'Nḥštk (Ezek. 16.36): Another Hebrew Cognate of Akkadian *naḥāšu*', in Maria de Jong Ellis (ed.), *Essays on the Ancient Near East, Festschrift for J.J. Finkelstein* (Memoirs of the Connecticut Academy of Arts and Sciences, 19; Hamden, CT: Archon Books, 1977), pp. 85-86.

21. *CAD* N/1, p. 42.

woman who suffers from *naḥšātu*: a woman during whose pregnancy blood keeps appearing'.[22] Given the Akkadian sense of discharge and the sexual context of Ezekiel 16, Greenberg concludes that הִשָּׁפֵךְ נְחֻשְׁתֵּךְ is a reference to 'copious distillation'. Thus the pouring out of a discharge could refer to the fluids produced at sexual arousal. Greenberg also cites *b. Sanh.* 92b, which says that the exilic men were so beautiful that the Chaldean women discharged copiously (זְבוּת שׁוּפְכוּת). David Halperin picks up on Greenberg's reading and writes: 'Her juice positively drips from her'.[23] Or, if we want to push the envelope a bit further, this phrase may have echoes of female ejaculation,[24] similar to the phrase שָׁפֵךְ תַּזְנוּת.

b. *Usurping the Phallus*
As YHWH continues to condemn his wife, he accuses her of cultic crimes. In v. 17, we encounter the phrase, צַלְמֵי זָכָר. The text reads:

וַתִּקְחִי כְּלֵי תִפְאַרְתֵּךְ מִזְּהָבִי וּמִכַּסְפִּי אֲשֶׁר נָתַתִּי לָךְ
וַתַּעֲשִׂי־לָךְ צַלְמֵי זָכָר וַתִּזְנִי־בָם

> You took your beautiful things, made of the gold and silver that I had given you and you made yourself phallic images and fornicated with them.

On one level of the metaphor, the accuser is referring to the corruption of the cult in Jerusalem; on another level, husband God is condemning wife Israel for having taken gifts of their courtship and having transformed them into instruments of unfaithfulness. Yet the phrase צַלְמֵי זָכָר has additional significance here. This clause is not a stock phrase for idol worship; in fact, it appears only here and has given rise to a scholarly debate on its meaning. The debate centers around the question of the meaning of זָכָר in this context. Is the statue a phallic image or a human (male) image?

---

22. *CAD* N/1, p. 41.
23. D.J. Halperin, *Seeking Ezekiel: Text and Psychology* (University Park, PA: Pennsylvania State University Press, 1993), p. 146.
24. The Greek physician philosophers debated whether women's ejaculations contained sperm or not. Avicenna, an Arabic physician, warns that men please their wives lest 'she does not emit sperm (*sperma*) and when she does not emit sperm a child is not made' (Thomas Laqueur, *Making Sex: Body and Gender from the Greeks to Freud* [Cambridge, MA: Harvard University Press, 1990], pp. 50-51). In antiquity, lesbians, *tribades*, were considered to be women with too much hot sperm; cf. K.J. Dover, *Greek Homosexuality* (London: Gerald Duckworth, 1978; updated with new postscript, Cambridge, MA: Harvard University Press, 1989), pp. 182-84.

The Hebrew word זכר generally means 'male' or 'man'; and it occurs especially to indicate gender.[25] It is often paired with its antonym, נקבה, which literally means 'one who is pierced'. Presumably, therefore, the male is the one who pierces. In cuneiform, the same sign is used to render 'penis', GÌŠ (= *išaru/mušaru/ušaru*) and 'male', NITA (= *zikaru*). In Isa. 57.8 we find a description of the worship of phalluses and this sets a precedent for taking our text as another example of the same phenomenon.

I would suggest that if we take the preposition ב in the word בם here in its use as a marker of instrumentality,[26] the translation of the second half of the verse reads: 'you made yourself phallic images and used them as instruments of fornication', that is, you gave yourself male genitalia, you usurped the power of the phallus![27]

The use of dildoes is scantily attested in antiquity. A text from third century BCE Egypt contains a discussion between two women about a dildo. The two women discuss their fondness for the sex toy and for the manufacturer of the product. One woman, Koritto, describes the phallus: 'what workmanship. You'd think Athena's hands, not Kerdon's went into it. I[...]he came bringing two of them, Metro. When I saw them, my eyes swam at the sight—men don't have such firm pricks. Not only that, but its smoothness is sleep, and its straps are like wool, not leather.'[28] Bernadette Brooten relates a Pseudo-Lucian dialogue on the relative merits of love of boys versus love of women. In a mocking tone, love between women is suggested: 'Let them strap to themselves cunningly contrived instruments of licentiousness, those mysterious monstrosities devoid of seed, and let women lie with women as does man'.[29] Brooten rightly notes that this text reflects more about male fantasies and assumptions that it does about actual practices between women; nonetheless, our concern is exactly with male projections of women's sexual activities.

25. It occurs 82 times in the Bible.

26. Cf., for example, Mic. 4.14, Eccl. 9.12.

27. Halperin (*Seeking Ezekiel*, p. 146) interprets this phrase to refer to phallic images with which women might masturbate. I am suggesting that the phallic images may not have been used simply for self-pleasure, but as instruments by which to penetrate men (or perhaps other women).

28. As quoted by Mary R. Lefkowitz and Maureen B. Fant, *Women's Life in Greece and Rome: A Source Book in Translation* (Baltimore: Johns Hopkins University Press, 1982), p. 108. Also, cf. Bernadette Brooten, *Love Between Women: Early Christian Responses to Female Homoeroticism* (Chicago and London: University of Chicago Press, 1996), p. 108 for a discussion of this text.

29. Brooten, *Love Between Women*, p. 54.

Additionally, Eva C. Keuls has collected visual representations (of the classical Greek period) of women engaged in sexual intercourse with each other with the use of dildoes. In most cases, the pictures show women engaged in masturbation.[30] At this time, the information from Mesopotamia is rather scant on this topic; however, Biggs makes reference to the discovery, near the Ishtar Temple in Assur, of stone models of erect penises with a hole in them, possibly worn as amulets.[31]

c. *The Violent Woman*

As we continue our reading to v. 21, we come across Ezekiel's accusation that wife Israel is slaughtering her own children.[32] The claim that a woman is slaughtering her own children is a powerful and horrific image; yet again, there is another reading to this verse. The verb שׁחט is usually used in a ritual context for the slaughter of animals.[33] An interesting exception to the ritual context of animal slaughter appears in Gen. 37.31, where Joseph's brothers slaughter an animal to use its blood on Joseph's coat. Although the polemic against child sacrifice appears with some frequency in biblical texts, the verb שׁחט is used only in Gen. 22.10 and Isa. 57.5 as well as in Ezek. 16.21 and 23.39. A more common use of the verb, outside of ritual contexts, is within the domain of men, war and extreme violence. Tribal conflicts in the premonarchic period lead to acts of slaughter;[34] Elijah's supporters slaughter the priests of Baal;[35] a dynastic rivalry within the Northern Kingdom leads to Jehu's slaughter of Ahab's extended family and supporters;[36] the Babylonians slaughter Zedekiah's sons before him;[37]

---

30. *The Reign of the Phallus: Sexual Politics in Ancient Athens* (Berkeley: University of California Press, 1984), pp. 82-86. Cf. also John Boardman, *Athenian Red Figure Vases: The Archaic Period* (New York: Oxford University Press, 1975), pls. 71 and 99.1. See Brooten, *Love Between Women*, pp. 152-54 for a discussion of dildoes in Greek and Roman society. Brooten knows of no vase painting 'that shows one woman penetrating another with a dildo' (p. 153). *b. Abod. Zar.* 44a mentions a female ruler who used a dildo every day.

31. Robert D. Biggs, *ŠÀ.ZI.GA: Ancient Mesopotamian Potency Incantations* (Texts from Cuneiform Sources; Locust Valley, NY: J.J. Augustin, 1967), p. 10 n. 57.

32. This reading follows manuscripts of the LXX which read בָנַיִךְ, 'your sons', rather than the MT בָּנַי, 'my sons'.

33. 37 times in the Pentateuch.

34. Judg. 12.6.

35. 1 Kgs 18.40.

36. 2 Kgs 10.7, 14.

37. 2 Kgs 25.7; Jer. 39.6, 52.10.

and Gedaliah's supporters are slaughtered by Ishmael son of Neta-
niah.[38] In each case, a rivalry between men vying for power gives rise
to the slaughter. Our text is the only one which attributes this activity
to a female. The power of this image is not only of a mother killing
her own children, but of a female slaughtering (שחט) at all.[39]

d. *Financial Independence*
Verse 30 offers another interesting twist. The second half of the verse
reads: מעשׂה אשׁה זונה שׁלטת. The translation provided in the JPS Tanakh
is 'the acts of a self-willed whore'. The seventeenth-century commentator Greenhill represents the most common interpretation of this
phrase:

> a woman that hath a domineering spirit; from שׁלט to domineer and
> exercise lordliness over others, to usurp authority... when the mask of
> modesty and bridle of continency are laid aside, and a bold forwardness
> to filthiness is manifested, when a woman doth not only expect and
> wait for her lovers, but desires, invites, and constrains them to satisfy
> her lusts, and will have no nay.[40]

More recently, Daniel Block understands the word to mean 'to gain
mastery over, domineer', but then translates it in the body of the text
as 'brazen woman'.[41] The scholarly discussion, I believe, is fueled by
the fact that the adjective derived from שׁלט is applied to a female only
here. The root שׁלט is attested in Aramaic, where it is rendered as 'to
exercise power over'. Based on a study of the root in the Elephantine
documents, Greenfield has argued that a woman holding the title of
שׁליטה is one who is financially independent. Placing this insight
within the context of gift giving, Greenfield argues that only a שׁליטה
could be in a position to give gifts to her lovers and to pay for sex.[42]

---

38. Jer. 41.7.

39. It is interesting to note that while some traditions extol Abraham for his
willingness to slaughter his son as a demonstration of his loyalty to God, wife
Israel's slaughter is here interpreted as a demonstration of her disloyalty.

40. Greenhill, *An Exposition of Ezekiel*, p. 376.

41. *The Book of Ezekiel, Chapters 1–24* (NICOT; Grand Rapids, MI: Eerdmans,
1997), p. 492.

42. C. Jonas Greenfield, 'Two Biblical Passages in Light of their Near Eastern
Background—Ezekiel 16.30 and Malachi 3.17', *Eretz Israel* 16 (1982), pp. 56-61, esp.
pp. 56-57 [Hebrew]. In addition to Greenfield's citations, cf. E.G. Kraeling's, *The
Brooklyn Museum Aramaic Papyri: New Documents of the Fifth Century B.C. from the
Jewish Colony at Elephantine* (Arno Press, 1969 [1953]), legal texts 2.11; 6.9, 10; 9.11-
15; 10.8-14 .

'In the first place, she burglarized his storeroom'.[43] In one Elephantine text, the term seems to have a broader meaning:

ל-ל-ה-ן לא שליטה יה[ן וישמע ל]-ה-ב-ע-ל-ה בעל אחר-ן

But Yehoishma shall not have the power to cohabitate [sic] with another man...[44]

That is, Yehoishma does not have the *legal right* to bring another man into her household, and breaking this agreement presumably abrogates her sole control over her household.

Akkadian šalāṭu refers to having authority to manage property,[45] but it also signifies independence and often appears in treaty contexts. One who acts independently is always the overlord.[46] In the Ezekiel text Jerusalem is playing the dominant role; thus, מעשׂה אשׁה זונה שׁלטת refers to a woman who is not only a prostitute out of necessity, but by her own choice. Financially and socially she is not only independent, but in a position to oversee or even dominate others. The woman of Ezekiel 16 revels in her independence.

e. *Inversion of Gender Order*
Most telling are vv. 30-34:

> How angry I became with you[47] declares YHWH God, when you did all those things, the acts of an independent prostitute, building your enclosure at every crossroad and setting your booth in every square! Yet you were not like a prostitute, for you reject fees; you were like the adulterous wife who welcomes strangers while under the authority[48] of her husband. Gifts are made to all prostitutes, but you have given gifts to all your lovers and have bribed them to come to you from every quarter with your promiscuous ways. Through your promiscuous ways, *you were the opposite of other women: you solicited instead of being solicited; you paid fees instead of being paid fees. Thus you were just the opposite!*

43. S. Greengus, 'A Textbook Case of Adultery in Ancient Mesopotamia', *HUCA* 40 (1969), pp. 33-44 (35).

44. Kraeling, *Aramaic Papers*, text 7.33.

45. *CAD* Š, p. 239, mng. 4.

46. *CAD* Š, pp. 238-39.

47. Interpretations of the phrase אמלה לבתך follow two basic lines: first לבה as a feminine form for heart and the verb as a qal participle of a by-form of מ-ל-ל, connected to Arab. *malla*, 'to be shaken with fever', thus yielding 'How lovesick was your heart'. The other reading connects לבה to Aramaic ל-ב-ה, 'wrath' and Akkadian *libbatu*, 'wrath', both of which appear with cognates of מ-ל-א. According to this line of thought, the verb should be pointed as a niphal, yielding, 'I am filled with wrath over you'. This suggests that the suffix is objective.

48. Instead of reading תחת אישׁה as 'instead/in place of her husband', we should read 'while under the authority of her husband'.

This passage speaks for itself: this female is aggressive, asserts power and independence. Interestingly, a recent comment on this passage points to the degree to which these verses are still powerful and threatening to men. Swanepoel writes: 'We are not even spared the greatest shock… That you pay your men instead of them paying you is surely the *summit of immorality*'.[49] And it is no accident that the word for opposite here is הפך, an overturning. From its contexts, the verb connotes not only a physical overthrow, but an inversion of nature where basic categories are subverted.

השמש יהפך לחשך והירח לדם לפני בוא יום יהוה הגדול והנורא

The sun shall turn into darkness and the moon into blood (Joel 3.4).

הפך ים ליבשה בנהר יעב׳רו ברגל שם נשמחה-בו

He turned the sea into dry land; they crossed the river on foot; we therefore rejoice in him (Ps. 66.6).

It is God who inverts darkness into light or who makes the sun become darkness. Zimmerli compares the word to the Greek phrase παρὰ φύσιν, found in Rom. 1.26 to describe homoerotic relationships, or an 'unnatural inversion of the human order'.[50]. Given this context, if the woman is opposite, this implies that she is no longer female, but male and that she is playing the role of God, inverting the 'natural order', or rather the divine order, by exhibiting male gender characteristics.

3. *Conclusions*

At a subtle level within the text of Ezekiel 16, wife Israel's crime is that she is trying to pass for a male. Like a male, she is associated with war and violence, she seeks multiple sexual partners,[51] she symbolically acquires male genitalia and ejaculates rather than receiving and containing fluids. Her תועבה, her abomination, is crossing gender boundaries. And it is no accident that the word תועבה is used here.

---

49. Swanepoel, 'Ezekiel 16', p. 89 (my italics). Unfortunately, he does not further explain what he understands by 'summit of immorality'.

50. W. Zimmerli, *Ezekiel 1: A Commentary on the Book of the Prophet Ezekiel Chapters 1–24* (trans. R.E. Clements; Hermeneia; Philadelphia: Fortress Press, 1979), p. 329.

51. Men could have multiple sexual partners, see Deut. 21.15-17; Ezek. 23 for examples of polygyny; for evidence of concubines see, for example, Gen. 16.3; 25.6; 30.3-10; 36.12; Judg. 8.30; 2 Sam. 3.7; 5.13; for female captives of war, see Num. 31.9; Deut. 20.14; 21.10-14; Judg. 5.30.

This word appears seven times in ch. 16.[52] תועבה indicates acts which violate God's nature, whether ethical (Prov. 17.15; 20.20) or cultic (Deut. 14.3, 17.1).[53] Cooke argues that the abomination is Baal-worship and participation in the Molech rites. Block points out that תועבה is usually cultic in Ezekiel, but that here 'there is a general shift in meaning': 'spiritual harlotry' is the sin.[54] Galambush disagrees with Block; she claims that the prophet is referring specifically to the abominations in the Temple.[55] But the offense against God lies in an even more profound place: Jerusalem has overstepped her limits vis à vis God. Where she should have been passive, dependent and connected only to YHWH, she became assertive, independent and non-monogamous. Her sins are against the 'natural' gender order, and her evils are so great, her actions so culturally male, that even her body is masculinized. Thomas Laqueur's observations are helpful here:

> it became increasingly clear that it is very difficult to read ancient, medieval, and Renaissance texts about the body with the epistemological lens of the Enlightenment through which the physical world—the body—appears as 'real', while its cultural meanings are epiphenomenal. Bodies in these texts did strange, remarkable, and to modern readers impossible things... There are numerous accounts of men who were said to lactate and pictures of the boy Jesus with breasts. Girls could turn into boys, and men who associated too extensively with women could lose the hardness and definition of their more perfect bodies and regress into effeminacy. Culture, in short, suffused and changed the body that to the modern sensibility seems so closed, autarchic, and outside the realm of meaning.[56]

The woman in vv. 14-43 takes what should be kept inside and brings it out, so to speak.

Again I return to my assertion at the outset of this essay: what is actually so remarkable about this text is that God does not have all the power! The story begins and ends in a fantasy or a myth of an all-powerful God and a completely submissive wife. However, the material embedded in this frame reveals a different dynamic. The

---

52. This word appears 43 times in the book of Ezekiel, almost all in the plural.

53. E. Gerstenberger describes תועבה as that which is 'incompatible with Yahweh's nature' ('תעב', *Theological Lexicon of the Old Testament* [eds. Ernst Jenni and Claus Westermann; trans. Mark E. Biddle; 3 vols.; Peabody, MA: Hendrickson Publishers, 1997], III, p. 1430).

54. Block, *Ezekiel*, p. 471.

55. Julie Galambush, *Jerusalem in the Book of Ezekiel: The City as Yahweh's Wife* (SBLDS, 130; Atlanta: Scholars Press, 1992).

56. Laqueur, *Making Sex*, p. 7.

center of the story expresses a much more volatile, chaotic relation-ship—one in which the deity does not have full control and in which wife Jerusalem is not completely submissive.

This radical admission is made even more radical by the metaphor in which it is expressed. The use of the marriage metaphor beckons us to read this text on more than one level. As we explore the power relationships between male and female, we are, in fact, exploring the power relationships between God and Israel. Additionally, Jerusalem is both female and male—female in relation to God, and male within the realm of human society. Jerusalem is at once powerful and utterly powerless. The male community, symbolically portrayed as a female, betrays its own maleness in Ezekiel 16. The marriage metaphor is not simply a vehicle, or a vessel for conveying a theological message. Ezekiel's use of the marriage metaphor embodies an outbreak of chaos. This is a story about cultural upheavals, social disintegration and theological crises, all expressed through the breakdown of one of the most fundamental cultural and social institutions: marriage and at its root, gender roles. At its core, this is a text about gender ambiguity and all its repercussions. Everything else flows out from this source.

Ezekiel's use of the marital metaphor in ch. 16 may be explained as follows: Ezekiel witnessed an age of extreme chaos—the experience of Exile, the destruction of Jerusalem and the Temple, and gender crisis.[57] He interpreted the chaos as a result of a disturbance of cosmic order. Ezekiel, like most thinkers of the biblical age, believed that the community of Israel had the power to invite chaos into the world. So, for example, Ezekiel's vision of the departure of YHWH's glory from the Temple is a direct result of the cultic and social crimes of his people (Ezek. 8–11). Similarly, Jacob Milgrom has shown how the priestly school held that God could be driven away from God's sancta by the introduction of contaminants.[58] The Deuteronomistic school believed that curses and calamities would befall the community should it turn away from God. Clearly, anxiety about the commun-ity's role in inviting chaos was prevalent among many schools of ancient Israel.[59]

Scholars generally agree that, on the historical level, Israel's crime is the forging of alliances with other nations and the desecration of the

---

57. For a more detailed discussion of the book of Ezekiel and emasculation, see my book, *Gender Reversal and Cosmic Chaos*.

58. Jacob Milgrom, *Leviticus 1–16* (AB; Garden City, NY: Doubleday, 1991).

59. Cf. also Jon Levenson, *Creation and the Persistence of Evil: The Jewish Drama of Divine Omnipotence* (Princeton, NJ: Princeton University Press, 1994 [1988]).

Temple cult. The punishment involves the divinely ordained invasion of the Babylonians into Jerusalem. The punishment having been carried out, Ezekiel is optimistic that order will return and that the people will return to the land of Israel and will be completely dependent on and loyal to God. The explicit metaphor of marriage is used to communicate the crimes of alliances and religious apostasy, but it does so by describing the people's actions as specific acts of infidelity. In this metaphor, the community invites chaos into the world by defiling its marriage to God.

In this essay I have argued that at a deeper level, beyond the marital metaphor, lies a profound anxiety regarding gender ambiguity. Thus, in Ezekiel 16, chaos emerges not only as a result of cultic and social crimes, but as a result of the subversion of gender order. On some level, Ezekiel believed that chaos began when female Israel started playing the role of a male—by acting as a sexually independent individual. The severity of the exilic experience could not be justified simply by the metaphor of an unfaithful wife, as other prophets had done; for Ezekiel's generation, the crime of the people had to strike at a deeper level—at the core of divinely sanctioned gender identities.

READING ZECHARIAH 5.5-11:
PROPHECY, GENDER AND (Ap)PERCEPTION*

Ulrike Sals

These notes treat one of the misogynist texts of the Old Testament: Zech. 5.5-11, the vision of the woman in the *ephah*.[1] In recent years interpretation of this text has been dominated by the question of whether this woman represents the goddess of another cult.[2] The following study will deal with several of the relevant aspects. After some introductory notes about Proto-Zechariah in general, I shall focus on the images in the text that provide us with the information about the woman in the *ephah*. Then I offer a text-immanent reading, and a consideration of the myth of Pandora before concluding with a short hermeneutical outlook.

Introduction: The Night Visions of Zechariah

The book of Zechariah is usually divided into three parts that are assumed to derive from three different sources: Proto-Zechariah (chs. 1–8); Deutero-Zechariah (chs. 9–11) and Trito-Zechariah (chs. 12–14). Our text, Zech. 5.5-11, is therefore a part of Proto-Zechariah.

After the Babylonian exile, Persian politics offered the Jews the possibility of returning to Israel. The questions of how, or even whether, this new beginning could be made was controversial (cf. Zech. 1.11; 2.11-12). Cultic questions, especially if and when there should be a

---

*   Many thanks to Charlotte Methuen for her help with the English.

1.   Throughout this article, the Hebrew איפה is transcribed as *ephah*.

2.   E.g. C.L. Meyers, E.M. Meyers, *Haggai, Zechariah 1–8* (AB, 25b; Garden City, NY: Doubleday, 1987); C. Uehlinger, 'Die Frau im Efa (Sach 5, 5-11): Eine Programmvision von der Abschiebung der Göttin', *BK* 49 (1994), pp. 93-103. M.H. Floyd reads Zech. 5.5-11 in the context of the two preceding night visions and assumes that the woman represents an alternative form of Judaism (M.H. Floyd, 'The Evil in the Ephah: Reading Zechariah 5.5-11 in its Literary Context', *CBQ* 58 [1996], pp. 51-68). These studies have given valuable impulses to my exegesis.

new Temple, were a part of this discussion. Both Zechariah and Haggai favoured a rapid rebuilding of the Temple and re-establishment of the Temple cult. For a short time these prophets achieved an enormous political influence.

> From the point of view of social history, the fundamental question is whether one should adapt to Persian sovereignty, allowing oneself to be restricted to a relative autonomy within the Province Judah, but achieving a stable political and religious environment, or whether one should dream of political independence, the re-establishment of the Davidic monarchy, the understanding of the Jerusalem Temple as the centre of the whole world, and all that bound together by world-wide peace and social justice.[3]

Whereas the former position is held by Ezra and Nehemiah, among others, the latter position is represented by prophets such as Haggai and Zechariah.[4] However, their interests are not identical: Haggai is primarily concerned with the Temple, while Zechariah considers all aspects of a return to Jerusalem and the introduction of a new political and cultic order.[5] The text of Proto-Zechariah recognizes that 'beginning' is a process rather than a state.

The textual structure of Proto-Zechariah is concentric: its beginning and end (1.1-6; 7.1–8.23) are related to each other. The centre of the text are the eight 'night visions', which are in their turn concentric too: the two outer visions I and VIII (1.7-17; 6.1-8) deal with an exploration of the whole earth; visions II (2.1-4) and VII (5.5-11) treat the peoples and countries who have suppressed Israel; while visions III (2.5-17) and VI (5.1-4) focus on Jerusalem's reconstruction and the treatment of internal foes. The textual and topographical centre of the sequence are visions IV (3.1-10) and V (4.1-14), which describe the purification of the high priest, the great menorah in holy peace and the legitimation of the leaders of Israel.[6]

---

3.   R. Kessler, 'Mirjam und die Prophetie der Perserzeit', in U. Bail and R. Jost (eds.), *Gott an den Rändern. Sozialgeschichtliche Perspektiven auf die Bibel* (Festschrift Willy Schottroff; Gütersloh: Chr. Kaiser Verlag, 1996), pp. 64-72 (68). See also the translation of Kessler's article in this volume.

4.   Kessler, 'Mirjam'.

5.   P. Marinkovic, 'What Does Zechariah 1–8 Tell Us about the Second Temple?', in T.C. Eskenazi and K.H. Richards (eds.), *Second Temple Studies 2: Temple and Community in the Persian Period* (JSOTSup, 175; Sheffield: Sheffield Academic Press, 1994), pp. 88-103. For Zechariah's place in the history of Israel's prophecy see J.E. Tollington, *Tradition and Innovation in Haggai and Zechariah 1–8* (JSOTSup, 150; Sheffield: Sheffield Academic Press, 1993).

6.   Some scholars assume Zech. 3.1-10 to be redactional, so they count only

The night visions are precisely dated: it is the twenty-fourth day of the eleventh month in the second year of the Persian King Darius, that is 15 February, 519 BCE.[7] The specificity of this date implies that the cycle presents a series of visions that seized the prophet in one night.

Zechariah 5.5-11

5   And the angel speaking to me came out and said to me:
    'Lift up your eyes and look: what is this coming out?'
6   And I said:
    'What is it?'
    and he said:
    'It is the ephah coming out',
    and he said:
    'It is their view in all the land'.
7   And behold a lead weight lifted itself up, and there was one woman sitting in the ephah.
8   And he said:
    'She is unrighteousness'.
    And he threw her into the middle of the ephah and he threw the lead stone on its mouth.
9   And I lifted up my eyes and looked, and behold, two women were coming out and they had wind in their wings — their wings were like stork's wings — and they lifted up the ephah between earth and heaven.
10 And I said to the angel speaking to me:
    'Where are they going to take the ephah?'
11 And he said to me:
    'To build her a temple in the land of Shinar and to establish it, and she will be set down on her base'.

seven night visions, seeing vision IV (Zech. 4.1-4) as the pivotal one. See e.g. K. Seybold, *Bilder zum Tempelbau: Die Visionen des Propheten Sacharja* (SBS, 70; Stuttgart: KBW, 1974), pp. 16-17; K. Elliger, *Das Buch der zwölf Kleinen Propheten*. II. *Die Propheten Nahum, Habakuk, Zephanja, Haggai, Sacharja, Maleachi* (ATD, 25; Göttingen: Vandenhoeck & Ruprecht, 8th edn, 1982), pp. 119-22; H.G. Reventlow, *Die Propheten Haggai, Sacharja und Maleachi* (ATD, 25.2; Göttingen: Vandenhoeck & Ruprecht, 9th edn, 1993), pp. 32-33; P.L. Redditt, *Haggai, Zechariah and Malachi* (NCB; Grand Rapids: Eerdmans, 1995), p. 41. Others remain with the text: D.L. Petersen, *Haggai and Zechariah 1–8: A Commentary* (OTL; Philadelphia: Westminster Press, 1984), p. 112; Meyers and Meyers, *Haggai, Zechariah 1–8*, p. 215; R. Hanhart, *Sacharja* (BKAT, 14.7; Neukirchen–Vluyn: Neukirchener Verlag, 1990), p. 213; B.C. Ollenburger, 'The Book of Zechariah: Introduction, Commentary and Reflections', in Leane E. Ked *et al.* (eds.), *The New Interpreter's Bible*, VII (Nashville: Abingdon Press, 1996), pp. 733-840 (737).
    7.   Hanhart, *Sacharja*, pp. 9-43.

This text dates to the end of the exile. Babylon had conquered Judah, destroyed Jerusalem and the Temple, and exiled many Judeans. Now the Persians are making a new beginning possible. It is precisely at this historical point that Zech. 5.5-11 presents a text about Shinar (Babylon) without significant recourse to traditional images of Babylon as they are found in the prophecies of Jeremiah or Isaiah. Instead the author constructs a relationship between place, gender and opposition to God by relating Babylon, woman and unrighteousness. Zechariah avoids the use of traditional images, but by different ways and means succeeds in achieving the same result: the corroboration of this relationship. By weaving together 'woman', 'unrighteousness' and 'Shinar' the text gives an aetiology of woman as evil. By explaining how the evil woman comes to Shinar, this passage provides a kind of birth story for the image of the whore of Babylon.[8] It locates sin in Shinar, placing the wicked things (evil and woman) where Zechariah believes them to belong.

(Ap)Perception in Zechariah 5.5-11

What The Text Says – And What it Does Not Say
Even more than other parts of the night visions, Zech. 5.5-11 is highly suggestive, as Floyd has pointed out:

> The few words of explanation given in the conversation between the angel and the prophet scarcely provide the reader with enough information to grasp the significance of the strange things that appear and happen. In order to make sense of the vision, the reader must presuppose some context in which to fit the fragmentary bits of imagery, action, and dialogue that are so starkly juxtaposed on so blank a background.[9]

The high tempo of this text leaves many blanks and gaps, giving few concrete indications but offering many subtle allusions to aid its interpretation.

The more closely the reader looks at the plot, the more gaps she sees. Right at the beginning the reader is not told where the angel 'comes out' (יצא) from. The same applies to the *ephah*: where does it come from and how does it move? Some scholars presume that it is flying,[10] but we are not told. The reader is literally left in the dark of

8.   Cf. H. Gese, 'Anfang und Ende der Apokalyptik, dargestellt am Sacharja-buch', *ZTK* 70 (1973), pp. 20-49 (31).
9.   Floyd, 'The Evil in the Ephah', p. 51.
10.   E.g. Ollenburger, 'Zechariah', p. 737; M.H. Floyd, 'Cosmos and History in

the vision. We are shown only the middle part of the whole process—or procession. The angel identifies the *ephah* as 'their view' or 'their sin' (see below) but does not give any clue about who 'they' are (v. 6). The action of v. 8 follows: the angel throws the woman into the *ephah*—but she is already sitting in it! Was she trying to escape or did he pull her out? Then the women with storks' wings appear—once more apparently from nowhere. We are told that they lift the *ephah*, but that they carry it away is indirect information assumed from the prophet's question in v. 10. Even v. 11—the focus of the whole section—is not clear: the sentence could refer to either the *ephah* or the woman. The final blank occurs outside the text, after v. 11: many modern commentators, and perhaps some ancient ones, complete v. 11 with 'and be worshipped', a conclusion clearly suggested but not explicitly expressed in the text.[11] The plot is at best a collection of still frames.

The images that appear in the vision are puzzling, at least to modern commentators, because they do not include classical theological motifs such as the shepherd. Here we have a woman shut up inside a grain measure that is closed with a lead lid, women with storks' wings and finally a pedestal of the type that used to stand in the Jerusalem Temple (2 Kgs 16.17).[12] Nor are the verbs used precise: they are few and used to refer to many different kinds of movement: the angel comes forth (5.5), as does the visionary object (5.5, 6, 9); the prophet lifts his eyes (5.5) just as the stork-winged women lift the *ephah* (5.9).[13]

The relation between the image and its interpretation provides for additional problems. In the first part of the text two components, the *ephah* and the woman, are interpreted by being named. The other images, especially the stork-winged women and their action, are not interpreted; nor is a summarizing interpretation offered. In the last

Zechariah's View of the Restoration (Zechariah 1.7–6.15)', in H.T. Sun *et al.* (eds.), *Problems in Biblical Theology: Festschrift Rolf Knierim* (Grand Rapids: Eerdmans, 1997), pp. 125-44 (135).

11. Petersen, *Haggai and Zechariah 1–8*, p. 262; Redditt, *Haggai, Zechariah and Malachi*, p. 74.

12. The precise meaning of מכונה in Zech. 5.11 is not clear. In 1 Kgs 7; 2 Kgs 16.17; 25.13, 16; and 2 Chron. 4.14 מכונה is a concrete object in the Temple (cf. also Jer. 27.19; 52.17, 20); in Ezra 3.3 it means 'place'; in Sir. 41.1; 44.6 it is used in a profane sense. Whether Zech. 5.11 is a late use of the older meaning or an early use of the younger 'place' is debated. For the word and its meanings see K. Koch, 'כון', in *ThWAT*, IV, cols. 95-107 (96).

13. Meyers and Meyers, *Haggai, Zechariah 1–8*, p. 306.

verse of the section the angel draws a cultic connection: in v. 11 the woman of the *ephah* is set up to be worshipped like a goddess. But it seems to me unclear whether the woman is a goddess during the whole process or whether she becomes one only when she arrives in Shinar. The reader is left with two small hints at the beginning of the passage to help her perceive and understand the rest of the action.

On the level of form and content, there is a contrast of movement and non-movement. Although the text depicts many movements, and is a truly dynamic vision, nearly all the verbs on the level of the vision are participles. Movements seem to be stiffened, whereas the tempo of the narrative is very fast, with its short sentences, its lack of description or illustration, and its rapid switches between speakers.

To make all this even more complex, the vision, its interpretation and its meaning are portrayed in terms of a dialogue between the two visionary figures, the prophet and the angel. Even more than in the other visions of Zech. 1–8, this vision takes place in dialogue.[14]

The highly suggestive effect of the text is demonstrated by interpretations that read into it details or descriptive elements which are simply not there. Thus we can read that the woman is very ugly[15] or that she must be imagined as a great beauty;[16] that the story is a merry parody,[17] or that it has an odour of something disreputable and forbidden.[18] The text includes the traps for these readings. Its meaning is illustrated by silence.

What the Prophet Sees – And What He Does Not See
The prophet's ability to see the vision is poor. Asked by the angel to look at what comes forth, either the prophet cannot see the *ephah*, or he cannot name it. This is all the more astonishing because an *ephah*

---

14. Cf. J.-M. Vincent, 'Von der feurigen Herrlichkeit JHWHs in Jerusalem: Eine Auslegung von Sach 2, 5-9', in *idem*, *Das Auge hört: Die Erfahrbarkeit Gottes im Alten Testament* (Biblisch-theologische Studien, 34; Neukirchen–Vluyn: Neukirchener Verlag, 1998), pp. 99-134, pp. 111-12 concerning 2.6: the dialogue between the measuring person and the prophet specifies the vision. What is seen needs a supplement in order to be seen correctly. Cf. Meyers and Meyers, *Zechariah 1–8*, p. 151.

15. K. Koch, *Die Profeten*. II. *Babylonisch-persische Zeit* (Stuttgart: Kohlhammer, 2nd edn, 1988), p. 173.

16. M. Haller, *Das Judentum: Geschichtsschreibung, Prophetie und Gesetzgebung nach dem Exil* (SAT, 2.3; Göttingen: Vandenhoeck & Ruprecht, 2nd edn, 1925), p. 104.

17. Seybold, *Bilder zum Tempelbau*, p. 56.

18. Uehlinger, 'Die Frau im Efa', p. 97. The citations are also used by Uehlinger.

was a common dry measure, an everyday object. This not-knowing or
not-being-able-to-see stands in contrast to the preceding vision, in
which the prophet saw a flying scroll with the dimensions of the
(Solomonic) Temple porch (Zech. 5.2; cf. 1 Kgs 6.3; Ezek. 40.49;
2 Chron. 3.4). Not only could Zechariah describe this unusual sight of
a flying scroll, he could also state exactly its enormous dimensions.

The prophet asks 'What is this?' (5.6). In fact, he asks this question
quite often, but in all other occurrences of the question he receives an
interpretation of the vision in response. In this vision the question is
answered by a description: it is thus not entirely clear whether the
ephah is the image or whether it is an interpretation that is subsequently interpreted a second time.

As is generally the case in the night visions, all the prophet's utterances are questions. 'Where are they taking the *ephah*?' he asks next.
The question is doubly astonishing: firstly, his sentence is grammatically incorrect, since he uses the masculine pronoun to refer to the
stork-winged women; and secondly he asks for a continuation of the
vision rather than for its interpretation. This question and the angel's
answer draw a parallel between this and the third vision (2.5-9) about
the measuring of Jerusalem.

What the Angel Interprets – And How He (Inter)Acts
The interpreting angel assumes many roles: he takes over the part of
the visionary (5.6), directs the prophet's attention, interprets some
elements of the vision, intervenes in the vision's action (5.8) and gives
the whole event a new meaning (5.11). The angel is the one who
connects 'woman', 'unrighteousness' and 'Shinar'.

In 5.5-11 the angel steps not only into the image but also into the
plot. By crossing the boundary between vision and reality, the angel
breaks up the vision. He is not only an interpreting angel but also an
interacting angel. The objects in the vision and the angel become connected in such a way that either the angel becomes a part of the vision
or the vision becomes a part of reality. In many ways the latter is
more likely, because it is hard to imagine that the messenger of God is
not real. The boundaries of vision and reality are also crossed by the
prophet himself in the third vision (2.5-9), when he sees a man with a
measuring line. 'Where are you going?' asks the prophet. 'To measure
Jerusalem!' responds the man – an object in the vision.

The angel's action thus implies that there is no longer a separate
visionary world. That he can act in this way shows that the vision is
reality; and this means in turn that this is a real woman. It is a real
woman whom he treats violently: the impression of brutality is

increased by the anthropomorphic description of the opening of the *ephah* as a 'mouth'. If the visionary images are part of reality this will have important consequences: the thieves and false-swearers of the preceding vision are really threatened death (5.4); and the woman who is identified with unrighteousness is really treated brutally. The angel is an interpreter of an image violating that image.

The prophet (and the reader) must rely entirely on the interpreting angel. This becomes especially clear in vv. 10-11, where the prophet's and the angel's ability to communicate with each other or with the reader seem to be lost. Grammatically v. 11 is not distinct, for the interpreter not only does not really answer the prophet's question, but also does not even utter a full sentence. Nevertheless, v. 11 contains the weight of the whole text and gives a second explication of the image and its meaning. The angel's answer to the prophet's question does not answer the question, but at the same time it contains more information than had been asked for. As well as naming the destination, it offers three additional bits of information which make the same point in ascending order: that the woman/unrighteousness will remain in Shinar for a long time; a house will be prepared for her; and she will be set up on a cultic device. Although the answer in v. 11 is a part of the image, it offers at the same time an important contribution to the interpretation of the image. The text claims that unrighteousness will be cultivated and worshipped in Shinar.

The Power of Definition

Through its many acts of naming, all pronounced in nominal sentences, the text reveals the extent to which prophecy is a translation. All the perspectives given in the text are male perspectives, while everything that is named is grammatically feminine. The feminine pronoun appears five times in these six verses. In Zech. 5.5 the genus of 'what is coming out there' is the only information we are given about it: 'The author built the reader's suspense by not identifying the *ephah* immediately, but he did employ feminine singular pronouns, anticipating the feminine singular noun *ephah*'.[19]

---

19. Redditt, *Haggai, Zechariah and Malachi*, p. 73. In Hebrew the grammatical feminine also signifies neuter, so that the question in 5.5 ('What is this?') can refer to something that is grammatically either neuter or feminine. In the other occurrences of זאת in Zech. 5.5-11 the reference is either to something grammatically feminine or to the opening question in v. 6. In all other occurrences of the question 'What is this?' the prophet uses the plural form מָה־אֵלֶּה (Zech. 2.2; 5.5, 13; 6.4). In two cases the personal pronoun is masculine (1.9; 4.5); this is the only use of the feminine. In all other occurrences where a personal pronoun singular is used, the

We do not have the woman's perspective, and in fact it is only as a consequence of the angel's definition and action that the woman appears to be a menace. Although she is the one who experiences violence, she is said to be dangerous. The angel's definition is performative language. As such it demonstrates the power of definition: the angel having defined the woman as unrighteousness, it is plausible to the reader that the woman should be treated badly. His definition is the explanation of his behaviour and his behaviour is the reason for the definition.

In this text we have a prophet who cannot see or explain and who is thus no prophet at all, an interpreting angel who is also an interacting angel, a bushel that may or may not be a view, and a real woman who is a gendered symbol. The ability to see, to name and to interpret prophecy is problematized in a dialogue in which sex and gender play an important role.

Text and Contexts of Zechariah 5.5-11

The Woman as Evil

The central image of the vision is that of a woman sitting in the *ephah*. The angel says of the woman: 'This is unrighteousness' (זֹאת הָרִשְׁעָה). What is he saying with the term 'unrighteousness'? The noun רִשְׁעָה occurs fourteen times in the Hebrew Bible, usually in explicit opposition to the term צְדָקָה (Exod. 18.20, 27; 33.12, 19; Prov. 11.5; 13.6; Deut. 9.4-5), and signifies the behaviour of a wicked person taken as a whole. Similar, and far more frequent, is the masculine רֶשַׁע.[20] Both words articulate Israelite mentality in that concrete behaviour is clearly signified by רֶשַׁע/רִשְׁעָה, but this behaviour is not explicitly defined. רִשְׁעָה is used three times to (dis)qualify foreign peoples' conduct and their laws (Deut. 9.4-5; Mal. 1.4; Ezek. 25.6). Applied to the people of Israel, it signifies abandoning God's laws and as such is judged worse than foreign peoples' conduct (Ezek. 5.5-9).

More information can be given about the meaning of רֶשַׁע, the wicked one, a conceptual opposite to צַדִּיק, the righteous one. רֶשַׁע is a broad term signifying certain (negatively assessed) behaviour and its consequences in questions of law, business and trade, in relationships with the righteous ones and with God. The wicked one is often

---

angel is speaking and he always knows what he is referring to. Therefore in 5.5 זאת refers to something that is feminine rather than neuter.

20. Ringgren, 'רשע', in *ThWAT*, VII, cols. 675-84 (682-83).

characterized as self-confident (Ps. 73.3, 75.5, 94.4-5 etc.).[21] Generally the term is applied to members of the people of Israel (exceptions are Ezek. 7.21; Ps. 9). Although the root רשע has some religious nuances — it characterizes the רָשָׁע's relation to God or marks bad behaviour in liturgical formulae (1 Kgs 8.47; 2 Chron. 6.37; Dan. 9.5, 15; Ps. 106.6; Neh. 9.33; Jer. 14.20) — there is only one *ex negativo* connection to idolatry: the righteous one abstains from idolatry (Ezek. 18.5-6); presumably the wicked one does not.

Zechariah 5.5-11 does not reflect a cultic connotation of the word רִשְׁעָה,[22] although it creates such a connotation in v. 11. Putting together the general semantics of the root רשע with Zech. 5.5-11 suggests that the juridical and ethical term generally used to indicate illegal and illegitimate conduct within the community is here connected with false cult. In this text the term, together with the woman it signifies, expands to occupy the entire spectrum of detestable behaviour.

Because רשע generally signifies public behaviour, it is not often used in biblical texts to refer to women.[23] Thus the identification of this woman with unrighteousness in Zech. 5.5-11 is surprising. We have here a constructed definition, that 'the woman is unrighteousness', which is not based upon a traditional *tertium comparationis* or even a possible one. Because the term 'unrighteousness' is personified in such a general way ('one woman'), unrighteousness is gendered as feminine. The identification has two important consequences. The text makes an anthropological statement about the woman, and it alienates the woman.

The woman in the *ephah* is carried into exile: unrighteousness is banished, but at the same time the woman is made the Strange Woman. In the historical situation of the text, that is, in the phase of return from the exile, such argumentation through gendered statements has enormous significance, for it acts to legitimate treatment of foreign women such as that portrayed later by the books Ezra and Nehemiah (Ezra 9, 10; Neh. 13). In this way the events portrayed in the historical books are given prophetic — even angelic — support.[24]

21. Ringgren, 'רשע', col. 679.

22. Against Meyers and Meyers, *Zechariah 1–8*, pp. 302-303.

23. One of the only two other texts is Qoh. 7.25-26. Here women in general are judged worse than death. The other text is a characterization of Athaliah. She is said to be המרשעת — 'the unrighteous' (2 Chron. 24.7), doing unrighteous things (2 Chron. 22.3).

24. Uehlinger's subtitle ('Eine Programmvision von der Abschiebung der Göttin') emphasizes that the deportation of people who are declared 'foreigners' is still a political problem which all too often receives theological support.

By mixing 'reality' and 'vision' the text claims the vision as reality. It anthropologizes its theme. What could have been 'only' a symbol becomes a characterization. This woman is passive and is described only as 'a woman': she has no specific attributes. It is easy for the reader to see her as Woman. Whereas in other prophetic texts leaving God or doing wrong is put in terms of the metaphor of a whoring woman (e.g. Ezek. 16; Jer. 2) whose actions cause her to be condemned, in this text the reference to a quite unspecified woman seems to suffice. The lack of any attributes makes it difficult or even impossible to identify this woman with any particular goddess or cult, but at the same time facilitates the interpretation of the image as an anthropological statement associating women and unrighteousness. The fact that no specific land is mentioned as a context places the prophet and vision in a visionary nowhere (or everywhere?) and serves to emphasize the association.[25] The text gives rise to the reading that the woman in the *ephah* is at one and the same time the strange woman *and* every woman, and that woman is intrinsically linked to unrighteousness.

It is important to note that this is an association drawn forth by the angel's interpretation of the image in the vision. Some scholars have tended to presume the association as a fact:[26] for instance, Rudolph connects the woman in the *ephah* with Eve.[27] Because the word 'Shinar' occurs here as well as in Gen. 11.1, Petersen assumes that Zech. 5.5-11 is connected with Genesis 3 and 6.1-4.[28] Although the text indeed suggests such a reading, it should be recognized that scholars do not interpret similar visionary associations with scrolls (5.1-4), riders (1.8) or smiths (2.1-4) as a basis for general assertions about the intrinsic character of scrolls, smiths or riders! Interestingly, the two stork-winged women in this vision are also not used as the basis for general statements about 'woman'.[29]

---

25. Although the night visions are precisely dated, it is not clear where the prophet is: still in Babylonia? In Israel? In between? Or somewhere else entirely? I understand this as a theological statement: it is unimportant where the Israelites are, but it is important that they can and will come back soon—so soon that the exact day is of importance.

26. E.g. Elliger, *Das Buch der zwölf Kleinen Propheten*, p. 112.

27. W. Rudolph, *Haggai – Sacharja 1–8 – Sacharja 9–14 – Maleachi* (KAT, 13.4; Gütersloh: Gerd Mohn, 1976), p. 120.

28. Petersen, *Haggai and Zechariah 1–8*, pp. 258-59.

29. Cf. Rudolph, *Haggai – Sacharja 1–8 – Sacharja 9–14 – Maleachi*, p. 120.

The Ephah

The first component of the vision (here treated second) is the *ephah* in which the woman sits. An *ephah* is a dry measure of about 22–40 litres. The unjust *ephah* (רשע איפה) was one cause of prophetic criticism (Amos 8.5; Mic. 6.10; Deut. 25.13-15; Prov. 20.10). Possessing a just *ephah* (צדק איפה) is connected with the Exodus, the giving of the Torah (Lev. 19.36-37), and promise of a long life in Israel (Deut. 25.15; cf. Ezek. 45.10): in short, the true and just measure is a guarantee that there will never again be an exile. Maybe in this text it is the unjust *ephah* that is taken away.[30]

The ephah in Zech. 5.5-11 is interpreted as עינם, a substantive singular with a masculine plural suffix. But there is no group in the text to which this suffix could apply. The suffix might indicate to everyone,[31] those who live in the land,[32] or the thieves and false-swearers of the preceding vision.[33] There is no compelling solution to this problem, but the suffix points to the representative character of the interpretation: the *ephah* is somehow related to a masculine marked group whose identity seems to be unimportant. The only information about this group is its masculine gender. (Grammatical) gender and sex seem to be important in this text, but the precise group to which the *ephah* is related seems to be less important than the interpretation of the woman who is in the *ephah*.

What does the substantive mean? The translation of עינם is 'their view' (in the sense of what their eyes see).[34] However, many exegetes follow the LXX and change this term to עונם, which means 'their sin'.[35]

---

30. This is already the interpretation in Targum Jonathan. For this see M. Delcor, 'La vision de la femme dans l'épha de Zach., 5, 5-11 à la lumière de la littérature hittite', *RHR* 187 (1975), pp. 137-45 (138-39). Cf. Petersen, *Haggai and Zechariah 1–8*, p. 258.

31. Elliger, *Das Buch der zwölf Kleinen Propheten*, p. 112; Uehlinger, 'Die Frau im Efa', p. 95.

32. Rudolph, *Haggai – Sacharja 1–8 – Sacharja 9–14 – Maleachi*, p. 119; Reventlow, *Die Propheten Haggai, Sacharja und Maleachi*, p. 66.

33. Floyd, 'The Evil in the Ephah', p. 59. Hanhart (*Sacharja*, p. 354) connects both possibilities: the suffix applies to the thieves and false-swearers, and they represent the sinful creation. Meyers and Meyers (*Haggai, Zechariah 1–8*, p. 298) consider the possibility of an old-fashioned dual that does not distinguish between masculine or feminine and which could, therefore, point to the two women. However, they themselves are not convinced by this interpretation.

34. O. Keel, *Deine Blicke sind Tauben: Zur Metaphorik des Hohen Liedes* (Stuttgart: Katholisches Bibelwerk, 1984), pp. 54-56.

35. E.g. Seybold, *Bilder zum Tempelbau*, p. 28; Rudolph, *Haggai – Sacharja 1–8 – Sacharja 9–14 – Maleachi*, p. 118; Elliger, *Das Buch der zwölf Kleinen Propheten*, p. 106;

The textual uncertainty at this point is unfortunate, because the text offers the reader only two hints for the interpretation of the image, and now one of them threatens to be useless. Furthermore, the text does not relate the image or its interpretation to a *tertium comparationis*, so we must appeal to text historical arguments. These do not resolve the discrepancy between the Hebrew text and the LXX,[36] but in fact the alternatives are not as far from each other as it might seem. Indeed, in one reading of the night visions they are juxtaposed: seven eyes of God are engraved in one stone; they roam through the whole earth and take away its sin on one single day (Zech. 3.9; 4.10).[37] Perhaps what is announced in 3.9; 4.10 is fulfilled in 5.5-11.

What are the consequences of a decision? If the text means that the *ephah* should be understood as 'their view in the whole earth', it implies that (female) unrighteousness, represented by the woman, lies in (male) eyes and demonstrates the way in which the process of seeing encloses and constitutes reality. This image sees the woman as object while males are subjects, as observers and definers. Reading the text as 'their view' doubles the act of viewing: the prophet is mirrored in his own vision. Changing the text to עונם, 'their sin' gives an explicit theological note to both interpretation and image. Different images (*ephah* and woman) represent similar interpretations (sin and unrighteousness).[38]

36. The discussion will not be rendered here, but see D. Barthélemy, *Critique textuelle de l'Ancient Testament*, III (OBO, 50.3; Fribourg: Editions Universitaires Fribourg Suisse; Göttingen: Vandenhoeck & Ruprecht, 1992), pp. 957-58; Meyers and Meyers, *Haggai, Zechariah 1–8*, p. 297-98; and Hanhart, *Sacharja*, p. 353. It is possible to understand *ephah* not as a Hebrew but as a Babylonian word *E-pa* 'summit house', denoting the shrine surmounting a zikkurat (Meyers and Meyers, *Haggai, Zechariah 1–8*, p. 296). 'If "Ephah" can be associated with a Mesopotamian shrine, the MT would correctly be referring to its visibility' (Meyers and Meyers, *Haggai, Zechariah 1–8*, p. 298).

37. It is likely that the position of 4.10 is the result of a scribe's moving it from its original position after 3.9. See commentaries to 3.9 and 4.10.

38. Petersen's semantic analysis concludes that רשעה and עונם are similar but represent different aspects: 'If רשע can be used to describe the improper act, then עונם refers to the sin guilt incurred by such action. The *ephah* with the woman inside, as guilt with sin inside it, represents the total package of error: the act and its consequences' (Petersen, *Haggai and Zechariah 1–8*, p. 257).

The Women with the Storks' Wings

The *ephah* with the woman inside is carried to Shinar by two women who are probably female angels. In common with the woman they carry, they are described only as 'women'. But it is not clear precisely what sort of beings they are, and this depends largely upon the meaning of the storks' wings. Should these be seen positively (storks are reliable migrant birds [Jer. 8.7])[39] or do they imply that these women are to be ridiculed (storks are unclean [Lev. 11.19; Deut. 14.18])?[40] This remains controversial. That they carry unrighteousness away is surely to Israel's advantage, whether they do it voluntarily or not, but it is not clear whether these women are to be associated with God or with the woman in the *ephah*.[41]

The text emphasizes that the woman in the *ephah* is *one* woman and the stork-winged women are *two* women. Although their identity remains mysterious they are active in the vision, and perhaps it is significant that in the prophet's eyes they are not really female. He asks 'Where are they going to carry the *ephah*?' (v. 10), and uses the masculine pronoun. The angel has no contact with them, and does not even mention them in his response. Although it is not clear what this non-existent connection between the male angel and the two female angels means, it can once more be seen that gender and sex are of great importance in this vision.

The Woman in Shinar

On her arrival in Shinar, the woman in the *ephah* remains passive; she is not acting but again being acted upon; her passiveness stands in sharp contrast to the activity of God's agents.[42] In v. 11 she is given a house and is settled there. She gains power but this takes place

39. Rudolph, *Haggai – Sacharja 1–8 – Sacharja 9–14 – Maleachi*, p. 120; Meyers and Meyers, *Haggai, Zechariah 1–8*, pp. 306-307; Hanhart, *Sacharja*, pp. 357-58; Reventlow, *Die Propheten Haggai, Sacharja und Maleachi*, p. 66. Butterworth considers that the root חסד may be understood as the opposite of רשׁע (M. Butterworth, *Structure and the Book of Zechariah* [JSOTSup, 130; Sheffield: Sheffield Academic Press, 1992], p. 135).

40. Petersen, *Haggai and Zechariah 1–8*, p. 260 assumes that the combination of both qualities makes the storks suitable for this purpose.

41. B. Schmitgen, 'Die Bücher Haggai und Sacharja: Neuer Tempel – neues Leben für alle', in L. Schottroff and M.-T. Wacker (eds.), *Kompendium Feministische Bibelauslegung* (Gütersloh: Chr. Kaiser Verlag/Gütersloher Verlagshaus, 1998), pp. 366-75 (373).

42. Schmitgen, 'Die Bücher Haggai und Sacharja', p. 373.

outside the boundaries of the text: after the end of v. 11 the woman is going to be worshipped as a goddess.

The Action – Carrying Unrighteousness to Shinar
Having looked at the images and their interpretations the question arises what this rather strange action can mean. Why does the angel treat the woman so badly? Why is she carried to Shinar, neither in earth nor in heaven, but between the two (v. 9b)?

The text of Zech. 5.5-11 can be convincingly read in terms of ritual laws and the associated acts. Some scholars have seen parallels between Zech. 5.5-11 and the rites of purification in Leviticus 14; 16,[43] believing that Zechariah shows the purification of God's community.[44] However, an essential component of the ritual in Leviticus 14 and 16 is the slaughtering of one of a pair of animals (birds in Lev. 14; rams in Lev. 16) for a blood rite,[45] while the other animal is set free to carry the sins of Israel away into the desert (Lev. 14.7, 53; 16.21-22).[46] The constellation in Zech. 5.5-11 is different: here the two stork-winged women both carry the woman in the *ephah* to Shinar. Moreover, there is no identity of terminology between Zech. 5.5-11 and the ritual processes in Leviticus.[47] The perspectives of Zech. 5.5-11 and Leviticus 14; 16 are also fundamentally different: whereas in the purification of Israel the object is sent away from the centre (the temple or the holy tent) into the nowhere of the desert (Lev. 16) or the open field (Lev. 14),[48] in Zech. 5.5-11 we witness an infection with sin, as the object is brought from nowhere to Shinar and fixed there.[49] But

43. E.g. Rudolph, *Haggai – Sacharja 1–8 – Sacharja 9–14 – Maleachi*, p. 121; Seybold, *Bilder zum Tempelbau*, p. 77; D.P. Wright, *The Disposal of Impurity: Elimination Rites in the Bible and in Hittite and Mesopotamian Literature* (SBLDS, 101; Atlanta: Scholars Press, 1987), p. 273 n. 150; Reventlow, *Die Propheten Haggai, Sacharja und Maleachi*, p. 67; Floyd, 'The Evil in the Ephah', p. 64.

44. Elliger, *Das Buch der zwölf Kleinen Propheten*, p. 112.

45. Cf. V. Haas, 'Ein hurritischer Blutritus und die Deponierung der Ritualrückstände nach hethitischen Quellen', in B. Janowski, K. Koch and G. Wilhelm (eds.), *Religionsgeschichtliche Beziehungen zwischen Kleinasien, Nordsyrien und dem Alten Testament: Internationales Symposium Hamburg 17.–21. März 1990* (OBO, 129; Freiburg: Universitätsverlag Freiburg/Schweiz; Göttingen: Vandenhoeck & Ruprecht, 1993), pp. 67-85 (69).

46. Cf. Wright, *The Disposal of Impurity*, pp. 25-30.

47. Lev. 16.22 is closest to Zech. 5.5-11 if one looks only at the words.

48. Cf. Wright, *The Disposal of Impurity*, pp. 78-80. In Mic. 7.19 God throws all sins into the deep sea.

49. This is the more striking since the use of יצא in the Hebrew Bible often names a starting point or at least hints at one; see H.D. Preuss, 'יצא', in ThWAT, III,

although there are no major correspondences between the *texts* of Leviticus 14; 16 and Zech. 5.5-11, the *processes* described in them do demonstrate functional, i.e. cathartic-eliminatory, parallels that can also be found in a number of other ancient Near Eastern texts.[50]

The most general intention of cathartic rites is the mobilization of impurity.[51] Impurity is understood as substantial. Generally there are two possibilities of mobilization: if the miasma is in finger-nails, saliva, or cleaning water or is transferred to one of these, the pollutant can be neutralized by enclosing it in a vessel. The same can be done with a god's or goddess's wrath (e.g. Telipinu KUB XVII, 10 or Lelwani Bo 7615).[52] In most of these texts, it is essential that the vessel be closed with a lead lid, well locked, and deposited far away in a safe place. All these characteristics can be found in Zech. 5.5-11.

A second possibility for getting rid of evil is to transfer it onto a living substitute. This is the ritual found in Leviticus 14; 16. There is the Hittite plague ritual (KUB IX, 32)[53] in which, after the performance of ritual actions, a ram and a woman are designated to carry the plague away into the enemy's land. The ram acts as a substitute for the camp's inhabitants and the woman substitutes its king. The following formula is spoken: 'Lo, the evil that was in this camp for people, cattle, sheep, horses, mules, and asses, lo, this ram and this

cols. 795-822 (798). By his use of this verb Zechariah draws attention to the starting point while at the same time refusing to name it.

50. For Lev. 16 and its religio-historical context see B. Janowski and G. Wilhelm, 'Der Bock, der die Sünden hinausträgt: Zur Religionsgeschichte des Azazel-Ritus Lev. 16, 10.21f', in Janowski, Wilhelm and Koch (eds.), *Religionsgeschichtliche Beziehungen*, pp. 109-69; for the blood rite in Lev. 14, the act in Zech. 5.5-11 and possible religio-historical parallels see Haas, 'Ein hurritischer Blutritus' and Delcor, 'La vision de la femme', pp. 139-43. For elimination rites in Hittite and Mesopotamian texts and their connection to Lev. 14 and 16 see Wright, *The Disposal of Impurity* and G. Wilhelm, 'Reinheit und Heiligkeit: Zur Vorstellungswelt altanatolischer Ritualistik', in H.-J. Fabry and H.-W. Jüngling (eds.), *Levitikus als Buch* (BBB, 119; Berlin and Bodenheim: Philo, 1999), pp. 197-217.

51. Wright, *The Disposal of Impurity*; Janowski and Wilhelm, 'Der Bock, der die Sünden hinausträgt', p. 154; Haas, 'Ein hurritischer Blutritus'; Wilhelm, 'Reinheit und Heiligkeit'.

52. Cf. Delcor, 'La vision de la femme', pp. 139-43; Haas, 'Ein hurritischer Blutritus', pp. 80-81. For the Lelwani text see H. Otten, 'Die Gottheit Lelwani der Boğazköy-Texte', *JCS* 4 (1959), pp. 119-36 (130-31).

53. H.M. Kümmel, 'Ersatzkönig und Sündenbock', *ZAW* 80 (1968), pp. 289-318 (310-11). Cf. H.M. Kümmel, W. Farber and W.H.P. Römer, *Rituale und Beschwörungen*, I (TUAT, 2.2; Gütersloh: Gütersloher Verlagshaus Gerd Mohn 1987), pp. 285-89.

woman carried that evil away from this camp; and whoever finds her, let this land take on this evil plague'.[54] There are many similarities between this kind of elimination ritual and Zech. 5.5-11, not least the fact that in the ritual a real woman is exiled into an enemy land.

Zech. 5.5-11 takes up these ritual traditions and changes them characteristically by connecting them so that the *living substitute* becomes *enclosed* in the vessel. As a consequence the woman concerned represents a double evil and a double 'impurity'. Taken together with the semantics of רִשְׁעָה, it is possible to see the unrighteousness of the woman as an ethical-juridical miasma.

The direction—and thus the intention—of the ritual is also altered in the ritual performance as it is depicted in the vision. In Zech. 5.5-11 the intention is not the *liberation* of a person or region, but the *infection* of a particular region with the personified unrighteousness. The origin of neither the *ephah* nor the woman is mentioned, nor is the prophet's position. The woman seems to be transported out of nowhere/everywhere to Shinar. Because Zech. 5.5-11 does not show a purification from sin but an infection with sin, it portrays the reversal of an elimination rite. Furthermore, it is a literary rite since it is contained in a (visionary) report and does not include any directions to be exercised. Besides, this ritual is unique because it takes place only once: unrighteousness in general is taken away. Elimination and purification may be necessary several times, but to infect someone/something with a miasma once is enough.

Here a very bad woman and a very wicked place come together. In v. 11 this text tells us about Babylonia, too. Those who live there, whether Babylonians, Persians or Israelites who do not want to return, cultivate and worship something which has been discarded by other countries: this is the place where miasma is adored, which means, a place where everything is wrong. So Zech. 5.5-11 functions both as a literary elimination rite—or infection rite—and as an aetiology that explains why Shinar is such a detestable place.

Modern and Ancient (Ap)Perception: Pandora as a Sister?

The function of an aetiology and the motifs of woman and evil are often assumed to be found in the story of Adam, Eve and the serpent in Eden (Gen. 3). Feminist exegesis has shown that many receptions have read much more into the text than it contains[55]—and we have

---

54. Kümmel, 'Ersatzkönig und Sündenbock', pp. 310-11.
55. H. Schüngel-Straumann, *Die Frau am Anfang: Eva und die Folgen* (Münster:

learned that Eve is no convincing intertextual parallel to Zech. 5.5-11. But the connection of woman, evil and a vessel immediately suggests the Pandora myth as a somehow parallel story. Indeed, scholars often assume that Hesiod's myth (*Theogony* 570-616; *Works and Days* 57-106) draws upon religious and historical motifs from the ancient Near East and, in particular, on concepts of anthropogony.[56] Fauth[57] sees Hittite concepts in the *pithos* in its function both as a place of assembly and as the starting point of ghostly roaming tormentors. Penglase,[58] Haas,[59] and Kübel[60] assume that Hesiod's story of Pandora and Zech. 5.5-11 share a historical origin.

However, content relations between the texts are few and historically may be none. In his Pandora myth Hesiod brings together three formerly independent and different motifs: the Prometheus tradition of the rivalry between god and man, the creation of the woman, and the aetiology of evil as locked up in a *pithos* and then released.[61] Hesiod changed the myths, but is himself reinterpreted in his own reception. Thus Erasmus of Rotterdam made a *pyxis*, a box, out of the *pithos*, the vessel. There is no disobedience against a prohibition in Hesiod's text, nor is female curiosity[62] shown as the motivation for opening the vessel and releasing evil into the world. The reception history has made of Pandora a Greek Eve—herself misunderstood (see above).

Shedding the dust of its reception does not make the text much nicer. In Hesiod's version, Prometheus cheats Zeus by offering something which seems valuable but which is in fact worthless. Zeus takes revenge and forms out of clay something that is meant to be similar: a woman, καζὸν κακὸν ἀντ᾽ ἀγαδοῖο, 'something beautiful and bad instead of something good' (*Theogony* 585). *Works and Days* tells how

LIT-Verlag, 2nd edn, 1997). Cf. the articles in *BK* 53.1 (1998).

56. P. Walcot, *Hesiod and the Near East* (Cardiff: Cardiff University Press, 1966), pp. 55-79; P. Kübel, 'Eva, Pandora und Enkidus "Dirne"', *BN* 82 (1996), pp. 13-20.

57. W. Fauth, 'Der Schlund des Orcus. Zu einer Eigentümlichkeit der römisch-etruskischen Unterweltsvorstellung', *Numen* 21 (1974), pp. 105-27 (123).

58. C. Penglase, *Greek Myths and Mesopotamia: Parallels and Influence in the Homeric Hymns and Hesiod* (London: Routledge, 1994).

59. Haas, 'Ein hurritischer Blutritus'.

60. Kübel, 'Eva, Pandora und Enkidus "Dirne"'. W. Oldfather ('Pandora', in *PW*, 18.2, pp. 529-48 [533-34]) assumes only Hesiod's misogyny to derive from the Orient.

61. Oldfather, 'Pandora', pp. 539-543.

62. D. Panofsky and E. Panofsky, *Die Büchse der Pandora: Bedeutungswandel eines mythischen Symbols* (Frankfurt and New York: Campus-Verlag, 1992 [1956]), esp. pp. 17-23.

this woman is married to Epimetheus, Prometheus's brother, and that she lifts the lid of the *pithos* to let out all the plagues, illnesses, pains and evils, that from now on torment all humankind (*Works and Days* 94-95).[63] All women descend from her, and like drones they sit in their husband's house and eat all he works for (*Theogony* 592-99).

The contents of the Pandora myth and Zech. 5.5-11 do share some characteristics. Both texts tell of a woman who is characterized only as 'woman';[64] in the *Theogony* she does not even have a name. Both connect a woman, a vessel and evil, which serves to characterize (the) woman as negative and harmful. But even here the differences between the two stories prevail. While Hesiod shows the creation and existence of woman as Prometheus's punishment, leading to the release of plagues and evil into the whole world when the woman opens the vessel, in Zech. 5.5-11 it is the woman herself who, *as* evil; is imprisoned in the vessel. Both women bring mischief but in Hesiod the woman brings evil to the whole world; in Zech. 5.5-11 the evil is brought to a certain place. Zech. 5.5-11 and the Pandora myth do share an aetiology in that they portray woman as fundamentally evil but while the latter seeks to explain how evil came into the world, the former shows evil being taken to Shinar. And while the Pandora myth functions as an aetiology, Zech. 5.5-11 shows both the functions of an aetiology and a literal elimination rite. Thus it seems that their intentions are rather different.

Moreover, from the religio-historical point of view, and that of the history of literature, an ancient Near Eastern origin for the *pithos*-myth does not really seem very likely. The inter-cultural contact must have taken place long before Hesiod wrote his texts. And we know too little about the myths that Hesiod changed. Did the myth portray the *pithos* being carried from the gods to humankind, when was it

---

63. For an interpretation of the *pithos*-myth as a myth about childbearing see F. Zeitlin, 'Das ökonomische Gefüge in Hesiods Pandora', in Walters Art Gallery Baltimore, Antikenmuseum Basel and the Ludwig Collection (eds.), *Pandora: Frauen im klassischen Griechenland* (Mainz: Von Zabern, 1995), pp. 49-55. Cf. F. Lissarague, 'Frauen, Kästchen, Gefäße: Einige Zeichen und Metaphern', in Walters Art Gallery Baltimore, Antikenmuseum Basel and the Ludwig Collection (eds.), *Pandora*, pp. 91-101.

64. The name Pandora means 'she who gives everything' and is an *epiklese* for chothonic goddesses or maybe the name of a goddess. Whether the (possible) goddess Pandora and Hesiod's Pandora depend on each other or are identical is under discussion. Oldfather ('Pandora') assumes a connection, as does Fauth ('Der Schlund des Orcus', pp. 122-23); M.L. West ([ed.], *Hesiod: Works and Days* [Oxford: Clarendon Press, 1978], pp. 164-66) votes for a homonym.

opened, and what was in it? I am sceptical that any real connection can be proved, especially as in these ancient Near Eastern traditions the elimination of evil seems to be the issue, while in this Greek myth the aetiology of good and bad is essential.

To think of Pandora when reading Zech. 5.5-11 is a result of our associations of 'woman—evil—vessel'. The history of the reception of these texts has diminished differences between famous 'bad' women and focused upon (possible and non-existent) similarities. This short comparison of Zech. 5.5-11 and Hesiod's Pandora myth shows that our own presuppositions, and the harmony in our own heads between misogynist texts, serve to obscure the texts themselves.

(Ap)Perceiving Gaps: Reading Zechariah 5.5-11

As I have shown, there are gaps in the text itself, gaps in the connections to other texts, and gaps between the text and us, its interpreters. 'Mind the gap!' is a warning in some London underground stations: there is a distance between the train and the platform, and one has to be careful stepping into or out of the train. 'Mind the gap!' can be a suitable warning for those of us who work with ancient texts in modern times. As in the underground station, we have to mind the gap: to know where it is, to look at it, and sometimes think about it. All this I have tried to show in these notes, mind the gap.

ON SAYING 'NO' TO A PROPHET[*]

Julia M. O'Brien

I

For reasons I am only beginning to understand, the first ten years of my academic career have centred on the biblical book of Malachi. While I have written on and reviewed others' work on different topics and while I have taught in areas as far afield from this little book as 'Women in the Christian Tradition', Malachi has been the pool to which I have returned when I have been able to wrestle from the demands of teaching and parenting time for my own work. To the incredulous inquiry of former professors who ask, wine glass in hand at SBL Meetings, 'Are you *still* working on Malachi?' I have had to respond with a sheepish, 'Yes'.

I would be the first to admit that the book of Malachi is not the most fascinating in the canon. It is short; it mentions few if any specific events; and it offers no 'prophetic personality' like that which readers experience through Jeremiah's gut-wrenchings and Ezekiel's visions. I also admit that the book has been well served by a growing corpus of articles and commentaries that address the historical and linguistic issues it raises.[1] So, why will this book not let me go? What could I possibly have to say about it that I—and its wealth of interpreters—have not already said?

For a long time, I attributed my failure to move onto other work as a function of my own inability to juggle the demands of heavy teaching loads, parenting, and life issues with the demands of scholarship. If my academic life was relegated to the wee hours of the morning, after my daughter was asleep, lunches made, papers graded, it

*   This article is a revision of a paper given to a session on the 'Ethics of Reading', co-sponsored by the 'Reading, Rhetoric and the Bible' and 'Semiotics and Exegesis' sections of the SBL, held in Philadelphia in November 1995, first published in *Semeia* 72 (1995). Printed by permission.

1.   An overview of recent scholarship on Malachi can be found in J.M. O'Brien, 'Malachi', *Currents in Research: Biblical Studies* 3 (1995), pp. 79-92.

seemed that my constant return to Malachi was a short cut back into writing: take what you know and do something new with it.

I don't discount that exhaustion has been a facilitator of my Mala-holism. But I have come to believe that something more has been going on, something about the evolving nature of my self-awareness that has found a helpful conversation partner in the book of Malachi. Indeed, from my current vantage point, I can trace how my reading of the book has both reflected and contributed to important changes in my life and in my soul.

I can identify (and am in the process of writing about) other times in which my understanding of Malachi has changed: after leaving graduate school, after giving birth to a daughter, after my first semester of teaching at a women's college. But I choose here to reflect on a particular year, 1995, in which I am aware of a significant shift in my reading: this change seems noteworthy both because it occurred in a relatively short period of time and because it correlates in a rather evident way with major developments in my life.

II

In March of 1995, I submitted an abstract to a session on 'The Ethics of Reading' co-sponsored by the 'Reading, Rhetoric and the Hebrew Bible' and 'Semiotics and Exegesis' sections of the SBL. In that abstract, I posited that Malachi is an abusive book and that a decon-structive reading of its gender hierarchies offers an ethical strategy by which to resist its abusive rhetoric.

That Malachi is an abusive book seemed clear to me. Malachi is an extended argument between God and the people.[2] It opens with God saying: 'I have loved you' (1.2). When Judah asks, 'how have you loved us?' the response blasts back, 'I have hated Esau; I have made his hill country a desolation and his heritage a desert for jackals' (1.2-3). Should Edom attempt a come-back, it will be in vain. 'They may build, but I will tear down, until they are called The Wicked Country, The People with Whom the LORD is Angry Forever' (1.4). The priests, who are charged with not paying the deity proper respect, are told, 'I will rebuke your offspring, and spread dung on your faces, the dung of your offerings, and I will put you out of my presence' (2.3). While Levi was a good priest, current priests will be despised

---

2. While most form critics follow Adrian Graffy (*A Prophet Confronts His People: Disputation Speech in the Prophets* [Rome: Biblical Institute, 1984]) in desig-nating the genre as 'disputation speech', few discuss the tenor of the attack.

and debased (2.4-9). The book's ending vision of restoration is no warm snuggle, either: 'Lo, I will send you the prophet Elijah before the great and terrible day of the LORD comes. He will turn the heart of fathers to their sons and the heart of sons to their fathers, lest I strike the land with a ban' (3.23-24; Eng. 4.4-6).

Throughout the book, the reader is invited, indeed forced, to envision the relationship between God and the people in terms of human relationships, father and son being the most frequent.[3] Once instructed to think of this dialogue as between humans, it sounds especially harsh: to a child who asks a parent 'do you really love me?', the answer is, 'I hated your brother, didn't I?' (So my father shows me he loves me by hating his other son?). And the favored son is shamed for asking the question in the first place: 'Son honors father; servant honors master. If I then am Father, where is my honor? And if I am master, where is my fear?' (1.6). Priests, those bad, bad boys, will have shit thrown in their faces, and the future restoration is a shoring up of the hierarchy between fathers and their properly subordinate sons. All that in response to Judah's question, 'how have you loved us?'

The book of Malachi argues that you will feel God's love if you behave. It defines the goal of life as knowing your place and staying there. To comply with Malachi is to comply with universal expectations, gender hierarchies, and physical punishment as justified, and it predicates abusive language as divine will. I could not, would not comply with any of that, and I found some encouragement in my resistance in the rubrics for reading the final verses of Malachi in the synagogue: 3.23 is repeated after 3.24, so that the book will not leave you cursed.

That deconstruction was a way to resist that rhetoric also seemed clear to me. I had recently completed an article in which I had offered a deconstructive reading of the gender and power hierarchies on which the book's argument relies.[4] To summarize a longer argument, this book, which relies on knowing your place and the expectations that come with it, manifests some problematic gender shifts. In a single verse (2.11), Judah is described as *she* who acted treacherously (בגדה), as *he* who profaned the Temple (חלל), and *he* who married (בצל) the daughter of a foreign god. The lack of gender agreement is

3. See David M. Bossman, 'Kinship and Religious System in the Prophet Malachi', in Jacob Neusner *et al.* (eds.), *Religious Writings and Religious Systems*, I (Atlanta: Scholars Press, 1989), pp. 127-41.

4. 'Judah as Wife and Husband: Deconstructing Gender in Malachi', *JBL* 115 (1996), pp. 243-52.

not, in itself, a problem; but it *is* problematic in a book structured by hierarchies of gender and social status, a book that demands that Judah act like a proper son. The gender shifts within Malachi leave Judah in a liminal state: both male and female, both God's erring wife and his son who has married someone else's daughter, thereby falling under the authority of *her* father.

Malachi's rhetoric also problematizes the gender of God. A dominant stream of the prophetic tradition describes Israel's fall as one of a pure youthful bride to an adulterous wife, using consistent vocabulary (בגדה, 'acted treacherously', almost always feminine; and Yahweh as בעל or 'husband'). In Mal. 2.15, however, this vocabulary is used to accuse *Judah* of acting treacherously (יבגד, masculine) against *his* youthful wife. This wife is also described as a 'covenant-wife', בריתך אשת, 2.14), strengthening the allusion of this image to the early covenant period of Israel's story. In putting standard prophetic language to a new use, Malachi's rhetoric feminizes God and, devastatingly for Malachi's argument, if God is feminine then God is not father at all.

Malachi is abusive, and its rhetoric falls under its own weight. In March, it all seemed so clear.

III

And then it was November. I sat down to write the paper for which I had prepared the abstract in March; my plan was to (1) isolate Malachi's most abusive passages; (2) consult the comments of other interpreters; (3) don my sassy metacommentary lenses and devastate all those interpreters who assume the moral rectitude of the text and thus comply (however unwittingly) with abuse. That scholars *do* assume the moral rectitude of the text was evident. To a person, commentators assume that the prophet's critiques are descriptive of actual practices in the post-exilic Judean community. For example, Glazier-McDonald writes (all emphases are mine):

> So, too, in Malachi's day, the priests *were* perfunctory in their duties (1.6-2.9). Paying little heed to the law, they reckon*ed* that any sacrifice was good enough for Yahweh (1.7-8). Adultery, perjury and victimization of the underprivileged *were* rife (3.5), as was the refusal to give Yahweh his due in the way of tithes and offerings (p. 274).[5]

5.　Beth Glazier-McDonald, *Malachi: The Divine Messenger: A Critical Appraisal* (SBLDS, 98; Atlanta: Scholars Press), p. 274.

In rationalizing God's behavior, Glazier-McDonald as well as other commentators often strain to explain which came first: the community's plight or its doubt in God's care:

> It is likely that *Yahweh's failure to provide for his people induced* them to better themselves through intermarriage with prominent, wealthy families the result of which was not only the divorce of Judean wives but the infiltration of foreign religious practices into Yahwism itself (2.10-16)... Malachi deplores the people's neglect and contempt of their religious duties not because they are important in and of themselves, but because such neglect reveals a lack of reverence, *faith and love* for Yahweh... Malachi demands a return to covenant law (3.22), a demand which involves no less than a wholehearted return to Yahweh himself (3.7b). *Only then* may Yahweh be counted on to fulfill all his promises made through the prophets'.[6]

Verhoef's rationalizations are similar:

> They must have become conscious of God's displeasure, because *they experienced failure of crops (3.10-12), and their prayers apparently were not heard.* Their religious activities amounted to nothing. The communication with the Lord was broken. That is why they now cover the altar with tears, with weeping and wailing. *We have every reason to believe that this sorrow did not come from a broken spirit and a contrite heart. It was not a 'godly sorrow' that brings repentance and leads to salvation (2 Cor 7.10; cf. Hosea 7.14), but rather a 'worldly sorrow', such as that of Cain (Gen 4.13, 14).*[7]

I was not surprised by what I found in the commentaries. But what did surprise me was my reaction in November to the passages I had read as abusive in March. In attempting to catalogue Malachi's most blatantly nasty passages, I found the book less harsh than I had remembered. Malachi did not sound so abusive to me any more. Even the 'dung in your face' sounded much tamer in the book than the way I had been retelling it; the threat at the end of the book also seemed, well, less threatening. It was as if Malachi itself was much less severe than it had become in my mind.

My first response was despair. What could I have been thinking? How could I have been so wrong? What was I to say to the SBL session?

But feminist, psychoanalytic and deconstructionist methods have, if nothing else, taught me to pay attention to changes, shifts, to see in the slips something important. And, in this case, too, observing change has proven instructive. I have come to believe that the shift in

---

6.   Glazier-McDonald, *Malachi*, pp. 274-75.
7.   Pieter Verhoef, *The Books of Haggai and Malachi* (NICOT; Grand Rapids, MI: Eerdmans, 1987), p. 273.

my reading is a manifestation of the shift in my location as a reader: not my social location, or my gender location, or my socio-political location, but my *personal* location.

March was an difficult time in my personal life. Although I had been separated from my husband for two years, I had been wrestling for months with my own inability to finalize a divorce. When I was honest with myself, I knew that the relationship could not help me thrive. What kept me from finalizing a divorce was guilt and fear: fear of another person's wrath, another person's pain; the fear of being yelled at, of being shamed, of being demeaned, of being wrong.

I was not physically abused as a child; I was not emotionally abused. But I listened to and watched my rebellious teenage sister bear the brunt of my parents' anger. I quickly mastered strategies for avoiding having that heat directed at me. I can remember at the age of eleven vowing that I would never do anything that would even invite dismay. What 'not inviting dismay' entails for a woman in the Southern United States is pretty broad. A good Southern woman can be strong, but never sassy or 'ugly' (a term that is used in the South for behavioral as well as aesthetic judgments, as in 'don't talk ugly to your teacher'). Nothing in my history could allow me to believe that acting on what benefited me at the expense of others was an acceptable thing to do.

Aware of my own fear, I had paid special attention in the weeks before the March abstract deadline when a friend heard me describing the negative rhetoric of Malachi and said 'that's abusive'. To be screamed at is 'abusive'? To accept that judgment not only changed how I perceived Malachi but also how I perceived my own relational situation. I might have been taught to avoid being 'ugly', but I also 'knew' that abuse is not justified. If I could believe that the rhetoric of Malachi is abusive, then I could perceive my deconstruction of the book as an ethical stance, destabilizing the power of its rhetoric; and if I could believe that the screaming that I was afraid of was not 'normal', 'rational', or 'self-evident', but 'abusive', then I might be able to say 'No' to it as well. To see in Malachi the aridness of a strictly intellectual argument about love, the truth that you can be shamed into guilt but not into love, helped me to see the same for my own life. Later that spring I filed for divorce.

In November, I still found Malachi harsh. I still believed that its heavy-handed argument collapses under its own weight. But what had shifted was my perception of *how* harsh it is. That is a function, I think, of my greater ability to observe, comment on, and act in opposition to the threatening voices in my own life. By November, with the marriage ended, Malachi had less to mirror, less fear to trigger.

And so, in the complicated relationship between me and this little book that I love (and hate), we inform one another, dancing within the 'hermeneutical circle' that Schüssler-Fiorenza describes:

> Understanding takes place in a circular movement: Interpretation and answer are to some extent determined by the question, which in turn is confirmed, extended, or corrected by the text. A new question then grows out of this understanding, so that the hermeneutical circle continues to develop in a never-ending spiral.[8]

IV

I continue to perceive how this unitary-but-increasingly-self-aware 'I' of which I have been speaking is itself a construct, one that assuages the Julia that values order and rationality and does not want to perceive herself as 'fickle' or 'non-committal'. But I also confess the heuristic value of such an 'I', at least in providing me the impetus to explore dimensions of the biblical text beyond the standard scholarship in which I was trained.

In seeking language and constructs with which to envision the interplay of my life and my reading of Malachi, I have found useful interpreters incorporating the insights of psychoanalysis. Exum's description of the thrice-told tale of the 'endangered ancestress' in Freudian terms sounds strangely similar to my own repetitive reading of Malachi, a manifestation of the 'repetition compulsion—the impulse to work over an experience in the mind until one becomes the master of it—whose locus, according to Freud, is the unconscious repressed. Repeating the story, working over the conflict until it is resolved, provides a semiotic cure for the neurosis'.[9]

Similarly, my own experience resonates with the observation of Miller that changes in thinking and behavior only emerge as the result of greater self-reflection. After pondering the statistic that 60 per cent of German terrorists in recent years have been the children of Protestant ministers,[10] she concludes:

8.   Elisabeth Schüssler-Fiorenza, *Bread Not Stone* (Boston: Beacon Press, 1984), p. 38.

9.   J. Cheryl Exum, 'Who's Afraid of "The Endangered Ancestress"?', in *idem* and David J.A. Clines (eds.), *The New Literary Criticism and the Hebrew Bible* (JSOTSup, 143; Sheffield: JSOT Press, 1993), p. 97.

10.   Alice Miller, *For Your Own Good* (trans. H. Hannun and H. Hannun; New York: Farrar, Strauss and Giroux, 1983), p. 65.

Both Hitler and Stalin had a surprisingly large number of enthusiastic followers among intellectuals. Our capacity to resist has nothing to do with our intelligence but with the degree of access to our true self. Indeed, intelligence is capable of innumerable rationalizations when it comes to the matter of adaptation. Educators have always known this and have exploited it for their own purposes.[11]

Rashkow, likewise, uses language I am willing to incorporate into my self-description:

...the reorganization of the role of a reader and a reader's relationship to a text affects something more fundamental than the experience of the character in the narrative or the plot alone: it touches the reader's *unconscious* and produces an effect on the reader's *self*-consciousness... As Holland observes..., individual reading responses disclose essential psychological characteristics; that is, readers 'use' literature to rediscover themselves through 'transactions' with texts. Each reader and each dreamer, in interpreting a text, makes it his or her own.[12]

Most helpful, however, in my search for language to describe the intertwining of reading and my life has been the work of Martha Nussbaum, whose powerful essays in *Love's Knowledge* explore 'the contribution made by certain works of literature to the exploration of some important questions about human beings and human life'.[13] A moral philosopher, Nussbaum reads the work not only of Aristotle and the Stoics, but also of William James and Marcel Proust 'as an "optical instrument" through which the reader becomes a reader of his or her own heart'[14] and asks of what she reads, 'What does all this mean for human life?'[15] The result of her efforts, I believe, is a powerful example of how reading contributes to ethical development, in contrast to the usual ethical enterprise of teasing out the values of a writer or judging the ethical worth of a text from the reader's ideological position. Nussbaum, in fact, believes we must go beyond judging texts according to prescribed ethical standards: 'In so far as

11. Miller, *For Your Own Good*, p. 43; quoted in Nel Noddings, *Educating for Intelligent Belief or Unbelief* (New York and London: Teachers College Press, Columbia University, 1993), pp. 59-60.

12. Ilona N. Rashkow, *The Phallacy of Genesis: A Feminist-Psychoanalytic Approach* (Literary Currents in Biblical Interpretation; Louisville, KY: Westminster/John Knox Press, 1993), pp. 23, 63. The reference is to Norman Holland, *5 Readers Reading* (New Haven: Yale University Press, 1975).

13. Martha Nussbaum, *Love's Knowledge: Essays on Philosophy and Literature* (Oxford: Oxford University Press, 1990), p. 5.

14. Nussbaum, *Love's Knowledge*, p. 47.

15. Nussbaum, *Love's Knowledge*, p. 12.

we train agents to think of ethical judgment as consisting simply in the application of [such] antecedently formulated rules we prepare them badly for the actual flow of life, and for the necessary resourcefulness in confronting its surprises'.[16]

Nussbaum is helpful in that she gives words to the process that I have been undergoing in these months, as the book of Malachi has changed on me. I hear myself in her description: 'the reader is at the same time a reader of his or her own life, bringing to the imagining the hopes and loves of real life'.[17] That my readings would change as my sense of life changes is acknowledged in her explanation that what we seek in our living and in our reading is some sense of coherence—reading, along with David Copperfield, 'as if for life':[18]

> For we do, in life, bring our experience, our active sense of life, to the different conceptions we encounter, working through them, comparing the alternatives they present, with reference to our developing sense of what is important and what we can live with, seeking a fit between experience and conception.[19]

I suspect that most thoughtful readers could name the same in themselves—how significant life events make everything, including the texts we study, look different.[20] The issue is not *whether* our personal location—as well as our historical, cultural, and gender location—as readers affects what we see but what to *do* with that recognition.

Discussing the personal dimension of texts within the academy raises an array of questions, questions that range from 'who *cares* about Julia's life?' to 'what kind of conversation can we have about it?' Many of those problematic issues were raised, in fact, in the discussion that followed the 'Ethics of Reading' session in which I

---

16. Nussbaum, *Love's Knowledge*, p. 38.
17. Nussbaum, *Love's Knowledge*, p. 355.
18. Nussbaum, *Love's Knowledge*, p. 10.
19. Nussbaum, *Love's Knowledge*, p. 25.
20. For example, in 'Elegiac Stanzas: Suggested by a Picture of Peele Castle, in a storm, Painted by Sir George Beaumont', Wordsworth ponders how the death of his brother altered his earlier evaluation of the painting as inappropriately 'dark':

> Such, in the fond illusion of my heart,
> Such Picture would I at that time have made:
> And seen the soul of truth in every part,
> A steadfast peace that might not be betrayed.
>
> So once it would have been—'tis so no more;
> I have submitted to a new control;
> A power is gone, which nothing can restore;
> A deep distress hath humanised my Soul...

presented an earlier version of this essay. My fears about reading a personal-disclosure paper were, initially, realized. While body language and eye contact during the presentation suggested that the paper was interesting, no one knew quite what to say afterward. One colleague ventured psychoanalytic insights into my personality, taking the life that I had laid bare and doing what academics do: making observations, offering insights, arguing. I got defensive.

But what happened next in our conversation convinced me that many of us are ready to talk about our lives and our work. In that room in Philadelphia, we thought that it might be acceptable to talk about the ethics of scholarly discussion; acceptable for the person whose life is at hand to say unashamedly which issues are too painful to discuss. We thought that academics might be able to find ways to talk to each other kindly.

I am aware of the problems of self-disclosure, the possibility that biblical studies could collapse into 'what the text means to me', into an orgy of the ego.[21] And yet I am uncomfortable with the alternative. Without some sense of the personal, I can imagine myself in a heated debate about whether Malachi is 'really' abusive or not, as if a definition or a method would answer the question. Such a conversation would be as intellectually dishonest as the way in which the judgements of white male Protestant scholars have long passed as objective scholarship: as in 'Ruth is an indictment of Israel's exclusivity',[22] or 'the post-exilic era was a dark age'.[23] Evaluative discourse implies an evaluator whose personal, historical, and social circumstances influence the evaluation, and to fail to acknowledge the power of the personal paradoxically grants it ultimate power — *uncontested* power.

21. The potential in post-colonial theory for solipsism is discussed by Russell Jacoby, 'Marginal Returns: The Trouble with Post-Colonial Theory', *Lingua Franca* (September–October 1995), pp. 30-37.

22. For example, H.J. Flanders, R.W. Crapps and D.A. Smith in discussing Ruth: 'In this light the particularism of the Jews is shown to be *shallow* and *selfish* and a stance that *should* be surrendered to a more hospitable attitude toward those Gentiles who desired to share blessings from Yahweh' (Henry Jackson Flanders, Jr, *et al.*, *People of the Covenant: An Introduction to the Old Testament* [New York: The Ronald Press, 2nd edn, 1973], p. 470).

23. Bernard W. Anderson, in discussing the post-exilic era, includes a section on 'The Weaknesses of Judaism' that includes these statements: 'Devotion to the Torah easily lapsed into legalism... We have only to read the New Testament to become aware of this weakness within Judaism... Preoccupation with the Torah seemed to stifle the spirit of prophecy' (*Understanding the Old Testament* [Englewood Cliffs, NJ: Prentice-Hall, 4th edn, 1986], p. 538).

The failure to acknowledge the personal also, I think, prevents us from appreciating the role of emotion in ethical judgment. Perhaps Nussbaum's most forceful apology is for the cognitive content of emotions: the way in which anger, disgust and delight tell us what we believe about how things are and what is important:

> ...emotions are not simply blind surges of affect, recognized, and discriminated from one another, by their felt quality alone; rather they are discrimination responses closely connected with beliefs about how things are and what is important...a certain belief or beliefs [is] at least a necessary condition for emotion... Because the emotions have this cognitive dimension in their very structure, it is very natural to view them as intelligent parts of our ethical agency, responsive to the workings of deliberation and essential to its completion...emotions are not only not more unreliable than intellectual calculations, but frequently are more reliable, and less deceptively seductive.[24]

Nussbaum also makes this argument in *The Therapy of Desire: Theory and Practice in Hellenistic Ethics* :

> ...passions such as fear, anger, grief, and love are not blind surges of affect that push and pull us without regard to reasoning and belief. They are, in fact, intelligent and discriminating elements of the personality that are very closely linked to beliefs, and are modified by the modification of belief.[25]

In my own change-of-reading, I recognize that it was my anger at the voices I could label abusive that empowered me to resist, to act. It was my anger that told me that such treatment of human beings is contrary to what I believe is appropriate. It seems difficult, if not impossible, to learn what emotions might teach us if we refuse to acknowledge the agents in whom those emotions are evoked.

V

The process of thinking/feeling through my life with Malachi may not always interest me. It may be, as I used to hate to hear my father say, that I am 'going through a stage'. And yet it is true that the questions that most interest me about biblical texts — and particularly prophetic texts — right now are: What do these texts claim about how to live that is useful, not only to those joined in believing communities, but other humans as well? Can they speak to the human

---

24. Nussbaum, *Love's Knowledge*, pp. 291, 293.

25. Martha Nussbaum, *The Theory of Desire: Theory and Practice in Hellenistic Ethics* (Princeton: Princeton University Press, 1994), p. 38.

questions of 'who am I?', 'how do I live?', outside of the rubrics of the faith communities that have preserved them?

Perhaps the more burning question for me is, 'with whom can I have this conversation?' While I am not confident that standard scholarship will ever have as much energy for self-disclosure as it does for the often violent disrobing of others' work and assumptions, I am grateful for literary critics[26] and the practitioners of auto-biographical criticism who can acknowledge the ways in which they too are obsessed—and mirrored—by the texts they study. Perhaps in on-going conversation with them and with my mirror Malachi, I will find other ways in which to read 'as if for life'.

26. Clines and Exum, for example, maintain: 'As long as we do not challenge the world views of our literature, as long as we limit our research merely to questions of meaning and refuse to engage with questions of value, it will become increasingly hard to for us to justify the place of biblical studies within the human sciences' (David J.A. Clines and J. Cheryl Exum, 'The New Literary Criticism', in Exum and Clines [eds.], *The New Literary Criticism*, p. 14).

IN RETROSPECT… SELF-RESPONSE
TO 'ON SAYING "NO" TO A PROPHET'

Julia M. O'Brien

Not long after 'On Saying "No"' was published, I accepted a position at a theological seminary. Before I even arrived on campus, the Dean phoned. 'Can we have students read your autobiographical piece as part of the first-year ministry seminar? The article would be perfect for our interdisciplinary exploration of "interpreting the self"'.

I said 'yes'—maybe because I felt in no position to say 'no' (yes, I hear the irony), maybe because I was flattered that 'On Saying "No"' would have more than the 1.2 readers of the average scholarly article. But, when I stood in front of a class of 30 students to talk about my piece, I realized just how complicated writing autobiographically can be.

On the one hand, I remained convinced that the article was one that I had needed to write. It marked an important step for me, both in distinguishing myself from the heavy linguistic/historical orientation of my academic training and in admitting, out loud and in print, that I cannot assent to everything in the Bible. There was, and there remains, power in naming those things, as well as the others that the article features.

On the other hand, teaching 'On Saying "No"' underscored the danger of the autobiographical style: it too easily allows a reader to dismiss the issues raised as 'only' personal experience. In the seminar, students limited their responses to my piece to the sharing of their own experiences (the power dynamics of the classroom, I suspect, made them reluctant to fish for more details about *mine*); they kept forgetting that the book of Malachi was integral to the interpretive process I had described, that there was something about this biblical book itself that invited my reflections about being shamed into con-formity. In writing, I had been interested in the interplay between scholarly study and life story, but, in reading, students never got past the autobiography.

In retrospect, this article was my first attempt to bring together the two approaches that most interest me: ideological criticism, reading biblical texts for their underlying assumptions about power and the 'proper' ordering of reality; and ethical concerns, engaging a text's ideologies in conversation with one's own values and convictions. My current work on Nahum and its relation to contemporary ideologies of violence manifests these two concerns, foregrounding questions about what reading this book does to and with the ethical imagination.

The article also marked the beginning of my awareness that while saying 'No' to texts may at times be necessary, especially for resisting ideologies that endanger human personhood, texts are not so easily contained, so readily silenced. Maybe as an outgrowth of my own attempts to respect and learn from otherness, I find myself less willing than in the past to write off texts that offend me, more open to the possibility that their ideologies might appropriately critique my own. These days, I do not pretend that I can say 'No' to texts or to the dynamics of my personal history. I tend to wrestle with them instead, hoping for – though not necessarily expecting – a blessing.

NINEVEH THE ADULTERESS

Mayer I. Gruber

The book of Nahum offers at one and the same time divine retribution to the Neo-Assyrian Empire and consolation to the nation-state of Judah. The Neo-Assyrian Empire is to be punished for its repressive treatment of people and nations. Judah is to be consoled in the knowledge that justice is about to be done to the evil empire that had carried away into captivity the Israelites of Samaria and subjugated Judah for a generation prior to the death of Assurbanipal in 628 BCE. In the book of Nahum, the Neo-Assyrian Empire or Assyria is represented by the personification of its capital Nineveh. The consolation of Judah in the Book of Nahum is epitomized by Nah. 2.1:

> Look! Atop the [Judean] mountains
> Are the feet of a herald
> Who announces well-being.[1]
> 'Celebrate your festivals, O Judah,
> Fulfill your vows
> Never again will personified wickedness[2] invade you
> He is altogether[3] eliminated.[4]

Hosea 1–2 offers an interesting parallel to Nahum's dual message of retribution and consolation. In its original form, Hosea 1–2 promises retribution to the Kingdom of Israel (Samaria) for its disloyalty to God. Its disloyalty is compared to a married woman's engaging in adulterous liaisons. The book of Hosea in its canonical form contains several Judahite glosses.[5] The Judahite gloss in Hos. 1.7 clearly suggests that the people of the southern kingdom are to be comforted in the knowledge that a well-deserved disaster such as befell Samaria in

---

1. שלום, which here means an end to the threat of repression; cf. Isa. 52.9, which is probably inspired by Nah. 2.1
2. בליעל; see T.H. Gaster, 'Belial', *IDB*, I, p. 377.
3. כלה, referring to Assyria.
4. נכרת; cf. Ps. 37.28: 'the progeny of wicked people is eliminated'.
5. See H.L. Ginsberg, 'Hosea, Book of', *EncJud*, VIII, pp. 1016, 1024.

722 BCE will not afflict Judah because, apparently, Judah is more virtuous than Israel:

> The House of Judah, however, I will love, and I will give them victory through the LORD their God. I will not give them victory by means of bow and sword and battle, by horses and cavalry (Hos. 1.7).

The resemblances between Hosea 1–2 and Nahum do not end here. Nah. 3.5 cannot help but remind one of Hos. 2.5. It is in Hos. 2.5 that God threatens publicly to abuse personified Israel sexually for her disloyalty to God. Throughout Hosea 1–3, with the possible exception of Hos. 1.4,[6] Israel's disloyalty to God consists of the worship of other deities, primarily various manifestations of the Canaanite storm god Hadad, commonly referred to by his epithet Baal, which means literally both 'lord' and 'husband'. In Hos. 2.4-5 God threatens his disloyal wife, i.e. personified Israel, that if she does not cease and desist from adultery (Heb. זנונים), God will publicly disgrace her as follows:

> …I will strip her naked,
> and I will exhibit her as on the day she was born (Hos. 2.5).

Later in that same chapter of Hosea God warns

> I will expose her genitals[7]
> in the sight of her lovers,
> and no one will rescue her from My power (Hos. 2.12).[8]

Public humiliation of Jerusalem is similarly portrayed in Jer. 13.22:

> It is because of your great iniquity
> that your skirts are lifted up,[9]
> your limbs[10] exposed.

---

6. 'I shall punish the dynasty of Jehu because of the blood of Jezreel' is probably a promise to avenge the blood of innocent scions of the Ahab dynasty, who were annihilated by Jehu in the Valley of Jezreel. Unlike Hosea, the author of 2 Kgs 10.30 holds that God looked favorably upon Jehu's atrocities.

7. Heb. נבלותה; see J. Cheryl Exum, 'Prophetic Pornography', in *idem*, *Plotted, Shot, and Painted: Cultural Representations of Biblical Women* (JSOTSup, 215; Gender, Culture, Theory, 3; Sheffield: Sheffield Academic Press, 1996), p. 104; so also Yehudah Qil, 'Commentary on the Book of Hosea', in *The Twelve Prophets*. I (Da'at Miqra; Jerusalem: Mossad Harav Kook, 1973), p. 13.

8. Heb. מידי, an inflected form of יד, 'hand', which here as in many cases stands for the metaphoric hand (in Akkadian usually *qātu*) rather than the anatomical hand (in Akkadian often *rettu*).

9. Heb. נגלו , a prophetic perfect, which literally means 'were exposed'. The same verb is employed in the same sense also in Nah. 3.5, quoted below. Common sense suggests that what is referred to in both cases is not exposing the skirt but lifting up the skirt to expose the genitals.

In Hos. 2.5, 12 and in Jer. 13.22 personified Israel and personified Jerusalem, respectively, are threatened with public humiliation, involving sexual molestation, which defies all Israelite notions of modesty. Likewise in Nah. 3.5 God threatens the personified city of Nineveh with punishment that involves sexual molestation:

> I shall lift up your skirts over your face,
> and I shall show nations your genitals
> and kingdoms your humiliation.

Just as in Hosea 2, the principle that operates is 'measure for measure'. In Hosea this principle is carried out as follows: 'You, personified Israel, acted immodestly by committing adultery. Therefore I am entitled to humiliate you.' Obviously the question arises, therefore, wherein is the breach of modesty, on the part of personified Nineveh, that would justify so humiliating her as to undress her in public so that strange men would have the opportunity to gaze with lust upon her breasts and genitals?[11] It is precisely this question that the prophetic author anticipates when he prefaces the divine promise publicly to undress Nineveh with the following declaration:

> I am against you, says the LORD of Hosts (Nah. 3.5a)
> because of the many acts of adultery
> on the part of an adulteress (Nah. 3.4a).[12]

Isa. 1.21 asserts that Jerusalem of the eighth century BCE had rightly been called 'the faithful city that was filled with justice (משפט), where personified justice (צדק) spent the night'. According to Isa. 1.21, when, however, the city of Jerusalem ceased to embody justice she became unfaithful. That is to say, she became like a woman who was unfaithful to her husband, which is to say זונה, the term that is commonly translated 'harlot'. In fact, this is the very same term that means 'adulteress' in Nah. 3.5. The masculine form of this noun is attested only once in all of Hebrew Scripture, in Hos. 4.15, referring disparagingly to a man who is unfaithful to his wife and nevertheless expects the women in his family to be faithful to their husbands.[13]

---

10. Literally, 'your heels'. As noted by Exum (*Plotted*, p. 107), 'limbs' or 'feet' often serve as euphemisms for 'genitals'; cf. Isa. 6.2: 'with two he [the seraph] covered his legs'.

11. On the ethical dilemma of Holy Scriptures' exposing female genitalia for public scrutiny see Exum, *Plotted*, pp. 102-103.

12. I have rearranged the clauses to reflect common English word order, in which adverbial prepositional phrases follow the predicate. In the Hebrew original of Nah. 3.4-5 the adverbial clause precedes the subject.

13. See Mayer I. Gruber, 'Marital Fidelity and Intimacy: A View from Hosea 4',

If in Isa. 1.21 it is Jerusalem's having abandoned its mission to embody and personify justice that made it unfaithfulness personified, i.e., the adulteress, it is the Neo-Assyrian Empire's devotion, over several generations, to repression and degradation of men and women that seem to have earned it, at least in the view of Nahum the Elkoshite, the title of adulteress. Typical of the pride the Assyrian kings and their scribes took in their repressive and violent policies is the following passage from the annals of Assurbanipal:

> I tore out the tongues of those whose slanderous mouths had uttered blasphemies against my god Ashur and had plotted against me, his god-fearing prince; I defeated them [completely]. The others, I smashed alive with the very same statues of protective deities with which they had smashed my own grandfather Sennacherib--now [finally] as a [belated] burial sacrifice for his soul. I fed their corpses, cut into small pieces, to dogs, pigs, *zîbu*-birds, vultures, the birds of the sky and [also] to the fish of the ocean. After I had performed this and thus made quiet [again] the hearts of the great gods, my lords, I removed the corpses of those whom the pestilence had felled, whose leftovers [after] the dogs and pigs had fed on them were obstructing the streets, filling the places [of Babylon], [and] of those who had lost their lives through the terrible famine.[14]

One of the positive consequences of the fact that the term for 'city' in Hebrew is feminine is that in Ruth 1.19 'the whole city' is represented specifically by the women of Bethlehem. Another consequence is that 'cities' that are unfaithful to the principles of common decency—be they eighth century BCE. Jerusalem or seventh-century BCE Nineveh—are compared by Israelite and Judean prophets to adulterous women.

Why, however, the threat of sexual abuse of persons or personified cities, who have been accused only metaphorically of adultery? Metaphorically or otherwise, to treat with immodesty those who have behaved immodestly is in keeping with a basic principle common to the Code of Hammurabi, the Middle Assyrian Laws and the laws contained in Hebrew Scripture. This principle is that the guilty should suffer in his or her person precisely what he or she perpetrated or sought to perpetrate. For example, Deut. 19.18-21 states the following:

---

in Athalya Brenner (ed.), *A Feminist Companion to the Latter Prophets* (The Feminist Companion to the Bible, 8; Sheffield: Sheffield Academic Press, 1995), pp. 169-79 (178).

14. 'The Death of Sennacherib', a passage from the annals of Assurbanipal from the Rassam Cylinder, col. iv, ll. 65-82; the translation is taken from A.L. Oppenheim, 'Babylonian and Assyrian Historical Texts', in *ANET*, 3rd edn, p. 288.

> If the witness is a false witness who testified falsely against a fellow human being, you shall do to him as he plotted for it to be done to his fellow human being. Thus you will eliminate evil from among you. Those who survive will take heed, and they will be afraid, and they will not continue to behave in such an evil manner among you. You must not show any pity: life for life, eye for eye, tooth for tooth, hand for hand, foot for foot.

Just as it apparently makes perfect sense that false witnesses in capital cases should be deterred by the threat of death, and just as it apparently makes sense that children who hit their siblings should be spanked, so does it seem to make sense that immodest persons and cities personified as immodest persons should be punished in kind. However, one of the things that parents and educators have learned over the years is that what children learn from verbal and physical violence emanating from the 'god-like' authority figures of parents and teachers is to adopt.[15] It has also been widely recognized in most advanced countries of the world that capital punishment is no deterrent to the crimes traditionally punished by death.[16] Increasingly, it has been recognized that home and school environments in which reasoned discussion, co-operation and compromise prevail produce children who grow into adults who eschew verbal and physical violence.

Nineveh, as represented by the passage quoted from the annals of Assurbanipal, certainly deserved to be humiliated. Nineveh, however, was about to be destroyed by the armies of the Medes just as Nahum the Elkoshite unleashed his verbal battering ram.[17] Once we fully understand the backdrop for what Nahum said, both in Nineveh's misbehaviour and in commonly held understandings of justice[18] as exemplified by Deuteronomy 19, we are in a position to relate critically to the full implications of what Nahum says in the name of God.

15. See the legal decision issued by Judge Neal Hendel in State of Israel vs. Morad handed down in the Beersheva (Israel) District Court, 1997.

16. See, *inter alia*, the decision of the Supreme Court of the Republic of South Africa in 1995 declaring capital punishment unconstitutional. I am most grateful to the Honorable Judge Neal Hendel of the Beersheva (Israel) District Court for supplying me with the references in this and the previous note.

17. Scholars are divided as to whether the vivid description of the fall of Nineveh in Nah. 2–3, which corresponds so closely to the descriptions written by the Greek historians Xenophon and Diodorus, was composed before, during or after the fall of Nineveh in August of the year 612 BCE. See D.J. Wiseman, *Chronicles of Chaldaean Kings* (London: British Museum, 1961), pp. 16-17; 58-61, reverse 38-45; see also commentaries.

18. See the classic discussion at the beginning of Plato, *The Republic*.

Nahum only wanted what many of us who have been wronged or have been pained by the wrong done to others want so desperately: justice. Experience, however, tells us that so often violence, even when employed for the sake of justice, breeds only more violence and more injustice and more undeserved suffering. Indeed, Nahum's diatribe against personified Nineveh exemplifies verbal and physical abuse of women rather than modesty. Hence, it may very well reinforce and encourage antisocial behaviour towards women rather than modesty and decency. In fact, Hebrew Scripture had already said as much:

> A gentle response turns away wrath,
> A harsh word produces anger (Prov. 15.1).

Part II

DANIEL

WHO'S AFRAID OF FEMINIST CRITICISM? WHO'S AFRAID OF BIBLICAL HUMOUR? THE CASE OF THE OBTUSE FOREIGN RULER IN THE HEBREW BIBLE[*]

Athalya Brenner

To the memory of a friend and colleague,
Dr Fokkelien van Dijk-Hemmes

Feminism, Humour and the Bible

Leaders and rulers, persons invested with authority over other persons, command respect and sometimes love but also, inevitably and especially in the case of foreign rule, encounter resentment and hostility. This inherent ambiguity of attitude often motivates and is expressed by jokes at the rulers' expense. Humorous depictions of rulers obtain in the Hebrew Bible, especially—but not only—in the case of foreign rulers. I will examine this humorous configuration of the obtuse foreign ruler from a feminist perspective (remembering that, undoubtedly, there are other feminist perspectives it can be viewed from). Some preliminary clarification regarding feminist criticism and biblical humour seems in order.

'Feminism', 'humour' and 'the Bible' might seem a strange triad. Feminists are by reputation angry, aggressive and serious individuals, mostly women, whereas humour is primarily associated with playfulness, joy and lightheartedness. The Bible is a supremely serious text for most of its readers—can there be humour in it? Should it be read for humour? Yet seemingly irreverent combinations may yield enjoyable results even within the sombre spheres of feminist interpretation and biblical studies.

* This paper is based on my inaugural lecture as Professor of the Feminism and Christianity Chair at the Catholic University of Nijmegen, The Netherlands. It was subsequently modified and presented to the summer Meeting of the (British) Society for Old Testament Study in Edinburgh, July 1994. First published in *JSOT* 63 (1994), pp. 38-54.

The position of feminist Bible criticism mirrors that of women and femaleness in society in general, and in academia in particular: it is far from secure; it is far from 'equal'. Today, at the close of the millennium and after a hundred and fifty years of feminist activism — decades after women in the western world have acquired the basic civil rights to vote and be elected for political office, decades after women in some relatively liberal groups in both Judaism and Christianity have been allowed to act as religious officials — feminist Bible scholarship is still widely unrecognized as academically significant by mainstream Bible scholarship. Neither is it welcomed by orthodox religious establishments, be they Jewish, Christian or Moslem. Attempts by women to appropriate the religious and cultural heritage embodied in the Bible are still met with stubborn resistance.

Actually, 'feminist Bible criticism' is not a good name. It hardly conveys the fact that, after twenty years of intensive work, feminists have evolved a polyvalence of approaches to the Bible. These approaches may be constructionist or reformist, Jewish or Christian, religious or secular, radical or moderate, motivated by gender — or class — or ethnic — or political — or other concerns. Be the perspective what it may, be the practitioners of whatever denomination or creed, their academic and/or religious acceptance is far from assured. And yet, feminist Bible criticism — like the socio-political contexts from which it springs — displays pioneering qualities that should not be underrated. Feminists are active in almost all fields of human knowledge, contributing some of the freshest angles and most innovative intuitions that are the prerequisites of scholarly progress. By and large, feminist critics espouse transdisciplinarity. Whereas this may seem like an academic deficiency to some, it may constitute a strength to others. Discrimination and subjectivity, two important issues on the feminist agenda, are at the foreground of contemporary scholarship in the humanities and the social sciences. It is therefore clear to feminists and their supporters that looking at the world, reading and studying as a woman[1] recreate it as a different and exciting place — and this

---

1. See for instance J. Culler, *On Deconstruction: Theory and Criticism after Structuralism* (London: Routledge & Kegan Paul, 1975), pp. 43-64 ('Reading as a Woman'); cf. also the concise sample of French feminist thoughts on gendered reading in English translation in E. Marks and I. de Courtivron (eds.), *New French Feminisms* (New York: Schocken Books, 1980), pp. 57-113; N.K. Miller, *Subject to Change: Reading Feminist Writing* (New York: Columbia University Press, 1988); E. Showalter (ed.), *The New Feminist Criticism: Essays on Women, Literature and Theory* (London: Virago, 1986); M. Humm, *Feminist Criticism: Women as Contemporary Critics* (London: Harvester Press, 1986); P.P. Schweickart, 'Reading Ourselves:

must be true for theology and biblical studies too. The pluralistic attitudes and innovative nature of feminist interpretations dictate that
inventive methodologies be developed; and we all know that imaginative thinking requires method to complement it, whereas method
without imagination accomplishes very little.

And what about humour in the Bible? 'Christians have often found
the subject of laughter an awkward one. Laughter seems the furthest
removed from reverence and piety, while humour seems to imply a
failure to take religious matters seriously'.[2] Humour and the comic in
the Bible were largely neglected in Christian tradition.[3] This seriousness reached its peak in Calvinism;[4] Judaism too, while recognizing
the possibility of God's laughter (*b. B. Meṣ.* 59b), came to exclude
humour from Scripture from talmudic times onwards.[5] It would
perhaps help to remember that equating humour exclusively with
play and laughter and jokes misses the mark. Paradoxically, humour
and seriousness are not necessarily opposites: '...humor gives us
nothing tangible, but it works with us and awakens us... And so it
makes sense to say that seriousness and humor are comrades for life'.[6]
Humour can be serious[7] and didactic, a great aid for living and for
teaching, including religious instruction.[8] In short, humour and wit
are tools for shaping opinion and for changing attitudes.

Nonetheless, understanding biblical humour may be difficult.
Humour is always culture-bound and, in the case of the Bible, there is
such a vast cultural distance between the text's creators and us, the
text's consumers (readers). We can only guess at the original, but lost,
situations and the authors' intent. Biblical humour is also 'serious'
humour. It consists less of joyous or non-tendentious, unconscious

Toward a Feminist Theory of Reading', in E.A. Flinn and P.P. Schweickart (eds.),
Gender and Reading: Essays on Readers, Texts and Contexts (Baltimore: Johns Hopkins
University Press, 1986), pp. 31-62.

2.   C. Hyers, 'Christian Humor: Uses and Abuses of Laughter', *Dialog* 22 (1983),
pp. 198-203 (198).

3.   Y.T. Radday, 'Introduction', in Y.T. Radday and A. Brenner (eds.), *On Humour
and the Comic in the Hebrew Bible* (JSOTSup, 92; Sheffield: JSOT Press, 1990), pp.
21-35.

4.   But see Gritsch's claim for Luther's humour in E.W. Gritsch, 'Luther's
Humor: Instrument of Witness', *Dialog* 22 (1983), pp. 176-81.

5.   Radday, 'Introduction', pp. 35-38.

6.   E. Bergravv, 'Humor and Seriousness', *Dialog* 22 (1983), pp. 206-10 (210).

7.   Cf. H. Kaasa, 'Confessions of a Serious-Minded Joker', *Dialog* 22 (1983),
pp. 171-75.

8.   J.E. Benson, 'The Divine Sense of Humour', pp. 191-97, and J. Vannorsdall,
'Humor as Content and Device in Preaching', pp. 187-190, both in *Dialog* 22 (1983).

joking and more of wilful and angry allusions expressing ridicule, spite, disrespect and other disparaging sentiments. One would do well, I think, to consult Freud on the function of such humour,[9] which is the release of social aggression that, simultaneously, exposes this same aggression. Hence biblical humour mostly assumes the literary forms of satire, parody, irony (which is not always humorous), grotesque presentations, burlesque and dark comedy. Light-hearted comedy is largely absent from biblical literature, although good fun can be obtained from witticisms, name- and word-play. In short, biblical humour, inasmuch as it is there, is of the contentious/ subversive kind. It undermines convention and authority, a property it shares with feminist criticism. It is born of anger and frustration, and it carries a sting. All these are shared, too. It is therefore important to utilize humour as an exegetical tool of feminist hermeneutics. The transdisciplinarity of feminist critiques allows for combining psycho-analytic observations, behavioural psychology, literary criteria (readerly response and deconstruction), art and sociology (underlying conventions and social norms). Let us see, then, how the combination of a feminist approach and the recognition of humour may work for a more complex, more gratifying understanding of some Hebrew Bible texts.[10] We shall focus on one issue: the link between gendered, specifically male, sexuality and socio-political authority in the biblical configuration of the obtuse ruler.

The Obtuse Ruler

One way of examining how sexuality is constructed in a culture is to analyse the sexual jokes in this culture's basic texts. Humour, especially sexual and toilet humour, is according to Freud a special case. Its overt motivation is never substantial. On the other hand, its covert significance is never completely hidden, exposed as it were by its underlying aggressiveness and the attempt to produce laughter and to influence through it. As it happens, sex and bodily secretions are part and parcel of the obtuseness attributed to some foreign rulers in the Hebrew Bible.

9.   S. Freud, 'Jokes as a Social Process', *Collected Works* (Standard Edition), VIII (1905), pp. 140-58. Cf. also S. Freud, *Jokes and their Relation to the Unconscious* (trans. J. Strachey; Penguin Freud Library, 6; Longman: Penguin, 1976 [originally 1905]).

10.   For a brief statement on humour in New Testament texts, see L. Nieting, 'Humor in the New Testament', *Dialog* 22 (1983), pp. 168-70.

Named foreign rulers configured as obtuse are supposedly Egyptian (the pharaoh of the oppression, Exod. 1–2), Moabite (Balak and his henchman Balaam, Num. 22–24; Eglon, Judg. 3), Canaanite (the king of Jericho, Josh. 2; Sisera, Judg. 4–5; Abimelek, Judg. 9), Babylonian (Nebuchadnezzar, Dan. 3; and Belshazzar, Dan. 5), and Persian (Ahasuerus, the book of Esther). To be sure, there are similar depictions of native (that is, Judahite) rulers, like Judah himself (and Tamar, Gen. 38), the womanizing King David, King Solomon and his fatal appetite for foreign women (in the Deuteronomistic report, 1 Kgs 11), Ahaz (Isa. 7), and Jehoiakim (Jer. 36). Traces of the configuration are also to be found in the portrayal of the foreign king in Jonah (ch. 3),[11] other kings in Daniel,[12] and elsewhere. The configuration applies, then, mainly to *foreign* rulers. Thus the Israelite kings Ahab (1 Kgs 16–22) and Jeroboam (1 Kgs 14), who are similarly described, belong to this same creed of foreign ruler, since biblical historiography is a mainly Judahite production in which Northern Kingdom rulers are considered usurping, anti-Davidic 'foreigners'.

Admittedly, not *every* foreign ruler is portrayed in this way. However, such portraits share the following themes. The ruler is of foreign territory and/or culture, if not always of foreign stock. He is represented as ludicrous, that is, with bitter humour bordering on malice, certainly with contempt for his (in)competence. His reported inadequacy is parodied or satirized by scornful allusions to his maleness or male sexuality, at times also to his elementary bodily functions. The ruler's ineptitude is mirrored negatively by some smart female actions. Since females are inferior social agents, their resourcefulness amplifies the foreign ruler's shortcomings.

Humour consists in the way that incongruity is suddenly recognized, and the recognition will extend to the cultural or physical norms that are breached. In this way humour can undermine the given world. The comic juxtapositions of ineffectual male ruler, his irregular sexuality/bodily functions and the nature of his affinities with females on the one hand, and of female aptitude on the other hand, are easily recognizable as inappropriate or ambiguous—hence

11. J. Mather, 'The Comic Art of the Book of Jonah', *Soundings* 65 (1982), pp. 280-91.

12. Cf., for example, on the device of humour in lists in Daniel, H.I. Avalos, 'The Comedic Function of the Enumerations of Officials and Instruments in Daniel 3', *CBQ* 53 (1991), pp. 580-88. Avalos's conclusion is relevant to the present study. He holds that the lengthy lists are satirical, and 'could be integrated in a socio-religious critique of pagan social institutions such as the Babylonian government bureaucracy' (p. 587).

comical—in an utterly patriarchal culture. The implied analogy between ruling but incompetent male, subordinate but competent female, signifies the ruler's virtual impotence. He is incapable of accomplishing his political tasks. Hence, his lot as narrated—whatever it turns out to be—constitutes a well-deserved serious joke. Let us now survey a few relevant narratives in some more detail.

The pharaoh of the oppression focuses on the Hebrew males. It takes women, Hebrew women as well as his own daughter and her servants, to subvert his intentions of genocide.[13] Ironically, had the pharaoh paid enough attention to the women to begin with, had he commanded every Hebrew *daughter* to be thrown into the Nile instead of every Hebrew son (Exod. 1.22), his design might have been better served. Was he being stupid? Yes and no. Yes, since this is borne out by the eventual outcome. No, since he follows the conventional social maxim: a social group's identity is discontinued when its *male* line is terminated. It takes feminist critics (like Exum and Siebert-Hommes) to point out that the pharaoh's error is made ludicrous by his adherence to gender conventions, and by the same social element that he considers of secondary consequence.

We now turn to Moabites and their rulers. Biblical attitudes toward Moab and Moabites are ambivalent. They are acknowledged as 'our' blood kin since they descend from Lot, 'our' ancestor Abraham's nephew. But Gen. 19.30-38 accuses this ethnic/territorial group (and the neighbouring Ammon) of sinister social and sexual practices, that is, lack of paternal respect and daughter–father incest initiated by the daughters. Thus Moab is posited as simultaneously kin and Other. The daughters' initiative is meaningful: the original sin of incest appears that much more base and preposterous by its attribution to resourceful females who dupe a weakling father. The same principle—Moabite males are weak; Moabite females are strong; this is not proper; ha-ha—recurs in other references to this foreign group.

King Balak hires Balaam the seer to curse Israel. The seer finally blesses instead of cursing, but not before his female ass is quicker to identify YHWH's presence than he is (Num. 22.22-35). He is a seer; she

13. Cf. J.C. Exum, '"You Shall Let Every Daughter Live": A Study of Exodus 1.8–2.10', originally published in *Semeia* 39 (1983), pp. 63-82, and reprinted with a self-response entitled 'Second Thoughts on Secondary Characters: Women in Exodus 1.8–2.10', in A. Brenner (ed.), *A Feminist Companion to Exodus – Deuteronomy* (The Feminist Companion to the Bible; Sheffield: Sheffield Academic Press, 1994). Cf. also J. Siebert-Hommes, 'But if she be a Daughter...She May Live!: "Daughters" and "Sons" in Exodus 1-2', in the same volume.

is a female animal. It's incongruous and funny that an animal speaks. We may add that a *female* animal's speech is funnier and more sub-versive of male authority still. The humour of the situation serves a purpose. It subverts the seer's authority and, by contiguity, also the authority of the king who employs him. Ultimately, Balak is the butt of the joke or, as Mary Douglas[14] calls it, political satire.[15] We might also interpret Ruth 3 as if Ruth the Moabite uses sex in order to seduce Boaz—there's gentle, teasing humour there too. In short, the socio-sexual humour deployed for depicting the foreign group Moab is well-established.

Since rulers epitomize their people, we would expect such configur-ations to carry the weight of the joke against those people. And indeed, the worst is reported of the Moabite king Eglon. Eglon is killed in a private chamber by Ehud son of Gera, who inserts a short double-edged sword into the fat king's stomach. Ehud then runs away, a feat made easier by the Moabite courtiers' wrong assumption (like ruler, like his advisers—this motif resurfaces in Esther) that the king is relieving himself in the toilet, and hence shouldn't be disturbed. By the time the courtiers realize their mistake, Ehud has already returned with re-enforcements (Judg. 3). As Alter writes, the assassination of Eglon 'is not simply a circumstantial account of the Moabite king's destruction but a satiric vision of it, at once shrewd and jubilant'.[16] Alter recognizes the sexual and secretion humour in this narrative. Eglon means 'big calf', an allusion to the king's obesity. 'Obese' is of course a cultural token of stupidity and vulnerability. Alter goes on,

> Perhaps it may also hint at a kind of grotesque feminization of the Moabite leader: Ehud 'comes to' the king, an idiom also used for sexual entry, and there is something hideously sexual about the description of the dagger-thrust. There may also be a deliberate sexual nuance in the 'secret thing' Ehud brings to Eglon, in the way the two are locked together alone in a chamber, and in the sudden opening of locked entries at the conclusion of the story.[17]

14. M. Douglas, *In the Wilderness: The Doctrine of Defilement in the Book of Numbers* (JSOTSup, 158; Sheffield: JSOT Press, 1993), ch. 12, pp. 216-25. The name of the chapter (pp. 216-34) is 'Balaam and Balak: A Political Satire'.

15. Moabite female involvement in ungodliness features in Num. 25.1-5 too: female temptation, sex and paganism merge in that passage.

16. R. Alter, *The Art of Biblical Narrative* (New York: Basic Books, 1981), p. 39.

17. Alter, *Biblical Narrative*, p. 39.

And, Alter continues, 'An enemy's obtuseness is always an inviting target for satire in times of war'.[18] It seems that the exposure of Moabite stupidity (as symbolized by the leader) functions to underline Moab's helplessness in war against YHWH.

Alter, who obviously recognizes the humorous properties of the passage in his inspiring analysis,[19] nonetheless doesn't go far enough. 'Fat' in the Bible does not imply simply and universally and gender-free 'stupid', nor specifically 'male-stupid'. By referring to Amos 4.1-3, which is addressed to the greedy 'female cows of the Bashan who live on the hill of Samaria', we gather that the obesity that symbolizes obtuseness/greed is associated specifically with women. Therein lies, at least in part, the feminization of the Moabite leader. The hinted homosexuality is certainly there. But, worse than that, the king is depicted not simply as a homosexual ('feminized' or 'effeminate'[20]) *man* but, distinctively, *as a woman*,[21] hence politically ineffectual. (Let us remember that the Hebrew Bible hardly acknowledges that a woman can be a reigning monarch; at least, it rejects the notion for its own culture.) Indeed, the narrative's intention is to ridicule the enemy. The success of this subversion of foreign political male superiority depends on the presentation of the victim's physical and sexual traits. However, without an understanding that the *man* is actually a *woman*,

18. Alter, *Biblical Narrative*, p. 40.
19. Alter, *Biblical Narrative*, pp. 37-41.
20. Cf. D. Boyarin, *Carnal Israel: Reading Sex in Talmudic Culture* (Berkeley: University of California Press, 1993), p. 208 n. 15: 'In the classical world, fat men are considered effeminate'. See the fascinating discussion of Nicole Loraux, 'Herakles: The Super-Male and the Feminine', in D.M. Halperin, J.J. Winkler and F. Zeitlin (eds.), *Before Sexuality: The Construction of Erotic Experience in the Ancient Greek World* (Princeton: Princeton University Press, 1990), pp. 21-52 (31-33); see also C. Paglia, *Sexual Personae: Art and Decadence from Nefertiti to Emily Dickinson* (New Haven: Yale University Press, 1990), p. 91; V. Traub, 'Prince Hal's Falstaff: Positioning Psychoanalysis and the Female Reproductive Body', *Shakespeare Quarterly* 40 (1989), pp. 456-75 (461-64).
21. In his text (*Carnal Israel*, p. 208), Boyarin himself writes in a discussion of *b. B. Meṣ.* 83b-85a and the fat R. El'azar's death, after Bakhtin's theory of the grotesque: 'The text produces another very intense image of a grotesque birth out of the flesh of a feminized male (dying) body... Moreover, obesity itself is an issue of gender, being associated with the maternal grotesque body.' Although Boyarin writes on talmudic culture his analysis is applicable to biblical narrative too. However, two problems remain. As in Alter, there seems to be no distinction between 'effeminate' and 'feminized'. Also, Boyarin seems to limit the 'effeminacy' or 'feminization' of fat males to the maternal aspect, while I want to draw attention to the sexual female image in its entirety (including female reproductive function).

the humour doesn't work to its full capacity. Feminist attention to this detail enhances the understanding of what Alter terms the 'modalities'[22] of the biblical story. The covert allusion to the king's bowel movements is anal humour which augments the sexual humour.

In Alter's reading, Ehud is an assassin, albeit a manly and patriotic one.[23] But does our hero remain untainted? Many feminists have written on Jael's killing of Sisera, the two accounts of which follow the Ehud and Eglon story in Judges (chs. 4 and 5). Here too a foreign leader is killed in sinister circumstances, with a woman and sexual undertones involved, which is of course a laughable end for a warrior. The narrative allows Jael to maintain stereotypic femininity as well as act in a male fashion: she seduces Sisera into her bed, then kills by sticking a phallic instrument into his anatomy. But reading her story as an intertext to Ehud's may not necessarily disclose a symmetrical inversion of gender roles in both.[24] In her deed, Jael acknowledges her female position of 'temptress' although she ultimately acts as a male. In Ehud's case, however, it is implied that Ehud pretends to act in a manner 'unnatural', that is, homosexual, for a male in order to achieve his goal. Read in the light of Jael's story, the Ehud narrative becomes more humane. Although foreign rulers are targeted in both, and those rulers' authority has to be eradicated, the local hero is satirized too: his success depends on deceptive sexuality first (a script usually ascribed to women as their most effective social weapon) and, only then, on his military skill. Although both males and females in the Bible may behave as tricksters, gender ideology still functions in their respective presentation, as it must;[25] and this gender differentiation may cut both ways.

Another foreign king, of Jericho (Josh. 2.2-7), is duped by Rahab, a prostitute who manages to save the Israelite spies; incidentally, the humour of this particular narrative is enhanced by the fun made of the Israelites themselves, who hurry to the local bordello instead of attending to their political and military mission.[26] Once more, while a target for satire is the foreign leader, source-group figures are

22. Alter, *Biblical Narrative*, p. 41.

23. Cf. O. Horn Prouser, 'The Truth about Women and Lying', *JSOT* 61 (1994), p. 26, and further references in nn. 32, 33 and 34 thereof.

24. But cf. M. Sternberg, *The Poetics of Biblical Narrative* (Bloomington: Indiana University Press, 1985), p. 282; and Prouser, 'Women and Lying', pp. 26-27.

25. *Contra* Prouser, 'Women and Lying'.

26. Y. Zakovitch, 'Humor and Theology, or the Successful Failure of the Israelite Intelligence (Josh. 2): A Literary-Folklorist Approach', in S. Niditch (ed.), *Text and Tradition: The Hebrew Bible and Folklore* (Atlanta: Scholars Press, 1990), pp. 75-98.

satirized too; and a female figure of enhanced sexuality plays a prominent subversive role in the comic representation. Ahab's childish response to Naboth's refusal to give up his vineyard—the king rejects food and retires to his bed—is made all the more ridiculous by his wife's resourceful actions. She gets the vineyard for him by seemingly legal means (1 Kgs 21). That the stakes here are political, a test case for the Israelite king's rights to land appropriation, has been noticed by numerous modern commentators, especially in the light of Ugaritic practices. For the presumed Judahite or Judaean editors of the Bible, Ahab the Israelite is a foreigner; and his wife Jezebel is even more so. The comic properties of the king's portrayal as petulant child are emphasized by the effective intervention of his female partner. Ahab's leadership is thus undermined: if a woman has to act for him in a legal matter of such import, then he is ineffectual. And the same goes for Jeroboam, who sends his nameless wife to question the man of god about their son's—his heir's—health and fate (1 Kgs 14). Thematically, men who behave like this are unfit for government. The motif of a woman's killing a leader—especially a military leader, like Abimelek (Judg. 9.50-57), Sheba (2 Sam. 20) or Sisera (Judg. 4–5)—is an extreme expression of this configuration and the vision of gender roles that motivate it.

Take the well-known example of Ahasuerus. He has woman trouble. Vashti (Est. 1) sabotages his authority by refusing his command to come. He loses face in public. He is a symbolic figurehead; his weakness is correctly diagnosed as legal vulnerability for himself and his subjects. He is portrayed as husband first, ruler later—is this how politics should work? Consequently, a special edict is issued so that male dominance over wives is assured throughout the empire. Instead of dealing with matters of state, the king occupies himself with choosing a new wife (ch. 2). Esther disobeys him too, in her case by coming to him unbidden (4.11; 5.1-2), then manipulates him to her own ends. Haman finally falls because the king imagines that Haman wants to 'rape' Esther (7.8). Mordecai achieves success and grandeur through Esther's agency. I would suggest (following Beal's analysis of Est. 1)[27] that all three leaders in Esther, the two foreign ones

27. T.K. Beal, 'Tracing Esther's Beginnings', in A. Brenner (ed.), *A Feminist Companion to Esther, Judith and Susanna* (Sheffield: Sheffield Academic Press, forthcoming; based on a paper delivered at the annual SBL meeting in Washington, 1993). Beal maintains that the ridiculed excesses of festivities and dealings in ch. 1 should be taken seriously and explored for their function within the overall story line of Esther.

(Ahasuerus and Haman) and the source-group one (Mordecai), are satirized by this plot line. In the Bible, women are by and large barred from direct political activities. When they engage in it—like in the cases of Deborah and Jael, Jezebel, Athaliah, Esther, even Miriam (Num. 12)—this reflects badly on the social and political fabric of their society.

My last example is from the Aramaic text of Daniel 5. King Belshazzar has a feast in which his advisers and women, inferior sexual companions, concubines and courtesans, participate. An orgiastic/ cultic element is strongly suggested (Dan. 5.1-4); the association of feast, women and alcohol, already encountered in Esther, sets a certain mood and certain readerly expectations. An enigmatic writing appears on the wall. What does the king do? Does he rise to the occasion, as a true leader should? No, he doesn't. He and his nobles are at once transformed from male sexual hedonists to confused cowards. The king and his governors are unable to confront the situation. The NEB translates, 'The king's mind was filled with dismay and he turned pale, he became limp in every limb and his knees knocked together' (v. 6).

This translation, however, masks the crude humour of the source text. The Aramaic of v. 6 is:

אדין מלכא זיוהי שנוהי ורעיונהי יבהלונה וקטרי חרצה משתרין
וארכבתה דא לדא נקשן

To translate, verbatim, 'Then the king's face changed, and his thoughts scared him, *and the knots of his loins became loose* [my italics], and his knees knocked together'. Now, the Aramaic word which I translated as 'loins', חרצה (and its Hebrew cognate חלצים) denotes 'hip' or 'loin', *not* 'every limb'. These terms are also euphemisms for the hip or loin as the anatomical locus of procreation, as in the biblical idiom 'son of the loins',[28] mostly used of male 'loins' as symbolic of male sexual virility.[29] In an allusive idiom, the 'girdle of the loins' (חלצים) is symbolic of military and political (that is, male) competence.[30] The equation between male virility and political power is obvious here as elsewhere: male ability to sire a male heir is considered an important component of his leadership potential in the Bible,[31] as in other

28. As in, for instance, 1 Kgs 8.19; 2 Chron. 6.9.
29. Gen. 35.11; Job 38.3; 40.4.
30. Isa. 5.27; 11.5.
31. Cf. the reiterated divine promises to the patriarchs in Genesis.

ancient literatures.[32] 'Loins' (חלצים) is indeed used once of a woman giving birth and holding on to her stomach while so doing (Jer. 30.6), which defines the anatomical part denoted as the seat of pain.[33] Thus it is parallel to the Hebrew מעים , 'bowels', a lexeme that exhibits the same contiguity of sense and range as חלצים/חרצה, 'loins' in Aramaic and Hebrew: an anatomical organ, the 'hips' or 'belly' or 'digestive system', but also the seat of procreative powers, again mostly male,[34] but female too.[35] Semantic analysis, then, shows that King Belshazzar does something much more definite than 'tremble in every limb'. He is hit exactly in the organs he has employed in his orgiastic drinking feast; instead of having sexual intercourse with his concubines, he becomes impotent; instead of eating and drinking, he loses control and becomes incontinent. He is demoted at once from sexual adult male to a an asexual child who can't control his bowel and/or bladder movements. This is the plain meaning of the text.

And who saves the situation? The queen does. She hears the commotion caused by the king and his advisers—all male, of course (vv. 8-9). She comes to the drinking house, calmly comforts the king and advises him to approach Daniel for an interpretation of the writing on the wall. Daniel is invited and delivers the interpretation that is catastrophic for Belshazzar; his prediction materializes that same night. The queen is right. She knows exactly who should be approached for advice, whose God should be consulted. She remains cool and presents her counsel to the king in a respectful manner, so that he can adopt her recommendation without losing face (vv. 10-12), to the point that he repeats her counsel to Daniel—as if it were his own idea, of course (vv. 13-16). The queen's dignified manner, her recognition of divine truth and its representatives, her remembrance of the state matters she alludes to[36]—everything she says and does satirizes the king and his 'wise men' further. She is the adult in court; she's the mature stateswoman, whereas they are frightened children. Such are the pagan rulers: they are unfit for government, for their wives are more astute than they are.[37] The difference between royal

32. Cf. the Ugaritic Keret and Daniel epics, where the reversal of the king's situation, from sonless hence ineffectual ruler to father to an heir, forms the linchpin of the unfolding action.

33. *BDB*, p. 323.

34. Gen. 15.4; 2 Sam. 7.12; 16.11; Isa. 48.19; 2 Chron. 32.21, and elsewhere.

35. Gen. 25.23; Isa. 49.1; Ruth 1.11.

36. The queen remembers Daniel's former position in the court during the reign of Nebuchadnezzar, the king's own father, v. 11.

37. The queen's words even contain a pun which the king unwittingly repeats,

husband and wife is stressed by her understanding of Daniel's
strength (v. 11) and by the king's offer of material rewards (v. 16),
which Daniel rejects (v. 17) and which, indeed, cannot be effective
because Belshazzar is killed that same night (v. 30). Clearly, the king
is dense. As is written in Qoheleth, 'Woe betide the land whose king
is a child and whose princes feast in the morning' (Qoh. 10.16),
instead of busying themselves with matters of state. Insinuations of
sexual misconduct and incontinence are made; moral, mental and
intellectual inferiority to a social subordinate, a woman, is attributed
to the king. Thus is the foreign ruler disqualified from office and his
fate justified. The sexual and toilet humour is dark and might not be
to our liking, but it achieves a serious critical aim: the subversion of
(proverbial) foreign powers who act against Jews and Judaism. Contempt is well-served by such a presentation, which allows verbal
aggression even where political conditions exclude physical retalia-
tion against foreign oppressors and their leaders. To impute impotence to somebody potent and powerful is almost the only kind of
revenge available to the impotent and the powerless.

This configuration of the ridiculed foreign ruler and, by implication, the foreign power he embodies, is significant for a reconstructed
sociology of ancient Israel, as it is narrated by Israel's own canonical
texts. First, once more a normative biblical attitude is revealed:
women are disqualified from government. Compare Isa. 3.12:
women's socio-political control is part of the nation's ills.[38] Secondly,
this presentation subverts precisely the cultural assumptions underlying it: when women are presented as more ingenious than some
men (rulers) in the public arena, this constitutes an implicit admission
that females may be politically competent (even while the framework
signifies denial of woman power). And thirdly, the configuration
illuminates an important aspect of community resistance to foreign
political power.

The Hebrew Bible and later Judaism and Christianity generally
view authority, including royal authority, as essential for social order
and community survival,[39] particularly so within a hostile political

be it a deliberate pun or otherwise, at his own expense. She defines Daniel, among
other things, as a man who 'unties knots', that is, 'solves problems'; the Aramaic
word for 'knots' here (קִטְרִין) is exactly that used for the loose 'knots' of the king's
'loins'.

38. Although some ancient versions attempt to remove the reference to women
here (cf. *BHS*), the following verses, 3.16–4.1—which predict a terrible fate for
Jerusalem's elite women—authenticate the sentiment expressed.

39. Cf., for instance, advice on this matter in Qoh. 8.2-4; 10.20.

environment. Restraint, obedience to and at least a modicum of outward respect for the ruler are usually advocated in situations of dependency. Humour, the weapon of the disadvantaged, is of great help in coping with such situations. It affords a certain release. It exposes the ruler's grotesque, absurd, comical, weak, childish, immature traits. Abusive humour may also subvert by paving the way for change: an ineffectual, ridiculous ruler run by women and controlled by his bodily functions is an unfit ruler. Thus, this satiric configuration is a double-edged sword reminiscent of the one stuck into Eglon's fat belly by Ehud. It is an ideological tool that serves endurance and acceptance, that is, passive resistance; but it also facilitates rebellion against its unworthy subverted object, that is, active resistance to an oppressive Other.

Josephus and some Biblical Foreign Rulers

But how do I know that my reading of the Obtuse Foreign Ruler configuration, a reading obviously motivated by my feminist concerns, is anchored in the cultural world of ancient Judaism and Christianity? I appeal to an ancient interpretation as an intertext. I appeal also to Flavius Josephus because he is an ancient, chronologically placeable commentator who undertook to retell biblical stories to foreigners in a foreign language.

In his *Jewish Antiquities*, Flavius Josephus introduces certain systematic modifications to some of the narratives mentioned. All traces of homosexual and secretion allusions are removed from his recounting of the Eglon and Ehud story.[40] Ahasuerus in Josephus is a reformed character, a more politically active and level-headed ruler than he is in the Esther Scroll. For instance, in the Bible Esther and Mordecai are commanded to write letters in order to revoke Haman's plan to exterminate the Jews, and they do so (Est. 8.7-14). In Josephus, the king himself sends a letter to all governors and provinces too, and Haman (rather than Esther and Mordecai) is defined as a foreigner.[41] Ahasuerus is humanized by other means also: love for Vashti and later pronounced domestic bliss with Esther are attributed to him. Josephus also omits the graphic description of Belshazzar's fear, makes him seem a much better ruler than the account in Daniel will have him, and cites the *king's old mother* (or grandmother) as the wise

40. *Ant.* 5.4.1-3.
41. *Ant.* 11.6.12, after the LXX?

female counselor instead of his *wife*,[42] against the plain meaning of 'queen' (מלכת) in the biblical text (Dan. 5.10). In short, Josephus goes out of his way to minimize the foreign rulers' sinister and comical properties.

Now why would Josephus do that? The reason should be sought in the ideological convictions manifest in his works. Now, in *The Jewish War against the Romans*[43] Josephus describes three 'philosophies', three ideological or religio-political factions in Judaism and Judah of his day, the first century CE: Pharisees, Sadducees and Essenes. In the *Jewish Antiquities* he adds a 'fourth philosophy', the Zealots or fundamentalists.[44] The latter are characterized by radicalism, especially a doctrine that rejects obedience to foreign (Roman) powers, recalling the biblical maxim that Israel owes veneration to YHWH alone (Num. 25.55), not to any other worldly or divine force. The religio-ideological debate on accepting or rejecting Roman authority during the Great Jewish Revolt was verbalized and enacted by the various factions, so that the ensuing civil strife excluded the feasibility of autonomy under the Pax Romana.[45]

Josephus himself was a beneficiary of Roman military leaders and emperors. He was a Jewish commander in the Revolt who went over to the other side after suffering military defeat. The Romans saved his life; in return, he glorified them or at least downplayed their attempts at devastating Jewish identity and political entity. His political vision is shrewd. However, he certainly sides with the foreign power, politically if not religiously. The configuration that represents foreign rulers as comical, sexually motivated morons prefigures the Zealots' ideology, but does not serve Josephus's purposes. This might be the reason why the configuration is omitted from his writings. His recounting is more favourable to the foreign rulers than the biblical accounts. Josephus appears to have falsified and modified the biblical texts in the name of his own ideology. In the process, the humour—cruel, abusive, low-brow—was eliminated and, therefore, the meaningful role of the females was minimized, repressed or suppressed.

Josephus's omissions seem to support my readings. He seems to have recognized the subversive potential of the humour involved; otherwise, why should he have bothered to remove all traces of it? It is funny how his ideological concerns and mine, which are as

---

42. *Ant.* 10.11.2-4.
43. *War* 2.8.1-14.
44. *Ant.* 18.1.1-6.
45. Hence, the Zealots even objected to the census (mentioned also in Lk. 2.1-5).

different as can be, appear to be anchored in the same understanding of the biblical texts and the gender norms that inform them.[46]

Concluding Remarks

Feminism coined the slogan, 'The personal is political'. I hope that I've managed to illustrate how this principle operates in biblical humour and, also, how it may be twisted and inverted: the political may become personal. In the Bible, in biblical interpretation and in theology, in religion and in religious texts, women and femininity and female sexuality may be loved; however, they are also and habitually marginalized into foreign Others. This ambivalence is a matter for concern, and anger, and laughter. The same can be said about the lack of acknowledgment and/or identification of biblical humour. It is funny, really, how insight and pleasure are denied in the name of outdated socio-religious attitudes and prejudice. Feminists may laugh as well as continue to be angry. By way of conclusion, I would like to quote from an interview with Gloria Steinem, a well-known American feminist and the editor of Ms magazine (in *The Sunday Times*, 15 May 1994). Ms Steinem is quoted as saying,

46. A discussion followed the reading of this paper at the SOTS meeting. I would like to respond here briefly to a few of the remarks made.

Professor Malamat said that, generally speaking, he views feminist Bible criticism as admissible (like other types of criticism) if and when it contributes to knowledge. I hope that my analysis shows how the questions we ask ourselves from our gendered reader location help to illuminate rarely explored facets of the biblical text and cultural world. Professor Greenfield attempted to fault my analysis on specific grounds. With regards to Dan. 5, he claims that the Aramaic words קטרי חרצה משתרין indeed signify (and also in Ugaritic) simply 'tremble in every limb'; however, this reading fails to acknowledge the linguistic movement from the specific/concrete (bodily function) to the metaphorized/general/abstract (trembling, fear). Greenfield also states that the 'queen' mentioned is, indeed, 'queen mother' in Babylonian texts. This is invalid for Dan. 5, in which 'Babylon' is remote and allegorical; that author or ancient readers of this text knew of Babylonian practice (assuming this was the case; there is some critical literature for the contrary) is at the very least implausible. Greenfield's contention that Josephus recounted biblical materials faithfully, according to the texts he had, is debatable. Professor Lambert accused me of eisegesis, whereas I imagined that a reader response perspective is a better description. It seems to me that these comments illustrate the difficulties feminist critics of the Bible and theology face when they enter the mainstream academic discourse, as implied by the title and the beginning of this paper. Other speakers suggested application of the Obtuse Foreign Ruler configuration and the self-criticism it incorporates to other Hebrew Bible and other biblical texts, notably Judith.

Humour has certainly always mattered to me very much... Of course, our image as feminists is that we don't have a sense of humour. I think there have been times in my life, especially in those early years when I was having such a hard time being taken seriously because there was so much ridicule, that I allowed it to happen. I allowed my humour to recede. And I missed it. Why should they take our humour away from us?

Why indeed?

SELF-RESPONSE TO 'WHO'S AFRAID OF FEMINIST CRITICISM?'

Athalya Brenner

It is the nature of things that returning to past writings is mostly done with reluctance. The feeling that it could be done at least differently, if not better, is a nagging presence. And this time, the revisit of my 'Who's Afraid' was conducted under the influence of re-reading Hans Deventer's 'Another Wise Queen (Mother) — Women's Wisdom in Daniel 5.10-12?', in this volume. So, in this revisit, I can't but think about the old Jewish adage: what are we looking at in any particular moment, the full or the empty half of the glass? This is a matter of choice as well as conscious or non-conscious motivation.

I chose to highlight my impression that women's wisdom, although acknowledged in the Hebrew Bible at times, more often than not is a handmaid to male authority, needs and aims. In Lacanian terms, wise women in the HB serve the Phallus that is denied them, by definition. This holds true also, perhaps especially, in relation to the queen of Daniel 5. She is pitched in between the cupidity and fear of one male camp, the king and his companions, on the one hand; and Daniel's wisdom and divine inspiration on the other hand. She is the mediator, and in that sense 'wise' and knowing. But, unlike the woman approaching David to restore Absalom (2 Sam. 14) or the woman from Abel (2 Sam. 20), her mediation brings no peace but a message of destruction. In between two named male camps, diametrically opposed to each other, she stands nameless. And, unlike a wise Esther, or a wise Rahab, we hear nothing of her escaping the king's fate. I therefore stick to my guns and repeat an earlier position. The queen, with all her wisdom, is there to serve as a reflection to the king: the 'wiser' she seems, the more obtuse, worthy of scorn and laughable he automatically becomes.

And I wonder, once again, why it is so much easier for (I earnestly beg to be excused) male commentators, from Josephus through Origen through Malamat and Greenfield and many others to Deventer, to attribute wisdom and a mediating position to the *queen mother* rather than to a *queen consort*, as clearly indicated by the biblical text. No amount of cognate materials can be convincing on this score: those cognate (and biblical) materials about the special position of a queen mother do not cancel out a similar position for a queen consort. The HB feels more at home with the authority of queen mothers; it allows for legitimate queen-consort authority in foreign contexts only. The same, it seems, is true of the Bible's commentators. A de-eroticized, partly de-sexualized (albeit still gendered) older wise woman, a *mother figure*, appears to be easier to cope with in a wisdom context. Why this should be so, when images of Wisdom as an erotic bride are to be found easily in Proverbs 1–9, is beyond the scope of feminist Bible criticism. The fact seems to be that a maternal type is better suited for the role. Is a de-sexualized, or post-sexual, female figure better suited to own the Phallus, by virtue of approaching the status of a male? This view of the queen as a once removed queen mother seems to invest her, whatever she may be, with authority. This is the half-full part. On the other hand, her removal to the House of Lords — so to speak — is a clear signifier of the half-empty part.

Images of capable women do appear in the HB. However, I remain convinced that, more often than not, such female images are there not in order to tell us something, anything, positive or otherwise, about femaleness and femininity, but as mirrors for male images and male behaviour. The more capable and wiser the female figure is, the more stupid the male counterpart she mirrors becomes. The myth of gender relations thus inscribed in the biblical text is based on a distorted reflection. If readers choose to lift the images out of this context and to read them separately, individually, as images positive for contemporary women's self-esteem, this is once again a case of privileging the half-full part. If commentators prefer to chastise, in the sense of imaging as presumably chaste, such female figures in order to cope with their power this, once again, is a matter of half-full or half-empty, depending on your personal viewpoint. The nameless 'queen' in Daniel 5, after all, is but the real messenger's shadow.

ANOTHER WISE QUEEN (MOTHER)—WOMEN'S WISDOM IN DANIEL 5.10-12?*

H.J.M. van Deventer

Introduction

The queen in Daniel 5 has been recognized as 'reminiscent of the Wisdom figure in Proverbs'.[1] In this study I want to highlight and elaborate on this reminiscence. Firstly, I present a brief survey of a few theoretical aspects related to gender criticism. Secondly, I discuss Wisdom texts outside the generally acknowledged 'wisdom corpus'. Thirdly, the focus shifts to the character of the queen (mother) in Daniel 5. Finally, I will conclude by referring to a South African context—and, more specifically, the context of the Lovedu people living in the Northern Province of South Africa.

Nowadays there are quite a number of studies available that survey the terrain of feminist readings of the Bible. At least two of these provide us with recent and positive critiques of the whole project of gender criticism. These two studies are discussed below and will form the parameters for my thinking in this regard from a specifically South African context.

The first study that receives our attention dates from the first half of the 1990s. In this contribution Alice Bach[2] addresses a number of important issues that demand the attention of the 'feminist guild'. She calls for a more dissonant 'buzz'[3] from this community. This buzz

---

*   A version of this paper was read at the 1999 Annual Meeting of the SBL held in Boston. I would like to thank Helen Efthimiadis-Keith, Frances Klopper and Christina Landman for reading through earlier drafts of this paper and for the valuable comments that they made.

1.   Cf. Athalya Brenner, 'Some Observations on the Figurations of Women in Wisdom Literature', in *idem* (ed.), *A Feminist Companion to Wisdom Literature* (Sheffield: Sheffield Academic Press, 1995), p. 65.

2.   Alice Bach, 'Reading Allowed: Feminist Biblical Criticism approaching the Millennium', *Currents in Research: Biblical Studies* 1 (1993), pp. 191-215.

3.   This relates to a beehive metaphor (from Derrida) that she quotes at the beginning of her article.

should be aroused by, among other things, the need to engage with philosophical and political issues; to tackle issues of race and ethnicity; and to re-examine the social construction of masculinity (especially on the part of male critics seeking a home within feminist critical theory). Bach also warns that '[i]f feminism is not to become boringly fashionable, each of us must contend with the ripples and waves of the dominant culture'.[4]

She outlines the development in feminist literary theory from the positivistic 'rhetorical' and text-centred readings, criticising these for not intending 'to topple the privileged and protected status of the biblical canon'.[5] She also warns against studies into the fragmented portraits of women in the Bible that either magnify them as heroines or deflate them as victims, *without* uncovering the social codes reflected in those texts.[6] The road ahead is envisaged as one on which the results of these studies are integrated by means of a cross-cultural comparison to the position of women in similarly constructed societies.[7]

The second study noted here is by Amador.[8] His main point of criticism of 'American feminists' biblical hermeneutics' is that this project ends in *meaning*, without indicating how that uncovered meaning is related to the Bible's rhetorical/ pragmatic function.[9] According to him, the focus on the biblical text and how to uncover its meaning creates barriers to addressing the issues of power that biblical feminist criticism should be focusing on.[10] Instead of concentrating on hermeneutics, Amador proposes a focus on *rhetoric* in which every kind of 'text' is understood as designed 'to persuade an audience to action in contexts of power'.[11]

---

4. Bach, 'Reading Allowed', pp. 191-95.

5. Bach, 'Reading Allowed', p. 197.

6. Bach, 'Reading Allowed', p. 199. She makes the apt remark that as the number of feminist scholars entering the field grows, so the number of female figures 'to [be] pumped up as heroes or to [be] deflated as victims of male authorship is dwindling'.

7. Anthony C. Thiselton (*New Horizons in Hermeneutics* [Grand Rapids: Zondervan, 1992], pp. 459), also refers to this social aspect when he describes what is labelled as socio-critical hermeneutics. It 'encourages questioning about the social order and social interests which texts may be deemed to presuppose or to legitimate'.

8. J.D.H. Amador, 'Feminist Biblical Hermeneutics: A Failure of Theoretical Nerve', *JAAR* 66/1 (1998), pp. 39-57.

9. Amador, 'Feminist Biblical Hermeneutics', p. 41.

10. Amador, 'Feminist Biblical Hermeneutics', p. 46.

11. Amador, 'Feminist Biblical Hermeneutics', p. 51.

Amador's criticism is to the point, albeit perhaps a little harsh. Of course, only correcting the 'patriarchal interpretive error' within a purely academic battleground (Amador's phrase) is not going far enough; but it may be a good place to start—especially for those within an academic profession. From the perspective of the South African, in which an unjust political system was toppled a few years ago, I feel confident to say that an adjustment to an interpretive stance definitely contributed towards the realization of this liberation. I feel just as confident that an unjust social system, although universal, may also be toppled with the contribution from feminist biblical inter-pretation. Interpretation does after all form part of the rhetorical act, although it is not the only part.[12]

This introduction would be incomplete without reference to a (South) African context, since I live and work in this context.[13] In an account of African women's theology, Christina Landman[14] sum-marizes some of the aims of this movement in the fields of theologies and ministries. Regarding theologies, '[t]he stories of people, espe-cially women, in the Bible, bind women from a variety of cultures in Africa together and provide a common source for their healing'; and regarding (healing) ministries it is believed that 'healing comes through telling one's story and listening to the previously muted voices of women who are harassed by unfriendly systems and cus-toms'. Although African women's theology centres on redefining theology in terms of African women's experiences, its methodology acknowledges the importance of integrating philosophical thinking and experience.[15]

To summarize, the aims of the rest of this study are twofold: not merely to provide an interesting (and interested) reading of a text

---

12. Dianne Bergent (*Israel's Wisdom Literature: A Liberation-Critical Reading* [Minneapolis: Fortress Press, 1997], p. 10), in a discussion of an interpretive method for her liberation-critical reading of Israel's wisdom literature, links interpretation and rhetoric. She maintains that 'the end of the entire interpretive endeavor is rhetorical. The Bible, if it is to be authentically the word of God, must transform the minds and hearts of those who hear it. That is the final and true goal of interpretation.'

13. For the following contextualization I have made use of a volume hailed by its editors as 'born and bred in Africa': Simon Maimela and Adrio König (eds.), *Initiation into Theology: The Rich Variety of Theology and Hermeneutics* (Pretoria: JL van Schaik, 1998), p. 3.

14. Christina Landman, 'African Women's Theology', in Maimela and König (eds.), *Initiation into Theology*, p. 139.

15. Landman, 'African Women's Theology', pp. 137-38.

(story), but also for this reading to have an effect within a real-life society; hence my attempts to link my interpretation of this story to other (real-life) 'stories' in similar contexts.

Women's Wisdom in the Hebrew Bible/Old Testament

It is not possible to treat the broader concept of 'wisdom' and its development in Israelite religion here.[16] This concept is manifested in Israelite religious literature in collections such as Proverbs, Job and Qoheleth. However, today studies that focus on the wisdom pheno-menon are not restricted to these texts.[17] 'Traces' of wisdom literature are also sought and (therefore?) found in other texts from the Hebrew Bible/Old Testament, although some reservations as to the method(s) employed in this regard have been voiced.[18]

Murphy outlines at least three criteria a text should be tested against before claiming wisdom influences.[19] These are vocabulary, literary form, and content. Even if a combination of these criteria is found, one should be careful not to claim wisdom influence as such, unless literary forms are made the monopoly of specific 'classes' in society. Therefore, Murphy is more at ease in referring to 'wisdom's echoes' in other parts of the Hebrew Bible/Old Testament. To avoid possible circular argumentation we should be careful not to describe texts outside the 'wisdom corpus' as wisdom compositions.[20]

Bearing this in mind, we can now look at the concept of women's wisdom as attested in the Hebrew Bible/Old Testament. We begin

---

16. A number of recent studies on the subject of wisdom literature and the wisdom tradition in the Hebrew Bible/Old Testament are available. Cf. Donn F. Morgan, *Wisdom in the Old Testament Traditions* (Atlanta: John Knox Press, 1981); Claus Westermann, *Wurzeln der Weisheit: Die ältesten Sprüche Israels und anderer Völker* (Göttingen: Vanderhoeck & Ruprecht, 1990); Joseph Blenkinsopp, *Wisdom and Law in the Old Testament: The Ordering of Life in Israel and Early Judaism* (Oxford: Oxford University Press, rev. edn, 1995); Ronald E. Murphy, *The Tree of Life: An Exploration of Biblical Wisdom Literature* (Grand Rapids: Eerdmans, 2nd edn, 1996).

17. This is already true of a collection from, the middle of the twentieth century; cf. some of the contributions in M. Noth and D.W. Thomas (eds.), *Wisdom in Israel and in the Ancient Near East: Presented to H.H. Rowley in Celebration of his Sixty-Fifth Birthday* (Leiden: E.J. Brill, 1955). Cf. also, more recently, Morgan, *Wisdom*; and J. Day, R.P. Gordon and H.G.M. Williamson (eds.), *Wisdom in Ancient Israel: Essays in Honor of J.A. Emerton* (Cambridge: Cambridge University Press, 1995).

18. Cf. Murphy, *Tree of Life*, pp. 98-102.

19. Murphy, *Tree of Life*, p. 98.

20. Murphy, *Tree of Life*, p. 221.

with Fontaine's analysis of Prov. 31.1-9[21] — a text reflecting the words of a queen mother addressing her son, King Lemuel. In this text Fontaine finds 'one instance within Israel's wisdom tradition where we might reasonably posit female authorship, or at least composition, if not the actual writing down of the text'.[22] This 'speech' by the queen mother, who, according to Fontaine, acts as a woman sage in the public domain, exhibits the following features:

1. She makes use of direct address and familial terms.
2. She makes direct admonitions and prohibitions using imperatives.
3. She expects her words to be heard and obeyed.
4. She takes up the usual themes of the wisdom genre by warning against drunkenness and women and giving advice about performing the tasks assigned to rulers.[23]

In uncovering an 'inner-Israelite basis' for the development of counselling wisdom, Schroer[24] discusses instances found in the Old Testament of wise counselling women, who include counselling wives and mothers of kings. Taking care to distinguish between 'historical or sociological data' and 'literary creations', Camp[25] identifies motherhood in her discussion of literary and theological developments of the historical phenomenon of 'the mother' as 'provid[ing] women with what was perhaps their primary source of authority within the Israelite community'.[26] However, when it comes to wise female counsellors in general she does not restrict counselling to the figure of the mother, but also includes the lover and wife as counsellors.[27] In the above discussion, we have noted how certain features within the Old Testament wisdom tradition have been linked to the role of women in society. The fact that these roles are also reflected in written material may point towards female (F) voices in the text. In an

21. Carole R. Fontaine, 'The Social Roles of Women in the World of Wisdom', in Athalya Brenner (ed.), *A Feminist Companion to Wisdom Literature* (Sheffield: Sheffield Academic Press, 1995), pp. 24-49.

22. Fontaine, 'Social Roles', p. 38.

23. Fontaine, 'Social Roles', p. 39.

24. Silvia Schroer, 'Wise and Counselling Women in Ancient Israel: Literary and Historical Ideals of the Personified Hokma', in A. Brenner (ed.), *A Feminist Companion to Wisdom Literature* (Sheffield: Sheffield Academic Press, 1995), pp. 67-84.

25. Claudia V. Camp, *Wisdom and the Feminine in the Book of Proverbs* (Sheffield: Almond Press, 1985), pp. 75-76.

26. Camp, *Wisdom and the Feminine*, p. 81.

27. Camp, *Wisdom and the Feminine*, p. 93.

important contribution to 'feminist' studies of the Hebrew Bible/Old Testament, Brenner and van Dijk-Hemmes introduced us to the re-routing of gender positions entrenched in the texts away from gender-ing authorship to gendering the text's authority. This route opened a quest for identifying so-called female/feminine (F) voices within the text.[28]

Brenner and van Dijk-Hemmes based their method on a study by Goitein, who did fieldwork among Yemenite people returning to Israel during 1949–50.[29] He studied the oral literature (mostly songs and poems) among the Yemenite women and sought to find remnants of similar genres in the Bible. However, his aim was not to 'discuss women as *authors*, but as creators of biblical literary *genres*'.[30] This entails the 'tracking down [of] biblical references to the literary trad-itions practised by women, and checking whether their remains have been preserved in the text'.[31] With regard to wise women in Israel, Goitein remarks that we have no written work of these women, but the writers of the texts put in their mouths what a reader in Israel expected to hear from such a woman.[32] This working hypothesis, set by Goitein, links this part of the present study to what Thiselton[33] refers to as 'socio-critical' hermeneutics that embody 'some trans-contextual, meta-critical principle of critique'.

In this section we noted literary evidence pointing towards the existence of an influential group of people in society. In some cases these people were affiliated to the royal court and exhibit character-istics that are also described in the wisdom literature. We have also noted how the voices of this group could have been preserved in the text. The next section relates these cases to the queen (mother) in Daniel 5, bearing in mind certain reservations we need to consider as regards a text's vocabulary, literary form and content.

The Queen (Mother) in Daniel 5

In the narrative of Daniel 5, King Belshazzar (here the son of the great King Nebuchadnezzar) is feasting together with his concubines. As

---

28. A. Brenner and F. van Dijk-Hemmes, *On Gendering Texts: Female and Male Voices in the Hebrew Bible* (Leiden: E.J. Brill, 1993), pp. 1-10.

29. S.D. Goitein, 'Women as Creators of Biblical Genres', *Prooftexts* 8 (1988), pp. 1-33 (orig. Hebr. 1957).

30. Goitein, 'Women as Creators', p. 5.

31. Brenner and van Dijk-Hemmes, *On Gendering Texts*, p. 90.

32. Goitein, 'Women as Creators', p. 10.

33. Thiselton, *New Horizons in Hermeneutics*, pp. 439-40.

they are drinking from the vessels that had been taken by his father from the Jerusalem Temple, their mood is suddenly soured. A hand appears and writes an indecipherable message on the wall. This leads to a comical situation. First, the king loses control over his bodily functions.[34] Then his wise men are unable to interpret the writing on the wall, and the queen (mother) has to come to his rescue by referring him to Daniel. Daniel in his turn reprimands the king for not humbling himself before the Most High God, and he prophesies that the kingdom will be taken away from Belshazzar. Daniel is rewarded for being the bearer of such bad tidings and receives a third of this kingdom, which is taken that very night by the Medes.

I will now focus on the queen (mother) in this text, hoping to point out that this text resembles what may be considered as a textual deposit of a strand of women's wisdom which can also be found in other parts of the Hebrew Bible/Old Testament. This character, however, raises a few questions that first need to be considered.

First of all, I refer to the queen (mother) although the text in Dan. 5.10 clearly reads only 'queen' (מלכה). This could perhaps be viewed as following in the tradition of Josephus, who minimizes or even suppresses the role of this female character.[35] Josephus found it more appealing to have Belshazzar corrected and counselled by his grandmother and not by his wife.[36] This tradition of viewing the queen as representing an older generation was upheld by a great number of commentators.[37] However, given their literal reading of the text, the

---

34. Cf. in this respect Athalya Brenner, 'Who's Afraid of Feminist Criticism? Who's Afraid of Biblical Humour? The Case of the Obtuse Foreign Ruler in the Hebrew Bible', *JSOT* 63 (1994), pp. 38-54 (reprinted in this volume); as well as Al Wolters, 'Untying the King's Knots: Physiology and Wordplay in Daniel 5', *JBL* 110 (1991), pp. 91-97.

35. Cf. Brenner, 'Who's Afraid', pp. 52-53.

36. Origen opts for Belshazzar's mother (cf. *Jerome's Commentary on Daniel* [trans. G.L. Archer; Grand Rapids: Baker Book House, 1958], p. 58).

37. Cf. S.R. Driver, *The Book of Daniel* (Cambridge: Cambridge University Press, 1900), pp. 64-65; J.A. Montgomery, *The Book of Daniel* (ICC; Edinburgh: T. & T. Clark, 1927), pp. 257-58; G.C. Aalders, *Daniël* (Kampen: Kok, 1962), p. 111; N.W. Porteous, *Daniel: A Commentary* (OTL; Philadelphia: Westminster Press, 1965), p. 79; J.G. Baldwin, *Daniel: An Introduction and Commentary* (TOTC; Leicester: Inter-Varsity Press, 1978), p. 122; L.F. Hartman and A.A. DiLella, *The Book of Daniel* (AB; Garden City, NY: Doubleday, 1978), p. 184; André Lacocque, *The Book of Daniel* (Atlanta: John Knox Press, 1979), p. 97; Robert A. Anderson, *Signs and Wonders: A Commentary on the Book of Daniel* (Grand Rapids: Eerdmans, 1984), p. 57; John E. Goldingay, *Daniel* (WBC; Dallas: Word Books, 1989), p. 109; John J. Collins, *Daniel* (Hermeneia; Minneapolis: Fortress, 1993), p. 248.

suggestion by Josephus and Origen was perhaps more aimed at smoothing the text than at stating a gender bias.[38]

Although we do not have access to the person[39] of the queen (mother) mentioned in Daniel 5 and therefore 'we cannot know whether...she is an accurate representation of a specific historical person',[40] I wish to argue that in order to address the the question of queen[41] or queen mother, the allusion to a historical figure may be of some help. This does not mean, however, that it will necessarily solve the problem.

It is almost universally accepted that the first six chapters in the book of Daniel do not come from the sixth century BCE. Along with Collins,[42] we may agree that the stories in Daniel 1–6 are 'considerably later than the Babylonian period' and possibly stem from the fourth or third century BCE. This dating could be extended even later for the final redaction of these chapters, along with the inclusion of the second ('apocalyptic') section of the book. It is suggested that the book in its final form dates from the second century BCE[43] and, more specifically, from the time just before and during the persecution of the Jews by Antiochus IV Epiphanes.

In 169 BCE, after Antiochus IV Epiphanes returned from a campaign against Egypt and restored Menelaus as high priest in Jerusalem, he received part of the Temple treasure[44] — a treasure also referred to in Dan. 5.2-3. If Antiochus IV Epiphanes is the foreign ruler whom the story in Daniel 5 has in mind (so Lacocque),[45] the

38. Although Jerome's recording of Porphyry's making fun of the fact that the queen knows more than her husband could also serve to lend weight to Brenner's argument (cf. *Commentary*, p. 58).

39. Cf. D.J.A Clines, 'Michal Observed: An Introduction to Reading her Story', in *idem* and T.C Eskenazi (eds.), *Telling Queen Michal's Story: An Experiment in Comparative Interpretation* (Sheffield: JSOT Press, 1991), pp. 24-63.

40. S. Bar-Efrat, *Narrative Art in the Bible* (Sheffield: Sheffield Academic Press, 2nd edn, 1997 [Hebr. orig. 1979]), p. 48.

41. Camp (*Wisdom and the Feminine*, p. 87), also treats the queen here as Belshazzar's wife in a section dealing with the wife as counsellor to her husband, which in turn is viewed as one 'of the expected responsibilities and modes of the Israelite wife' (p. 85).

42. Collins, *Daniel*, p. 37.

43. Lacocque, *Daniel*, pp. 7-8.

44. W.W. Tarn, *Hellenistic Civilisation* (London: Edward Arnold, 3rd edn, 1952), p. 215.

45. Lacocque (*Daniel*, p. 92) remarks that 'it is possible to see Antiochus behind the Belshazzar of this chapter'.

character of the queen mentioned in the text might be explored in light of evidence from the second century BCE.

Furthermore, it is striking that Antiochus IV was born of a marriage between Antiochus III and a certain Laodice.[46] Later Antiochus IV also married a woman by the name of Laodice. She was probably the widow (and sister) of his elder brother, who—just to complicate matters further—was also named Antiochus. Thus, the mother and the wife of Antiochus IV were both named Laodice.[47] Although this evidence is too meagre to form the basis of a concrete theory, it could be put forward as part of an argument that we need not make a final decision on the issue of the queen or the queen mother in Daniel 5.

We should also look briefly at the social role of a queen mother. In this regard our character echoes the (influential) character of the גבירה (sometimes translated as 'lady') mentioned in the Hebrew Bible/Old Testament (cf. 1 Kgs 15.13; 2 Kgs 10.13; Jer. 13.18, 29.2).[48] The queen mother is also pictured as a female counsellor to the king along the lines of Lady Wisdom in Proverbs.[49]

Moving on from the historical aspects, I now want to consider the literary aspects of the queen (mother). Although the literary function of the queen (mother) in the narrative has been argued to be parallel to that of Arioch in Daniel 2 (who also introduces Daniel to the king to solve his problem, cf. 2.25),[50] care should be taken not to '[relegate] characters to being mere functions in the plot'.[51] It would be worthwhile, therefore, to compare the character of Arioch in Daniel 2 to that of the (unnamed) queen (mother) in Daniel 5.

---

46. Laodice, married to Antiochus III, is praised by her husband for her exemplary conduct and her piety towards the gods. Cf. Grace H. Macurdy, *Hellenistic Queen: A Study of Woman-Power in Macedonia, Seleucid Syria and Ptolemaic Egypt* (New York: AMS Press, 1977 [1932]), p. 93.

47. Cf. Pieter van't Hof, 'Bijdrage tot de kennis van Antiochus IV Epiphanes koning van Sirië' (DLitt dissertation, Vrije Universiteit Amsterdam, 1955), pp. 14-15.

48. For a discussion of the גבירה cf. N.-E. A. Andreasen, 'The Role of the Queen Mother in Israelite Society', *CBQ* 45 (1983), pp. 179-94; A. Brenner, *The Israelite Woman: Social Role and Literary Type in Biblical Narrative* (Sheffield: JSOT Press, 1985); Z. Ben-Barak, 'The Status and Right of the *Gebîrâ*', in A. Brenner (ed.), *A Feminist Companion to Samuel and Kings* (Sheffield: Sheffield Academic Press, 1994), pp. 170-85.

49. Andreasen, 'Role', p. 188.

50. Lacocque, *Daniel*, p. 97; Andreasen, 'Role', p. 57; D.N. Fewell, *Circle of Sovereignty: Plotting Politics in the Book of Daniel* (Nashville: Abingdon Press, 1991), p. 88.

51. D.M. Gunn and D.N. Fewell, *Narrative in the Hebrew Bible* (Oxford: Oxford University Press, 1993), p. 48.

An initial reading points out the following differences:

1. Arioch is a man, the queen a woman.
2. Arioch is an insider 'going out' (כפק) to kill the sages, while the queen is an outsider 'going in' (אללח) to the 'dampened' festivities.
3. Arioch is named and given a title ('chief of the royal executioners'), the queen has only a title and no name—the only unnamed speaking character in this tale.
4. Arioch acts on orders (cf. 2.13-14; 24-25), while the queen acts independently.
5. Arioch is addressed for the most part (2.14-15, 24), the queen addresses the king (5.10-12).
6. Arioch has a short speech mostly put in his mouth by Daniel (2.25), but the queen has a much longer speech, of which only the introduction is influenced by the previous narration.
7. Arioch's speech ends abruptly, despite his claim to fame ('I have found a man from the exiles of Judah' [2.25]), with the king addressing Daniel in the next verse (2.26); the queen's speech ends with an order (imperative) (5.12) which is executed in the next verse (5.13).[52]

Leaving the suggested literary connection between the queen (mother) in Daniel 5 and Arioch in Daniel 2 at that, I shall now address the role of this character within the narrative. In her first sentence the queen seems to be following protocol uttering the phrase, 'O king, live forever' (cf. 2.4). That this utterance is in fact meant to be ironic is indicated by the content of the rest of her speech, the fact that Daniel, a minor subject, is not reported as making the same utterance (5.17), and the fact that, in the context of the rest of the story, this wish is frustrated in the last verse, which reports the death of the king. Her next sentence echoes the narrator's earlier report concerning the king's condition and serves to inform the reader that the queen's perception of his condition is correct.[53]

The queen's next sentence echoes the exact words of king Nebuchadnezzar in the previous chapter (cf. 4.5 MT). This introduces us to an aspect of the queen's speech that Fewell describes as doing more than it is saying.[54] In this verse there are three references to Daniel (as yet unnamed). Two of these references echo the words of

52. Cf. Fewell, *Circle of Sovereignty*, p. 90.
53. Fewell, *Circle of Sovereignty*, p. 88; cf. Bar-Efrat, *Narrative Art*, p. 59.
54. Fewell, *Circle of Sovereignty*, p. 89.

King Nebuchadnezzar in Daniel 4.5, 6. The fact that Daniel is perhaps not the primary referent here is stressed by the five direct references to Belshazzar's father, identified in the narrative as King Nebuchad-nezzar.[55] Fewell opines that the queen's speech undermines the kingship of Belshazzar, identifying it even with the voice of the dead King Nebuchadnezzar.[56]

In the second part of this speech (v. 12) the queen names Daniel as able to interpret the writing on the wall. However, the context in which this is done, and especially the words used, echo the under-mining spirit of the first part (v. 11). Earlier in the narrative we learned that the joints (lit. knots) of the king's loins were loosened (v. 6), a euphemism for losing bladder and bowel control. In the second part of her speech the queen refers Daniel's ability to loosen knots, a wordplay on the loosening of the king's joints (knots). As Fewell wittingly asks: 'If the handwriting on the wall has 'loosened the knots of the king's loins', what does the queen think Daniel's interpretation will do?'[57]

In this section I elaborated on a few historical and literary aspects related to the character of the queen (mother) in Daniel 5. In the next section I shall try to point out the connections between the issues raised thus far.

Tying a Few Knots

From the discussion above we see how the speech of the queen has a broader function: she does not merely introduce Daniel to the king. Let us consider the following: her words are a direct address in which familial terms (cf. 'your father') are used; he takes control of the situation and makes use of imperatives; her words are not only heard, but also obeyed without any further ado; and although she does not take up the usual themes of the wisdom genre (such as warnings

---

55. The glorification of the time of the king's father by the queen (mother) as well as by Daniel is also echoed in an episode from the second century BCE. We learn about Antiochus III that, after extending the Seleucid Empire to include Judea, he did the following: he promised to provide supplies for religious cere-monies in the Temple, restored sacred buildings, remitted taxes for three years and granted the Jewish community the right to live according to their ancestral reli-gion, as well as prohibiting foreigners from entering the holy areas in Jerusalem. Cf. Otto Markholm, *Antiochus IV of Syria* (Copenhagen: Gyldendalske Boghandel, 1966), p. 135.

56. Fewell, *Circle of Sovereignty*, p. 89.

57. Fewell, *Circle of Sovereignty*, p. 89.

against drunkenness and women), the context suggests an atmosphere in which such a warning is to be expected (cf. below).

Furthermore, a number of words that are closely related to the wisdom tradition are heard in her speech. The most important of these is, of course, חכמה (5.11).[58] Taking the context within which this narrative is set into consideration, we find an almost orgiastic atmosphere created by the introductory verses (5.1-2). In this atmosphere there is present a king, concubines and wine. Within a wisdom tradition this king is in need of a rebuke, most probably from his mother (cf. Prov. 31.3, 4).[59] Thus, in the words of Camp, we find here a wise woman (along the lines of either a mother or wife — perhaps purposely ambiguous). She stems from a wisdom background that is not only theoretical in this instance but, borrowing from the theory, is also placed within a 'performance context' where she is easily recognizable.[60]

In the narrative she is paving the way for a second 'rebuke' — this time from Daniel. I do not think that the role of the queen (mother) — here challenging male control along acceptable social lines — should be viewed negatively. Although she challenges the king, the queen (mother) in Daniel 5 is not a sorceress.[61] What we have here is most probably an F voice in the text that is not merely being used in the narrative for the patriarchal (?) aim of the narrator (to belittle someone). This F voice also represents a recognizable strand within the Jewish society that could be contextualized within present-day societies when commenting on this text.

Returning to Africa

The well-known African theologian, Mercy Amba Oduyoye, wrote that 'Doing theology involves knowing what others have written on the subject, doing your own research, listening and studying the contemporary scene and context and finally having something to say on

---

58.   R.N. Whybray, *The Intellectual Tradition in the Old Testament* (Berlin: W. de Gruyter, 1974), pp. 75-76; cf. Robert P. Gordon, 'A House Divided: Wisdom in Old Testament Narrative Traditions', in Day, Gordon and Williamson (eds.), *Wisdom in Ancient Israel*, p. 96.

59.   Goitein ('Women as Creators', p. 12) refers to warnings against the temptations of women and against drinking wine as part of the repertoire of the Hebrew 'rebuker'.

60.   Cf. Camp, *Wisdom and the Feminine*, pp. 166, 177.

61.   Fontaine, 'Social Roles', p. 48.

the subject.'[62] In order to explain how what has been said relates to an African context, I would like to return to Landman's summary of the aims of African women's theology[63]. These include 'inculterating' religious beliefs (i.e. 'to confront culture with belief, but also to accommodate the one within the other'), whereby 'liberative' models are reclaimed from scriptures and applied to traditional cultures; and seeking to empower women against women-unfriendly systems, again by reclaiming models from the official scriptures. In light of this, it is possible to relate this wise queen (mother) in Daniel 5 to the influential figure of Modjadji, the rain-queen of the Lovedu people in Southern Africa.[64] Such a comparison might serve to satisfy (at least to some extent) the aims of 'incultration' and empowerment mentioned by Landman.

The Lovedu society is located in the Northern Province of South Africa.[65] As early as the late sixteenth century they migrated south across the Limpopo River (currently the border between South Africa and Zimbabwe). After an initial period of strife during which they established themselves in their new environment, a period of political stability was heralded by the accession of the first woman chief, Modjadji, around 1800. During the latter half of the nineteenth century friction was stirred up again through contact with white settlers migrating northward. The coming of the settlers left Modjadji with about a tenth of the area she formerly ruled. Furthermore, tax measures introduced by the whites led to the Lovedu men seeking wage-labour on farms and in towns, thus abandoning to a certain degree a long-standing cultural legacy. Within the Lovedu society two aspects stand out: the importance of women in the social

62. Mercy Amba Oduyoye, 'African Women's Hermeneutics', in Maimela and König (eds.), *Initiation into Theology*, p. 364.

63. Landman, 'African Women's Theology', p. 140.

64. The Lovedu people live in the low veld of the Northern Province in South Africa. Since the beginning of the nineteenth century they have been ruled by a female chief. Cf. Patricia Davidson, 'The Material Culture of the Lobedu: A Museum and Field Study' (MA dissertation thesis, University of Stellenbosch, 1979), p. 8.

65. The following discussion is based upon the work of Davidson, 'Material Culture; E. Jensen Krige, 'Medicine, Magic and Religion of the Lovedu' (DLitt thesis, University of the Witwatersrand); E. Jensen Krige and J.D. Krige, *The Realm of a Rain-Queen: A Study of the Pattern of Lovedu Society* (London: Oxford University Press, 1943); Elfriede Höckner, *Die Lobedu Südafrikas: Mythos und Realität der Regenkönigin Modjadj* (Stuttgart: Franz Steiner Verlag, 1998).

structure, and power and influence of Modjadji, the so-called rain-queen. Only the latter aspect will receive a brief comment here.

The Lovedu economy centres on agriculture. Meat and milk do not form a significant part of the diet. In an agricultural setting rain is of the utmost importance — it is the life-giving force on which people are dependent. But rain is more than this in the Lovedu society — it is a symbol of spiritual well-being and a manifestation that the social order is operating smoothly. Heat and drought are seen as destructive forces leading to disharmony. In this context the chief plays a significant role. She is a ruler by divine right and her power is centred in rainmaking. This is achieved through a complex rain cult in which she is the chief actor.

This rain cult exhibits, amongst others, the following features:

1. Its observances must be kept at all times, not only during times of drought.
2. The queen is viewed as having a sort of general control over the season and not every fall of rain is attributed to a special activity on her part.
3. It is not merely composed of a few magical passes made by the queen.
4. In times of drought headmen and councillors will approach her with gifts, while asking for help.
5. This may be followed by people dancing before the queen, in order to express their hardship and soften her heart towards them.
6. Modjadji does not work alone in 'transforming the clouds', but is assisted by one of the so-called rain-doctors. His work is to discover the causes of drought, i.e. what is hindering the queen's power in being effective.
7. The queen uses obscure objects and medicines to perform her work — these, however, are enshrouded in great secrecy.

A great variety of steps can be taken to produce rain, depending on what is believed to be the cause of the drought — for instance, the queen being displeased over something, wrongful practices in the community, or the ancestors being displeased. Despite certain cultural changes over the past decades, there is still an implicit belief among the Lovedu people in the power of their queen to make rain, to 'transform' the clouds. Her superior position in society is mirrored in the role women play within the rest of the social structure.

Conclusion

Does Africa have anything to do with Babylon or, for that matter, Palestine? I believe it does. The South African society of the Apartheid period has been described as one in which patriarchy was one of the few non-racial institutions. Today this institution of patriarchy is still very much alive and very well.

However, our understanding of the role women played in ancient societies, linked to the role women still play in less male-dominated present-day societies (such as the Lovedu society), could set the tone for effecting change in the oppressive societies many women and children inhabit.

DANIEL, BELSHAZZAR, AND JULIA: THE REDISCOVERY AND VINDICATION OF THE TRANSLATIONS OF JULIA E. SMITH (1792–1886)

Emily Sampson

> The Church of England appointed two groups of scholars in 1870 to prepare a revision [of the King James Version]. Similar groups were formed in America yet no woman was invited to participate, either here or abroad. American women had expected that at least Julia Smith would be included. Unassisted, she had made five translations of the Bible from the Hebrew, Greek and Latin, considered by some scholars to be the most literal translations to date.[1]

When I read these words I was stunned. I was nearing the end of my career as a doctoral student and I had never heard of this woman. My amazement was quickly followed by anger, for I certainly could have used such a role model. This anger has never completely dissipated for, as I began to investigate the story of Julia Smith, the lack of attention that had been given her accomplishment seemed to epitomize the contempt with which intellectual women have been, and sometimes still are, treated.

She was born in 1792, hardly a time when women would have received schooling in Greek, Hebrew and Latin. How had she been able to acquire knowledge of these languages? In 1876 she published a very literal translation of the Bible. Such scant information as I found focused mainly on Smith's activities in the suffragist movement and gave far more attention to her younger sister, Abby. Finally, in the appendix to the 1895 edition of *The Woman's Bible*, I found a few pages of tribute written by one of Smith's contemporaries, Frances Ellen Burr.

In the century that has followed this tribute, little has been written on the subject of Smith's Bible. There are only two book-length

---

1. Eleanor D. Bilimoria, in Elizabeth Cady Stanton *et al.*, *The Woman's Bible* (Seattle: Coalition Task Force on Women and Religion, 1974 [1895]), p. vii.

studies of her life, both written in the late twentieth century.[2] Neither of these books was written by a biblical scholar, and neither focused on her translation. The few words accorded her by biblical scholars have been dismissive and often inaccurate.

This brief study has two goals: first, to acquaint scholars with the work of Julia Smith, thereby remedying to some degree the wrong done her by the academic community; second, to alert scholars to a trove of unexamined material available for analysis.

Consider the historical context in which her intellect developed. When Julia Evelina Smith was born in Glastonbury, Connecticut, in 1792, Louis XVI and his queen, Marie Antoinette, awaited their execution in a Parisian prison, the fall of Robespierre and the rise of Napoleon were on the horizon, and George Washington was completing his first term as president of the new United States. She was the fourth daughter of remarkable parents, Hannah Hadassah Hickock Smith and Zephaniah Hollister Smith. Her mother, the only child of a country schoolmaster, was unusually accomplished for the time and was known as a linguist, poet, astronomer and mathematician. Her father had trained at Yale to be a clergyman but abandoned that career early when, under the influence of Glasite-Sandemanian theology, an extremely conservative Protestant view, he embraced the belief that a minister should not be paid as this might influence the direction he gave his congregation. After a brief stint as a merchant, Zephaniah Smith became a lawyer and rose in local politics to become a representative in the Connecticut legislature.

Julia appears to have been the most linguistically gifted of the five sisters. She had probably been exposed to the French language from an early age. Both her father and her maternal grandfather had the reputation of speaking French like Frenchmen. As a schoolgirl, she had studied Greek at the local academy, that of Sarah Pierce in Litchfield.[3] Although her father appears to have been unusually supportive

---

2.   Kathleen Housley, *The Letter Kills But the Spirit Gives Life: The Smiths — Abolitionists, Suffragists, Bible Translators* (Glastonbury, CT: The Historical Society of Glastonbury, 1993); and Susan J. Shaw, *A Religious History of Julia Evelina Smith's 1876 Translation of the Holy Bible: Doing More than Any Man Has Ever Done* (San Francisco: Mellen Research University Press, 1992). Housley's work,which was the basis of Shaw's, focuses on the family and emphasizes the contributions of Julia and her sister, Abby, to the burgeoning suffragist movement. Shaw's book emphasizes the unusual religious background of the family (Sandemanian) and the events that brought about Smith's translations.

3.   This assertion is uncertain. Julia wrote of having learned Greek as a girl 'at our academy', but this might refer to home schooling. In 1806 Hannah wrote about

of the intellectual pursuits of his daughters, Julia recounted an anec-
dote in which he appears to have opposed, though somewhat mildly,
her linguistic studies:

> When I was fourteen, my teacher...wanted me to study Latin grammar.
> My father thought it was not necessary, but I teased him so much that
> he said I could have his; but I told him that [it] was all Latin, without a
> bit of English. Finally he said that he would buy me one the next time
> he went to Hartford. So when he went, I was very eager to have him get
> back with the new grammar, but when he came he said he had for-
> gotten it. That was a bitter disappointment to me.[4]

Not easily deterred, Julia hitched up the family horse and rode from
Glastonbury to Hartford to collect the precious Latin grammar for
herself. The local boys teased her when she began this study: 'They
said ironically that I must be going to college. But the more they
plagued me, the more it spurred me up to get ahead of them in the
study; and I did.'[5] A more poignant version of these incidents was
revealed in a letter to an unnamed correspondent:

> It was altogether an unheard of thing in our academy, when I went to
> school, for a girl to study the languages, but somehow I always wanted
> to do something contrary to the common course, and, though laughed
> at, stood it out bravely, never letting it be known how much I was
> mortified.[6]

At the age of eighteen, Julia went to board with the family of Jean
Pierre Victor Value, Haitian refugees who taught French and dancing.
After leaving them she kept up both her acquaintance and correspondence with them and, in order to maintain her proficiency in the
language, kept her diary in French for more than thirty years.

When Julia was thirty-one (in 1823)[7] she was invited to teach
French at Emma Willard's seminary in Troy, New York, one of the
earliest establishments for the higher education of women in the
United States. In return for her labors, she was to receive instruction

---

the girls studying Greek (Shaw, *A Religious History*, p. 98). But Julia's diaries show
that her father bought her a Greek grammar on 20 February, 1816.

4.   Frances Ellen Burr, 'Obituary: Julia E. Smith Parker', *Hartford Daily Times*, 8
March 1886.

5.   Burr, 'Obituary'.

6.   Julia E. Smith, *Abby Smith and Her Cows, with a Report of the Law Case Decided
Contrary to Law* (New York: Arno Press, repr. 1972 [1877]), p. 64. This book is made
up of letters and articles compiled by Julia relating to their tax rebellion.

7.   In her conversations with Frances Burr, Julia remembered herself as much
younger at this time, twenty. This discrepancy was caught by Shaw (*A Religious
History*, p. 123 n. 44).

in mathematics. For once Julia seems to have loathed her studies. Her health suffered; she wrote of insomnia, headaches, stiff neck, and other unspecified illnesses. It is uncertain whether these were exacerbated by her dislike of Euclid, the unhappiness occasioned by separation from her family, or perhaps Mrs Willard's insistence that she wear a corset.[8] Although Mrs Willard tried to induce her to stay, offering her a salary of $200, a handsome salary for the time, Julia returned home after only two terms.[9]

An amusing, though probably apocryphal, story is connected with her return home:

> She found for fellow travelers a certain chancellor, accompanied by one of his learned friends... They, wishing to converse on some private business, began to talk in French, and were surprised to hear from the unknown woman the remark, 'Excuse me, but I understand French'. They resumed their conversation in Latin, but were soon again interrupted by the remark, 'Excuse me, gentlemen, I know the Latin'. A good deal astonished, this time, they looked at the unknown in silence, but then once more fell to conversing, but this time in Greek. 'If you'll excuse me', said the unknown woman, 'I also understand the Greek.' Thoroughly amazed, the chancellor turned to her with the exclamation, 'Who the d—l are you?'[10]

Julia returned home to a disciplined life of study and domesticity. Her diary entry for 1 December 1824 states, 'Began algebra today. I have planned to study two hours a day every day this winter'. The rather convent-like life that she appears to have led is underscored by the reminiscence of a cousin who noted that the sisters 'all wore white dresses which were expected to stay clean for four days with reasonable care regardless of what chores were assigned'.[11]

In February 1836, Zephaniah died of complications of a broken thigh. Though financially secure, the family was now in a tenuous

---

8.   On 24 September, 1823, Julia wrote in her diary that Mrs Willard had once 'called [her] to her room to ask [her] if [she] needed/wanted some corsets'. Julia continued, 'She told me I must wear them and I finally consented'.

9.   Diary entry 11 March, 1824. This was a very good salary. According to another entry made by Julia (13 June, 1823; Shaw, *A Religious History*, p. 123 n. 43), Laurilla earned two dollars a week at this establishment. Therefore, the offer of a salary of $200 would have represented a great desire on Mrs Willard's part to retain Julia's services.

10.   *The Hartford Daily Times*, 11 December 1875, cited in Smith, *Cows*, p. 63.

11.   Lillian E. Prudden, 'Memoirs', typed document, 1949, Smith Family Papers, Historical Society of Glastonbury, CT.

position for they had no male relative to represent their interests in the community. Yet, for the time being, the Smith women were able to continue life as usual, centered on domestic, intellectual, and charitable activity among both blacks and whites. The family became prominent in the Abolitionist movement. Although she was initially reluctant to take up a life of teaching after her return from Willard's academy, Julia's diaries record intermittent periods of teaching lasting through the end of 1842.

In the 1840s New England and New York were swept with the prophecies of William Miller that the Second Coming would soon take place. Though initially reluctant to give a definite date, Miller was finally pressed into stating that the great event would occur in 1843. Julia's diary for the end of 1842 demonstrates dramatically the impact of these prophecies on her life. The entries for November and most of December reflect the concerns of ordinary life—the killing of hogs for winter meat, painting the house, teaching, and sewing. Christmas Day fell on Sunday, the day Julia devoted time to religious reading, though not church attendance. That Christmas Day she read three issues of the *Midnight Cry*, a newly organized Millerite publication. From that date to the end of the year, her diary records intense interest in Miller's message, culminating in the final entry:

> I was upstairs all daylong except I went below in the afternoon to see Henry Welles. I read the Bible almost all day. I have eaten nothing since yesterday noon. It is the last day of the year and we can all be prepared to enter the new year of 1843 which, according to Mr. Miller, could be the last year of this world. May the Great Lord give us faith to be always ready for his second coming.

With this last dramatic entry, Julia appears to have abandoned the diary which she had kept in French for thirty-two years.[12]

The faithful waited until 22 October 1844, a time known as 'The Great Disappointment'. Significantly, by the spring of 1845, six

---

12. The accepted interpretation of her behavior is that Julia saw no point in keeping a diary since the end of the world was imminent. Yet she continued to keep records of the weather. Since there are no family records at all from this period, I believe that they may well have been destroyed in an attempt to distance themselves from the movement because Millerites were popularly thought to have been insane, a view challenged by Ronald and Janet Numbers in their article 'Millerism and Madness: A Study of "Religious Insanity" in Nineteenth-Century America', in Ronald L. Numbers and Jonathan M. Butler (eds.), *The Disappointed: Millerism and Millenarianism in the Nineteenth Century* (Bloomington: Indiana University Press, 1987), pp. 92-118.

months after, Julia had completed her translation of the Greek New Testament and begun work on the Septuagint.[13]

In her latter years Julia described the supportive circle in which this work was done:

> This translation was made for the gratification of six persons, the five sisters Smith and one friend. They were all much interested…in searching the Scriptures after the *notorious* [my emphasis] Miller doctrine came out, and they met weekly for that purpose.[14]

Her motivation was further clarified in an interview granted a reporter for the *New York Sun*:

> It struck me that, if we could consult the original text whenever any passage in the Bible was referred to, it would be a good thing and so I determined to make a literal translation for that sole reason at least of the Greek of the Septuagint and the New Testament.[15]

As has been shown above, Julia was familiar with Latin and Greek from her early years, but Hebrew posed a new challenge. She turned to Samuel Farmar Jarvis, one of the most prominent scholars of the language in this country at the time, for advice.

> I wrote to him that I wanted to learn the meaning of the proper names in the Bible and asked if I could not find them in St. Jerome? He replied that St. Jerome's works were in numerous volumes and that he could not lend them, but if I would come to Middletown I could have the use of any of them. 'But', he added, 'why don't you study Hebrew yourself and learn the meaning?'[16]

In the *New York Sun* interview Julia recounted that Jarvis had counseled her:

> '[Hebrew] is a very simple language and soon learned. The Bible is the only pure ancient Hebrew extant, and that is all you need to study in the language. You would then be able to see with your own eyes, and not with the glasses of your neighbors.' Then he wrote about the

---

13. This LXX, currently held by the Connecticut Historical Society, consists of 268 numbered, undated booklets. On 30 April 1846 Julia noted at the end of booklet 133 (Job), 'Wrote the bible from the Septuagint as far as thru the 30th chapter of Job in one year'.

14. Julia Smith, 'The Smith Bible', *Springfield Union*, 27 November 1875, repr. in Smith, *Cows*, p. 62. The friend was Emily Moseley, with whom Julia quarreled when criticized for her behavior after her marriage in 1879 at the age of 87!

15. 'The Bible in a New Dress', *New York Sun*, no author, no date, repr. in *The Woman's Journal*, 1 January 1876.

16. Burr, 'Obituary'.

cognate languages—Chaldee, Syriac and Arabic—and advised me what
books to purchase. Well, I acted upon his advice and set to work studying Hebrew from the element [*sic*]. I used Stewart's grammar and the
lexicons of Parkhurst and Gesenius. I found Prof. Jarvis was right. I had
no difficulty in studying the language.[17]

Julia's studies in Hebrew must have advanced very rapidly: the first
booklet of a Hebrew translation bears the date 18 January 1847. Perhaps as important as his advice in the purchase of textbooks was
Jarvis's encouragement that she see with her own eyes, a reinforcement of the intellectual independence stressed in her Sandemanian
background. Now equipped to deal with the Masoretic Text as well as
the New Testament, Julia recalled, 'A most delightful work it was,
making the whole agree, taking the New Testament from Geneses
[*sic*] to Revelation.'[18] She found her labors so absorbing that she often
did not hear the dinner bell and had to be called to the table by her
sisters.[19] This first Hebrew translation was completed on 11 July 1848.

Julia then undertook a translation of the Vulgate, a testimony to the
thoroughness that she brought to her studies. This translation
occupied her attention from 1 August 1848,until 30 June 1849. From 4
July through 25 July she continued with the Prayer of Manasses, 3 and
4 Esdras, Prefaces of Holy Jerome, and Jerome to Paulinus. At the end
of Revelation Julia noted, 'Finished comparing the three translations
May 15, 1850.'[20]

Slightly less than one year after making this comparison, Julia
undertook a second Hebrew translation which occupied her from
1 May 1851 through 10 July 1853. On 16 July she undertook a second
translation of the Septuagint at which she worked in a much more
desultory fashion, finishing in 1860.[21] To summarize her work: in a
period of fifteen years she translated the Septuagint twice, the New
Testament once, the Masoretic Text twice, and the Vulgate once, an

17. 'The Bible in a New Dress'.

18. Smith, *Cows*, p. 62.

19. *Hartford Daily Times*, 11 December 1875, cited in Smith, *Cows*, pp. 62-64.

20. This may refer to the notations she made in a King James Version currently
in the collection of the Olin Library, Special Collections, Wesleyan University,
Middletown, Connecticut. These notations are color coded: blue for Hebrew, red
for Latin, black for Greek. Pages have been tipped in where the changes were too
extensive for marginal notation.

21. This translation is incomplete; parts 1-68 and 79-85 (2 Esdras) are held by
the Connecticut Historical Society.

accomplishment that surely supported her boast that she had done 'more than any man'.[22]

All this was done as a labor of love for the intimate circle that surrounded her. These translations, meticulously numbered and/or dated were written in small hand-stitched booklets folded to make an eight page volume, 20 × 16 cm. After completing her translations, Julia bound them in red ribbons and put them aside where they remained untouched for more than twenty years. The gap between the motivation which inspired her labor and that which brought about the publication of her Bible is a source of difficulty in assessing her work.

It is unlikely that the translations of Julia Smith would ever have been seen had she not felt unjustly treated by the local tax authorities. In 1872, Julia and her younger sister Abby were the only remaining members of the immediate family. When their taxes were increased by one hundred dollars, Julia, who was by then more than eighty years old, inquired to see if the same had been done elsewhere. Her investigations revealed that only their property and that of two widows had been so assessed; no man had been similarly treated. Though Julia counseled submission, Abby spoke against this treatment before the town meeting in November 1873, in a fiery speech which compared their situation with that of southern slaves. In January 1874 seven of their cows, which had been raised by Julia more as pets than as farm animals, were taken to be auctioned to pay their debt. The sisters were shocked to find that, after a lifetime of community service, their neighbors were willing to take advantage of their situation and purchase the animals at a ridiculously low price. The animals were restored to their home by the device of having a hired hand purchase them for the sisters. Thus, the debt was collected yet the sisters felt that they had not yielded to an unjust demand. This charade, which was to continue for a number of years, became an immediate sensation. The *Springfield Republican* declared that the sisters 'as truly stand for the American principle as did the citizens who ripped open the tea chests in Boston harbor or the farmers who leveled their muskets at Concord'.[23] Souvenir flowers made from the hair of the cows' tails appeared as far west as Chicago.[24] Perhaps, had the centennial of the American Revolution not been imminent, events would have passed differently, but once again the cries of 'No

22. Smith, *Cows*, p. 57.

23. 'Abby Smith's Cows', 6 January 1874, repr. in Smith, *Cows*, p.14.

24. 'A Work of Art From A Cows [sic] Tail', *The Hartford Times*, June 1874, repr. in Smith, *Cows*, pp.42-43.

taxation without representation' were raised, this time as an appeal
for women's suffrage. The Smith sisters' battle became a *cause célèbre*.

Yet, even while support from the outer world increased, the position in Glastonbury deteriorated. The tax collector next seized eleven
acres of their land although such a practice was against the law. This
triggered a series of lawsuits which lasted for more than three years
before the rights of the sisters were upheld.

It was the juxtaposition of these events, the approaching centennial
and the experience of unjust treatment, that moved Julia to bring forth
the work that she had done thirty years earlier and begin preparations
for the publication of a new translation of the Bible: 'We thought it
might help our cause to have it known that a woman could do more
than any man has ever done [i.e., translate the entire Bible without
assistance].'[25] The sisters commissioned the American Publishing
Company of Hartford, Connecticut to print one thousand copies of
Julia's Bible. When the sisters were reproached for spending four
thousand dollars in such a manner rather than contribute more
directly to the suffragist cause, their reply left no doubt as to their
motivation:

> If it be wrong to take a man's property without his consent, [it] must be
> equally wrong to take a woman's property without her consent; and the
> men, therefore, must take it from her on the ground that her intellect is
> not as strong as theirs; the women are not as capable of going into all
> kinds of knowledge as the men are, (and which is required of men to
> govern;) that men are able to search deeper into every kind of learning.
> Now there is no learning that is so much respected by the whole
> world—let their religious belief be what it may—as the knowledge of
> the most ancient languages, in which the Bible was written—the three
> over the head of our Saviour.
>
>   They must have been given by God; for the instruction of all three are
> so perfect they could not, possibly, be altered, and they are now dead
> languages, and can never be changed by speaking, as modern languages
> are. And here is a woman, with no motive but the love of doing it, and
> no instructions since her school-days, has gone further, alone, in trans-
> lating these languages, than any man has ever gone, and without any of
> his help, and no law of the land gives her any protection... If this be not
> robbery, there is no such thing as robbery...[26]

The translation bore the title *The Holy Bible: Containing the Old and New
Testaments Translated Literally from the Original Tongues*; it used Julia's
first Hebrew translation.

   25. Abby and Julia Smith, Letter to an unnamed man, 20 July 1875, printed in
People, 15 August 1875, repr. in Smith, *Cows*, p. 57.
   26. Smith, *Cows*, p. 57.

One can only speculate on what might have happened had Julia chosen to publish her second Hebrew translation instead of the first. In the first translation, Julia deliberately chose to ignore the practice of *consecution*, the convention that translates a verb preceded by a waw in the same temporal aspect as the verb which precedes it. This played havoc with the temporal aspects of her translation:

> Two men were in one city; one rich and one poor. To the rich was sheep and oxen exceeding many: And to the poor, not anything except one little ewe lamb which he found and he will save it alive; and it will grow with him and with his sons together (2 Sam. 12.1-3).

> And queen Sheba heard the report of Solomon for the name of Jehovah, and she will come to try him in enigmas (1 Kgs 10.1).

One effect of this peculiarity of Smith's translation is that it makes historical narrative read as though it were predictive:

> And a man from the house of Levi will go and take a daughter of Levi. And the woman will conceive and will bring forth a son; and she will see him that he is good, and she will hide him three months. And she will not be able anymore to hide him, and she will take for him an ark of bulrush, and will pitch it with bitumen and with pitch (Exod. 2.1-2).

> And it will be at the time of the evening, and David will rise from off his bed, and will go upon the roof of the king's house: and he will see from the roof a woman washing herself; and the woman good of aspect exceedingly (2 Sam. 2.1-2).

The magnitude of the effect of Julia's rejection of the waw consecutive can be easily seen when one recognizes that approximately 42 per cent of the verbs in the Hebrew Bible are so classified.[27] As a consequence the readers, who had no knowledge of the principles of Hebrew, and even the scholars, who should have had, believed that the roughness of her translation arose from a poor understanding of the language. Yet it was not Julia's command of Hebrew that governed her stance but her desire to produce the most literal translation possible for reasons of piety:

> It is very possible that the readers of this book may think it strange that I have made such use of the tenses, going according to the Hebrew grammar. It seems that the original Hebrew had no regard to time, and that the Bible speaks for all ages. If I did not follow the tenses as they are, I myself should be the judge, and man must not be trusted with regard to the word of God. I think that the promiscuous use of the

---

27. Bruce K. Waltke and M. O'Connor, *An Introduction to Biblical Hebrew Syntax* (Winona Lake, IN: Eisenbrauns, 1990), p. 456.

tenses shows that there must be something hidden, that we must search out...[28]

This struggle toward independent interpretation is surely a reflection of the characteristic intellectual climate of New England in which she had been raised, for not only had her Sandemanian upbringing urged her to read for herself, but the Episcopalian Samuel Jarvis had, as we have seen, encouraged her to read with her own' spectacles', and not those of her neighbors. One should also note her rather mystical attitude toward the text, that it contained something hidden, to be searched out. Finally, one must mark the humility of her approach: 'If I did not follow the tenses as they are, I myself should be the judge and man must not be trusted with regard to the word of God.' Surely the psychological framework in which her work was undertaken should be considered in its evaluation. Yet, uniformly, those few people who have troubled to examine her translation have completely neglected to extend her this courtesy. Moreover, her work has rarely been judged within the intellectual context of the nineteenth century, a period of time characterized by the historian Eugen Weber as one that 'savored exactness and positive knowledge'.[29] In Julia Smith, the nineteenth century's tension between traditional piety and the enthronement of the new god, Science, are perfectly met. And they are met in the parlor of a New England farmhouse in the person of a woman denied access to the academic community.

In assessing Smith's approach to biblical Hebrew one must take into account the fact that at one time scholars attributed the peculiarities of the Greek of the New Testament to the 'influence of the Holy Spirit'.[30] Against this background, Julia's attitude toward the Hebrew tenses seems less quixotic. One might also note the numerous cases of books of the Bible that begin with an imperfect consecutive that has no preceding perfect verb. This is explained by Gesenius as a sign of 'close connexion with the historical books now or originally preceding them'.[31] Yet some of these appear to be independent documents, which indicates that, in an early stage of transmission, the decision

---

28. Julia E. Smith, *The Holy Bible: Containing the Old and New Testaments, Translated Literally from the Original Tongues* (Hartford, CT: American Publishing, 1876), Preface.

29. Eugen Weber, *Apocalypses: Prophecies, Cults, and Millennial Beliefs through the Ages* (Cambridge, MA: Harvard University Press, 1999), p. 15.

30. Ernest Colwell, 'Greek Language', in *IDB*, pp. 479-87. The German scholar who articulated this point of view also argued that 'the Holy Spirit changed the language of any people who received a divine revelation'.

31. GKC, 2nd edn, p. 133 n. 1.

was made to replace certain imperfect verbs with imperfect consecutives. Furthermore, in the instances in which whole books begin with the imperfect consecutive, normal translation practice is suspended because of convention. It was precisely this sort of arbitrary decision that Julia, in her pious approach to the text, was unwilling to accept:

> It was not man's opinion that I wanted as to construction or rendering, but the literal meaning of every Hebrew word and that I wrote down, supplying nothing and paraphrasing nothing, so everybody may judge the meaning for himself by the translation, precisely as those familiar with the Hebrew may construe the original.[32]

Elsewhere Julia indicated that she believed that the marginal readings and italicized words of the KJV indicated that its translators had not been 'exactly satisfied'.[33]

Perhaps the second greatest problem with Julia's published Hebrew translation was her refusal to add words for the sake of smooth reading: 'All the italicized words in the King James version, inserted to fill out the meaning according to the construction of the translators, have been omitted by me. Let every reader supply them for himself, as these translators did.'[34] Yet, as any Hebrew reader knows, that language does not express the present tense of the verb 'to be'. Therefore, Abraham replies to God, 'Behold, here I' (Gen. 22.1), which gives Julia's translation a rather 'pidgin-English' feel. Again, Joseph's brothers 'will take him and will throw him into the pit and the pit empty; water not in it' (Gen. 37.24).[35]

Another awkwardness arising from the refusal to supply words, such as the impersonal pronoun 'who', is found in such phrases as:

> He separating himself will seek according to desire (Prov. 18.1).

> He finding a wife found good (Prov. 18.22).

> He dwelling in the covering of the Most High, in the shadow of the Almighty shall he lodge (Ps. 91.1).

> And remember him creating thee in the days of thy youth (Eccl. 12.1).

---

32. 'The Bible in a New Dress'.
33. Smith, *Cows*, p. 62.
34. 'The Bible in a New Dress'.
35. Julia admitted in her Preface that she had not been completely successful: 'There may be some little inaccuracies, like putting the verb to be, for is, in a few instances...' This does not quite describe what she has done. Examples are found in Ps. 1.2, Prov. 20.1, and Song 5.10.

A third factor in Julia's translation was her use of concordant congruence, the consistent use of the same receptor word in rendering the original: 'So, too, with all circumlocutory phrases to express the meaning of single words, varying in different places according to the conception of the translators, I have translated every such word in the same way whenever found.'[36] Yet in this aspect she was not so completely consistent has she claimed in her Preface. For example, she used both 'wife' and 'woman' for אשה.

Literal translation is always a disaster when it encounters an idiom, risking incomprehension or the provocation of laughter: Moses was placed 'by the lip of the river' (Exod. 2.3) and the graceful 'apple of thine eye' was rendered as a tortured 'pupil of the daughter of the eye' (Ps. 17.8). Sarah died 'in the city of four' (Gen. 37.3). Yet even in this Julia was not perfectly consistent and one is surprised that she has not translated a name such as Abimelech when she did translate the forementioned Kiriath-arba.

Though her translation presents many difficulties, it also has its virtues. In a time when some sought to soften readings that were offensive to the nineteenth-century sensibilities, Julia's handling was brisk and forthright:

> Thus will God do the enemies of David and thus will he add if I shall leave from all which is to him till the light of morning, him pissing against the wall (1 Sam. 25.22).

> And Rabshakeh will say to them, To thy lord and to thee did my lord send me to speak these words: is it not to the men sitting upon the wall to eat their dung and to drink their piss with you? (2 Kgs 18.27)

Surely, this reflects the rough speech of war better than the English Revised Version's circumlocutions 'one man child' or 'drink their own water'. One can also see the process of bowdlerization in *The Woman's Bible*, which, though it claimed to use the Smith translation as its authority, rendered the entreaty of Potiphar's wife, 'Lie with me' (Gen. 39.7) as 'and she solicited him'. Similarly, the reference to birthing stools (Exod. 1.16) must have been considered indelicate by Stanton and her committee, for they have omitted these words. Julia's translation made no such concessions.

For all its faults, there are features that are outstanding about Smith's Hebrew translation. First, she used the word 'Jehovah' for the Tetragrammaton instead of the traditional 'LORD' of the King James Version. In this she not only anticipated the American Standard

36.   Smith, *Bible*, Preface.

Version by more than half a century but produced a more comprehensible translation of Ps. 110.1, 'Jehovah spake to my Lord', than had the translators of the KJV, 'The LORD said to my Lord'. This also gives a more accurate picture of the religious practice of early Israel. Furthermore, Julia's translation also uses the shorter form 'Jah', which in the following example allows more insight into the poetic interplay of that name and 'Jehovah':[37]

Psalm 135

KJV		Smith
Praise ye the LORD, Praise ye the name of the LORD; praise *him*, O ye servants of the LORD.		Praise ye Jah. Praise ye the name of Jehovah; praise, ye servants of Jehovah,
Ye that which stand in the house of the LORD, in the courts of the house of our God,	2	Standing in the house of Jehovah, in the enclosures of the house of our God.
Praise the LORD; for the LORD *is* good: sing praises unto his name; for *it is* pleasant.	3	Praise ye Jah; for Jehovah is good, play on the harp to his name, for it is pleasant.[38]
For the LORD hath chosen Jacob unto himself, *and* Israel for his peculiar treasure.	4	For Jah chose to himself Jacob;[39] Israel for his property.
For I know that the LORD is great, and *that* our Lord is above all gods.	5	For I knew that great is Jehovah, and our Lord above all gods.

Although the familiar KJV falls more pleasantly on the ear, the substitution of 'the LORD' vitiates the Hebrew poetry.

The second innovation of Smith is the substitution of the word 'Life' for the name Eve'. 'And Adam will call his wife Life, for she was the mother of all living' (Gen. 3.20); 'And Adam knew Life, his wife' (Gen. 4.1). This translation has appealed to both the first and second waves of feminist biblical scholars.[40]

---

37. The statement that the use of 'Jehovah' was an innovation may be misleading. The *Bay Psalm Book*, for example, frequently used 'Jehovah' for 'LORD'. Others using the name included Lowth (*Isaiah*, 1778), Blaney (*Jeremiah and Lamentations*, 1784), and Newcome (*Minor Prophets*, 1785). The KJV uses 'Jehovah' four times (Exod. 6.3; Ps. 83.18; Isa. 12.2; 26.4). What sets the Smith translation apart is its regular use of the name. Of those who came after Julia, the Swedenborg Bible and the American Standard Version also used it regularly.

38. This is but one more example indicating that the pull of the verb of existence was too strong for Julia. It does not exist in the Hebrew text.

39. This is but a small example of the stubbornness of contextual congruence!

40. *The Woman's Bible* made much of this. Latest to appreciate this facet of

The third innovation in the Smith translation is a modest attempt to modernize the language. Although she retained the archaic –*st* ending of the second person singular, she rejected the -*th* ending of the third person.

One of the ironies of Smith's work is that her idiosyncratic treatment of Hebrew occasionally works in her favor. The best examples of this are found in The Song of Solomon where the absence of theverb of existence accentuates the breathlessness of the lover and heightens the sexual tension of the poetry:

> Behold thee beautiful, my friend, behold thee beautiful; thine eyes doves; from behind to thy veil: thy hair as a herd of goats which lay down from mount Gilead.
> 2 Thy teeth as a herd of the shorn which came up from the washing; all of them bearing twins, and none barren among them.
> 3 As a scarlet thread thy lips, and thy speech becoming: as a piece of pomegranate, thy temples from behind thy veil.
> 4 As the tower of David thy neck, built for the weapons; a thousand shields hung upon it, all shields of the powerful.
> 5 Thy two breasts as two fawns, twins of the roe deer feeding among the lilies.
> 6 Till the day shall breathe, and the shadows fled away, I will go for myself to the mountain of myrrh, and to the hill of Lebanon.
> 7 All of thee beautiful, my friend, and no blemish in thee.
> 8 Thou shalt come with me from Lebanon, O bride, with me from Lebanon: thou shalt go round about the head of faith, from the head of Shenir and Hermon, from the dwellings of lions, from the mountains of panthers.
> 9 Thou didst rob me of the heart, my sister, O bride; thou didst rob me of the heart with one of thine eyes, with one necklace of thy neck (Song 4.1-9).

Or,

> 10 My beloved is white and ruddy, bearing the standard of ten thousand.
> 11 His head purified gold, his locks waving branches, black as a raven.
> 12 His eyes as doves upon channels of water washed with milk, sitting upon fulness.
> 13 His cheeks as beds of spices, towers of aromatic herbs: his lips lilies, dropping overflowing myrrh… (5.10-13).[41]

Smith's translation is Marla J. Selvidge, *Notorious Voices: Feminist Biblical Interpretation 1500–1920* (New York: Continuum Paragon House, 1996).

41. As noted, although Julia attempted to reproduce the Hebrew by omitting the missing present tense verb of existence, she could not always sustain the effort. This passage is another example in which her results are mixed.

There is a breathlessness in such passages that is all the more striking when one remembers that they came from the pen of a middle-aged New England spinster.

One of the few scholars to acknowledge the Smith translation in the nineteenth century, John Wright, included a mention of its existence in his work *Early Bibles of America* (New York: Thomas Whittaker, 1894) in a chapter titled 'Curious Versions'. This acknowledgment consists of a report of publication, along with a quotation from the Preface, and nine citations, perhaps chosen to illustrate the more bizarre passages, for example:

> Good a ration of herbs and love there, above an ox of the stall and hatred with it (Prov. 15.17).

> And he having answered, said to them, It being evening, ye say, Calm weather for the heaven is fiery red. And in the morning, Today wintry weather: for heaven being sad is fiery red (Mt. 16.2-3).

Against this I wish to place the Smith translation of Daniel 5, so that the reader may make her own evaluation:

DANIEL 5

> Belshazzar the king made great food for a thousand of his nobles, and before the thousand he drank wine.
> 2 Belshazzar said, in tasting the wine, to bring in for the vessels of gold and silver that Nebuchadnezzar his father brought forth from the temple that was in Jerusalem; and in them the king and his nobles, his wives and his concubines, will drink.
> 3 At that time they brought the vessels of gold that were brought forth from the temple of the house of God which was in Jerusalem; and in them they drank, the king and his nobles, his wives and his concubines.
> 4 They drank wine, and praised to the gods of gold and silver, brass, iron, wood and stone.
> 5 In the same moment went forth fingers of a man's hand and wrote before the candlestick upon the lime of the wall of the temple of the king: and the king saw the palm of the hand that wrote.
> 6 The king's brightness changing, and his thoughts will terrify him, and the knots of his loins breaking forth, and his knees knocked this upon that.
> 7 The king called with strength to bring up the enchanters, the Chaldeans and the diviners. The king answered and said to the wise of Babel, Whatever man that shall read this writing, and will show to me its interpretation, shall be clothed with purple, and a necklace of gold upon his neck, and shall rule the third in the kingdom.
> 8 Then came in all the king's wise ones: and they were not able to read the writing and to make known the interpretation to the king.

9 Then king Belshazzar being greatly terrified, and his brightnesses being changed upon him, and his nobles being perplexed.

10 The queen, on account of the king's words and his nobles, came in to the house of drinking: the queen answered and said, O king, live forever: thy thought shall not terrify thee, and thy brightnesses shall not be changed:

11 There is a man in thy kingdom that the spirit of the holy gods in him; and in the days of thy father, his light and his understanding and wisdom according to the wisdom of the gods was found in him; and king Nebuchadnezzar thy father, the king thy father, set him up leader of the sacred scribes, the enchanters, the Chaldeans, the diviners:

12 Because that an excellent spirit and knowledge, and his understanding interpreting dreams, and showing of enigmas, and solving knotty questions, was found in him, in Daniel whom the king set his name Belteshazzar: now Daniel shall be called, and he will show the interpretation.

13 At that time Daniel came in before the king. The king answered and said to Daniel, Is it thou, Daniel, which is from the sons of the captivity of Judah, whom the king my father brought from Judah?

14 I heard concerning thee that the spirit of the gods is in thee, and his light and his understanding and excellent wisdom was found in thee.

15 And now the wise ones, the enchanters, were brought in before me that they shall read this writing, and to make known to me its interpretation: and they were not able to show the interpretation of the word:

16 And I heard concerning thee, that thou wilt be able to interpret interpretations, and solve knotty questions: now if thou shalt be able to read the writing, and to make known to me its interpretation, thou shalt be clothed in purple, and a necklace of gold upon thy neck, and thou shalt rule the third in the kingdom.

17 At that time Daniel answered and said before the king. Thy gifts be to thyself, and give thy presents to another; but I will read the writing to the king, and make known to him the interpretation.

18 Thou, O king, God most high gave a kingdom and greatness and honor and splendor to Nebuchadnezzar thy father:

19 And from the greatness that he gave to him, all peoples, nations and tongues, were trembling and fearing from before him: whom he was willing he killed; and whom he was willing, he was setting up; and whom he willed he was humbling.

20 And when his heart was lifted up, and his spirit was strong for pride, he was brought down from the throne of his kingdom, and they took away his honor from him.

21 And he was driven from the sons of men, and his heart was made level with the beasts, and with the wild asses his dwelling: they will feed him with the green herb as oxen, and from the dew of the heavens his body will be wet; till that he knew that God the Most High ruled in the kingdom of men, and to whom he will, he will set up over it.

22 And thou his son, O Belshazzar, didst not humble thy heart because that thou knewest all this;

23 And against the Lord of the heavens thou didst lift up thyself; and for the vessels of his house they brought before thee, and thou and thy nobles, and thy wives, and thy concubines, drinking wine in them; and to the gods of silver and gold, brass, iron, wood, and stone, who see not, and hear not, and know not, thou didst praise: and to the God whom thy breath in his hand, and all thy ways to him, thou didst not honor.

24 At that time from before him was sent the palm of the hand, and this writing written.

25 And this the writing that was written: MENE, MENE, TEKEL and PHARSIN.

26 This the interpretation of the word: Mene; God numbered thy kingdom and complete it.

27 Tekel; Thou shalt be weighed in the balances and bef ound wanting.

28 Pharsin; Thy kingdom was divided, and it shall be given to the Medes and to Persia.

29 At that time Belshazzar said, and they clothed Daniel with purple, and a necklace of gold upon his neck, and they cried out concerning him, for him to rule the third in the kingdom.

30 In that night Belshazzar king of the Chaldeans was killed.

One can see from the last verse that Smith has followed the chapter division of the Masoretic Text. If we had her Bible before us, we would see that she has also accepted the order of the *Tanakh*, for the book is found between Esther and Ezra rather than between Ezekiel and Hosea, as it is in the Protestant canon. This must have been a surprise to most of her readers. The narrative reads surprisingly smoothly. The temporal flow is interrupted only in vv. 2, 6, 21 and 27. Her translation shows that she was not daunted that the text is in Aramaic.

Space allows but limited opportunity to examine her technique, which is revealed by a comparison of her translation with the KJV. In v. 1 she has chosen 'a great food' rather than 'a great feast', yet her 'for a thousand' reads more smoothly than the KJV 'to a thousand'; in v. 2 note the literal use of the *beth*, 'in tasting the wine'/'whiles he tasted the wine'. It is surprising to find 'was' in v. 2aβ; this demonstrates the difficulty she had in omitting the verb of existence when it was not found in the text. In contrast, note the repetitious 'of' (v. 4), which could be omitted for stylistic reasons. Given her intention to be literal, it is disconcerting,that she has used *Pharsin* instead of *Peres* (v. 28). In numerous cases she has asserted her independence of the KJV vocabulary, and often her choices are the clearer ones: nobles/princes, lords (vv. 3, 10, 23); lime/plaster (v. 5); palm of the hand/part of the hand (v. 5); and *Pharsin/U-PHARSIN* (v. 25).

Is there anything that can be construed as 'feminist' in the present-day understanding of the term? 'The king said...to the wise of Babel' (v. 7), and 'wise ones' (vv. 8, 15), never 'wise men', though this is offset by 'Whatever man shall read'/Whosoever (v. 7). Smith's nineteenth-century feminism is best reflected in her distrust of previous male scholarship; in her assertion of her right to raise her own questions; in her confidence in her own ability to translate; in her relationship to the nurturing circle of women for which her work was done; and, ultimately, in her insistence on the intellectual equality of women that gave her the courage to publish.

Largely because of her treatment of the Hebrew verbal system, Smith's Bible was a disappointment. She was criticized for her arrogance in presuming to undertake such work and the translation appears to have been something of an embarrassment to the suffragist movement. *The Woman's Journal*, which had trumpeted the forthcoming publication did not even review it when it finally appeared. It was at best an oddity, described by a contemporary as a translation *into* three different languages and clearly of less interest than the seven-thousand-piece silk bed quilt that she had also wrought.[42]

But what if she had published the second translation? This has lain unexamined since it was tied with red ribbon and put away in 1853. Space, as well as accessibility limits examples that can be cited in this article. Yet consider how much more smoothly the second translation reads than the first.

Translation I   Translation II

GENESIS
Chapter 1

In the beginning God formed		In the beginning God formed
the heavens and the earth.		the heavens and the earth.
And the earth was	2	And the earth was
desolation and emptiness, and		wasteness and emptyness and
darkness over the face of the deep:		darkness upon the face of the deep.
and the spirit of God moved over the	2 3	and the spirit of God causing to
face of the waters.		shake the face of the waters.[43]

42. E.V.H., 'A Visit to the Misses Smith and their Cows', *Nantucket Inquirer and Mirror*, 4 April 1874, repr. in Smith, *Cows*, pp. 36-37.

43. The oddity of numbering here is that of the translation, not a mistake in transcription.

And God will say there shall be light, and there shall be light.

And God will see the light that it is good, and God will separate between the light and between the darkness.

And God will call the light day and the darkness he called night: and the evening shall be, and the morning shall be one day.

3 4 And God said there shall be light and there was light.

4 and God saw the light that it *was* good and God separated between the light and between the darkness

5 and God called the light day and the darkness he called night and the evening and the morning was one day.

GENESIS

Chapter 3

And to Adam he said, Because thou didst listen to the voice of thy wife, and thou wilt eat from the tree which I commanded thee, saying, Thou shalt not eat from it; cursed the earth for thy sake; in labor shalt thou eat of it all the days of thy life;

And thorns and weeds shall it cause to spout forth to thee; and thou shalt eat the green herb of the field.

In the sweat of thy face thou shalt eat food until thy turning back to the earth; for out of it thou wert taken; for dust thou art, and to dust shalt thou turn back.

And Adam will call his wife's name Life, for she was the mother of all living.

17 and to the man he said because thou heardst to the voice of thy wife and didst eat from the tree which I commanded thee in saying thou shalt not eat from cursed the earth for thy sake and in pain shalt thou eat it all the days of thy life

18 thorns and weeds shalt it bring forth to thee and thou shalt cut the herb of the field.

19 in the sweat of thy face shalt thou eat bread till thy turning back to the earth for from it were thou taken, for dust thou, and to dust shalt thou turn back.

20 and the man called his wife's name life, for she was the mother of all living/life.

From these brief examples it can be seen that the second avoids much of the difficulty of temporal dislocation. One can also discern the continuing struggles of the translator to find the correct word. Although Smith followed more closely the conventional use of the waw conversive in her second translation, she was clearly ill at ease in doing do, for above each 'deviation' in tense, she has indicated the original. Moreover, in the few instances in which she inserted a verb of existence, she underlined it, a practice also seen in her diary when she used any word that she regarded as irregular.

At this point the reader might ask, 'Of what use could such a literal translation be? Perhaps the work of Smith is deservedly, if not mercifully, obscure?' If for no other reason than recognition of the magnitude of her accomplishment, the Smith translations should be known. But there is yet another value to be gained from them: a translation such as Julia's challenges complacency. A public familiar with the words of the KJV, RSV or the new Jewish Publication Society translation are surprised, perhaps shocked, to find how much the scholars have supplied. Julia Smith's translation, rough though it is, challenges smooth readings and provides a warning against the smugness that leads a casual reader to don the prophetic mantle too quickly and to pronounce too facilely, 'Thus says the Lord', a practice I find all too often in the United States.

The Bible abounds in agricultural metaphors. Therefore, it seems appropriate to observe that biblical scholars often seem like farmers who have inherited a farm and plow the same fields over and over. As farmers continually find new stones that have risen during the winter, so we find nuggets to explore, clods of insights to break apart by analysis. The translations of Julia Smith offer us new opportunities for cultivation; perhaps they are the treasures beneath the soil we till or perhaps they are long-sown seeds waiting only cultivation, which process begins with our attention.[44] Whatever view is taken, seed or precious stone, much awaits scholars in the archives of the Connecticut Historical Society. There are to be found not only the unpublished second Hebrew translation, but two Septuagints and a translation of the Vulgate that await the opening of their decaying red ribbons. Smith's personal Bible, a KJV carrying color-coded annotations marking deviations noted in the MT, LXX and Vulgate, awaits the scholar who would assess the work of one of the earliest text critics in the United States.[45] Surely these documents merit serious study and offer us the opportunity to share with an interested public new insights. May the reputation of Julia Smith, proto text critic and *savante extraordinaire*, blossom from these endeavors; the seeds of her sowing have waited far too long for harvest.

---

44. Some work has begun to appear, such as that of Housley, Shaw and, as noted above, Selvidge in *Notorious Voices*, though I find myself in disagreement with much of her interpretation. Janet Larson PhD of Rutgers University has also done some literary analysis of the Smith translation ('Julia E. Smith's Holy Bible of 1876: The Literal, the Symbolic and Representations of the Female Translator', paper presented to American Bible Society Symposium, 14 September 1998; *Journal for Scripture and Media*, forthcoming). However, little attention has been given by those who have expertise in biblical languages. My dissertation, 'Her Works Shall Praise Her: The Biblical Translation of Julia Evelina Smith' (1998) is only a beginning to the work that should be done.

45. This Bible carries extensive additions, passages not covered in the Protestant canon, written over the center 'family record' pages, as well as tipped-in pages. See n. 21.

BIBLIOGRAPHY

Aalders, G.C., *Daniël* (Kampen: Kok, 1962).

Ackerman, S., ' "And the Women Knead Dough": The Worship of the Queen of Heaven in Sixth-Century Judah', in P.L. Day (ed.), *Gender and Difference in Ancient Israel* (Minneapolis: Fortress Press, 1989), pp. 109-24.

—*Under Every Green Tree: Popular Religion in Sixth-Century Judah* (HSM, 46; Atlanta: Scholars Press, 1992).

—'Isaiah', in C.A. Newsom and S.H. Ringe (eds.), *The Women's Bible Commentary* (Louisville, KY: Westminster/John Knox Press, 1992), pp. 162-68.

—*Warrior, Dancer, Seductress, Queen* (New York: Doubleday, 1998).

Albertz, Rainer, *A History of Israelite Religion in the Old Testament Period* (Louisville, KY: Westminster / John Knox Press, 1994).

Albright, W.F., *Yahweh and the Gods of Canaan* (London: University of London, 1968).

Alter, R., *The Art of Biblical Narrative* (New York: Basic Books, 1981).

Althusser, Louis, *Lenin and Philosophy* (trans. Ben Brewster; London: Monthly Review Press, 1971).

Amador, J.D.H., 'Feminist Biblical Hermeneutics: A Failure of Theoretical Nerve', *JAAR* 66.1 (1998), pp. 39-57.

Anderson, Bernhard W., *Understanding the Old Testament* (Englewood Cliffs, NJ: Prentice–Hall, 4th edn,1986).

Anderson, Robert A., *Signs and Wonders: A Commentary on the Book of Daniel* (Grand Rapids: Eerdmans, 1984).

Andreasen, N.-E.A., 'The Role of the Queen Mother in Israelite Society', *CBQ* 45 (1983), pp. 179-94.

Anon, 'The Bible in a New Dress', *New York Sun*, no date, repr. *The Woman's Journal*, 1 January 1876.

Archer, G.L. (trans.), *Jerome's Commentary on Daniel* (Grand Rapids: Baker Book House, 1958).

Avalos, H.I., 'The Comedic Function of the Enumeration of Officials and Instruments in Daniel 3', *CBQ* 53 (1991), pp. 580-88.

Bach, A., 'Reading Allowed: Feminist Biblical Criticism Approaching the Millennium', *Currents in Research: Biblical Studies* 1 (1993), pp. 191-215.

Bail, U., *Gegen das Schweigen klagen: Eine intertextuelle Studie zu den Klagepsalmen Ps 6 und Ps 55 und der Erzählung von der Vergewaltigung Tamars* (Gütersloh: Chr. Kaiser Verlag/Gütersloher Verlagshaus, 1998).

Bal, Mieke, *Murder and Difference: Gender, Genre and Scholarship on Sisera's Death* (trans. Matthew Gumpert; Bloomington and Indianapolis: Indiana University Press, 1988), pp. 111-34.

—'Metaphors He Lives By', *Semeia* 61 (1993), pp. 185-207.

Baldwin, J.G., *Daniel: An Introduction and Commentary* (TOTC; Leicester: Inter-Varsity Press, 1978).

Baltzer, K., *Deutero-Jesaja* (KAT, 10.2; Gütersloh: Gütersloher Verlagshaus, 1999).

Bar-Efrat, S., *Narrative Art in the Bible* (Sheffield: Sheffield Academic Press, 2nd edn, 1997 [Hebr. orig. 1979]).

Barnett, R.D., 'From Arad to Carthage: Harvest Rites and Corn-Dollies', *Eretz-Israel* 20 (1989), pp. 1*-11*.

Barthélemy, D., *Critique textuelle de l'Ancient Testament*, III (OBO, 50.3; Fribourg: Editions Universitaires Fribourg Suisse; Göttingen: Vandenhoeck & Ruprecht, 1992).

Bauer, A., *Gender in the Book of Jeremiah: A Feminist-Literary Reading* (Studies in Biblical Literature, 5; New York: Peter Lang, 1999).

Baumann, G., 'Connected by Marriage, Adultery and Violence: The Prophetic Marriage Metaphor in the Book of the Twelve and in the Major Prophets', SBLSP 1999, pp. 552-69.

—*Liebe und Gewalt: Die Ehe als Metapher für das Verhältnis JHWH-Israel in den Prophetenbüchern* (SBS, 185; Stuttgart: Katholisches Bibelwerk, 2000).

Beal, T.K., 'Tracing Esther's Beginnings', in Brenner (ed.), *A Feminist Companion to Esther, Judith and Susanna* (Sheffield: Sheffield Academic Press, 1995), pp. 87-110.

Beck, J.T., *Erklärung der Propheten Micha und Joel nebst einer Einleitung in die Propheten* (Gütersloh: C. Bertelsmann, 1898).

Ben-Barak, Z., 'The Status and Right of the *Gebîrâ*', in Brenner (ed.), *A Feminist Companion to Samuel and Kings*, pp. 170-85.

Benson, J.E., 'The Divine Sense of Humor', *Dialog* 22 (1983), pp. 191-97.

Benveniste, Emile, *Problems in General Linguistics* (trans. Mary Elizabeth Meek; Coral Gables, FL: University of Miami Press, 1971).

Bergent, Dianne, *Israel's Wisdom Literature: A Liberation-Critical Reading* (Minneapolis: Fortress Press, 1997).

Bergravv, E., 'Humor and Seriousness', *Dialog* 22 (1983), pp. 206-10.

Berquist, Jon L., *Surprises by the River: The Prophet of Ezekiel* (St Louis: Chalice Press, 1993).

Beuken, W.A.M., 'Isaiah XIV: The Multiple Identity of the Person Addressed', *OTS* 19 (1974), pp. 29-70.

—*Jesaja deel II B* (POT; Nijkerk: Callenbach, 1983).

Biddle, Mark E., *A Redaction History of Jeremiah 2.1–4.2* (ATANT; Zürich: Theologischer Verlag, 1990).

—'The Figure of Lady Jerusalem: Identification, Deification and Personification of Cities in the Ancient Near East', in K.L. Younger, Jr, W.W. Hallo and B.F. Batto (eds.), *The Biblical Canon in Comparative Perspective* (Scripture in Context, 4; Ancient Near Eastern Texts and Studies, 11; Lewiston, NY: Edwin Mellen Press, 1991), pp. 173-94.

—'Lady Zion's Alter Egos: Isaiah 47.1-15 and 57.6-13 as Structural Counterparts', in R.F. Melugin and M.A. Sweeney (eds.), *New Visions of Isaiah* (JSOTSup, 214; Sheffield: Sheffield Academic Press, 1996), pp. 124-39.

—*Polyphony and Symphony in Prophetic Literature: Rereading Jeremiah 7–20* (Studies in Old Testament Interpretation, 2; Macon, GA: Mercer University Press, 1996).

Biggs, Robert D., *ŠÀ.ZI.GA: Ancient Mesopotamian Potency Incantations* (Texts from Cuneiform Sources; Locust Valley, NY: J.J. Augustin, 1967).

Binns, L.E., *The Book of the Prophet Jeremiah* (London: Methuen, 1919).

Bird, P.A., ' "To Play the Harlot": An Inquiry into an Old Testament Metaphor', in P.L. Day (ed.), *Gender and Difference in Ancient Israel* (Minneapolis: Augsburg Fortress, 1989), pp. 75-94 (also in: P.A. Bird, *Missing Persons and Mistaken Identities: Women and Gender in Ancient Israel* [Minneapolis: Fortress Press, 1997], pp. 219-36).

—'The Place of Women in the Israelite Cultus', in *idem, Missing Persons and Mistaken Identities: Women and Gender in Ancient Israel* (Overtures to Biblical Theology; Minneapolis: Fortress Press, 1997), pp. 81-102.

—'Images of Women in the Old Testament', in *idem, Missing Persons and Mistaken Identities: Women and Gender in Ancient Israel* (Overtures to Biblical Theology; Minneapolis: Fortress Press, 1997), pp. 13-51.

Black, M., *Models and Metaphors: Studies in Language and Philosophy* (Ithaca, NY and London: Cornell University Press, 1962).

Blenkinsopp, Joseph, *Ezekiel* (Interpretation; Louisville: John Knox, 1990).

—*Wisdom and Law in the Old Testament: The Ordering of Life in Israel and Early Judaism* (Oxford: Oxford University Press, rev. edn, 1995).

Block, Daniel, *The Book of Ezekiel, Chapters 1–24* (NICOT; Grand Rapids, MI: Eerdmans, 1997).

Boardman, John, *Athenian Red Figure Vases: The Archaic Period* (New York: Oxford University Press, 1975).

Bossman, David M., 'Kinship and Religious System in the Prophet Malachi', in Jacob Neusner *et al.* (eds.), *Religious Writings and Religious Systems*, I (Atlanta: Scholars Press, 1989), pp. 127-41.

Bowen, Nancy R., 'The Daughters of Your People: Female Prophets in Ezekiel 13:17-23', *JBL* 118.3 (Fall 1999), pp. 417-33.

Boyarin, D., *Carnal Israel: Reading Sex in Talmudic Culture* (Berkeley: University of California Press, 1993).

Braulik, Georg, *Deuteronomium 1–16,7* (NEB, 15; Würzburg: Echter Verlag, 1986).

Brenner, A., *The Israelite Woman: Social Role and Literary Type in Biblical Narrative* (Sheffield: JSOT Press, 1985).

—'Who's Afraid of Feminist Criticism? Who's Afraid of Biblical Humour? The Case of the Obtuse Foreign Ruler in the Hebrew Bible', *JSOT* 63 (1994), pp. 38-54.

—'Some Observations on the Figurations of Women in Wisdom Literature', in *idem* (ed.), *A Feminist Companion to Wisdom Literature*, pp. 50-66.

—'On Prophetic Propaganda and the Politics of "Love": The Case of Jeremiah', in *idem* (ed.), *A Feminist Companion to the Latter Prophets*, pp. 256-74.

—'Identifying the Speaker-in-the-Text and the Reader's Location in Prophetic Texts: The Case of Isaiah 50', in *idem* and C. Fontaine (eds.), *A Feminist Companion to Reading the Bible: Approaches, Methods and Strategies* (The Feminist Companion to the Bible, 11; Sheffield: Sheffield Academic Press, 1997), pp. 138-50.

—*The Intercourse of Knowledge: On Gendering Desire and 'Sexuality' in the Hebrew Bible* (Biblical Interpretation Series, 26; Leiden: E.J. Brill, 1997).

Brenner, A. (ed.), *A Feminist Companion to Samuel and Kings* (The Feminist Companion to the Bible, 5; Sheffield: Sheffield Academic Press, 1994).

—*A Feminist Companion to Exodus to Deuteronomy* (The Feminist Companion to the Bible, 6; Sheffield: Sheffield Academic Press, 1994).

—*A Feminist Companion to Esther, Judith and Susanna* (The Feminist Companion to the Bible, 7; Sheffield: Sheffield Academic Press, 1995).

—*A Feminist Companion to the Latter Prophets* (The Feminist Companion to the Bible, 8; Sheffield: Sheffield Academic Press, 1995).

—*A Feminist Companion to Wisdom Literature* (The Feminist Companion to the Bible, 9; Sheffield: Sheffield Academic Press, 1995).

Brenner, A., and F. van Dijk-Hemmes, *On Gendering Texts: Female and Male Voices in the Hebrew Bible* (Leiden: E.J. Brill, 1993).

Bresciani, E., and M. Kamil, 'Le Lettere aramaiche di Hermopoli', in E. Volterra, S. Moscati, and G.L. Della Vida (eds.), *Atti della Accademia Nazionale dei Lincei: Rendiconti Mem. Scienze Morali 1966* (Ser. 7, 12.5; Rome: Accademia Nazionale dei Lincei, 1966), pp. 359-428.

Bright, J., *Jeremiah* (AB; Garden City, NY: Doubleday, 2nd edn, 1965).

—'The Date of the Prose Sermons of Jeremiah', in L.G. Perdue and B.W. Kovacs (eds.), *A Prophet to the Nations: Essays in Jeremiah Studies* (Winona Lake, IN: Eisenbrauns, 1984), pp. 193-212.

Broome, Edwin C., 'Ezekiel's Abnormal Personality', *JBL* 65 (1946), pp. 277-92.

Brooten, Bernadette, *Love Between Women: Early Christian Responses to Female Homoeroticism* (Chicago and London: University of Chicago Press, 1996).

Brueggemann, W., 'At the Mercy of Babylon: A Subversive Rereading of the Empire', *JBL* 100 (1991), pp. 3-22.

—*A Commentary on Jeremiah: Exile and Homecoming* (Grand Rapids, MI: Eerdmans, 1998).

Burns, Rita J., *Has the Lord Indeed Spoken Only Through Moses? A Study of the Biblical Portrait of Miriam* (SBLDS, 84; Atlanta, GA: Scholars Press, 1987).

Burr, Frances Ellen, 'Appendix', in Stanton, *et al.*, *The Woman's Bible*.

Butterworth, M., *Structure and the Book of Zechariah* (JSOTSup, 130; Sheffield: Sheffield Academic Press, 1992).

Camp, Claudia V., *Wisdom and the Feminine in the Book of Proverbs* (Sheffield: Almond Press, 1985).

—'Wise and Strange: An Interpretation of the Female Imagery in Proverbs in Light of Trickster Mythology', *Semeia* 42 (1988), pp. 14-36.

—'What's So Strange About the Strange Woman?', in David Jobling, Peggy L. Day and Gerald T. Sheppard (eds.), *The Bible and the Politics of Exegesis: Essays in Honor of Norman K. Gottwald on His Sixty-Fifth Birthday* (Cleveland: Pilgrim Press, 1991), pp. 17-31.

—'1 and 2 Kings', in C.A. Newsom and S.H. Ringe (eds.), *The Woman's Bible Commentary* (Louisville, KY: Westminster/John Knox Press, 1992), p. 109.

—'Metaphor in Feminist Biblical Interpretation: Theoretical Perspectives', *Semeia* 61 (1993), pp. 3-36.

Carley, Keith W., *The Book of the Prophet Ezekiel* (Cambridge Bible Commentary; (Cambridge: Cambridge University Press, 1974).

Carroll, R.P., *From Chaos to Covenant: Uses of Prophecy in the Book of Jeremiah* (London: SCM Press, 1981).

— *Jeremiah: A Commentary* (OTL; Philadelphia: Westminster Press, 1986).

Cassem, Ned H., 'Ezekiel's Psychotic Personality: Reservations on the Use of the Couch for Biblical Personalities', in Richard Clifford (ed.), *The Word in the World* (Cambridge, MA: Weston College Press, 1973), pp. 59-63.

Cazelles, H., 'Jeremiah and Deuteronomy', in L.G. Perdue and B.W. Kovacs (eds.), *A Prophet to the Nations: Essays in Jeremiah Studies* (Winona Lake, IN: Eisenbrauns, 1984), pp. 89-111.

Clines, D.J.A, 'Michal Observed: An Introduction to Reading Her Story', in *idem* and T.C. Eskenazi (eds.), *Telling Queen Michal's Story: An Experiment in Comparative Interpretation* (Sheffield: JSOT Press, 1991), pp. 24-63.

Clines, D.J.A., and J. Cheryl Exum, 'The New Literary Criticism', in *idem* (eds.), *The New Literary Criticism and the Hebrew Bible* (JSOTSup, 143; Sheffield: JSOT Press, 1993), pp. 12-25.

Cody, Aelred, *Ezekiel: With an Excursus on Old Testament Priesthood* (Old Testament Message: A Biblical Theological Commentary, 11; Wilmington, DE: Michael Glazier, 1984).

Cogan, M., *Imperialism and Religion: Assyria, Judah and Israel in the Eighth and Seventh Centuries BCE* (SBLMS, 19; Missoula, MT: Scholars Press, 1974).

Collins, John J., *Daniel* (Hermeneia; Minneapolis: Fortress Press, 1993).

Colwell, Ernest, 'Greek Language', in *IDB*, pp. 479-87.

Cooke, G.A, *A Critical and Exegetical Commentary on the Book of Ezekiel* (ICC; Edinburgh: T. & T. Clark, 1967 [1936]).

Cooper, Lamar Eugene, Sr, *Ezekiel* (The New American Commentary, 17; Nashville: Broadman & Holman, 1994).

Couturier, G.P., 'Jeremiah', in R.E. Brown, J.A. Fitzmyer and R.E. Murphy (eds.), *Jerome Biblical Commentary* (Englewood Cliffs, NJ: Prentice–Hall, 1968), pp. 300-36.

Cowley, A.E., *Genesius' Hebrew Grammar* (ed. E. Kautsch; Oxford: Clarendon Press: Oxford, 1910 [1957]).

Craigie, Peter C., *Ezekiel* (Daily Study Bible Series; Philadelphia: Westminster Press, 1983).

Craigie, Peter C., P.H. Kelley and J.F. Drinkard, Jr, *Jeremiah 1–25* (WBC, 26; Dallas: Word Books, 1991).

Crenshaw, James L., *Prophetic Conflict: Its Effect Upon Israelite Religion* (Berlin: W. de Gruyter, 1971).

Crüsemann, Frank, *The Torah: Theology and Social History of Old Testament Law* (trans. Allan W. Mahnke; Minneapolis: Fortress Press, 1996).

Culican, W., 'A Votive Model from the Sea', *PEQ* 108 (1976), pp. 119-23.

Culler, J., *On Deconstruction: Theory and Criticism after Structuralism* (London: Routledge & Kegan Paul, 1975).

Cunliffe-Jones, H., *The Book of Jeremiah* (London: SCM Press, 1960).

Dahood, M., 'La Regina del Cielo in Geremia', *RevistB* 8 (1960), pp. 166-68.

Darr, K.P., 'Like Warrior, Like Women: Destruction and Deliverance in Isaiah 42:10-17', *CBQ* 49 (1987), pp. 560-71.

—'Ezekiel's Justifications of God: Teaching Troubling Texts', *JSOT* 55 (1992), pp. 97-117.

— *Isaiah's Vision and the Family of God* (Literary Currents in Biblical Interpretation; Louisville, KY: Westminster/John Knox Press, 1994).

—'Ezekiel', in Carol A. Newsom and Sharon H. Ringe (eds.), *Women's Bible Commentary: Expanded Edition* (Louisville, KY: Westminster/John Knox Press, 1998).

Davidson, Patricia, 'The Material Culture of the Lobedu: A Museum and Field Study' (MA dissertation, University of Stellenbosch, 1979).

Day, J., R.P. Gordon and H.G.M. Williamson (eds.), *Wisdom in Ancient Israel: Essays in Honor of J.A. Emerton* (Cambridge: Cambridge University Press, 1995).

Delaney, C., *The Seed and the Soil: Gender and Cosmology in Turkish Village Society* (Berkeley: University of California Press, 1991).

Delcor, M., 'La vision de la femme dans l'épha de Zach., 5,5-11 à la lumière de la littérature hittite', *RHR* 187 (1975), pp. 137-45.

—'Le culte de la "Reine du Ciel" selon Jer 7,18; 44,17-19, 25 et ses survivances', in W.C. Delsman *et al.* (eds.), *Von Kanaan bis Kerala* (AOAT, 211; Kevelaer: Butzon & Bercker; Neukirchen–Vluyn: Neukirchener Verlag, 1982), pp. 101-22.

Diamond, A.R.P., and K. O'Connor, 'Unfaithful Passions: Coding Women Coding Men in Jeremiah 2–3 (4:2)', *BibInt* 4 (1996), pp. 288-310.

Dijk-Hemmes, F. van, 'The Imagination of Power and the Power of Imagination: An Intertextual Analysis of Two Biblical Love Songs: The Song of Songs and Hosea 2', *JSOT* 44 (1989), pp. 75-88.

—'The Metaphorization of Woman in Prophetic Speech: An Analysis of Ezekiel 23', *VT* 43 (1993), pp. 162-70; also in Brenner (ed.), *A Feminist Companion to the Latter Prophets*, pp. 244-55.

—'Traces of Women's Texts in the Hebrew Bible', in Brenner and van Dijk-Hemmes, *On Gendering Texts Female and Male Voices in the Hebrew Bible* (Leiden: E.J. Brill, 1993).

—'The Great Woman of Shunem and the Man of God: A Dual Interpretation of 2 Kings 4.8-37', in Brenner (ed.), *A Feminist Companion to Samuel and Kings*, pp. 218-30.

Dijkstra, M., 'Goddess, God, Men and Women in Ezekiel 8', in B. Becking and M. Dijkstra (eds.), *On Reading Prophetic Texts: Gender-Specific and Related Studies in Memory of Fokkelien van Dijk-Hemmes* (Leiden: E.J. Brill, 1996), pp. 83-114.

Douglas, M., *Purity and Danger* (London: Routledge and Kegan Paul, 2nd edn, 1978).

—*In the Wilderness: The Doctrine of Defilement in the Book of Numbers* (JSOTSup, 158; Sheffield: JSOT Press, 1993).

Dover, K.J., *Greek Homosexuality* (London: Duckworth, 1978; updated with new postscript, Cambridge, MA: Harvard University Press, 1989).

Driver, S.R., *The Book of Daniel* (Cambridge: Cambridge University Press, 1900).

—*The Book of the Prophet Jeremiah* (London: Hodder and Stoughton, 1906).

E.V.H., 'A Visit to the Misses Smith and their Cows', *Nantucket Inquirer and Mirror*, 4 April 1874, repr. in Julia E. Smith, *Abby Smith and her Cows*, pp. 36-37.

Edelman, Diana, 'Huldah the Prophet—of Yahweh or Asherah?', in Brenner (ed.), *A Feminist Companion to Samuel and Kings*, pp. 231-50.

Eichrodt, Walther, *Ezekiel: A Commentary* (Philadelphia: Westminster Press, 1970).

Eilberg-Schwartz, H., 'God's Body: The Divine Cover-Up', in J.M. Law (ed.), *Religious Reflexions on the Human Body* (Bloomington: Indiana University Press, 1995), pp. 137-48.

Ellermeier, Friedrich, *Prophetie in Mari und Israel* (Theologische und Orientalistische Arbeiten, 1; Herzberg: Verlag Erwin Jungfer, 1968).

Elliger, K., *Das Buch der zwölf Kleinen Propheten*. II. *Die Propheten Nahum, Habakuk, Zephanja, Haggai, Sacharja, Maleachi* (ATD, 25; Göttingen: Vandenhoeck & Ruprecht, 8th edn, 1982).

Eskenazi, Tamara C., 'Out From the Shadows: Biblical Women in the Post-Exilic Era', in Brenner (ed.), *A Feminist Companion to Samuel and Kings* (Sheffield: Sheffield Academic Press, 1994), pp. 252-71.

Eslinger, L., 'The Infinite in a Finite Organical Perception (Isaiah VI 1-5)', *VT* 45 (1995), pp. 145-73.

Exum, J. Cheryl, 'Who's Afraid of "The Endangered Ancestress"?', in *idem* and David J.A. Clines (eds.), *The New Literary Criticism and the Hebrew Bible* (JSOTSup, 143; Sheffield: JSOT Press, 1993), pp. 91-113.

—' "You Shall Let Every Daughter Live": A Study of Exodus 1:8–2:10', in Brenner (ed.), *A Feminist Companion to Exodus to Deuteronomy* (originally in *Semeia* 28 [1983], pp. 63-82).

—'Second Thoughts About Secondary Characters', in Brenner (ed.), *A Feminist Companion to Exodus to Deuteronomy* (Sheffield: Sheffield Academic Press, 1994), pp. 75-87.

—*Plotted, Shot and Painted: Cultural Representations of Biblical Women* (JSOTSup, 215; Gender, Culture, Theory, 3; Sheffield: Sheffield Academic Press, 1996).

Fauth, W., 'Der Schlund des Orcus: Zu einer Eigentümlichkeit der römisch-etruskischen Unterweltsvorstellung', *Numen* 21 (1974), pp. 105-27.

Feinberg, C.L., *Jeremiah: A Commentary* (Grand Rapids, MI: Zondervan, 1982).

Fewell, D.N., *Circle of Sovereignty: Plotting Politics in the Book of Daniel* (Nashville: Abingdon Press, 1991).

Fischer, I., 'Das Buch Jesaja: Das Buch der weiblichen Metaphern', in L. Schottroff and M.-T. Wacker (eds.), *Kompendium Feministische Bibelauslegung* (Gütersloh: Chr. Kaiser Verlag/Gütersloher Verlagshaus, 2nd edn, 1999), pp. 246-57.

Fitzmyer, J.A., 'The Phoenician Inscription from Pyrgi', *JAOS* 86 (1966), pp. 285-97.

Flanders, Henry Jackson, Jr, *et al.*, *People of the Covenant: An Introduction to the Old Testament* (New York: The Ronald Press, 2nd edn, 1973).

Floyd, M.H., 'The Evil in the Ephah: Reading Zechariah 5.5-11 in its Literary Context', *CBQ* 58 (1996), pp. 51-68.

—'Cosmos and History in Zechariah's View of the Restoration (Zechariah 1.7–6.15)', in H.T. Sun *et al.* (eds.), *Problems in Biblical Theology: Festschrift Rolf Knierim* (Grand Rapids: Eerdmans, 1997), pp. 125-44.

Fontaine, Carole R., 'The Social Roles of Women in the World of Wisdom', in Brenner (ed.), *A Feminist Companion to Wisdom Literature*, pp. 24-49.

Foster, J.A., 'The Motherhood of God: The Use of *hyl* as God-Language in the Hebrew Scriptures', in L.M. Hopfe (ed.), *Uncovering Ancient Stones: Essays in Memory of H.N. Richardson* (Winona Lake: Eisenbrauns, 1994), pp. 93-102.

Franke, C.A., 'The Function of the Satiric Lament over Babylon in Second Isaiah (XLVII)', *VT* 41 (1991), pp. 408-18.

—*Isaiah 46, 47, and 48: A New Literary-Critical Reading* (BJSUCA, 3; Winona Lake: Eisenbrauns, 1994).

Franzmann, M., 'The City as Woman: The Case of Babylon in Isaiah 47', *ABR* 43 (1995), pp. 1-19.

Freedman, D.N., 'The Biblical Idea of History', *Int* 21 (1967), pp. 32-49.

Freud, S., 'Jokes as a Social Process', in *Collected Works* (Standard Edition), VIII (1905), pp. 140-58.

—*Jokes and their Relation to the Unconscious* (trans. J. Strachey; Penguin Freud Library, 6; Longman: Penguin, 1976 [1905]).

Frevel, C., *Aschera und der Ausschliesslichkeitsanspruch YHWHs*, I (BBB, 94.1; Weinheim: Beltz Athenäum, 1995).

Fuchs, E., 'Who is Hiding the Truth? Deceptive Women and Biblical Androcentrism', in Adela Y. Collins (ed.), *Feminist Perspectives on Biblical Scholarship* (Chico, CA: Scholars Press, 1985), pp. 137-44.

—' "For I Have the Way of Women": Deception, Gender, and Ideology in Biblical Narrative', in J. Cheryl Exum and Johanna W.H. Bos (eds.), *Reasoning with the Foxes: Female Wit in a World of Male Power* (Semeia, 42; Society of Biblical Literature, 1988), pp. 68-83.

Fuhs, Hans Ferdinand, *Ezechiel 1–24* (NEB, 7; Würzburg: Echter Verlag, 1984).

Galambush, J., *Jerusalem in the Book of Ezekiel: The City as Yahweh's Wife* (SBLDS, 130; Atlanta: Scholars Press, 1992).

Galling, Kurt, *Hesekiel* (HAT; Tübingen: Mohr, 1936).

—*Die Bücher der Chronik, Esra, Nehemia* (ATD, 12; Göttingen: Vandenhoeck & Ruprecht, 1954).

Gaster, T. H., 'Belial', in *IDB*, I.

Gerstenberger, E., '[תב]', *TLOT*, III, p. 1430.

Gese, H., 'Anfang und Ende der Apokalyptik, dargestellt am Sacharjabuch', *ZTK* 70 (1973), pp. 20-49.

Ginsberg, H.L., 'Hosea, Book of', *EncJud*, VIII.

Girard, René, *Violence and the Sacred* (trans. Patrick Gregory; Baltimore: Johns Hopkins University Press, 1977).

—*Things Hidden Since the Foundation of the World* (trans. Stephen Bann and Michael Metteer; London: Athlone Press, 1987).

—'Generative Scapegoating', in Robert G. Hamerton-Kelly (ed.), *Violent Origins* (Stanford: Stanford University Press, 1987).

Glazier-McDonald, Beth, *Malachi: The Divine Messenger, A Critical Appraisal* (SBLDS, 98; Atlanta: Scholars Press, 1987).

Goitein, S.D., 'Women as Creators of Biblical Genres', *Prooftexts* 8 (1988), pp. 1-33 (orig. Hebr. 1957).

Goldingay, John E., *Daniel* (WBC; Dallas: Word Books, 1989).

Gordon, P., and Washington, H.C., 'Rape as a Military Metaphor in the Hebrew Bible', in Brenner (ed.), *A Feminist Companion to the Latter Prophets*, pp. 308-25.

Gordon, R.P., 'Aleph Apologeticum', *JQR* 69 (1978), pp. 112-16.

—'A House Divided: Wisdom in Old Testament Narrative Traditions', in Day, Gordon and Williamson (eds.), *Wisdom in Ancient Israel*.

Gowan, Donald E., *Ezekiel* (Atlanta: John Knox, 1985).

Graetz, Naomi, *Silence is Deadly: Judaism Confronts Wifebeating* (Northvale, NJ: Jason Aronson Press, 1998).

Graffy, Adrian, *A Prophet Confronts His People: Disputation Speech in the Prophets* (Rome: Biblical Institute, 1984).

Greenberg, M., '*Nhšk* (Ezek. 16:36): Another Hebrew Cognate of Akkadian *nahāšu*', in M. de J. Ellis (ed.), *Essays on the Ancient Near East: Festschrift for J.J. Finkelstein* (Hamden, CT: Archon Books, 1977), pp. 85-86.

—*Ezekiel 1–20: A New Translation with Introduction and Commentary* (AB, 22; Garden City, NY: Doubleday, 1983).

Greenfield, C. Jonas, 'Two Biblical Passages in Light of their Near Eastern Background: Ezekiel 16.30 and Malachi 3.17', *Eretz Israel* 16 (1982), pp. 56-61 (Hebrew).

Greengus, S., 'A Textbook Case of Adultery in Ancient Mesopotamia', *HUCA* 40 (1969), pp. 33-44.

Greenhill, W., *An Exposition of Ezekiel* (Edinburgh and Carlisle, PA: Banner of Truth Trust, 1645-67).

Gritsch, E.W., 'Luther's Humor: Instrument of Witness', *Dialog* 22 (1983), pp. 176-81.

Gruber, M.L., 'The Motherhood of God in Second Isaiah', *RB* 90 (1983), pp. 351-59.

—'Marital Fidelity and Intimacy: A View from Hosea 4', in Brenner (ed.), *A Feminist Companion to the Latter Prophets* (Sheffield: Sheffield Academic Press, 1995), pp. 169-79.

Gunn, D.M., and D.N. Fewell, *Narrative in the Hebrew Bible* (Oxford: Oxford University Press, 1993).

Haag, H., *Der Gottesknecht bei Deuterojesaja* (EdF, 233; Darmstadt: Wissenschaftliche Buchgesellschaft, 2nd edn, 1993).

Haas, V., 'Ein hurritischer Blutritus und die Deponierung der Ritualrückstände nach hethitischen Quellen', in B. Janowski, K. Koch and G. Wilhelm (eds.), *Religionsgeschichtliche Beziehungen zwischen Kleinasien, Nordsyrien und dem Alten Testament: Internationales Symposium Hamburg 17.–21. März 1990* (OBO, 129; Freiburg: Universitätsverlag Freiburg/Schweiz; Göttingen: Vandenhoeck & Ruprecht, 1993), pp. 67-85.

Habel, N.C., *Jeremiah, Lamentations* (Concordia Commentary; St Louis: Concordia, 1968).

Hadley, J.M., 'The Fertility of the Flock? The De-Personalization of Astarte in the Old Testament', in B. Becking and M. Dijkstra (eds.), *On Reading Prophetic Texts: Gender-Specific and Related Studies in Memory of Fokkelien van Dijk-Hemmes* (Leiden: E.J. Brill, 1996), pp. 115-33.

—'The De-Deification of Deities in Deuteronomy', paper delivered at the 16th Congress of the International Organization for the Study of the Old Testament (Oslo, Norway, 1998).

—*The Cult of Asherah in Ancient Israel and Judah: Evidence for a Hebrew Goddess* (Oriental Publications, 57; Cambridge: Cambridge University Press, 2000).

Haller, M., *Das Judentum: Geschichtsschreibung, Prophetie und Gesetzgebung nach dem Exil* (SAT, 2.3; Göttingen: Vandenhoeck & Ruprecht, 2nd edn, 1925).

Hallo, W.W. (ed.), *The Context of Scripture*, II (Leiden: E.J. Brill, 2000)

Halperin, David J., *Seeking Ezekiel: Text and Psychology* (University Park, PA: Pennsylvania State University Press, 1993).

Hals, Ronald M., *Ezekiel* (FOTL, 19; Grand Rapids: Eerdmans, 1989), p. 109.

Hanhart, R., *Sacharja* (BKAT, 14.7; Neukirchen–Vluyn: Neukirchener Verlag, 1990).

Haran, M., 'The Disappearance of the Ark', *IEJ* 13 (1963), pp. 46-58.

Hardmeier, Christof, *Prophetie im Streit vor dem Untergang Judas: Erzählkommunikative Studien zur Entstehungssituation der Jesaja und Jeremiaerzählungen in II Reg 18–20 und Jer 37–40* (BZAW, 187; Berlin and New York: W. de Gruyter, 1990).

Harrison, R.K., *Jeremiah and Lamentations* (TOTC; London: The Tyndale Press, 1973).

Hartman, L.F., and A.A. DiLella, *The Book of Daniel* (AB; Garden City, NY: Doubleday, 1978).

Häusl, M., 'Die Klagelieder: Zions Stimme in der Not', in L. Schottroff and M.T. Wacker (eds.), *Kompendium Feministische Bibelauslegung* (Gütersloh: Chr. Kaiser Verlag/Gütersloher Verlagshaus, 2nd edn, 1999), pp. 270-77.

Held, M., 'Studies in Biblical Lexicography in the Light of Akkadian', *Eretz-Israel* 16 (1982), pp. 76-85 (in Hebrew).

Hobbs, T.R., 'Jeremiah 3.1-5 and Deuteronomy 24.1-4', *ZAW* 86 (1974), pp. 23-29.

Höckner, Elfriede, *Die Lobedu Südafrikas: Mythos und Realität der Regenkönigin Modjadj* (Stuttgart: Franz Steiner Verlag, 1998).

Hof, Pieter van't, 'Bijdrage tot de kennis van Antiochus IV Epiphanes koning van Sirië' (DLitt dissertation, Vrije Universiteit Amsterdam, 1955).

Holladay, W.L., *Jeremiah 1: A Commentary on the Book of the Prophet Jeremiah Chapters 1–25* (Hermeneia; Philadelphia: Fortress Press, 1986).

—*Jeremiah 2: A Commentary on the Book of the Prophet Jeremiah Chapters 26–52* (Hermeneia; Minneapolis: Fortress Press, 1989).

—*Jeremiah: A Fresh Reading* (New York: Pilgrim Press, 1990).

Holland, Norman, *5 Readers Reading* (New Haven: Yale University Press, 1975).

Holt, E.K., 'The Chicken and the Egg—Or: Was Jeremiah a Member of the Deuteronomist Party?, *JSOT* 44 (1989), pp. 109-22.

Housley, Kathleen, *The Letter Kills But the Spirit Gives Life: The Smiths—Abolitionists, Suffragists, Bible Translators* (Glastonbury, CT: Historical Society of Glastonbury, 1993).

Houtman, C., 'Queen of Heaven', in K. van der Toorn, B. Becking and P.W. van der Horst (eds.), *Dictionary of Deities and Demons in the Bible* (Leiden: E.J. Brill, 1995), cols. 1278-83.

Huey, F.B., Jr, *Ezekiel, Daniel* (Layman's Bible Commentary, 12; Nashville: Broadman, 1983).

Hugenberger, G. P., *Marriage as Covenant: A Study of Biblical Law and Ethics Governing Marriage Developed from the Perspective of Malachi* (VTSup, 52; Leiden: E.J. Brill, 1994).

Humm, M., *Feminist Criticism: Women as Contemporary Critics* (London: Harvester Press, 1986).

Hunter, M.J., *A Guide to Jeremiah* (Theological Education Fund Study Guide, 30; London: SPCK, 1993).

Hvidberg, F.F., *Weeping and Laughter in the Old Testament* (Leiden: E.J. Brill, 1962).

Hvidberg-Hansen, F.O., *La déesse Tnt, un étude sur la religion canaanéo-punique*, I (Copenhagen: Gad, 1979).

Hyatt, J.P., 'Jeremiah and Deuteronomy', in L.G. Perdue and B.W. Kovacs (eds.), *A Prophet to the Nations: Essays in Jeremiah Studies* (Winona Lake, IN: Eisenbrauns, 1984), pp. 113-27.

—'The Deuteronomic Edition of Jeremiah', in L.G. Perdue and B.W. Kovacs (eds.), *A Prophet to the Nations: Essays in Jeremiah Studies* (Winona Lake, IN: Eisenbrauns, 1984), pp. 247-67.

Hyers, C., 'Christian Humor: Uses and Abuses of Laughter', *Dialog* 22 (1983), pp. 198-203.

Irigaray, Luce, 'When Our Lips Speak Together', in *This Sex Which is Not One* (trans. Catherine Porter; Ithaca, NY: Cornell University Press, 1985), pp. 205-18.

Isaksson, A., *Marriage and Ministry in the New Temple: A Study with Special Reference to Mt. 19.3-12 and 1. Cor. 11.3-16* (ASNU, 24; Lund: Gleerup, 1965).

Jacoby, Russell, 'Marginal Returns: The Trouble with Post-Colonial Theory', *Lingua Franca* (Sept.–Oct. 1995), pp. 30-37.

Janowski, B., and G. Wilhelm, 'Der Bock, der die Sünden hinausträgt: Zur Religionsgeschichte des Azazel-Ritus Lev. 16,10.21f', in B. Janowski, G. Wilhelm and Klaus Koch (eds.), *Religionsgeschichtliche Beziehungen zwischen Kleinasien, Nordsyrien und dem Alten Testament: Internationales Symposium Hamburg 17.–21. März 1990* (OBO, 129; Freiburg: Universitätsverlag Freiburg/Schweiz; Göttingen: Vandenhoeck & Ruprecht, 1993), pp. 109-69.

Janzen, J.G., *Studies in the Text of Jeremiah* (HSM, 6; Cambridge, MA: Harvard University Press, 1973).

Jones, D.R., *Jeremiah* (NCB Commentary; Grand Rapids, MI: Eerdmans, 1992).

Jost, R., *Frauen, Männer und die Himmelskönigin: Exegetische Studien* (Gütersloh: Chr. Kaiser Verlag/Gütersloher Verlagshaus, 1995).

Joyce, Paul, *Divine Initiative and Human Response in Ezekiel* (JSOTSup, 51; Sheffield: Sheffield Academic Press, 1989).

Junker, H., 'Die Frau im alttestamentlichen ekstatischen Kult', *TGl* 21 (1929), pp. 68-74.

Kaasa, H., 'Confessions of a Serious-Minded Joker', *Dialog* 22 (1983), pp. 171-75.

Kaiser, B.B., 'Poet as "Female Impersonator": The Image of Daughter Zion as Speaker in Biblical Poems of Suffering', *JR* 67 (1987), pp. 164-82.

Kaiser, O., *Der Prophet Jesaja: Kapitel 13–39* (ATD, 18; Göttingen: Vandenhoeck & Ruprecht, 2nd edn, 1976).

—*Das Buch des Propheten Jesaja: Kapitel 1–12* (ATD, 17.5; Göttingen: Vandenhoeck & Ruprecht, 5th edn, 1981).

—'Klagelieder', in H. Ringgren, W. Zimmerli and O. Kaiser, *Sprüche. Prediger. Das Hohe Lied. Klagelieder. Das Buch Esther* (ATD, 16; Göttingen: Vandenhoeck & Ruprecht, 3rd edn, 1981), pp. 291-386.

Kamionkowski, S. Tamar, 'Gender Ambiguity and Subversive Metaphor in Ezekiel 16' (PhD dissertation, Brandeis University, 2000).

Keel, O., *Deine Blicke sind Tauben: Zur Metaphorik des Hohen Liedes* (Stuttgart: Katholisches Bibelwerk, 1984).

Keel, O., and C. Uehlinger, *Gods, Goddesses, and Images of God in Ancient Israel* (trans. H. Trapp; Edinburgh: T. & T. Clark, 1998).

Keown, G.L., P.J. Scalise and T.G. Smothers, *Jeremiah 26–52* (WBC, 27; Dallas: Word Books, 1995).

Kessler, R., 'Mirjam und die Prophetie der Perserzeit', in U. Bail and R. Jost (eds.), *Gott an den Rändern: Sozialgeschichtliche Perspektiven auf die Bibel* (Festschrift Willy Schottroff; Gütersloh: Chr. Kaiser Verlag, 1996), pp. 64-72.

Keuls, Eva C., *The Reign of the Phallus: Sexual Politics in Ancient Athens* (Berkeley: University of California Press, 1984).

King, P.J., *Jeremiah: An Archaeological Companion* (Louisville, KY: Westminster/John Knox Press, 1993).

Koch, K., 'כדן', in *ThWAT*, IV, cols. 95-107.
—'Aschera als Himmelskönigin in Jerusalem', *UF* 20 (1988), pp. 97-120.
—*Die Profeten*. II. *Babylonisch-persische Zeit* (Stuttgart: 2nd edn, 1988).
Koole, J.L., *Isaiah 40–48* (HOT, 3.1; Kampen: 1997).
—*Isaiah 49–55* (HOT, 3.2; Leuven: 1998).
Korpel, M.C.A., 'The Female Servant of the Lord in Isaiah 54', in B. Becking and M. Dijkstra (eds.), *On Reading Prophetic Texts: Gender-Specific and Related Studies in Memory of Fokkelien van Dijk-Hemmes* (Biblical Interpretation Series, 18; Leiden: E.J. Brill, 1996), pp. 153-67.
Kraeling, E.G., *The Brooklyn Museum Aramaic Papyri: New Documents of the Fifth Century BC from the Jewish Colony at Elephantine* (Arno Press, 1969 [1953]).
Krige, E. Jensen, 'Medicine, Magic and Religion of the Lovedu' (DLitt thesis, University of the Witwatersrand).
Krige, E. Jensen, and J.D. Krige, *The Realm of a Rain-Queen: A Study of the Pattern of Lovedu Society* (London: Oxford University Press, 1943).
Kübel, P., 'Eva, Pandora und Enkidus "Dirne"', *BN* 82 (1996), pp. 13-20.
Kümmel, H.M., 'Ersatzkönig und Sündenbock', *ZAW* 80 (1968), pp. 289-318.
Kümmel, H.M., W. Farber and W.H.P. Römer, *Rituale und Beschwörungen*, I (TUAT, 2.2; Gütersloh: Gütersloher Verlagshaus/Gerd Mohn, 1987).
Lacocque, André, *The Book of Daniel* (Atlanta: John Knox Press, 1979).
Lakoff, G., and Johnson, M., *Metaphors We Live By* (Chicago and London: University of Chicago Press, 1980).
Lanahan, W.F., 'The Speaking Voice in the Book of Lamentations', *JBL* 93 (1974), pp. 41-49.
Landman, Christina, 'African Women's Theology', in Maimela and König (eds.), *Initiation into Theology*.
Laqueur, Thomas, *Making Sex: Body and Gender from the Greeks to Freud* (Cambridge, MA and London: Harvard University Press, 1990).
Larson, Janet, 'Women and Bible Translation—The 1876 Translation of Julia E. Smith', paper presented to American Bible Society Symposium, 14 September 1998; *Journal for Scripture and Media*, forthcoming.
Lefkowitz, Mary R., and Maureen B. Fant, *Women's Life in Greece and Rome: A Source Book in Translation* (Baltimore: Johns Hopkins University Press, 1982).
Lincoln, Bruce, *Discourse and the Construction of Society: Comparative Studies of Myth, Ritual, and Classification* (New York: Oxford University Press, 1989).
Levenson, Jon, *Creation and the Persistence of Evil: The Jewish Drama of Divine Omnipotence* (Princeton, NJ: Princeton University Press, 1994 [1988]).
Lissarague, F., 'Frauen, Kästchen, Gefäße: Einige Zeichen und Metaphern', in Walters Art Gallery Baltimore, Antikenmuseum Basel and the Ludwig Collection (eds.), *Pandora: Frauen im klassischen Griechenland* (Mainz: Von Zabern, 1995), pp. 91-101.
Long, Burke O., 'The Stylistic Components of Jer. 3.1-5', *ZAW* 88 (1976), pp. 376-90.
Loraux, N., 'Herakles: The Super-Male and the Feminine', in D.M. Halperin, J.J. Winkler and F. Zeitlin (eds.), *Before Sexuality: The Construction of Erotic Experience in the Ancient Greek World* (Princeton: Princeton University Press, 1990), pp. 21-52.
Loretz, O., *Ugarit und die Bibel: Kanaanäische Götter und Religion im Alten Testament* (Darmstadt: Wissenschaftliche Buchgesellschaft, 1990).

Macurdy, Grace H., *Hellenistic Queen: A Study of Woman-Power in Macedonia, Seleucid Syria and Ptolemaic Egypt* (New York: AMS Press, 1977 [1932]).

Magdalene, F.R., 'Ancient Near-Eastern Treaty-Curses and the Ultimate Texts of Terror: A Study of the Language of Divine Sexual Abuse in the Prophetic Corpus', in Brenner (ed.), *A Feminist Companion to the Latter Prophets*, pp. 326-52.

Maier, C., 'Jerusalem als Ehebrecherin in Ezechiel 16: Zur Verwendung und Funktion einer biblischen Metapher', in H. Jahnow *et al.*, *Feministische Hermeneutik und Erstes Testament: Analysen und Interpretationen* (Stuttgart: Kohlhammer, 1994), pp. 85-105.

Maimela, Simon, and Adrio König (eds.), *Initiation into Theology: The Rich Variety of Theology and Hermeneutics* (Pretoria: JL van Schaik, 1998).

Malul, Meir, 'Adoption of Foundlings in the Bible and Mesopotamian Documents: A Study of Some Legal Metaphors in Ezekiel 16.1-7', *JSOT* 46 (1990), pp. 97-126.

Marinkovic, P., 'What Does Zechariah 1–8 Tell Us about the Second Temple?', in T.C. Eskenazi and K.H. Richards (eds.), *Second Temple Studies 2: Temple and Community in the Persian Period* (JSOTSup, 175; Sheffield: Sheffield Academic Press, 1994), pp. 88-103.

Markholm, Otto, *Antiochus IV of Syria* (Copenhagen: Gyldendalske Boghandel, 1966), p. 135.

Marks, E., and I. de Courtivron (eds.), *New French Feminisms* (New York: Schocken Books, 1980).

Martin, James D., 'The Forensic Background to Jeremiah III 1', *VT* 19 (1969), pp. 82-92.

Mather, J., 'The Comic Art of the Book of Jonah', *Soundings* 65 (1982), pp. 280-91.

McKane, W., 'Relations Between Poetry and Prose in the Book of Jeremiah with Special Reference to Jeremiah iii 6-11 and xii 14-17', *VTSup* 32 (1981), pp. 220-37.

—in Leo G. Perdue and Brian W. Kovacs (eds.), *A Prophet to the Nations: Essays in Jeremiah Studies* (Winona Lake: Eisenbrauns, 1984), pp. 269-84.

—*A Critical and Exegetical Commentary on Jeremiah. I. Introduction and Commentary on Jeremiah I–XXV* (ICC; Edinburgh: T. & T. Clark, 1986).

—'Worship of the Queen of Heaven (Jer 44)', in I. Kottsieper, J. van Oorschot, D. Römheld and H.M. Wahl (eds.), *'Wer ist wie du, HERR, unter den Göttern?' Studien zur Theologie und Religionsgeschichte Israels für Otto Kaiser zum 70. Geburtstag* (Göttingen: Vandenhoeck & Ruprecht, 1994), pp. 318-24.

—*A Critical and Exegetical Commentary on Jeremiah. II. Commentary on Jeremiah XXVI–LII* (ICC; Edinburgh: T. & T. Clark, 1996).

Merendino, R.P., 'Jes 49,14-26: Jahwes Bekenntnis zu Sion und die neue Heilszeit', *RB* 89 (1982), pp. 321-69.

Mesnil du Buisson, R. du, *Etudes sur les dieux phéniciens hérités par l'empire romain* (Etudes préliminaires aux religions orientales dans l'Empire romain, 14; Leiden: E.J. Brill, 1970).

—*Nouvelles études sur les dieux et les mythes de Canaan* (Etudes préliminaires aux religions orientales dans l'Empire romain, 33; Leiden: E.J. Brill, 1973).

Mettinger, T.N.D., *A Farewell to the Servant Songs: A Critical Examination of an Exegetical Axiom* (SMHVL 1982–1983, 3; Lund: Gleerup, 1983).

Meyers, C.L., 'Everyday Life: Women in the Period of the Hebrew Bible', in C.A. Newsom and S.H. Ringe (eds.), *The Woman's Bible Commentary* (Louisville, KY: Westminster/John Knox Press, 1992), pp. 244-51.

—'Miriam the Musician', in Brenner (ed.), *A Feminist Companion to Exodus to Deuteronomy*, pp. 207-30.

Meyers, C.L., and E.M. Meyers, *Haggai, Zechariah 1–8* (AB, 25b; Garden City, NY: Doubleday, 1987).

Milgrom, Jacob, *Leviticus 1–16* (AB; Garden City, NY: Doubleday, 1991).

Milik, J.T., 'Les Papyrus araméens d'Hermoupolis et les cultes syro-phéniciens en Egypte perse', *Bib* 48 (1967), pp. 556-64.

Miller, Alice, *For Your Own Good* (trans. H. Hannun and H. Hannun; NY: Farrar, Strauss and Giroux, 1983).

Miller, N.K., *Subject to Change: Reading Feminist Writing* (New York: Columbia University Press, 1988).

Moi, Toril, *Sexual/Textual Politics: Feminist Literary Theory* (London: Routledge, 1985).

Montgomery, J.A., *The Book of Daniel* (ICC; Edinburgh: T. & T. Clark, 1927).

Morgan, Donn F., *Wisdom in the Old Testament Traditions* (Atlanta: John Knox Press, 1981).

Morgan, G.C., *Studies in the Prophecy of Jeremiah* (London and Edinburgh: Oliphants, 1955).

Müller, Hans-Peter, 'כביא', *ThWAT*, V (1984), p. 160.

Mürkholm, Otto, *Antiochus IV of Syria* (Copenhagen: Gyldendalske Boghandel, 1966).

Murphy, Ronald E., *The Tree of Life: An Exploration of Biblical Wisdom Literature* (Grand Rapids: Eerdmans, 2nd edn, 1996).

Naidoff, B.D., 'The Twofold Structure of Isaiah 45, 9-13', *VT* 31 (1981), pp. 180-85.

Newsom, Carol, 'Woman and the Discourse of Patriarchal Wisdom: A Study of Proverbs 1–9', in Peggy L. Day (ed.), *Gender and Difference in Ancient Israel* (Philadelphia: Fortress Press, 1989), pp. 142-60.

Nicholson, E.W., *The Book of the Prophet Jeremiah Chapters 1–25* (Cambridge: Cambridge University Press, 1973).

—*The Book of the Prophet Jeremiah Chapters 26–52* (Cambridge: Cambridge University Press, 1975).

Niditch, Susan, 'Eroticism and Death in the Tale of Jael', in Peggy L. Day (ed.), *Gender and Difference in Ancient Israel* (Minneapolis: Fortress Press, 1989), pp. 43-57.

Nielsen, K., *There is Hope for a Tree: The Tree as Metaphor in Isaiah* (JSOTSup, 65; Sheffield: Sheffield Academic Press, 1989).

Nieting, L., 'Humor in the New Testament', *Dialog* 22 (1983), pp. 168-70.

Noddings, Nel, *Educating for Intelligent Belief or Unbelief* (New York and London: Teachers College Press, Columbia University, 1993).

Noth, Martin, and D.W. Thomas (eds.), *Wisdom in Israel and in the Ancient Near East: Presented to H.H. Rowley in Celebration of his Sixty-Fifth Birthday* (Leiden: E.J. Brill, 1955).

Nötscher, Friedrich, 'Prophetie im Umkreis des alten Israel', *BZ* NS 10 (1966), pp. 161-97.

Numbers, Ronald L., and Janet S. Numbers, 'Millerism and Madness: A Study of "Religious Insanity" in Nineteenth-Century America', in Ronald L. Numbers and Jonathan M. Butler (eds.), *The Disappointed: Millerism and Millenarianism in the Nineteenth Century* (Bloomington: Indiana University Press, 1987), pp. 92-118.

Nussbaum, Martha, *Love's Knowledge: Essays on Philosophy and Literature* (Oxford: Oxford University Press, 1990).

—*The Therapy of Desire: Theory and Practice in Hellenistic Ethics* (Princeton: Princeton University Press, 1994).

O'Brien, Julia M., 'Malachi', *Currents in Research: Biblical Studies* 3 (1995), pp. 79-92.

—'Judah as Wife and Husband: Deconstructing Gender in Malachi', *JBL* 115 (1996), pp. 243-52.

O'Connor, K.M., *The Confessions of Jeremiah: Their Interpretation and Role in Chapters 1–25* (SBLDS, 94; Atlanta: Scholars Press, 1988).

—'Jeremiah', in C.A. Newsom and S.H. Ringe (eds.), *The Women's Bible Commentary* (London: SPCK; Louisville, KY: Westminster/John Knox Press, 1992), pp. 169-77.

—'Lamentations', in C.A. Newsom and S.H. Ringe (eds.), *The Women's Bible Commentary* (London: SPCK; Louisville, KY: Westminster/John Knox Press, 1992), pp. 178-82.

Oduyoye, Mercy Amba, 'African Women's Hermeneutics', in Maimela and König (eds.), *Initiation into Theology*.

Oldfather, W., 'Pandora', in PW, 18.2, pp. 529-48.

Ollenburger, B.C., 'The Book of Zechariah: Introduction, Commentary and Reflections', in *The New Interpreter's Bible*, VII (Nashville: 1996), pp. 733-840.

Olyan, S., 'Some Observations Concerning the Identity of the Queen of Heaven', *UF* 19 (1987), pp. 161-74.

Oppenheim, A.L., 'Babylonian and Assyrian Historical Texts', in *ANET*.

Otten, H., 'Die Gottheit Lelwani der Boğazköy-Texte', *JCS* 4 (1959), pp. 119-36.

Paglia, C., *Sexual Personae: Art and Decadence from Nefertiti to Emily Dickinson* (New Haven: Yale University Press, 1990).

Panofsky, D., and E. Panofsky, *Die Büchse der Pandora: Bedeutungswandel eines mythischen Symbols* (Frankfurt and New York: Campus-Verlag, 1992 [1956]).

Parrot, A., 'Les fouilles de Mari', *Syria* 18 (1937), pp. 54-84.

—*Mission Archéologique de Mari*. II. *Le Palais. Documents et Monuments* (BAH, 70; Paris: Librairie Orientaliste Paul Geuthner, 1959).

Peake, A.S., *Jeremiah*, I (The Century Bible; Edinburgh: T.C. & E.C. Jack, 1910).

—*Jeremiah and Lamentations*. II. *Jeremiah XXV to LII and Lamentations* (The Century Bible; Edinburgh: T.C. & E.C. Jack, n.d.).

Penglase, C., *Greek Myths and Mesopotamia: Parallels and Influence in the Homeric Hymns and Hesiod* (London: Routledge, 1994).

Petermann (Bathmartha), I.J., 'Machen Geburt und Monatsblutung die Frau "unrein"? Zur Revisionsbedürftigkeit eines mißverstandenen Diktums', in L. Schottroff and M.-T. Wacker (eds.), *Von der Wurzel getragen: Christlich-feministische Exegese in Auseinandersetzung mit Antijudaismus* (Biblical Interpretation Series, 17; Leiden: E.J. Brill, 1996), pp. 43-60.

Petersen, D.L., *Haggai and Zechariah 1–8: A Commentary* (OTL; London: 1985).

Porten, B., *Archives from Elephantine* (Los Angeles and Berkeley: University of California, 1968).

Porteous, N.W., *Daniel: A Commentary* (OTL; Philadelphia: Westminster Press, 1965).

Preuß, H.D., 'יעץ', in *ThWAT*, III, cols. 795-822.

Prouse, O. Horn, 'The Truth about Women and Lying', *JSOT* 61 (1994).

Prudden, Lillian E, 'Memoirs', typed document, 1949, Smith Family Papers, Historical Society of Glastonbury, CT.

Qil, Yehudah, 'Commentary on the Book of Hosea', in *The Twelve Prophets. I. Da'at Miqra* (Jerusalem: Mossad Harav Kook, 1973).

Radday, Y.T., 'Introduction', in *idem* and A. Brenner (eds.), *On Humour and the Comic in the Hebrew Bible* (JSOTSup, 92; Sheffield: JSOT Press/Almond Press, 1990), pp. 21-38.

Rashkow, Ilona N., *The Phallacy of Genesis: A Feminist-Psychoanalytic Approach* (Literary Currents in Biblical Interpretation; Louisville, KY: Westminster/ John Knox, 1993).

Rast, W.E., 'Cakes for the Queen of Heaven', in A.L. Merrill and T.W. Overholt (eds.), *Scripture in History and Theology: Essays in Honor of J. Coert Rylaarsdam* (Pittsburgh: Pickwick Press, 1977), pp. 167-80.

Redditt, P.L., *Haggai, Zechariah and Malachi* (NCB; Grand Rapids: Eerdmans, 1995).

Reventlow, H.G., *Die Propheten Haggai, Sacharja und Maleachi* (ATD, 25.2; Göttingen: Vandenhoeck & Ruprecht, 9th edn, 1993).

Ricoeur, P., *The Rule of Metaphor: Multi-Disciplinary Studies of the Creation of Meaning in Language* (London: Routledge & Kegan Paul, 1977).

—'The Metaphorical Process as Cognition, Imagination, and Feeling', *Critical Inquiry* 5 (1978), pp. 143-59.

Ringgren, H., 'ישע', in *ThWAT*, VII, cols. 675-84.

Rousselle, Aline, *Porneia: On Desire and the Body in Antiquity* (Oxford: Basil Blackwell, 1988).

Rudolph, W., *Haggai – Sacharja 1–8 – Sacharja 9–14 – Maleachi* (KAT, 13.4; Gütersloh: Gerd Mohn, 1976).

Rudolph, W., *Jeremia* (HAT; Tübingen: J.C.B. Mohr [Paul Siebeck]).

Russell, L.M. (ed.), *Feminist Interpretation of the Bible* (Oxford: Basil Blackwell, 1985).

Rüterswörden, Udo, 'Die Prophetin Hulda', *Festschrift H. Donner* (1995).

Sampson, Emily, ' "More Than Any Man Has Ever Done": Julia Smith's Search for the Meaning of God's Word', *BR* 14.2 (1998), pp. 41-54.

—'Her Works Shall Praise Her: The Biblical Translation of Julia Evelina Smith' (1998).

Sawyer, J.F.A., 'Daughter of Zion and Servant of the Lord in Isaiah: A Comparison', *JSOT* 44 (1989), pp. 89-107.

Schmitgen, B., 'Die Bücher Haggai und Sacharja: Neuer Tempel—neues Leben für alle', in L. Schottroff and M.-T. Wacker (eds.), *Kompendium Feministische Bibelauslegung* (Gütersloh: Chr. Kaiser Verlag/ Gütersloher Verlagshaus, 1998), pp. 366-75.

Schmitt, J.J., 'The Motherhood of God and Zion as Mother', *RB* 92 (1985), pp. 557-69.

Schmitz, P.C., 'Queen of Heaven', in *ABD*, V, pp. 586-88.

Schoors, A., *I am God Your Saviour: A Form-Critical Study of the Main Genres in Is. XL–LV* (VTSup, 24; Leiden: E.J. Brill, 1973).

Schottroff, Luise, *Lydia's Impatient Sisters: A Feminist Social History of Early Christianity* (trans. Barbara Rumscheidt and Martin Rumscheidt; Louisville, KY: Westminster/John Knox Press, 1995)

Schroer, S., *In Israel gab es Bilder: Nachrichten von darstellender Kunst im Alten Testament* (OBO, 74; Fribourg: Editions universitaires; Göttingen: Vandenhoeck & Ruprecht, 1987).

—'Wise and Counselling Women in Ancient Israel: Literary and Historical Ideals of the Personified Hokma', in Brenner (ed.), *A Feminist Companion to Wisdom Literature*, pp. 67-84.

Schulte, H., 'Beobachtungen zum Begriff der Zônâ im Alten Testament', *ZAW* 104 (1992), pp. 255-62.

Schulz-Rauch, M., *Hosea und Jeremia: Zur Wirkungsgeschichte des Hoseabuches* (CThM, 16; Stuttgart: Calwer, 1996).

Schüngel-Straumann, H., 'Mutter Zion im Alten Testament', in T. Schneider and H. Schüngel-Straumann (eds.), *Theologie zwischen Zeiten und Kontinenten: Für Elisabeth Gössmann* (Freiburg: Herder, 1993), pp. 19-30.

—'God as Mother in Hosea 11', in Brenner (ed.), *A Feminist Companion to the Latter Prophets*, pp. 194-218.

—*Die Frau am Anfang: Eva und die Folgen* (Münster: LIT-Verlag, 2nd edn, 1997).

Schüssler-Fiorenza, Elisabeth, *Bread Not Stone* (Boston: Beacon Press, 1984).

Schwartz, Regina, *The Curse of Cain: The Violent Legacy of Monotheism* (Chicago and London: The University of Chicago Press, 1997).

Schweickart, P.P., 'Reading Ourselves: Toward a Feminist Theory of Reading', in E.A. Flinn and P.P. Schweickart (eds.), *Gender and Reading: Essays on Readers, Texts and Contexts* (Baltimore: Johns Hopkins University Press, 1986), pp. 31-62.

Seifert, E., *Tochter und Vater im Alten Testament: Eine ideologiekritische Untersuchung zur Verfügungsgewalt von Vätern über ihre Töchter* (Neukirchener Theologische Dissertationen und Habilitationen, 9; Neukirchen–Vluyn: Neukirchener Verlag, 1997).

Seitz, C.R., *Theology in Conflict: Reactions to the Exile in the Book of Jeremiah* (Berlin and New York: W. de Gruyter, 1989).

Selvidge, Marla, *Notorious Voices: Feminist Biblical Interpretation 1500–1920* (New York: Continuum/Paragon House, 1996).

Setel, T.D., 'Prophets and Pornography: Female Sexual Imagery in Hosea', in Russell (ed.), *Feminist Interpretation of the Bible*, pp. 86-95.

Seybold, K., *Bilder zum Tempelbau: Die Visionen des Propheten Sacharja* (SBS, 70: Stuttgart: KBW, 1974).

Shaw, Susan Jean, *A Religious History of Julia Evelina Smith's 1876 Translation of the Holy Bible: Doing More Than Any Man Has Ever Done* (San Francisco: Mellen Research University Press, 1992).

Sherwood, Y., *The Prostitute and the Prophet: Hosea's Marriage in Literary-Theoretical Perspective* (JSOTSup, 212; Gender, Culture, Theory, 2; Sheffield: Sheffield Academic Press, 1996).

Shields, M.E., 'Circumcision of the Prostitute: Gender, Sexuality, and the Call to Repentance in Jeremiah 3.1–4.4', *BibInt* 3 (1995), pp. 61-74 (repr. in this volume).

—'Circumscribing the Prostitute: The Rhetorics of Intertextuality, Metaphor and Gender in Jeremiah 3.1–4.4' (PhD dissertation, 1996; a revised version is forthcoming in the JSOTSup series).

—'Multiple Exposures: Body Rhetoric and Gender Characterization in Ezekiel 16', *JFSR* 14 (1998), pp. 5-18 (repr. in this volume).

—'An Abusive God? Identity and Power, Gender and Violence in Ezekiel 23', in *Postmodern Interpretations of the Bible: A Reader*. Ed. A.K.M. Adam (St Louis: Chalice Press, 2001), pp. 129-51.

Showalter, E. (ed.), *The New Feminist Criticism: Essays on Women, Literature and Criticism* (London: Virago, 1986).

Siebert-Hommes, J., ' "But If She Be a Daughter…She May Live": "Daughters" and "Sons" in Exodus 1–2', in Brenner (ed.), *A Feminist Companion to Exodus to Deuteronomy*.

Simon, U., 'The Poor Man's Ewe Lamb', *Bib* 48 (1967), pp. 207-42.

Skinner, J., *Prophecy and Religion: Studies in the Life of Jeremiah* (Cambridge: Cambridge University Press, 1926).

Smith, Julia E., *The Holy Bible: Containing the Old and New Testaments, Translated Literally from the Original Tongues* (Hartford, CT: American Publishing, 1876).

—*Abby Smith and her Cows, with a Report of the Law Case Decided Contrary to Law* (New York: Arno Press [1877]).

—'Diaries: 1810–1842', written in French in the hand of Julia Smith, translated by Olive Rhines, typed document, no date, Connecticut Historical Society, Hartford, CT.

Smith, M., 'The Veracity of Ezekiel, the Sins of Manasseh, and Jeremiah 44.18', *ZAW* 87 (1975), pp. 11-16.

Smith, M.S., *The Early History of God: Yahweh and the Other Deities in Ancient Israel* (San Francisco: Harper & Row, 1990).

Soggin, J., 'The Ark of The Covenant, Jeremiah 3,16', in P.-M. Bogaert (ed.), *Le Livre de Jérémie* (Leuven: Leuven University Press, 1981), pp. 215-21.

Soskice, J.M., *Metaphor and Religious Language* (Oxford: Clarendon Press, 1985).

Spieckermann, Hermann, *Juda unter Assur in der Sargonidenzeit* (FRLANT, 129; Göttingen: Vandenhoeck & Ruprecht, 1982).

Stanton, Elizabeth Cady *et al.*, *The Woman's Bible* (Seattle: Coalition Task Force on Women and Religion, 1974 [1895]).

Steck, O.H., 'Zion als Gelände und Gestalt: Überlegungen zur Wahrnehmung Jerusalems als Stadt und Frau im Alten Testament', *ZTK* 86 (1989), pp. 261-81.

Sternberg, M., *The Poetics of Biblical Narrative* (Bloomington: Indiana University Press, 1985).

Streane, A.W., *The Book of the Prophet Jeremiah together with the Lamentations* (Cambridge: Cambridge University Press, 1913).

Stulman, L., *The Prose Sermons of the Book of Jeremiah: A Redescription of the Correspondences with the Deuteronomistic Literature in the Light of Recent Text-Critical Research* (SBLDS, 83; Atlanta: Scholars Press, 1986).

Swanepoel, M.G., 'Ezekiel 16: Abandoned Child, Bride Adorned or Unfaithful Wife?', in Philip R. Davies and David J.A. Clines (eds.), *Among the Prophets: Language, Image and Structure in the Prophetic Writings* (JSOTSup, 144; Sheffield: JSOT Press, 1993), pp. 84-104.

Tarn, W.W., *Hellenistic Civilisation* (London: Edward Arnold, 3rd edn, 1952).

Taylor, John B., *Ezekiel* (TOTC; Downer's Grove, IL: InterVarsity Press, 1969).

Thiel, Winifrid, *Die Deuteronomistische Redaktion von Jeremia 1–25* (Neukirchen–Vluyn: Neukirchener Verlag, 1973).

Thiselton, Anthony C., *New Horizons in Hermeneutics* (Grand Rapids: Zondervan, 1992).

Thistlethwaite, Susan Brooks, 'Every Two Minutes: Battered Women and Feminist Interpretation', in Russell (ed.), *Feminist Interpretation of the Bible*.

Thompson, J.A., *The Book of Jeremiah* (Grand Rapids, MI: Eerdmans, 1980).

Tollington, J.E., *Tradition and Innovation in Haggai and Zechariah 1–8* (JSOTSup, 150; Sheffield: Sheffield Academic Press, 1993).

Törnkvist, R., *The Use and Abuse of Female Sexual Imagery in the Book of Hosea: A Feminist Critical Approach to Hos. 1–3* (AUU, Uppsala Women's Studies, A. Women in Religion, 7; Uppsala: Uppsala University Press, 1998).

Traub, V., 'Prince Hal's Falstaff: Positioning Psychoanalysis and the Female Reproductive Body', *Shakespeare Quarterly* 40 (1989), pp. 456-75.

Trible, P., *God and the Rhetoric of Sexuality* (Philadelphia: Westminster Press, 1978).

—'Bringing Miriam Out of the Shadows', in Brenner (ed.), *A Feminist Companion to Exodus to Deuteronomy*, pp. 166-86.

Uehlinger, C., 'Die Frau im Efa (Sach 5,5-11): Eine Programmvision von der Abschiebung der Göttin', *BK* 49 (1994), pp. 93-103.

Unterman, Jeremiah, *From Repentance to Redemption* (JSOTSup, 54; Sheffield: Sheffield Academic Press, 1987).

Vannorsdall, J., 'Humor as Content and Device in Preaching', *Dialog* 22 (1983), pp. 187-90.

Vawter, B., 'Yahweh: Lord of the Heavens and the Earth', *CBQ* 48 (1986), pp. 461-67.

Verhoef, Pieter, *The Books of Haggai and Malachi* (NICOT; Grand Rapids, MI: Eerdmans, 1987).

Vieweger, D., *Die literarischen Bezüge zwischen den Büchern Jeremia und Ezechiel* (BEAT, 26; Frankfurt: Peter Lang, 1993).

Vincent, J.-M., 'Von der feurigen Herrlichkeit JHWHs in Jerusalem: Eine Auslegung von Sach 2,5-9', in *idem, Das Auge hört: Die Erfahrbarkeit Gottes im Alten Testament* (Biblisch-theologische Studien, 34; Neukirchen–Vluyn: Neukirchener Verlag, 1998), pp. 99-134.

Volz, P., *Studien zum Text des Jeremia* (BWAT, 25; Leipzig: J.C. Hinrichs, 1920).

Vriezen, K.J.H., 'Cakes and Figurines: Related Women's Cultic Offerings in Ancient Israel?', in B. Becking and M. Dijkstra (eds.), *On Reading Prophetic Texts: Gender-Specific and Related Studies in Memory of Fokkelien van Dijk-Hemmes* (Leiden: E.J. Brill, 1996), pp. 251-63.

Wacker, M.-T., 'Traces of the Goddess in the Book of Hosea', in Brenner (ed.), *A Feminist Companion to the Latter Prophets*, pp. 219-41.

—*Figurationen des Weiblichen im Hosea-Buch* (HBS, 8; Freiburg: Herder, 1996).

Walcot, P., *Hesiod and the Near East* (Cardiff: Cardiff University Press, 1966).

Walker, Lenore E., *The Battered Woman* (San Francisco: Harper and Row, 1979).

Waltke, B.K., and M. O'Connor, *An Introduction to Biblical Hebrew Syntax* (Winona Lake: Eisenbrauns, 1990).

Weber, Eugen, *Apocalypses: Prophecies, Cults and Millennial Beliefs through the Ages* (Cambridge, MA: Harvard University Press, 1999).

Weems, R.J., 'Gomer: Victim of Violence or Victim of Metaphor?', *Semeia* 47 (1989), pp. 87-104.

—*Battered Love: Marriage, Sex, and Violence in the Hebrew Prophets* (Minneapolis: Augsburg Fortress, 1995).

Weider, A., *Ehemetaphorik in prophetischer Verkündigung: Hos. 1–3 und seine Wirkungsgeschichte im Jeremiabuch. Ein Beitrag zum alttestamentlichen Gottes-Bild* (FzB, 71; Würzburg: Echter Verlag, 1993).

Weinfeld, M., 'The Worship of Molech and of the Queen of Heaven and its Background', *UF* 4 (1972), pp. 133-54.

Wenham, G.W., 'The Restoration of Marriage Reconsidered', *JJS* 30 (1979), pp. 36-40.

West, M.L. (ed.), *Hesiod: Works and Days* (Oxford: Clarendon Press, 1978).

Westermann, C., *Das Buch des Propheten Jesaja: Kapitel 40–66* (ATD, 19; Göttingen: Vandenhoeck & Ruprecht, 4th edn, 1981).

—*Wurzeln der Weisheit: Die ältesten Sprüche Israels und anderer Völker* (Göttingen: Vandenhoeck & Ruprecht, 1990).

—*Basic Forms of Prophetic Speech* (Louisville: Westminster Press, 1991).

Wevers, John W., *Ezekiel* (The Century Bible; London: Thomas Nelson and Sons, 1969).

White, R.E.O., *The Indomitable Prophet* (Grand Rapids, MI: Eerdmans, 1992).

Whybray, R.N., *The Intellectual Tradition in the Old Testament* (Berlin: W. de Gruyter, 1974).

—*Isaiah 40–66* (NCB; London: Oliphants, 1975).

Wilhelm, G., 'Reinheit und Heiligkeit: Zur Vorstellungswelt altanatolischer Ritualistik', in H.J. Fabry and H.W. Jüngling (eds.), *Levitikus als Buch* (BBB, 119; Berlin and Bodenheim: Philo, 1999), pp. 197-217.

Willey, P.T., *Remember the Former Things: The Recollection of Previous Texts in Second Isaiah* (SBLDS, 161; Atlanta: Scholars Press, 1997).

Williams, James, *The Bible, Violence and the Sacred* (San Francisco: Harper, 1991).

Wilshire, L.E., 'The Servant-City: A New Interpretation of the "Servant of the Lord" in the Servant Songs of Deutero-Isaiah', *JBL* 94 (1975), pp. 356-67.

Wilson, 'Prophecy and Ecstasy: A Reexamination', *JBL* 98 (1978), pp. 321-37.

Winter, U., *Frau und Göttin: Exegetische und ikonographische Studien zum weiblichen Gottesbild im Alten Israel und in dessen Umwelt* (OBO, 53; Fribourg: Editions universitaires; Göttingen: Vandenhoeck & Ruprecht, 1983).

Wiseman, D.J., *Chronicles of Chaldaean Kings* (London: British Museum, 1961).

Wolters, Al, 'Untying the King's Knots: Physiology and Wordplay in Daniel 5', *JBL* 110 (1991), pp. 91-97.

Wright, D.P., *The Disposal of Impurity: Elimination Rites in the Bible and in Hittite and Mesopotamian Literature* (SBLDS, 101; Atlanta: Scholars Press, 1987).

Yarbro Collins, A., 'Feminine Symbolism in the Book of Revelation', *BibInt* 1 (1993), pp. 20-33.

Yaron, R. 'The Restoration of Marriage', *JJS* 17 (1966), pp. 1-11.

Yee, G.A., 'Hosea', in C.A. Newsom and S.H. Ringe (eds.), *The Women's Bible Commentary*, pp. 195-202.

Zakovitch, Y., 'Humor and Theology, or the Successful Failure of the Israelite Intelligence (Josh. 2): A Literary-Folklorist Approach', in S. Niditch (ed.), *Text and Tradition: The Hebrew Bible and Folklore* (Atlanta: Scholars Press, 1990), pp. 75-98.

Zeitlin, F., 'Das ökonomische Gefüge in Hesiods Pandora', in Walters Art Gallery Baltimore, Antikenmuseum Basel and the Ludwig Collection (eds.), *Pandora: Frauen im klassischen Griechenland* (Mainz: Von Zabern, 1995), pp. 49-55.

Zimmerli, W., *Ezechiel 1–24* (BKAT, 13.1; Neukirchen–Vluyn: Neukirchener Verlag, 1969).

—*Ezekiel 1: A Commentary on the Book of the Prophet Ezekiel Chapters 1–24* (trans. R.E. Clements; Hermeneia; Philadelphia: Fortress Press, 1979).

INDEXES

INDEX OF REFERENCES

BIBLE

INDEXES

INDEX OF AUTHORS

FEMINIST THEOLOGY TITLES

Individual Titles in Feminist Theology
Linda Hogan, *From Women's Experience to Feminist Theology*
Lisa Isherwood and Dorothea McEwan (eds.), *An A–Z of Feminist Theology*
Lisa Isherwood and Dorothea McEwan, *Introducing Feminist Theology*
Kathleen O'Grady, Ann L. Gilroy and Janette Patricia Gray (eds.), *Bodies, Lives, Voices: Gender in Theology*
Melissa Raphael, *Thealogy and Embodiment: The Post-Patriarchal Reconstruction of Female Sacrality*
Deborah Sawyer and Diane Collier (eds.), *Is There a Future for Feminist Theology?*
Lisa Isherwood (ed.), *The Good News of the Body: Sexual Theology and Feminism*
Alf Hiltebeitel and Kathleen M. Erndl, *Is the Goddess a Feminist? The Politics of South Asian Goddesses*

Introductions in Feminist Theology
Rosemary Ruether, *Introducing Redemption in Christian Feminism*
Lisa Isherwood and Elizabeth Stuart, *Introducing Body Theology*
Melissa Raphael, *Introducing Thealogy: Discourse on the Goddess*
Pui-lan Kwok, *Introducing Asian Feminist Theology*
Janet H. Wootton, *Introducing a Practical Feminist Theology of Worship*
Mary Grey, *Introducing Feminist Images of God*
Mercy Amba Oduyoye, *Introducing African Women's Theology*

Feminist Companion to the Bible (1st Series)
Athalya Brenner (ed.), *A Feminist Companion to the Song of Songs*
Athalya Brenner (ed.), *A Feminist Companion to Genesis*
Athalya Brenner (ed.), *A Feminist Companion to Ruth*
Athalya Brenner (ed.), *A Feminist Companion to Judges*
Athalya Brenner (ed.), *A Feminist Companion to Samuel–Kings*
Athalya Brenner (ed.), *A Feminist Companion to Exodus–Deuteronomy*
Athalya Brenner (ed.), *A Feminist Companion to Esther, Judith and Susanna*
Athalya Brenner (ed.), *A Feminist Companion to the Latter Prophets*
Athalya Brenner (ed.), *A Feminist Companion to the Wisdom Literature*
Athalya Brenner (ed.), *A Feminist Companion to the Hebrew Bible in the New Testament*
Athalya Brenner and Carole Fontaine (eds.), *A Feminist Companion to Reading the Bible: Approaches, Methods and Strategies*

Feminist Companion to the Bible (2nd Series)
Athalya Brenner and Carole Fontaine (eds.), *Wisdom and Psalms*
Athalya Brenner (ed.), *Genesis*
Athalya Brenner (ed.), *Judges*
Athalya Brenner (ed.), *Ruth and Esther*
Athalya Brenner (ed.), *Samuel and Kings*
Athalya Brenner (ed.), *Exodus–Deuteronomy*
Athalya Brenner (ed.), *Prophets and Daniel*